SERVICE BANKING

The All-Purpose Bank

Also by the same author:

Moneyguide: The handbook of personal finance
Kluwer Publishing Ltd. 1981

Dictionary of Banking and Finance
Pitman 1985

Service Banking

The All-Purpose Bank

D. G. HANSON, LLM, Hon FCIB
of Lincoln's Inn, Barrister

With a Foreword by
The Lord Seebohm

Third edition

The Chartered Institute of Bankers

10 Lombard Street, London EC3V 9AS

First published in 1979 by The Institute of Bankers
Second Edition 1982
Third Edition 1987 published by Bankers Books Ltd.

Chartered Institute of Bankers (CIB) Publications are published by Bankers Books Limited under an exclusive licence and royalty agreement. Bankers Books Limited is a company owned by The Chartered Institute of Bankers.

Enquiries should be sent to the publishers at the undermentioned address:

BANKERS BOOKS LIMITED
c/o The Chartered Institute of Bankers
10 Lombard Street
London
EC3V 9AS

ISBN Hbk 0 85297-200-8
Pbk 0 85297-192-3

Typeset in 11pt on 12pt Century Schoolbook by
Staples Printers Rochester Limited.

Printed and bound in England by
Staples Printers Rochester Limited, Love Lane, Rochester, Kent.

Foreword by the Lord Seebohm

The first edition of *Service Banking* by Derrick Hanson was, I believe, the first book to be devoted to the less traditional services of the clearing banks. I said at the time that it was a very welcome addition to banking literature for all those who were studying or working in the business of banking. So much happened in the late '60s and throughout the '70s in the business of banking that the book filled a significant gap in the material available for all those who were interested, either professionally or academically, in the various services that banks had to offer to their customers.

After the very considerable success of the first and second editions of *Service Banking*, it is a special pleasure for me to commend this new edition to what I believe will be a very wide readership. The author has extended the text to include the many and varied developments in recent times. The book is skilfully and at times entertainingly written and the fact that the author has had long and deep experience of managing many of these services comes through in almost every chapter.

Many of us who have spent our lives in banking and can look back over many years have wondered whether the wide diversity of services which this book reveals was altogether wise. Could branch managers give the time to sell so many different products? How would they adjust to so many different markets? How could managers and their staffs be kept up-to-date and well-informed in so many areas? Was it right to trespass on the ground of other specialist institutions who historically were better equipped to deal with some of these services? Would there be an adequate return on the resources employed? These and many related questions have been posed over the last two decades for they have been a time of immense diversification and development within the banks. In more recent times the banking system has undergone great change, partly because of the intense competition for personal savings and partly because of the great strains on the cheque-clearing system and the challenges of new technology. More particularly, as this new edition is being published we are at the height of the financial services revolution in this country. It must be doubtful whether even the author with his background of experience in financial services could have foreseen the upheaval which is taking place, nor could anyone necessarily have foreseen the changing face of the City with its emphasis on financial services and the passing, in 1986, of the Building Societies Act and the Financial Services Act.

These pages describe many of the services which have now become central to the City revolution and the author gives the reader a remarkable insight into the diversity of our modern banking business. Once again, we are in Mr Hanson's debt for a most readable and far-ranging contribution to banking literature.

Frederic Seebohm

A Personal Note

There can be few major activities which have changed so much in such a short time as British banking. It so happened that I spent a large part of my banking career in the so-called service departments and I was privileged not only to observe at first hand many of the developments described in these pages, but also to be involved in a modest way in the changing scene. Like many others, I believed that banks should move into the field of total financial management and this very largely is what has now happened. Some problems remain and some questions remain unanswered, but the remarkable thing is that so much has been achieved by the banks in such a short time. The banker of today has to have a working acquaintance with a range of financial services far beyond anything which would have been expected of him years ago. Both as a student and in his bank duties, he will have to learn of banking activities which would have been quite unfamiliar to a former age. The public too can be confused at the proliferation of bank services and it is hoped that these pages may be helpful to the man in the street as well as to the career banker. I have not set out to teach the experts anything about their own subjects, but rather to describe to the layman (and in this sense we are all laymen) something of what goes on in the present day business of banking. Thus I offer this modest work as a kind of compendium of all that banks do and I have tried to deal with each subject from the 'service' standpoint.

I have thought it right to arrange the chapters under the broad headings 'Personal Services' and 'Business Services'. In modern banking this is increasingly the division which is followed, both in the structure of the branch system and in the marketing of the services. Nevertheless, there are certain subjects which transcend this dichotomy and which have, therefore, been dealt with separately.

In the previous editions of this work I acknowledged with much gratitude the help I had received from a very long list of friends. Perhaps I may be allowed to say again how very much I appreciated their help and that of many others who have assisted me in this revised and enlarged edition and how grateful I am to the banks who have so readily opened their doors for my enlightenment. I am particularly indebted to my secretary Shelagh Page, for typing this new edition and to my wife Patricia for reading the proofs.

D. G. Hanson
November 1987

Contents

Thirty Years of British Banking - Chronology (i)

Chapter 1 1

Service Banking – what is a bank? – the all-purpose bank – terminology — innovation and diversification – the competition for savings – moves towards new services – retail banking competition – the purpose of this book.

Chapter 2 19

Deposit Banking – historical note – the sources of deposits – constraints on deposit-taking – the competition for deposits – building societies – The Building Societies Act 1986 – National Savings – the Trustee Savings Bank – National Girobank – the Co-operative Bank – the Yorkshire Bank – money shops – licenced deposit-takers – in-store banking – types of account – rates of interest and bank charges – the banking habit – some legal aspects – the Banking Acts – the banker/customer relationship – associated services.

Chapter 3 57

The Lending Banker – training and experience – the development of lending business – the nature of bank lending – analysis of lending – lending to the business sector – lending for house purchase – constraints on lending – the principles of lending – unsecured loans – secured loans – credit scoring – interest rates.

PERSONAL SERVICES (CHAPTERS 4–13)

Chapter 4 83

Administration of Estates – an anomaly – historical background – the trade of a trustee – the growth of executorship business – trust business today – executorships and administrations – the choice of executor – a question of costs – the employment of solicitors – profitability – some related benefits – the system of charging – the market – marketing methods – some conclusions.

Chapter 5 **103**

Private Trusts – the origin of the trust – private and corporate trusts – settled estates – lifetime trusts – discretionary trusts – banks as trustees – investment matters – older fee scales – charitable trusts – living trusts – trust policies – conclusion.

Chapter 6 **117**

Investment Services – a changing scene – custodian services – nomineeships – valuation services – negotiable certificates of deposit – market rate deposits – deposit receipts – purchase of Stock Exchange securities – local authority investments – Treasury Bills – insurance contracts – advice on investments – management of investments – discretionary accounts – personal equity plans – investment policy – institutional business – some problems of investment management – smaller portfolios – profitability – administrative problems – possible conflicts – the Gower Report – the market.

Chapter 7 **141**

Unit Trusts – the banks' involvement – the growth of the movement – the nature of a unit trust – the unit price – authorisation of trusts – savings plans – withdrawal plans – share exchange schemes – unitisation of investment companies – linked life assurance – unit trusts for children – exempt unit trusts – investment aspects – advantages of unit trust investment – the Unit Trust Association – the market for unit trust sales – unit trust charges – profitability – unauthorised trusts – the financial services legislation.

Chapter 8 **165**

Life Assurance – the banks' involvement – linked life assurance and conventional life assurance – some historical aspects – categories of life assurance – the purpose of life assurance – categories of linked life assurance – personal pension plans – selling methods – counter sales – sales representatives – sales through brokers – sales by advertisement – profitability – 'spin-off' business – the risks – statutory provisions – consumer protection – banking and insurance.

Chapter 9 **193**

Insurance Broking – the role of the broker – the professional bodies – categories of insurance broking – Lloyd's of London – a widespread business – the banks' involvement – the reasons why – some criticisms – customer attitudes – the market – profitability – registration of insurance brokers – the Financial Services Act 1986.

Chapter 10 213

Credit Cards – early developments – categories of cards – travel and entertainment cards – cheque cards – credit cards – credit cardholders – the merchants – the card companies – the market – company cards – in-house cards – some risk aspects – a code of practice – the monopoly aspect – some legal aspects – profitability – premium cards – smart cards – pinpoint machines – petrol cards – Cardlink – credit balances – debit cards – the future.

Chapter 11 243

Hire Purchase and Consumer Credit – the Crowther Committee – the nature of hire purchase – historical note – the hiring of railway wagons – the finance houses – categories of instalment credit – consumer hire purchase – business credit – profitability – the market – the clearing banks' involvement.

Chapter 12 259

Personal Advisory and Agency Services – the reluctant banks – specialist departments – taxation services – the competition – costs and profitability – the contribution of tax business – personal financial planning – other specialist schemes – the financial services legislation – banks as agents – estate agencies.

Chapter 13 275

Money and Travel – some bank services for the traveller – foreign currency – open credits – overseas payments – telegraphic transfers – postcheques – eurocheques – credit cards – travellers' cheques – the travel business – bureaux de change.

BUSINESS SERVICES (CHAPTERS 14–22)

Chapter 14 289

Merchant Banking – the princes of the financial world – the accepting houses – capital issues – diversity of business – good times and bad corporate advice – the clearing banks – the bidding subsidiaries – mergers and acquisitions – the issuing houses – rights issues – capital issues – management buy-outs – the Unlisted Securities Market – the receiving banker – some special characteristics – equity participation – some possible conflicts – insider dealing.

Chapter 15 313

Share Registration and Computer Services – some legal requirements – the role of the registrar – some benefits to the banks – typical charges – the banks' share of the market – level of activity – other computer services – payroll services – stock control – accounting systems – industrial and professional services – cash management services.

Chapter 16 325

Leasing and Industrial Hire Purchase – an unfamiliar concept – some history – the nature of leasing – taxation aspects – a source of finance – types of contract – the clearing banks – the lease-buy decision – growth of business – industrial hire purchase – the motor industry – block discounting – the market.

Chapter 17 345

Factoring – historical background – the nature of factoring – debt administration – credit protection – factor financing – some legal aspects – the involvement of the banks – the Association of British Factors – the banker/factor relationship – the risks – profitability – international factoring — the potential.

Chapter 18 369

Corporate Trusteeships – pension funds – the Social Security Acts – custodian trustees – debenture trusts – consortium trusts – unit trusts – the Financial Services Acts – other corporate trusteeships.

Chapter 19 387

Pensions Services – some traditional attitudes – the State schemes – the Social Security Act 1986 – insured schemes – managed funds – self-administered schemes – schemes for executives and directors – personal pension plans – trusteeship for pension schemes – pension fund surpluses – investment management – the provision of investment vehicles – pension fund structure and administration – insurance schemes – the market – fund management.

Chapter 20 407

Business Advisory Services – businesses in the United Kingdom – the Bolton Committee – the services developed by the banks – large and small companies – public and private – some categories of advice – benefits to the banks – economic information.

Chapter 21 **421**

Off-shore Services – the Channel Islands and the Isle of Man – the popular image – the role of the banks – the meaning of off-shore – personal services (trusts, investment companies, portfolio management and off-shore funds) – corporate services (company registration, invoicing, captive insurance companies, cash management) – the banks' involvement – banking business.

Chapter 22 **433**

The Finance of Foreign Trade – bills of exchange – overseas trade – categories of export finance (cash or deposits, open account, bills of exchange, documentary letters of credit, acceptance credits, forward contracts and export guarantees) – ECGD insurance cover – ECGD guarantees – ECGD support services – buyer credit guarantees – export finance houses – export factoring – import finance – other supporting services – a forfait finance.

Chapter 23 **447**

Money Transfer – moneyness – payments in cash – automated teller machines – payments by cheque – Bankers' Clearing House – the credit clearing – Bankers' Automated Clearing Services Limited (BACS) – Clearing House Automated Payments System (CHAPS) – bank charges – plastic money – Electronic Funds Transfer Point of Sale (EFTPOS) – the 'Connect' card – home banking – the future.

Chapter 24 **469**

Selling the Services – the marketing function – bankers as salesmen – the need to sell – the markets – customer response – the branch network – advertising – direct mail – sales representatives – the role of the bank manager – 'polarisation' – branch re-organisation – packaged services – new relationships – the bank account – postscript.

Table of Statistics **493**

Appendix **497**

The Financial Services Act 1986 – the Act – the previous legislation – the scope of the Act – investment business – exemptions – the concept of authorisation – the consequences of carrying on investment business without authorisation – the Securities and Investment Board – the self-regulating organisations – applications for authorisation – the Conduct of Business Rules – the business plan –

'know your customer' – the customer agreement – a self-regulatory system – the enforcement of the statutory powers – the right of appeal – the Compensation Fund – the effect on banks and other financial institutions – 'polarisation' – the effect of 'polarisation' – the duality of role – the sale of pension plans – direct marketing – Personal Equity Plans (PEPs) – banks as investment managers – the management of pension fund investments – banks acting as trustees of other funds – advertisements – investments sold 'off the page' – unsolicited calls – cancellation rights – clients' accounts – compliance – insider-dealing – unit trusts – the official listing of securities.

Further Reading 513

Index 519

Thirty Years of British Banking

Chronology of Principal Events 1958–1987

1958

'Personal loans' introduced
The banks acquired interests in finance houses
Variation of Trusts Act
Prevention of Fraud (Investments) Act

1959

Publication of the Report of the Radcliffe Committee

1960

The Payment of Wages Act
The centralised credit clearing set up
Factoring operations developed in the UK

1961

The Trustee Investments Act

1962

National Provincial Bank acquired District Bank

1963

The Protection of Depositors Act

1964

The clearing banks moved into leasing

1965

Cheque cards introduced
Westminster Bank acquired 40 per cent of Diners' Club
Westminster Bank issued debenture stock for Tecalemit Limited

1966

Short term export credits introduced under ECGD guarantees
Barclays Bank launched Barclaycard
Lloyds Bank entered the unit trust management field
The National Savings Bank introduced investment accounts

1967

The Prices & Incomes Board Report on bank charges
First introduction of cash dispensers
Martins Bank acquired 75 per cent of Unicorn Securities
Midland Bank acquired a one-third interest in Montagu Trust

1968

National Provincial Bank became the first UK bank to enter the factoring field
Barclays Bank acquired Martins Bank
District Bank, National Provincial Bank and Westminster Bank merged to establish National Westminster Bank
Inter-Bank Computer Bureau set up (the forerunner of BACS)
The National Giro commenced business

1969

Barclays Bank sold the British Linen Bank to the Bank of Scotland in exchange for a 35 per cent shareholding
The banks introduced Saturday closing
Department for National Savings established
National Westminster Group announced that County Bank would undertake merchant banking

1970

The Eurocheque scheme introduced
The National Commercial Banking Group merged with Williams Deacon's Bank, Glyn Mills & Co. and the National Bank to form Williams & Glyn's Bank
National Westminster Bank acquired Lombard Banking, forerunner of Lombard North Central
Banks first disclosed full profits
Medium term lending developed
Barclays Insurance Services Company incorporated

1971

Competition and Credit Control introduced
The Report of the Crowther Committee published
Barclays Bank DCO became a wholly-owned subsidiary of Barclays and its name changed to Barclays Bank International
Barclays established business advisory service
Capital allowances introduced under Finance Act
Williams & Glyn's Insurance Consultants established
The Report of the Bolton Committee published
Lloyds Bank Insurance Department established
Building societies overtook banks as primary repository of personal savings
The Co-operative Bank incorporated

1972

Bank rate replaced by minimum lending rate
Midland Bank acquired a controlling interest in Thomas Cook
Access credit cards introduced by Lloyds, Midland, National Westminister and Williams & Glyn's Banks
Midland Bank Insurance Services set up
Barclays Bank (London & International) (now Barclays Merchant Bank) entered the field of merchant banking
Capital allowances increased to 100 per cent of acquisition costs

1973

Interest limited to 9½ per cent on bank deposit accounts up to £10,000 in order to protect flow of money to building societies
The Supplementary Special Deposit Scheme (the 'Corset') introduced by the Bank of England
Midland Bank acquired remaining capital of Montagu Trust
The Report of the Page Committee published
National Westminster Insurance Services established
The Fair Trading Act
Finance Act widened pensions opportunities for 'controlling' directors
Finance for Industry established as holding company for Finance Corporation for Industry and the Industrial and Commercial Finance Corporation
Report of the Scott Committee published re Equity-Linked Life Assurance

1974

Consumer Credit Act
The Co-operative Bank and the Central Trustee Savings Bank became members of the Bankers' Clearing House
Insurance Companies Act

1975

The 'Corset' was suspended
Mercantile Credit became wholly-owned by Barclays Bank
Royal Commission on the Distribution of Income and Wealth
Social Security Pensions Act

1976

The 'Corset' was re-introduced
The Trustee Savings Bank Act
Stock Exchange (Completion of Bargains) Act

1977

The Wilson Committee established
Society for Worldwide Inter-Bank Financial Telecommunications (SWIFT) established
The 'Corset' again suspended
Lloyds Bank Insurance Services Limited incorporated
Clearing House Automated Payments System (CHAPS) agreed
Insurance Brokers (Registration) Act
Insurance Brokers' Registration Council established
British Linen Bank became the merchant banking arm of Bank of Scotland

1978

The Price Commission reported on Bank Charges
Trustee Savings Banks introduced Trustcard
Barclays Bank introduced Barclaycare Scheme
Social Security Pension Act, 1975 became effective
Finance Act introduced taxation relief for profit-sharing schemes
Post Office announced Viewdata Service

1979

The Banking Act
Midland Bank Insurance Brokers Limited incorporated
Visa Group commenced marketing of travellers' cheques

1980

Report of the Wilson Committee published licensing provisions of the Banking Act, 1979 came into effect
Royal Commission on Legal Services reported on Non-Contentious Probate Rules
Report of the Monopolies and Mergers Commission on credit cards
Mastercard introduced Master's travellers' cheques
The Unlisted Securities Market (USM) introduced
Prestel Service introduced by Post Office
TSB Holdings acquired 51% of United Dominions Trust

1981

Banks entered house mortgage field
Small Firms Loan Guarantee Scheme introduced
Barclays terminated Barclaycare Scheme
Euro Travellers' Cheques International (ETCI) formed
Thomas Cook joint venture with Mastercard announced
Lloyds Bank acquired 51% in Lloyds & Scottish Finance Company
TSB Holdings acquired whole of United Dominions Trust
American Express introduced the Gold Card in co-operation with Lloyds Bank

Midland Bank introduced the Premium Card jointly with Mastercard

1982

The Deposit Protection Scheme came into effect

Lloyds Bank acquired estate agency businesses

Barclays Bank announced opening of some branches on Saturdays from August

The Gower Review of Investor Protection published

Barclaycard launched the Premium Visa card

Midland Bank announced pilot project in a move towards home banking

1983

Nottingham Building Society/Bank of Scotland launched home banking scheme with Prestel, to be known as Homelink

Barclays, Lloyds, Williams & Glyn's, The Royal Bank of Scotland and Bank of Scotland announced plans for the sharing of their cash dispensing machines

Abbey National Building Society launched a cheque account

Lord Richardson (Governor of the Bank) warned building societies against too rapid an expansion into the banking business. He spoke of the 'very special confidence' which the general public placed in the building society movement and cautioned against undermining that confidence.

Barclays announced re-structuring of branch network – a 5-step tier of branch offices from small, part-time agencies up to large 'key' branches

Barclaycard and Amoco (UK) Limited announced the introduction of Cardpump service for payment of petrol by means of inserting a Barclaycard in the petrol pump

Bristol and West Building Society and Standard Chartered Bank introduced a combined savings account and cheque book scheme known as Moneylink, with provision for cheque guarantee cards and overdraft facilities

Citibank applied for membership of the bankers' clearing house

National Girobank introduced Flexiplan to enable customers to have borrowing facilities linked to the customer's current account

The Secretary of State for Social Services issued consultative document on pensions for 'early leavers'

National Consumer Council published a report on banking services and recommended *inter alia* that a banking ombudsman be appointed

Mr Alex Fletcher, Minister at the Department of Trade & Industry with special responsibility for City affairs, suggested that the

separation of financial institutions in their present form had probably had its day and that there was a need for conglomerates
Bank of England in Quarterly Bulletin favoured a trend towards 'new associations with financial intermediaries or institutions straddling the conventional boundaries between different financial activities'
National Consumer Council published report 'Banking Services and the Consumer'

1984

The final draft of the Gower Report was published
The Building Societies Association published discussion document 'New Legislation for Building Societies', proposing new powers for building societies
High Interest Cheque Account introduced by the Midland Bank
The Secretary of State for Social Services issued consultative document on 'greater security of the rights and expectations of members of occupational pension schemes'
Barclays announced agreement in principle to become 29.9 per cent limited partner in Wedd Durlacher and in stockbrokers, De Zoete & Bevan
The ten clearing banks agreed to undertake a major review of the clearing system
Samuel Montagu acquired 29.9 per cent of Stockbrokers, W. Greenwell
Discussion document published by the Stock Exchange on the subject of 'dual capacity' and abolition of fixed commissions. Full ownership of Stock Exchange firms by outsiders also contemplated
Natwest announced agreement to buy 5 per cent of stockbrokers, Fielding Newson-Smith (later to be followed by full ownership), and 29.9 per cent of jobbers, Bisgood Bishop
The Government published proposals for portable pensions
TSB announced the opening of branches on Saturdays for full personal banking services with effect from April 1985
Midland announced free banking on current accounts maintained in credit
Midland announced that 50 branches will open on Saturday mornings during 1985 and a further 150 branches during 1986
National Westminster Bank offered retired customers, aged 55 and over, free banking if accounts maintained in credit
Barclaycard announced insurance scheme for cardholders in the event of collapse of tour operators
The clearing banks published the Child Report on the future membership of the clearing system

1985

Natwest announced the opening of 200 branches on Saturday mornings

Lloyds Bank announced opening of 75 branches on Saturdays, to be followed by the opening of another 125 by the end of the year

Co-operative Bank claimed to be the first UK bank to introduce a VISA 'electron' card, designed to operate cash machines as well as serving as a credit card

National Westminster Bank introduced 'Special Reserve Accounts', a high interest deposit account for personal customer, minimum balance £2,000

The Bank of Scotland announced Home Banking Service

The LINK Organisation (National Girobank, Abbey National Building Society, Co-operative Bank, Nationwide Building Society and a consortium of 17 other institutions) proposed to provide a shared ATM network throughout Britain

The banks announced their commitment to EFTPOS and anticipated a pilot project being operational within two years

Royal Bank of Scotland acquired Charterhouse Japhet

Lloyds Bank launched new high interest cheque account – the first occasion of a clearing bank offering both cheque facilities and a cash card on an interest bearing account. Minimum balance £2,500

Marks & Spencer announced the introduction of a credit card (following six months' trial in Scotland)

Littlewoods Stores, House of Fraser and Burton Group all announced plans for providing financial services for customers through their retail outlets

Midland Bank and Tesco announced plans for the opening of Midland Bank branches at three Tesco stores with possible extension to all the new Tesco 'superstores'

Barclays launched higher rate deposit account (minimum balance £1,000)

National Girobank announced plans to enter the home mortgage market

Barclays attracted £1 billion of personal account funds into new Higher Rate Deposit Accounts in 10 weeks

National Westminster Bank announced reorganisation of bank network, with the creation of 150 'corporate' branches to serve business customers, the new development to take place between 1986 and 1990. The existing system of 'service' branches to be expanded in about 300 locations

Lloyds Bank set up a merchant bank subsidiary to be known as Lloyds Merchant Bank

Prudential Corporation announced plans to acquire an estate agency business

Co-operative Bank announced plans to launch a chain of 'several hundred' money shops throughout Co-operative stores

Samuel Montagu became wholly owned by Midland Bank (by Midland's re-purchase of the 40 per cent stake it sold to Aetna Life and Casualty of the U.S. in 1982)

Social Security Act 1985 passed (mostly coming into force on 1 January 1986)

Williams & Glyn's Bank and the Royal Bank of Scotland merged to become the Royal Bank of Scotland PLC

National Girobank announced the introduction of Visa credit card

Debenhams, Oxford Street, announced sales of stocks and shares 'over the counter'

National Westminster Bank formed NatWest Investment Bank, incorporating County Bank, Bisgood Bishop, the jobbing firm, and Fielding Newson-Smith, stockbrokers

National Girobank became a public limited company

The Department of Trade and Industry authorised 'fund of funds' type of unit trust

Royal Bank of Scotland combined National Commercial & Glyn's and Charterhouse into one merchant banking subsidiary to be known as Charterhouse Development

Formation of Committee of London and Scottish Bankers, a merger of Committee of London Clearing Bankers and Committee of Scottish Clearing Bankers

Anglia Building Society launched England's first cashless shopping scheme, in Northampton

First banking ombudsman appointed from January 1986

Building Societies Bill published

Financial Services Bill published

1986

Social Security Bill published, including provision for changes in SERPS (state earnings-related pensions scheme)

Chancellor announces introduction of Personal Equity Plans from January 1987

Building Societies Bill receives Royal Assent

Department of Trade and Industry, and Bank of England announce membership of the Securities and Investments Board Ltd. (SIB)

TSB public flotation

Financial Services Act receives Royal Assent

1987

Building Societies Act 1986 came into effect 1 January

The Securities and Investments Board publishes its rule book on investor protection

Barclays Bank introduce 'Connect' card
TSB move into 'offshore' banking
National Westminster Bank sells unit trusts subsidiary
Midland Bank announce extension of hours

Supplement to the Chronology

Events subsequent to the printing of the main text

(CHAPTER 2)
October 1987. The Treasury announce proposed changes to the Building Societies Act, 1986 to enable building societies (a) to issue credit cards in their own name, (b) to buy unit trusts on behalf of customers direct from a fund manager (instead of merely through a broker) and (c) to give advice on financial investments.

(CHAPTER 6)
August 1987. The Institute for Fiscal Studies suggests that 19.5 per cent of British adults are holders of shares in public companies, but one-half of these hold shares only in one company: the *proportion* of share values held by private individuals continues to fall.

October 1987. Barclays Bank extend Barclayshare Service to enable investors to deal through their branches in UK equities, gilts and unit trusts with a portfolio administration service and, if desired, an investment advisory service.

(CHAPTERS 6 AND 7)
October 1987. Stock Market crash.

(CHAPTERS 6, 7 AND 14)
October 1987. TSB acquire Hill Samuel.

December 1987. County Natwest acquire stockbrokers, Wood MacKenzie.

(CHAPTER 7)
September 1987. National Westminster Bank sell unit trust subsidiary to Britannia Arrow Holdings.

October 1987. The Securities and Investments Board announces new proposals for changing the method of pricing of unit trusts, i.e. to move from an historic to a forward pricing system so that unit trust transactions would be conducted at the next dealing price quoted by the management company instead of dealing at the last price made.

(CHAPTER 8 AND APPENDIX)

October 1987. Midland Bank announce the setting-up of a life assurance company jointly with Commercial Union Assurance in order to offer life assurance products through Midland Bank branches.

(CHAPTERS 10 AND 13)

October 1987. Leading retail banks in Europe propose to introduce compatibility for their cash cards and credit cards. This would involve 40 banks from 17 countries and would initially extend to holders of cards issued by VISA, Eurocard, Mastercard and Eurocheque. In November 1987 the European Commission institute an enquiry into this proposal.

(CHAPTERS 10 AND 23)

November 1987. Lloyds Bank introduce a debit card through the VISA group, thus becoming the first British bank to be a member of both VISA and Access card companies.

(CHAPTER 12)

September 1987. Abbey National Building Society announce their intention to develop an estate agency network with 1,000 branches over the next 5 years.

October 1987. TSB England & Wales announce development of a network of estate agency offices.

(CHAPTER 19)

August 1987. The Government announce that the starting date for the new Personal Pensions legislation is to be put back 6 months to 1 July 1988.

November 1987. The Sex Discrimination Act, 1986, came into force, giving employees, whether male or female, the right to retire at the same age, i.e. it became no longer possible to compel a woman to retire at, say, 60 if the normal retirement age for men in a particular scheme was 65.

(CHAPTER 20)

November 1987. Midland announce launching of Credo, a banking and advisory service for new customers starting up businesses. The service includes general advice, business training, accounting and planning and also provides free banking for a 6-month period.

(CHAPTER 23)

October 1987. National Westminster Bank introduce BankLine, an electronic banking service for small business customers, linked to the use of personal computers.

November 1987. Midland Bank announce joint scheme with British Coal Computer Bureau, Compower, to develop a point of sale "cashless" shopping facility using a debit card to be known as Transact.

November 1987. J. Sainsbury PLC and Girobank PLC announce an EFTPOS trial based on the LINK National Cash Network.

(CHAPTER 24)

September 1987. Barclays Bank announce a further rationalisation of branch network, accelerating the division between corporate and personal banking services.

October/November 1987. Barclays, Midland and Lloyds Banks announce extended opening hours on weekdays.

'Banking is a trade.'

CHAPTER 1

Service Banking

What is a bank?

The year 1986 will be remembered as the year of the Big Bang. Strictly speaking, the term relates to the date in October when 'single capacity' and minimum commissions were abolished on the Stock Exchange. The origins and impact of that event are discussed later in this chapter and again in Chapter 6 under the heading of Investment Services.

In practice, the Big Bang became associated with those other changes in the City which crystallised in 1986 – the ownership of stockbrokers and stock jobbers by large banks, the passing of the Financial Services Act of 1986, the setting up of the regulatory agencies under that Act, the passing of the Building Societies Act, 1986, the intensifying of competition and the abolition of many lines of demarcation which had existed for over a century. Thus, for many years 1986 will be recalled as the high-water mark of the financial services revolution.

Earlier editions of this work began with the observation by Lord Denning, then Master of the Rolls, in United Dominions Trust Limited v. Kirkwood that 'Like many other beings, a banker is easier to recognise than to define.'[1] In that celebrated case, his Lordship and his colleagues enunciated a number of essential requirements if one was to enjoy the title of 'banker', but drew back from offering any precise definition. Indeed the statutory definitions are those which describe 'banker' as 'any person or corporation carrying on the business of bankers'.[2] The Banking Act, 1979, conferred on the Bank of England the power to recognise an institution as a 'bank' provided certain criteria were satisfied (see Chapter 2). The Act also prohibited the use of the name 'bank' or 'banker' in the course of a business activity except within a narrow range of exceptions listed in the Act. The 1987 Banking Act also prohibits the use of such names except for institutions authorised under the Act.

If Lord Denning were speaking today he might not feel that banks were all that easy to 'recognise'. Indeed, they, like other institutions, have become financial conglomerates. A banker returning from the past might find it difficult to believe that banks are now engaged in almost every field of financial activity. One bank, for example, owns the largest travel agency in the country, another bank has the largest life assurance broking business and yet another bank owns a large estate agency. All the large banks have more home loans on their books than all but the largest building societies, one bank owns the largest leasing operation in the United Kingdom and another is the largest in the business of factoring. On the stock exchanges of the world, the large banks following the Big Bang are among the largest dealers in securities, both in bonds and equities, whether for their own account or for their clients. Nor is this movement all one way. Some insurance companies have substantial stakes in banking or deposit-taking institutions, building societies have obtained statutory powers to move into banking activities and in recent years, 300 or so non-bank institutions have been licensed to accept deposits.

One might also reflect on whether the 'business' of banking is a trade, a profession or an industry. Certainly a former Lord Chief Justice, Lord Goddard, considered that 'ordinarily speaking, banking is a trade' and that 'a banker in the proper way refers to his *customer* because he is carrying on the *trade* of a banker – old bankers never refer to their clients – that was left to hairdressers and dressmakers.'[3] Nowadays, in addition to customers banks have clients, cardholders, beneficiaries, policyholders, unitholders and indeed many other relationships outside that of banker and customer. We are tempted to say that banking is what one cares to make it. Perhaps a better definition is that banking is the business of finance.

It is of course well established that the traditional trade or business of banking is that of taking deposits, lending money and providing a money transmission service. The first edition of this book was concerned exclusively with *other* aspects of present-day banking. It set out to describe for the first time under one cover those services, which were in themselves a departure from the traditional banking functions. It was customary at one time to refer to these non-banking activities as 'ancillary services', but this is no longer acceptable, for ancillary means 'subservient or subordinate' and this would never do.

A collective term used by the National Westminster Bank for some years was 'related banking services' and this is usefully explicit although probably inaccurate because presumably what it meant was 'services related to banking'. At least one senior banker used the description 'service banking', and this is a useful title although subject to the criticism that all banking is a service.

It is a little paradoxical that whereas these adjuncts of banking were known for many years as 'service departments', the City, the public and Parliament now refer to 'financial services' of which banking is but a part! Thus our title has taken on a new significance.

Not all these services are new. The executor and trustee services of the banks have been operating for nearly seventy years. The Midland Bank Executor and Trustee Company Limited (now Midland Bank Trust Company Limited) was established in 1909 and on the occasion of its Jubilee was referred to with some affection by the then Chairman of the Midland Bank, Viscount Monckton, as 'our earliest subsidiary'. Indeed, it must be one of the oldest subsidiary companies of any British banking group.

For the most part, however, it has been in the last three decades that the British clearing banks have come out in a rash of new services. There are now approximately 300 separately identifiable services available over the counters of the United Kingdom banks. It has been a truly remarkable phenomenon and one without any precise counterpart elsewhere in the world.

The All-Purpose Bank

A former Governor of the Bank of England remarked that 'the supremacy of London as an international banking centre is founded on a freedom from banking legislation equalled in few countries in the world', and on the same occasion referred to 'the arrival of the all-purpose bank in the United Kingdom'.[5] Certainly the freedom of the British banks to engage in almost any business activity of their choosing made it possible for them to embark on the proliferation of their services.

Thus, the second edition of this book was enlarged to take in the more traditional services of deposit banking, lending and money transmission as well as some other specialist services, which were consciously omitted from the earlier book. The name 'Service Banking' remains appropriate because it is the service aspect of banking in all its forms with which we are concerned. The aim is to describe what bankers do rather than teach bankers how to do it. It is an attempt to describe the all-purpose bank in the United Kingdom.

Terminology

The word 'bank' was used in everyday language in these Islands to describe the joint stock banks, whether in England (i.e. Barclays, Coutts, Lloyds, Midland, National Westminster, Williams & Glyn's), or in Scotland (i.e. Bank of Scotland, Clydesdale Bank and Royal Bank of Scotland), or the Trustee Savings Banks or the Co-operative Bank, or the Yorkshire Bank, or the National Girobank. The term 'clearing bank' is ambiguous. The 'old' clearing banks were the joint stock banks, but nowadays the Trustee Savings Bank, Co-operative Bank and Girobank are all members of the Clearing House. Only the old clearing banks were all-purpose banks in the true sense.

In September 1985 the Committee of London Clearing Banks and the Committee of Scottish Clearing Banks merged to form the Committee of London & Scottish clearing Banks consisting of

Bank of Scotland
Barclays
Lloyds
Midland
National Westminster
Royal Bank
Standard Chartered, and
TSB

totalling, at the end of 1986, approximately 13,700 branches.

Some of the other banks have developed and are developing a wide range of services and thus, wherever appropriate, reference is made to them in the text.

The services described are those offered in the United Kingdom to residents of the United Kingdom and thus, no attempt is made to describe truly international banking. Off-shore services are, however, included because of their proximity to these Islands and because they are home-based in origin.

Innovation and diversification

Those given to long-term strategy would no doubt like to think that all this happened like the unfolding of some master plan. It is true that today corporate planning forms an essential part of the decision-making process in the British clearing banks, but it was comparatively unknown until the '70s. The banks tended to pursue an empirical, even pragmatic approach to the development of their business. More particularly, banks were not great originators. They did not necessarily have any occasion to diversify into other activities, nor did they see any particular reason for departing from traditional concepts. That was equally true across the Atlantic. Professor Paul Nadler wrote a few years ago of American banks that 'banking's motto has long been "Never do something for the first time"'.[6]

One may speculate on the reasons for the gradual and in some cases reluctant diversification into financial services which began in the late 1960s. Some may regard it as no more than a normal organic or evolutionary process, a kind of blossoming to crown the years of sturdy but unexciting growth. Such an idealistic, even poetic, view is probably far from the truth. Until the middle 1960s few, if any, saw banks in the role of financial supermarkets. Not a word in the banking publications of thirty to forty years ago contemplated, even in part, the cluster of services which eventually emerged. Banks were banks and that was an end to the matter. Less than thirty years ago, a commentator was able to write: 'Unlike manufacturers, banks are not continually developing new products or improvements upon existing products which can be made the subject of an advertisement or a series of advertisements.'[7] In certain respects, the American banks were ahead of their British counterparts, despite their legal limitations on diversification, but some of their innovations were thought not to be appropriate to the traditional view of banking in Britain.

For the first sign of change we need look no further than the monetary climate of the 1960s. The three basic ingredients which we have already mentioned, viz: deposit taking, lending and money transmission, all seemed to be severely threatened albeit for different reasons. With regard to deposits it is now well known that the clearing banks' share of new personal savings diminished very significantly over the post-war years. This was well recognised in the 1950s and 1960s but the trend continued. For example, in 1972 the increase in banking deposits from the personal sector amounted to £1·7 billion against a figure of £5 billion for growth in savings through building societies, life assurance and pension funds. By 1976, the increase in personal bank deposits was down to a level of £1·3 billion compared with over £9 billion placed with building societies, life companies and pension funds.[8] More graphically, the evidence of the clearing banks to the Wilson Committee[9] showed that among the deposit-taking institutions in the United Kingdom, the clearing banks' share of deposits fell from 48·8 per cent in 1962 to 35·4 per cent in 1976. Over the same period, the building societies' share of deposits increased from 21·2 per cent to 37·7 per cent and the share of all other banks in the United Kingdom, including overseas banks operating in the UK, rose from 3·8 per cent to 12·5 per cent. In their evidence, the banks also commented on the fact that in the twenty or so years since the Radcliffe Committee reported in 1959, the total number of commercial banks, both domestic and foreign, operating in the United Kingdom had expanded from 125 to over 300. In the same period, as a result of the mergers of the late 1960s, the number of clearing banks had been reduced from eleven to six. By the end of 1986 building society savings in the UK accounted for over 52 per cent of the liquid assets of the personal sector, whereas bank deposits (including all banks) had fallen to approximately 33 per cent.

As regards the flow of money into pension funds and insurance companies, it must be acknowledged that these constitute a large part of the long-term savings market whereas the banks traditionally are in the market for short-term savings. Such a generalisation may, however, be partly fallacious, because a large proportion of bank deposits tends to be long term. In any case, there is only so much disposable income at any one time and that part which goes into long-term savings is obviously not lying in personal banking accounts.

Over the years, the volume of money in private hands has increased enormously, but as we have seen the banks' share of this has diminished. For many years the attitude of the banks was comparatively passive. They showed little aggression in the competition for private savings and the word 'marketing' was not heard in the corridors of British banks until the mid-1960s. Nowadays, the competition is intense and the banks naturally felt aggrieved at the taxation advantages and the comparative freedom from regulation enjoyed by some of their competitors. They were to say with some force in their evidence to the Wilson Committee.

> 'At present, the national savings movement, the building societies and the life assurance companies in particular can attract deposits and savings on the basis of fiscal and regulatory advantages not available to other types of institution. Such differentiation may have made sense when the roles of the various institutions were more clear-cut than they are today. But now that institutions are increasingly competing with one another in the same market places, the differentiation has become discriminatory and undoubtedly lessens the efficiency of the financial system as a whole."[9]

While the deposit-taking business was losing ground to competition, the banks' role as lenders was more overtly threatened. For most of the post-war years and certainly from 1951, credit squeezes were successive features of monetary policy. For most of that time, bank lending was subject to qualitative constraints and from 1957 onwards there were quantitative controls. Only for a comparatively brief period, from 1958 to 1960, were restrictions on bank credit removed – long enough for a great upsurge in lending, the advent of personal loans, the new concept (for banks) of fixed-term loans for consumer durables and with that the gradual turning of the banks towards involvement in hire purchase finance. With the return of lending 'ceilings' in 1960, it seemed to many that lending constraints must forever be a feature of the mixed economy.

The third area of traditional banking, the transmission of

money, was not and probably could never be a profitable activity in itself, but it is of course an essential aspect of current account management – and even that area was coming under threat from the National Giro (now Girobank plc).

The threats to traditional banking were very real and bank profits seemed to be a hostage to bank rate. In some banks it was calculated that a return to a period of 'cheap money' would prevent the continuance of profitable trading. Not unnaturally, all the banks, no doubt with varying degrees of conviction, turned their minds to the more profitable use of resources. In the mid-1960s there were approximately 12,500 banking branches throughout the United Kingdom and the staffs of the clearing banks totalled something over 150,000. If conventional banking activities were to be circumscribed, it was essential to use some of those resources in new, profitable channels. It was also thought at the time that automation would release staff to deal with higher grade duties, although it is doubtful whether in the event this happened. In any case, costs were increasing rapidly and it was only a few years later in 1971 that Sir John Thomson in his address to Barclays Bank shareholders said, 'We must continue to supplement our retail service by developing less labour intensive activities, which will gather some of their business from the network of 5,000 branches in the Group'.

Thus the banks began to look in a number of directions at once, but they showed neither unanimity nor uniformity. In November 1954, the Commercial Bank of Scotland had acquired the share capital of Scottish Midland Guarantee Trust and Second Scottish Midland Guarantee Trust, but it was not until 1958 that the English clearing banks took any major investment in hire purchase houses. In July of that year, Barclays bank and British Linen Bank acquired 25 per cent of the share capital of United Dominions Trust, described by the then Barclays Bank Chairman as arising from 'an unexpected opportunity'.[10] A month later, in August 1958, Westminster Bank and Martins Bank announced the acquisition of 20 per cent each in the equity of Mercantile Credit Limited; National Provincial Bank acquired the whole of the capital of North Central Wagon and Finance; Midland Bank acquired the whole of Forward Trust; Royal Bank of Scotland acquired 40 per cent of British Wagon Company; Lloyds Bank acquired 25 per cent of Bowmaker and

30 per cent of Olds Discount; District Bank acquired 33⅓ per cent of Astley Industrial Trust; and Bank of Scotland acquired the whole of North West Securities. It was a busy month! The *Bankers' Magazine* was prompted to declare:

> 'The celerity with which the schemes have appeared certainly suggests that in modern times an association of banking with hire purchase finance is regarded as a natural and desirable development.'

The total investment by the clearing banks in hire purchase companies at that time came to approximately £23 million.

Among the services which had their inspiration outside the United Kingdom – in this case the United States – was the credit card. Here again, however, the banks chose to go in quite diverse ways. Early in 1965 Westminster Bank announced the purchase of 40 per cent (later 48·7 per cent) of The Diner's Club with its international credit card business. In October that year, the first cheque card was introduced by National Provincial Bank, guaranteeing payment of cheques up to £30. Before the year was out, Barclays Bank had developed 'Barclaycard', a true credit card on the American pattern, regarded by Barclays Bank in their announcement 'as a natural extension of ordinary banking facilities'. In March 1966, Midland Bank introduced their cheque card and the following month Lloyds Bank and Martins Bank, together with nine other English and Irish banks, announced the introduction of the 'Bankers' Card'.

There was a similar confluence of activity in the matter of unit trusts. Almost simultaneously with an internal decision in Martins Bank that they would not then go into the management of unit trusts, Lloyds Bank announced its decision to do so. The first issue of Lloyds Bank units was made in October 1966. The following July, Westminster Bank moved into unit trust management jointly with Hambros Bank and within a few months Martins Bank announced the acquisition of 75 per cent of Unicorn Securities. With commendable single-mindedness Midland Bank chose not to enter the field of unit trust management, but to concentrate on the role of trustee. Possibly Midland Bank thought there was the risk of conflict in being managers of their own unit trusts whilst being trustee of others, although other banks seemed to resolve this problem. However,

'Banking Supermarkets.'

in due time through the acquisition of Montagu Trust and the Drayton Group, Midland Bank found themselves in the business of unit trust management and so they remain.

There we have but a few examples. As we shall see, the banks turned their thoughts in a short space of years to insurance broking, life assurance, advisory services, merchant banking, leasing, factoring and almost every other legitimate financial activity. Sometimes the banks went by different routes to the same terminus. An outside observer may be forgiven for thinking that there were times when the banks did not know their own mind. They moved in no time at all from talk of 'sticking to their lasts' to such terminology as 'one stop banking' and 'banking supermarkets'. It must have seemed to many bank managers that service was piled on service and they must have longed to cry halt. On an old sign on the M6 motorway approaching Carlisle, the plea of many a bank manager was graphically summed up – 'no more services'. Indeed, a survey among bank managers (see p. 472) elicited at least two graphic comments: 'banks shouldn't sell specialist services' and 'ancillary services are a pain in the neck'!

Although in their evidence to the Wilson Committee the clearing banks refer to the 'diversification into a wide range of financial activities not previously associated with clearing banking', they go on to say:

> 'The clearing banks have developed along lines much closer to those of the continental "universal" banks than before, aiming to provide a comprehensive range of domestic and international financial services within a single group of companies. But the blurring of traditional demarcation lines between the clearing banks and other institutions does not mean that they either seek or expect to dominate all the diverse financial markets, old and new, in which they now operate. Deposit banking remains the staple of their existence and conditions all other banking activities. In particular, it means that by far the largest part of their banking business must be conducted with due regard to the essentially short-term nature of their deposit base.'

And again:

> 'It is their (the clearing banks) intention to continue to adapt to changing circumstances and needs and to compete robustly with

one another and with other institutions. But in so doing they cannot afford to neglect the basic clearing banking services which remain the foundation of their business.'

Retail banking competition

Far from neglecting the basic services, the joint stock banks have in recent times intensified their efforts through the retail branch network to increase their business in the personal sector. Their market shares, both of deposit banking and personal lending, are discussed in Chapters 2 and 3. In particular, the high street banks entered the house mortgage field in a highly competitive way with considerable initial success. They have also continued to explore the problems of payment of wages by cheque or credit transfer. The branch network is costly and, not surprisingly, the banks are looking for an improved return on the very considerable resources, in terms of both staff and premises, absorbed in the branch system. The competition for personal savings became intense, partly from the building societies, partly from the Trustee Savings Banks and partly from the Department for National Savings. By the mid 1980s, there were approximately 50,000 retail outlets of financial institutions in the United Kingdom. The total number of money shops is now over 1,000 and there is increasing competition from those retail stores who have seen the opportunity to provide their own banking services.

The building societies remain the largest single competitor in the group. They are the recipients of approximately one-half of the total private savings in this country, and an increasing number of building society investors use the building societies as banks. Traditionally, they have not offered anything approaching the range of services of the all-purpose bank but with their new statutory powers the building societies are now able to widen their product base as discussed in the next chapter.

The City Revolution

The evolution of British banking towards the 'all-purpose bank' over little more than two decades was fascinating to observe. It proceeded in a gradual, almost organic, fashion, sometimes haphazardly and impulsively but on the whole predictably, once the concept of diversification had been accepted. It must be doubtful however, whether anyone did predict or could have predicted the confluence of events which culminated in 1986 in what has come to be known as the City Revolution, to which we have made reference on the opening page of this book. The concurrent factors were:

(i) The re-structuring of the Stock Exchange leading up to the "Big Bang" in October 1986,
(ii) the general climate surrounding the subject of investor protection and the eventual passing of the Financial Services Act 1986,
(iii) the enlargement of the powers of building societies by the Building Societies Act 1986, and
(iv) the increased competition (to which the Government and the Bank of England gave encouragement) and the resulting mergers and crossing of traditional boundaries.

These subjects are dealt with in their place throughout this work, but it may be appropriate here to refer to the events which led up to the Big Bang.

The Fair Trading Act 1973, extended the jurisdiction of the Restrictive Practices Court to financial and commercial operations and in 1976 the Office of Fair Trading embarked on an examination of the Stock Exchange's rule book. As many as 170 rules were challenged and in general the Stock Exchange was considered to be operating restrictive practices for three reasons, viz (i) commissions were levied according to a fixed scale and not negotiated, (ii) membership of the Exchange was exclusive and outside corporations were prohibited from membership, and (iii) the separation of the functions of jobbers and stockbrokers (known as 'single capacity') resulted in a two-tier system of expenses and profits.

As a result, restrictive practice proceedings were initiated against the Stock Exchange in 1979. The prospect of these proceedings was hanging over the Stock Exchange, and therefore the City, for the next four years, i.e. until agreement was reached between the Stock Exchange and the then Secretary of State for Trade and Industry to the effect that the restrictive practices proceedings would be withdrawn and the Stock Exchange, for its part, would abolish its system of fixed commissions and also allow non-members to join the Stock Exchange Council and some of its committees. It was envisaged at that stage that 'single capacity' would continue. It was argued however, that the abolition of fixed commissions would so constrict brokers' margins that they would deal among themselves and cut out the jobbers. The theory was advanced therefore that single capacity should be abolished and all firms would become dual capacity broker-dealers.

It must be doubtful whether this internal restructuring would of itself have led to the resultant upheaval but it coincided with a number of factors which at the time were exercising the minds of City people. We can only list those factors briefly and in no particular order. These factors, taken together with the Stock Exchange's internal reorganisation, resulted in the ultimate solution which was to be so dramatic and which set the pattern of securities dealings for the future. They were these:

1. Technological development had made it possible for the major international financial centres to deal in securities virtually round-the-clock.

2. For that and other reasons, overseas dealing in London stocks had increased considerably and were being dealt in outside London.

3. Equity finance for large corporations was increasingly being raised across international borders, whereas a few years ago such issues would have been confined to home markets.

4. There was increased 'securitisation' of debt: this meant that large corporations were raising money by the issue of securities rather than by loans from the commercial banks. This led to increased activity on the stock markets of the world (some of which was in danger of bypassing London) and it gave the banks an added reason for becoming involved in the Stock Exchange as the relationship of bank loans and the raising of securitised debt became more apparent.

5. Few firms had the financial resources to conduct the large-scale research necessary in present day markets.

6. There was an increasing tendency to conduct bargains away from the floor of the Stock Exchange which was regarded by some as a threat to the jobbing system in this country.

7. There was pressure for 'negotiated commissions' in the gilt-edged market (the third largest government securities market in the world after the USA and Japan) and the threat that gilts would be traded off the floor of the House as in America.

The resulting structure arrived by co-operation between the Bank of England and the Stock Exchange may be summarised as follows:

(i) minimum commissions were abolished with effect from 27 October 1986.

(ii) From the same date 'dual capacity' was introduced and all firms were deemed to become broker-dealers or market-makers.

(iii) All market-makers would be required to maintain a two-way price system, i.e. buying and selling prices on the Stock Exchange's automated quotation system (SEAQ), the development of which was one of the main reasons for deferring the Big Bang until October 1986.

(iv) In the gilts markets there would be four categories of membership, viz:

(a) Market-makers, of whom in the result there were 27, who would deal direct with the Bank of England and would be obliged to maintain continuous two-way prices at which they must be prepared to deal in the gilts market.
(b) Money brokers, who would act as intermediaries between market-makers and the institutions.
(c) Inter-dealer brokers who would provide dealing facilities between the market-makers.
(d) Broker-dealers who generally would deal in transactions too small for the wholesale market-makers.

(v) The Stock Exchange amended their rules to permit corporate membership and total ownership of jobbers and brokers by institutions.

In the result, within a comparatively short space of time, all the major firms of jobbers and stockbrokers (with the notable exception at the time of writing of Messrs. Cazenove) had been acquired by financial institutions. The extent of that involvement is discussed in Chapter 6 under the heading of Investment Services. In March 1984, Barclays acquired the then permitted maximum stake of 29·9 per cent in jobbers Wedd Durlacher Mordaunt & Co., and stockbrokers De Zoete & Bevan, and announced their intention of acquiring from 75 per cent to 80 per cent of these firms when the rules permitted. Barclays was thus the first of the London banks to announce this threefold association between a clearing bank, a stock jobber and a stockbroker. Shortly afterwards Midland Bank, through their associated merchant bank, Samuel Montagu, announced the acquisition of an interest in W. Greenwell & Co., stockbrokers, but chose not to acquire a stake in a jobbing firm. In July 1984 National Westminster Bank acquired a minority stake in stockbrokers, Fielding, Newson-Smith, having already acquired 29·9 per cent of jobbers, Bisgood, Bishop. Lloyds Bank indicated that it would develop its own securities business through Lloyds merchant bank. Of the remaining clearing banks only the Royal Bank of Scotland took a similar step – in February 1986 they acquired an interest in a Liverpool-based firm of stockbrokers, Tilney & Co. Over the two years or so in which such alliances were possible a number of merchant banks, overseas banks and other business houses acquired significant stakes in firms of both stockbrokers and jobbers to the point where, as mentioned above, nearly all the major Stock Exchange firms became part of large institutional groupings.

These matters are discussed further in Chapter 6 under the heading of Investment Services. It is interesting and a little surprising that the area in which banks traditionally trod with most caution and even reluctance, i.e. that of investment business, has become suddenly and dramatically the main development of recent years. Whilst one tends to think of the business of banking having evolved over a long history it is not surprising that the City talks not of evolution but of revolution.

For the student of banking the following pages are designed to serve as a guide to the activities of the high street banks in the United Kingdom. An attempt is made to describe each service in substance; to discuss in each case the market for the service and the environment in which it is offered; to consider the attendant problems and pose some questions for the future; and to look at the structure or framework within which each service operates.

For the practising banker here is something in the nature of a refresher course. In his everyday business the bank official has the seemingly impossible task of assimilating the details of a great number of diverse financial services, seeing each one in its place in the total spectrum of banking activities and calling up the relevant information from the recesses of his memory depending on the needs and circumstances of the customer. Furthermore, for a long time to come, bank officials will be required to attend courses and other meetings to discuss the range of products offered by their group and to consider the marketing and profitability of this or that service.

Finally, this commentary may also be of interest to the external observer of British banking. If it helps the enquirer to appreciate, in the comfort of his armchair, something of the role of the all-purpose bank in the United Kingdom in the field of 'service banking' and if in turn that stimulates imitation, imagination or even inspiration, it will have been a useful exercise.

References

1 United Dominions Trust Ltd v Kirkwood (1966) 1 All. E.R., at page 979.
2 Bankers' Books Evidence Act 1879 *and* Companies Act 1948, s. 432.
3 Regina v Industrial Disputes Tribunal *ex parte* East Anglian Trustee Savings Bank (1954) 1 W.L.R. 1093.
4 L. C. Mather: *Commercial Banks: Evolution of Services.* International Banking Summer School, Oxford, July 1970. The Institute of Bankers, 1970.
5 Lord (then Sir Leslie) O'Brien speaking to the The Institute of Bankers in Scotland, January 1973.
6 P. S. Nadler: *Banking.* Girard Bank, February 1972.
7 G. Riley: 'Banks and Advertising'. *Journal of The Institute of Bankers,* August 1959.
8 Central Statistical Office: *Economic Trends.* January 1978.
9 Committee of London Clearing Bankers: *The London Clearing Banks – Evidence to the (Wilson) Committee to Review the Functioning of Financial Institutions.* Longman, 1978.
10 A. W. Tuke: Address to the Stockholders of Barclays Bank Limited, 12 January 1959.

CHAPTER 2

Deposit Banking

In *The Principles and Practice of Banking* (1871), J. W. Gilbart tells us that:

> 'The exchanging of money; the lending of money; the borrowing of money; the transmitting of money, are the four principal branches of the business of modern banking.'

Indeed, this seems to have been the order of historical development of banking in most countries and it seems well established that money changing began when Edward II granted land in the City of London to the Lombardy goldsmiths in order to encourage them to settle here. Although, in time, the goldsmiths being men of substance became the repositories for other people's money and although they lent money 'at interest', it was not until the second half of the sixteenth century that deposit banking as such began. We are told that Sir Thomas Gresham, 'the father of English banking' was the goldsmiths' banker at the sign of the Grasshopper in Lombard Street from 1549 onwards and that he was not only a lender of money, but was also paying interest on deposits.[1]

Although the early goldsmith bankers may well have been lenders of (their own) money before they became borrowers of money on deposit, modern banking in this country has traditionally worked in the reverse order, i.e. the joint stock banks have in general been deposit-driven. They have taken money in and then sought ways in which to deploy it. This traditional attitude has been modified in more recent times. With the development of the wholesale money markets, the banks can usually lend money knowing that they can borrow it, if necessary, in the market. Indeed, some commercial banks conduct a 'wholesale' banking business in this way without a customer deposit base as such.

Nevertheless, the flow of customer deposits has been the life blood of the UK clearing banks over the years and will no doubt continue to be the main source of the banks' funds.

The sources of deposits

The main source of sterling deposits for the UK banks has been, and still is, the private sector. Approximately 80 per cent of all bank accounts are held by private individuals and private unincorporated businesses. These account for approximately two-thirds of total resident sterling deposits. In general, the network of branch banks has been set up across the country over the years as a deposit-gathering exercise. It is true that some branches have become lending branches in the sense that, because of their particular environment, their loans have far exceeded their deposits. From the customer's point of view, the attraction of having an account with a clearing bank was primarily the facility for making payments by cheque. The joint stock banks in Britain were probably unique in that the money transmission system which they initiated through the Bankers' Clearing House became a central feature of the financial system.

The second main source of deposits is that of industrial and commercial companies. Approximately one-quarter of the sterling deposits of the London clearing banks comes from this source. The remaining sterling deposits come from other financial institutions and from the public sector, representing between 5 per cent and 10 per cent of the total.

The deposits of the London and Scottish clearing banks include at any one time an increasingly high proportion of currency deposits. At the end of 1986, out of total deposits of £235b, sterling deposits amounted to £157b and foreign currency deposits amounted to £79b.

Constraints on deposit-taking

We have already said that the major part of sterling deposits of the UK banks comes through the retail operations of the branch network, whether from private individuals or from industry and commerce. It follows that the major constraint on the banks' ability to gather deposits is the general economic environment and, in particular, the general level of national income. In the private sector, the level of personal savings, i.e. the difference between total personal disposable incomes and consumer expenditure, has varied in recent years from approximately 16½ per cent as a percentage of disposable incomes in 1980 down to approximately 7 per cent in 1985. It varies from time to time, depending primarily on savers' expectations. In the business sector, the level of liquidity will vary also according to the overall economic climate, the nature of the business, the terms of trade, the cost of money and, for example, the commitment to capital expenditure.

Other constraints on the ability of individual banks to attract deposits have arisen over the years, either from inter-bank agreements, principally the interest rate cartel which existed until the introduction of Competition and Credit Control in 1971[2] and also the monetary controls imposed by the Bank of England from time to time as part of overall government policy. In this category, there was the 'corset' introduced in November 1973, the effect of which was to impose penalties on banks which increased their interest-bearing liabilities above a prescribed ceiling. The other example was the constraint imposed between September 1973 and February 1975 on the ability of the banks to pay more than 9½ per cent per annum interest on deposits, in order to protect building societies from the effect of high interest rates then current.

The competition for deposits

The total of sterling deposits held by financial institutions in this country (excluding deposits held on behalf of other banks) has increased substantially over the years, as one would expect, from a total of £24·5b in 1964 to £89b in 1978 and approximately £272b in 1986. The following table shows the percentage of deposits held by the various institutions competing for sterling deposits in the United Kingdom in recent years.

The figures in the table include deposits from both personal and corporate sources and we may consider these in turn. Taking first the corporate sector, the main competition for deposits from companies and other incorporated institutions comes from overseas banks now operating in London. At the

Per cent of total sterling deposits of UK residents at end year				
	1972	**1977**	**1982**	**1986**
London & Scottish clearing banks	42·4	38·5	33·6	39·9
Other UK monetary sector institutions	13·0	12·9	18·5	12·8
Building societies	35·6	40·6	42·4	43·3
National Savings Bank	4·9	3·8	3·4	2·9
Treasury Bills, UK non-bank holders	0·1	1·2	0·2	0·1
Local authority temporary debt	4·0	3·0	1·9	1·0
Total Deposits	100·0	100·0	100·0	100·0
£ billion	40·4	79·3	159·5	271·6

[Source: *CLSB Statistical Unit*]

time of writing, there are approximately 350 branches or representative offices of overseas banks in London, compared with only half that number 10 years ago. A degree of competition for corporate deposits came, however, from the National Savings Bank when the maximum deposit on investment account was raised to £250,000 at very competitive rates of interest. The maximum is now £100,000.

It is in the personal sector that the competition for sterling deposits has been most intense. The repositories for personal savings in Britain are the following:

the high street banks,
National Savings,
Girobank,
other banks,
money shops,
building societies,
life assurance,
pension schemes,
stocks and shares (including unit trusts).

A distinction may be drawn here between short-term savings (or cash deposits) and longer term savings consisting principally of endowment assurance and pension schemes. These are all parts of the savings media, whether long-term or short-term, but for practical purposes we may assume that the banks are in competition with other savings institutions for cash deposits, i.e. after savers have put aside a proportion of their disposable income for pension or life assurance purposes. Nevertheless, the more people who are inclined to save through these longer term media, the less there is available in the short-term deposit market.

Building societies

The building society movement is the largest competitor of the banks in the deposit-taking business. Indeed, in aggregate, the building societies are now the major repository of personal savings, having passed the banks for the first time in 1971.

Building societies grew out of the spirit of self-help in the late eighteenth century, the first society being created in Birmingham in 1775. The early societies were small and local. The members would subscribe funds, which would be used first to buy some land and then to build a house. Further money would be used to buy further land and build further houses. The houses would be allocated by ballot among the members or, in some cases, the right to a house would be sold by auction among the members. In time, money was subscribed by other people who had funds to invest, but did not necessarily wish to buy a house through the society. Thus, the members of a building society became its investors and its borrowers, and this is still the situation today.

At the turn of the century, there were 2,286 building societies in existence, but with terminations and mergers the number had reduced to 149 by the end of 1986.

It is an indication of the growth of the building society movement that, in 1930, their total assets were £370m; at the time of the Radcliffe Committee[3] in 1958, total assets were £2,400m; by 1978 (figures quoted in evidence to the Wilson Committee), the figure was approximately £40,000m and by the end of 1985, total assets had passed the £120,000m mark.

By the end of 1986, building societies were operating approximately 40 million accounts through 7,000 branches.

Various reasons have been advanced for the growth of building society savings at the expense of the joint stock banks. They may be summarised thus:

All building society accounts earn interest: It seems that a large number of people prefer to have an interest-bearing account with a building society, even for short-term savings, rather than the traditional non-interest-bearing current account with a bank, notwithstanding the money transmission facilities which a current account offers.

The income tax treatment of building society interest: It is a feature of building societies in the United Kingdom that the societies pay to the Inland Revenue income tax at a 'composite rate' on the interest which they allow to their investors. The rate is calculated each year according to a number of factors, including the basic rate of tax currently in force, the reliefs available and the typical income levels of a cross-section of building society investors. This arrangement is not intended to give building society investors any special relief from tax, but rather to calculate in a composite way the level of taxation which would be payable if interest were paid gross to individual investors. Thus, the building societies pay the income tax and the investor is not liable for any further tax at the basic rate. Investors who are liable for higher rates of income tax will, however, have to pay the higher rate tax. The effect of all this is that the main body of building society investors are not troubled with income tax in relation to their building society interest. And so it is that building societies, in general, have always been able to show in their advertisements the gross equivalent before basic rate tax of the rates of interest they are paying.

This difference in treatment between building societies and banks was removed with effect from the fiscal year 1985/86 when all banks and licenced deposit takers became subject to a composite rate of tax in relation to personal accounts. The system operates in the same way as described above for building societies and, in fact, for the first three years the composite rate was arrived at by reference to the available data applicable to building societies. For all practical purposes therefore, the treatment of interest on personal bank accounts is now the same as for building society accounts.

The convenience of building societies: In general, the hours of business of building societies have been more convenient to the public than those of banks. In particular, the employment of part-time staff by building societies enabled them to provide a service to the public on Saturday mornings.

Branch design: For the most part, building societies have adopted the 'potted plant' shop-front style of branch which presents a friendlier, more welcoming image than most of the older designs of bank premises.

The availability of mortgages: Many people have been encouraged to save in their early years with building societies in the belief, with some justification, that they would more readily be able to obtain a mortgage loan for house purchase. Any such advantage diminished, however, with the entry of the banks into the house mortgage business.

Freedom from controls: The building societies were not brought within the system of monetary or credit control operated by the Bank of England in accordance with the policies of successive governments. Thus, the building societies have, for the most part, been free from contraints on either their deposit-taking or lending policies, whereas the banks have been subject over the years to quantitative and qualitative controls and certain other restrictions on their ability to take deposits, such as the 'corset' mentioned on page 21.

Simplicity: On the whole, building society services are simple and understandable to the public, whereas to many people bank services appear more sophisticated, more diverse and at times a bit of a mystery.

A mortgage monopoly: Building societies have traditionally been the main source of finance for house purchase in this country and, until recently, approximately 94 per cent of all home mortgages were granted through building societies. That figure was reduced to approximately 80 per cent with the entry of the banks into house mortgage business. It may be argued that the absence of competition enabled the building societies to fix their mortgage interest rates at a level which enabled them to maintain competitive investment rates, (although it must be said that the cost of borrowing money for house purchase in this country has not been historically high). With the widening of competition for mortgage business, there is an additional constraint on what building societies may charge for mortgage loans and, therefore, on the rates they can pay to investors.

No doubt other reasons may be advanced for the comparative success of the building societies. One thing is certain – they have been used increasingly as banks by their investors. A large number of salary cheques are paid into building societies and a large number of household bills are met out of building society accounts. The 'turnover' of building society balances is enormous, something not remotely contemplated in the early days of the movement. In a typical year, the withdrawals from building societies may be as much as, and sometimes in excess of, 80 per cent of new investment.

In recent years not only have the public used building societies as banks, but the societies themselves have tended to become more like banks in the development of their services. However, the powers of building societies were somewhat proscribed by statute, notably the Building Society Act 1962. For example, a building society was unable to issue a credit card because this could result in the granting of unsecured loans and under the Act a society could lend money only on the security of a first mortgage of freehold or leasehold property. Under the Building Societies Act 1986, societies were given increased powers to undertake a range of financial services. The legislation provides that building societies may make unsecured advances within certain statutory limits, to own and develop land primarily for residential purposes, to raise non-retail funds subject to a maximum (which may be varied) of 20 per cent of liabilities and to offer a wide range of financial services including money transmission, foreign exchange, the administration of pension schemes, the provision of insurance services and the ability to undertake estate agency and conveyancing services. The legislation also includes new provisions for investor protection similar to those contained in the Banking Act 1979 (see page 45) and provides for the setting up of a Building Societies Commission with wide powers of supervision of the building society movement.

Not all societies will have the capital and human resources to embark on such a wide range of financial services. Nevertheless, the capacity to offer banking services such as personal loans, money transmission and credit cards must necessarily enhance the ability of some societies to compete for customer deposits. A survey by the Inter-Bank Research Organisation shows that 51 per cent of all adults already have accounts with building societies. (This compares with a figure of only 15 per cent some 15 years earlier.)

Perhaps of particular interest is the power contained in the new legislation to enable building societies (subject to very stringent voting requirements) to become public limited companies (PLC). If in time some societies choose to follow that route, we may well see mergers between such PLC 'societies' and other financial institutions. Whether or not that happens there will no doubt be more mergers among the building societies themselves in order to gain extra strength to take advantage of the new powers.

National savings

The Department for National Savings was established on 1st October 1969. It had hitherto been the Post Office Savings Department and had been part of the Post Office. The Department has a responsibility for the following:

National Savings Bank;
Premium Savings Bonds;
British Savings Bonds (no longer on sale);
Certain government stocks;
National Savings Certificates;
National Savings Income Bonds;
National Savings Deposit Bonds;
National Savings Yearly Plan;
The Save-As-You-Earn Service.
Index-linked schemes

Total balances outstanding with the National Savings Department as at December 1986 were £31,000m. The major items in terms of competition for short-term savings were:

National Savings Certificates	£17,100m
National Savings Bank	£7,300m

National savings have not historically been a major source of competition to the clearing banks in the personal savings sector. Until 1979, Trustee Savings Bank balances were included in the national savings figures and so comparison with past years is difficult. Approximately 20 years ago, the Trustee Savings Bank and National Savings Bank accounted for 20 per cent of sterling deposits in the United Kingdom, but both the Trustee Savings Banks (see below) and the National Savings Bank lost ground to the building societies. By 1976, the balances of the National Savings Bank accounted for only a little over 3 per cent of total sterling deposits. For most people, national savings meant the purchase of National Savings Certificates but with the high level of inflation in the 1970s, they lost much of their attraction, notwithstanding that the interest was tax-free.

In more recent times, increased emphasis has been placed on national savings as a factor in financing the central government's borrowing requirement, and this has led to the introduction of Index-Linked Savings Certificates and the payment of competitive rates of interest on National Savings Bank investment accounts. The following are now the main factors in the overall competitiveness of the National Savings Department:

From September 1981, Index-Linked Savings Certificates became available for purchase by any persons regardless of age, up to £5,000 per person;

Interest on National Savings Bank investment accounts, at the time of writing, is higher than that available from the commercial banks or building societies;

The first £70 per person of interest on a National Savings Bank *ordinary* account is exempt from income tax;

Depositors may hold up to £100,000 in a National Savings Bank *investment* account.

The National Savings Bank was formerly the Post Office

Savings Bank. It has approximately 21 million customers, who pay into or draw out of their National Savings Bank accounts at any of the 22,000 or so offices of the Post Office throughout the country. It has traditionally been a small saver's bank, the average balance in the ordinary accounts being approximately £70. In the investment department, however, the number of accountholders now exceeds three million and total balances exceed £5,000m. The National Savings Bank does not lend money, but it provides two of the basic ingredients of banking, i.e. the taking of deposits and the transmission of payments.

The Trustee Savings Bank

The first Trustee Savings Bank was founded by Reverend Henry Duncan in Dumfriesshire in 1810 to provide a haven for the savings of the poor. In the following year, a considerable number of savings banks were set up in Scotland, England and Wales.

The Trustee Savings Banks were based on the principle that the depositors' money is held in trust for the depositors by a Board of Trustees. Thus, the basic relationship was not that of debtor and creditor as in commercial banking and it was not contemplated that the deposits of customers would be onward-lent to other customers.

The movement developed so rapidly that in 1817 an Act of Parliament was passed, establishing a Fund for the Banks for Savings to serve as a repository for Trustee Savings Bank deposits. The number of Trustee Savings Banks increased to 465 by 1819, but a number were closed when the Post Office Savings Bank was established in 1861. The special investment departments were set up from 1870 onwards to take in funds which were subject to notice of withdrawal and which were invested not in the Fund for the Banks for Savings, but in other government securities. It was this development which was largely responsible for the substantial growth of the Trustee Savings Banks.

There were 73 Trustee Savings Banks in existence when the Page Committee[4] reported in 1973 on its review of national savings. The Committee recommended that the banks should merge to form not more than 20 separate units and that they should become the basis of the 'third force' in banking in this country. The general recommendations of the Page Committee were put into effect in the Trustee Savings Bank Act of 1976 which provided for the setting-up of the Trustee Savings Bank Central Board. Within a short space of time, the 73 banks merged into 17 local banks and then into four main regional banks, viz. England & Wales, Scotland, Northern Ireland and the Channel Islands. Under the 1985 legislation the Trustee Savings Bank incorporated as a public liability company with the four regional subsidiaries incorporated and having their head offices in their respective countries. The public flotation of the bank took place in October 1986.

The Trustee Savings Bank has approximately six million customers and operates through 1,700 or so branches throughout the country.

Until September 1979, the Trustee Savings Banks functioned as a part of the Department for National Savings. The Central Trustee Savings Bank is now a separate statutory creation, however, and is a member of the Bankers' Clearing House and a member of the Committee of London and Scottish Bankers. Throughout this work therefore, the Trustee Savings Bank is grouped with the other clearing banks in this country.

The Trustee Savings Banks used to have a 'down-market' image compared with that of the joint stock banks – indeed this was natural, bearing in mind that the banks were set up to assist the poor. In their evidence to the Wilson Committee, the London Clearing Banks showed that only 28 per cent of Trustee Savings Bank customers were in the AB/C1 socio-economic group, compared with a corresponding figure of 56 per cent among clearing bank current accountholders. Nevertheless, in terms of actual account-holders, the Trustee Savings Bank has more customers than any other bank in the country apart from the National Savings Bank, which some would argue is not a bank in the strict sense.

Like the building societies, the Trustee Savings Banks were not within the monetary control exercised by the Bank of England. When they were part of the Department for National Savings, their customers enjoyed exemption from tax on the first £70 of bank interest, but this no longer applies.

Girobank plc.

Girobank, formerly the National Giro was set up in October 1968 to provide a money transmission service on a national basis as an alternative to the cheque-clearing service provided by the commercial banks. This, in turn, necessitated offering account facilities to customers and, up to the present time, National Girobank has attracted approximately one million accounts. Like the National Savings Bank, it operates through offices of the Post Office. The bank has developed a number of financial services, including the provision of cheque account facilities and personal loans. It is a member of the Bankers' Clearing House.

The Wilson Committee agreed that, on the surface, 'it does seem irrational for there to be two separate public sector banks both operating across Post Office counters' (i.e. National Girobank and National Savings Bank) but, on balance, could not see any great advantage flowing from a merger. At the present time, Girobank does not present a major threat to the other clearing banks in the deposit-taking field. Girobank has not been particularly successful in attracting personal savings, the larger share of its business coming from nationalised institutions and some large corporations who use its money transfer service but do not maintain large balances as such. Nevertheless, Girobank has opened a number of regional offices and as it extends its banking services, it may well become a more significant competitor in the deposit-taking arena.

The Co-operative Bank

The Co-operative Bank was incorporated by Act of Parliament in 1971. Prior to that, it was the banking department of the Co-operative Wholesale Society handling the house cash and banking arrangements of the Co-operative Societies around the country. It now has well over one million customers and approximately half the bank's total deposits come from the personal sector, the remainder coming from trade unions, local authorities and retail co-operative societies. The bank has approximately 4,000 cashpoints (Handybanks) in stores around the country; it operates current and deposit accounts, grants personal loans and has its own credit card (Handycard). The bank is a member of the Bankers' Clearing House. It has approximately 80 branches and operates a number of financial centres in Co-operative stores around the country.

The Yorkshire Bank

The Yorkshire Bank, formerly the Yorkshire Penny Bank, is owned by Barclays, Lloyds, National Westminster and Royal Bank of Scotland. It has just over 200 branches in England and offers a range of banking services comparable to the main clearing banks. At the end of 1985, the bank had deposits of approximately £1,500b.

Money shops

We have referred to the growth of foreign banks in London, most of which concentrate on wholesale banking and borrow from the money market in order to finance their lending. The overseas banks have not, for the most part, developed a branch network in this country, nor engaged in retail banking as such. A handful of institutions, usually of American origin or parentage, have developed the money shop concept in Britain. The principal operators are Citibank; Western Savings & Trust and H.F.C. (Household Finance Corporation of Illinois). In 1982 the Standard Chartered Bank announced that their instalment credit subsidiary, Chartered Trust, planned to open 12 or so money shops in the UK. There are approximately 1,000 money shops either in being or in prospect throughout the country. They offer basic financial facilities and have set out to provide the customer with three basic needs, viz: interest on current accounts, automatic or easily arranged credit facilities and convenient hours of business. Whilst not presenting a serious threat to the clearing banks, they appear to have found a gap in the market and it will be interesting to observe their progress.

Licensed Deposit-Takers

At the present time there are approximately 300 institutions licensed by the Bank of England to take deposits under the Banking Act 1979 (see page 45). These include the retail money shops mentioned above but the majority of licensed deposit takers do not have a branch network. Under the Banking Act of 1987 the distinction between licensed deposit takers and banks will to some extent disappear but there will be stringent requirements to be observed before any deposit taker may use the description 'bank'.

In-store banking

This is one of the most significant developments in the field of competition for retail banking deposits. In-store banking may mean two things. The term is applied to those cases where a bank opens a branch in a retail store as, for example, Midland Bank have opened a small number of branches in Tesco stores. The term also applies however, to the development of financial services, including the taking of deposits, by retail stores within their own organisations. Perhaps the most quoted example is that of Sears Roebuck in the United States, a merchandising operation which has become one of the largest financial institutions in America. It has approximately 40 million credit cardholders and it owns an insurance company, a real estate agency and a large firm of share-brokers.

A number of stores in this country have moved in varying ways and at varying speeds into financial services. Debenhams, for example, operate money centres and home centres (through their subsidiary Wellbeck Finance) and in recent times have established a link with a leading firm of stockbrokers in order to sell stocks and shares through at least one of the Debenhams retail stores. Marks & Spencer have expressed interest from time to time in the development of financial services and in particular, have now promoted their credit card to a point where they have approximately 1 million cardholders operating on 700,000 or so accounts. Sainsburys do not at present operate a credit card themselves but they are developing automated teller machines in their stores, an operation which is self-financed by the Group. Other leading stores, Burtons, Littlewoods and John Menzies have all announced their intention to move into the supply of financial services and in June 1985 the Co-operative Society said that they proposed to launch several hundred money shops in their stores throughout this country. Other examples are Harrods, who operate their own credit card and provide a range of financial services and the House of Fraser store, Rackhams, who have also moved into the financial services scene.

Other stores have developed links with existing financial institutions, e.g. British Home Stores operate money centres in co-operation with Boston Trust and Savings and the Anglia Building Society, and the Asda Group have arrangements with a number of banks for the provision of in-store banking.

Arguably the oldest in-store bank is Lewis's Bank, acquired by Martins Bank many years ago and subsequently sold to Lloyds Bank when Lewis's were taken over by House of Fraser. Lloyds Bank still operate Lewis's Bank in Lewis's stores.

The trend towards electronic funds transfer and the development of automated teller machines, both discussed in Chapter 23, point to the extensive development of in-store financial services and this may well become a major factor in the changing pattern of personal banking habits throughout the United Kingdom.

Total financial outlets

It is believed that the financial outlets of all these competitive institutions amount to approximately 50,000, including the Handybanks of the Co-op and the 22,000 or so National Savings Bank and Girobank outlets through the Post Office – a financial port of call for every 900 or so adults!

Types of account

British retail banking has developed on the basis of two categories of account, i.e. the current account and the deposit account, known historically but not in recent times as Drawing Accounts and Deposit Receipts. Deposit Receipts or deposit accounts were subject to a period of notice, traditionally 7 days, although it has long been the practice to waive notice on request on payment of an interest penalty. Until the late 1960s, nearly all clearing bank deposits were on either current account or deposit account. This was partly because of the interest rate cartel, which had operated over the years and partly because of the difficulty of employing more costly deposits, e.g. higher rates for a longer term, on a profitable basis when the banks were required to maintain a 28 per cent liquidity ratio. However, in more recent years and particularly with the introduction of Competition and Credit Control in 1971, the banks have competed extensively for deposits in the money markets and have sought larger deposits on a 'wholesale' basis through the branch network. The banks bid for these larger sums on a competitive basis and will quote the appropriate rate, either through the branch network or direct to the customer depending on the size of the deposit and its term.

In addition, the principal banks issue sterling certificates of deposit, which are payable to bearer and which are negotiable. A certificate of deposit has the advantage that it may be held until maturity, or sold on the secondary market operated by the banks and discount houses. A large proportion of the certificates of deposit in issue at any one time is held by the banks themselves as part of the inter-bank deposit market.

Most forms of bank deposit follow these basic patterns, although the terminology varies from bank to bank. The principal categories are, therefore:

Current accounts: These are essentially drawing or running accounts and no interest is paid on the balances. Approximately one-half of the retail deposits of the London Clearing Banks tend to be on current account. The balances are withdrawable on demand and may be used to meet cheques, standing orders, direct debits and similar money transfers through the banking system. A current account may be in credit or in debit, the term 'overdraft' being normally used to denote an overdrawn current account. The figures quoted for total banking deposits include only those current accounts which are in credit, overdrawn current accounts being reflected in the total of loans and advances.

Deposit accounts: These are normally on seven days' notice and, as described above, bear interest at the London Bankers' Deposit Rate (see below). The balances are not normally available for money transfer purposes, e.g. the drawing of cheques.

Higher rate deposit accounts: From 1984 onwards most of the banks introduced some form of higher rate deposit account, usually with a minimum deposit, e.g. £1,000, in order to counteract the continuing loss of deposits to the building societies. These accounts have various names, e.g. Midland and Lloyds Banks operate High Interest cheque accounts, Barclays have a Higher Rate deposit account and a Prime account, the Bank of Scotland operate a Money-market account and Royal Bank of Scotland have a premium account. In some cases, a limited number of cheques may be drawn on these higher rate accounts: in other cases transfers must be made first to the current account of the customer. The introduction of these accounts resulted in the transfer of very substantial new funds to the clearing banks, although inevitably there would also be the transfer of some balances within each bank in order to take advantage of the higher rate of interest.

Savings accounts: These represent only a tiny proportion of total bank deposits in this country. They take various forms, but usually provide for regular saving at a deposit account rate of interest with limited arrangements for withdrawals.

Investment accounts: These are the larger retail deposits, as described above, and are in the nature of wholesale deposits in that the rate of interest reflects current market rates. They are usually for a period of months, but may be for fixed terms of one to five years. They are also known by such names as Option Deposits (Lloyds Bank), Capital Investment (Midland Bank), High Yield Deposit Scheme (Royal Bank of Scotland), Short-Term Deposit (Co-operative Bank), and Term Deposits (Trustee Savings Bank).

Money Market deposits: These, sometimes known as Treasurer's Deposits, are similar to investment deposits except that the rate of interest is normally variable according to market rates and is useful where a fixed term deposit is not necessarily appropriate.

Most other forms of bank account are variations on these themes. For example, Barclays, Midland and Trustee Savings Bank all operate Home Savings Plans which, at the end of a stipulated saving period, virtually guarantee the customer a house mortgage up to an agreed multiple of the amount saved.

Some banks have Budget Accounts designed to assist customers in spreading their normal living expenses evenly over the year, and some banks have special accounts to enable employees to set aside regular amounts out of earnings.

The current account is perhaps the dominant feature of British banking. We have said that the money transfer system built up by the joint stock banks over the years is central to the whole financial system, and one effect of this is that current account balances are so readily available for the payment of debts that they are almost as good as cash. In fact, current account balances are included in the narrowest definition of the money supply (M1) along with notes and coin in circulation. And so, Mr Gilbart was able to tell us over 100 years ago that:

> 'were every man to keep a deposit account at a bank and make all his payments by cheques, money might be superseded and cheques become the sole, circulating medium.'

Of course, Mr Gilbart was wrong because cheques will disappear before cash. Nevertheless, it is the convenience of the money transfer system developed by the banks (see Chapter 23) which has enabled them to build up large volumes of credit balances on current account without the payment of interest. The 'endowment' or 'bounty' effect of these large interest-free balances has been an important item in the development and profitability of the British banks, particularly in times of high interest rates. On the other hand, the rising costs of money transfer and indeed the whole operation of current accounts, currently estimated to be of the order of 9 per cent of the balances on hand, leaves little scope for the payment of interest when the general level of interest rates is not so high. The high interest rates and levels of inflation in the 1970s have, however, emphasised to the British public the value of money and so there is less inclination to leave large balances interest-free on current account. The introduction in the United States of NOW (Negotiated Order of Withdrawal) accounts, which are virtually interest-earning accounts with withdrawal facilities, appears to have met with a high degree of acceptance and to some extent this idea has been adopted by the United Kingdom banks with their higher rate deposit accounts mentioned above. The payment of interest on current accounts as we know them in this country could presumably be justified only if it resulted in a substantial increase in the overall level of deposits, something which must be improbable with so many competitive forces at work.

There has been a fairly modest step towards the payment of interest on current accounts in that a number of banks have introduced special categories of accounts which provide for the payment of interest whilst allowing limited withdrawal facilities. The Co-operative Bank has marketed an interest-bearing current account through its finance house subsidiary, First Co-operative Finance. The other banks do not, however, offer the Co-operative Bank cheque-cashing facilities so that, in practice, the Co-operative Bank cheques drawn on the interest-bearing accounts may be encashed only at branches of the Co-operative Bank or through the Handybanks and cheque-cashing points in Co-operative stores. The Royal Bank of Scotland also operate a scheme, known as 'Cashline', which provides customers with interest on current accounts whilst allowing facilities for the withdrawal of cash through the bank's cash dispensers. In May 1982, Midland Bank announced a similar scheme 'Readicash', offering the payment of interest on this special category of account and allowing withdrawals of cash by means of a Readicash card through the bank's cash dispensers, as well as the payment of regular household accounts by means of standing orders or direct debits. Lloyds Bank also offer a cashflow account on similar lines, backed up by their cheque guarantee card which enables Lloyds Bank cheques drawn on cashflow accounts to be cashed at other banks. Similarly, the National Westminster Bank introduced in May 1983 their Cashwise account – a type of current account on which credit interest is paid. The customer may draw on the account in the ordinary way and receive a Cashwise card which serves as a cheque guarantee card and which enables cash to be obtained from the bank's cash dispensers.

Rates of interest

Prior to the introduction of Competition and Credit Control in 1971, the rate of interest on seven day deposit accounts (the London Bankers' Deposit Rate) was agreed among the London Clearing Banks and was traditionally 2 per cent below the level of Bank Rate. Since 1971, banks have been free to fix their own interest rates, but inevitably the degree of competition in such a highly developed market prohibits any wide divergence on rates from one bank to another.

The rates of interest paid by the clearing banks have not always been competitive with for example building societies, local authorities and even the National Savings Bank. We have already referred to the increased share of the savings market gained by building societies over the last 20 years or so and, more recently, the increased emphasis on national savings. On page 23, we have considered the reasons for this. On the whole, the banks did not fall behind because of disadvantageous interest rates. In fact, among bank customers, i.e. those who have developed a banking habit, there was little tendency to transfer funds to other avenues of saving merely to take advantage of an interest rate differential. This was partly no doubt because of a natural inertia, but it is more particularly because of customer loyalty based on a long tradition of convenience, accessibility and absolute safety.

The ultimate factor in determining the level of interest rates on bank deposits is the ability of the banks to deploy the funds profitably. Thus, there has always been a relationship between deposit rates of interest and the rates obtainable by the banks on advances. The differential between deposit rate and base lending rate has been as low as 1½ per cent, but has tended over the years to vary between that figure and 4½ per cent with a tendency for the margin to widen in recent times. An increasingly important factor is the level of interest rates in the wholesale money market. But here the differential has tended to narrow in recent years. The awareness of the higher money market rates has encouraged finance directors and treasurers to place wholesale deposits through the banks rather than leaving the money on seven-day deposit at lower rates. Among personal customers, however, perhaps because of the tradition referred to in the previous paragraph, there has been less marked switching of retail branch deposits to the 'wholesale' side of the house.

We have referred on page 35 to the introduction by the clearing banks of term deposits under such names as Investment

Accounts and High Interest Deposit Accounts. There has not, however, been a tradition of term deposit business in this country because of the availability of other attractive avenues for medium-term savings. It is exceedingly difficult for the banks to compete in terms of interest rates on medium-term savings against such highly developed areas as the market for government stocks and the life assurance market. Furthermore, the building societies have moved increasingly into the medium-term savings markets with Term Shares and Escalating Bonds, offering competitive (and increasing) rates of interest up to five year periods. Few, if any, other countries have developed these three alternative savings markets to such a high degree of sophistication and thus, the banks in those other countries have been able to compete more successfully for medium-term savings. It is no doubt also one of the reasons for the greater development of the banking habit in some overseas countries.

The term 'bank charges' is used colloquially to mean interest on loans and overdrafts (see Chapter 3) as well as the 'commission' charges made by the banks for the operation of current accounts. Bank charges in this latter (and more correct) sense relate almost entirely to the costs of money transfers and are dealt with under that heading in Chapter 23. Nevertheless, in any consideration of deposit banking it is appropriate to touch on the cost to both the bank and the customer in maintaining current accounts. From the customer's standpoint, there is a traditional reluctance to pay bank charges and over the years many customers have enquired a little ruefully why they should pay banks to look after their money. Viewed from the banks' position, however, the cost of operating current accounts has escalated enormously to the level, which we have already quoted, of approximately 9 per cent of the current account balances. The system of charging is discussed in Chapter 23. In essence, all the banks developed systems for waiving commission charges on personal accounts where there was a minimum balance, usually of the order of £50 or £100. In more recent times the minimum balance has been reduced to zero so that most banks will now operate current accounts free of charge provided accounts do not become overdrawn. As part of this arrangement, there is often a notional allowance for interest on the average credit balance on current account, even where a charge is being made, perhaps because the balance has fallen at some point below the required minimum or has become overdrawn. One of the quirks of this system is that the customer receives some benefit for the balance he carries in his account without being taxed on it. If the banks were to pay interest on current account balances, such interest would be *prima facie* taxable in the customers' hands and the commission charges, which would no doubt be at a much higher and economic rate, would, as the law stands at present, be payable out of taxed income, i.e. the commission charges would not be offset against the earned interest.

Bank charges used to be calculated on a rather unscientific basis. Twice a year, the manager of a banking branch would look through the ledger account of each customer and mark an appropriate half-yearly charge. This would be based on the activity on the account, the behaviour of the customer in conducting his account, the turnover and the value of the connection in general to the bank. It tended to be a very subjective appraisal. In April 1978, the Price Commission reported on bank charges and suggested improved ways of dealing with them.[5]

In addition to those charges which a bank makes for the operation of a current account and which may be waived as explained above if a minimum credit balance is maintained, a bank will also charge for such as the following:

> obtaining a credit reference on another person or company, holding items in safe custody, allowing the use of the bank's nominee company, returning vouchers to the customer, supplying travellers' cheques and foreign currency, and lengthy correspondence or interviews with the manager or a senior official.

The banking habit

The use of current accounts with the clearing banks has not developed among private customers in this country to the same extent as it has in some countries overseas. It is believed that less than 50 per cent of the adult population have accounts with the old clearing banks. Nearly half the adult population have accounts with the building societies and six million or so have accounts with the Trustee Savings Banks. There is of course a considerable overlapping of the figures and many customers of the joint stock banks or the Trustee Savings Banks will also have accounts with building societies. Also, the increased use of credit cards has reduced the need for current accounts as such. The following table shows the proportions of bank accountholders among the working and non-working sections of the population.

	Non-working				**Working**			
	1981		**1984**		**1981**		**1984**	
	m	%	**m**	%	**m**	%	**m**	%
Current accountholders	8·9	47	9·8	50	16·9	72	18·2	77
Non-current accountholders	9·9	53	9·9	50	6·5	28	5·5	23
All adults	18·8	100	19·7	100	23·4	100	23·7	100

[Source 1981: *Inter-Bank Research Organisation.*]
[Source 1984: *Association for Payment Clearing Services.*]

Recent times have seen a considerable thrust by the joint stock banks to extend the banking habit to those who have become affectionately known as 'the great unbanked'. This usually, but not necessarily, means in this country the so-called blue collar workers. Approximately 40 per cent of employees in the United Kingdom receive their wages paid weekly in cash. (The figure in 1976 was approaching 60 per cent and thus the proportion has come down substantially). They are not necessarily 'unbanked' because some of these workers or their wives do have accounts with the joint stock banks. A much larger proportion of them have accounts with the Trustee Savings Banks or with building societies, but very few conduct current accounts as such with the old clearers. In discussions on this subject, it has become the fashion to draw distinctions between the United Kingdom and other countries. We are told, for example, that in France only 25 per cent of the workforce is paid in cash, in Germany 5 per cent and in the United States as few as 1 per cent. There are in fact two aspects of the matter. One is the frequency of the wage payment, i.e. weekly or monthly and the other is the nature of the payment, i.e. cash, cheque or credit transfer. In France, for example, owing to government action almost the entire workforce is now paid monthly (although 25 per cent as mentioned above still receive payment in cash). In Holland, approximately 85 per cent of the workers are paid monthly (or four weekly), the great majority by transfer to banking accounts. In Norway, one-half of the working population is paid by credit transfer monthly and in Sweden, nearly all the work people are paid in this way. The table below shows the change in the pattern of wage and salary payments to working adults in Great Britain over the years to 1984.

Wage/salary payment by all working adults in Great Britain

	1976	**1979**	**1981**	**1981**	**1984**	**1984**
	%	%	%	m	%	m
Cash	59	54	44	10·2	39	9·5
Cheque	12	14	14	3·4	16	3·9
Bank credit transfer	27	31	38	8·9	43	10·5
Other	2	1	4	0·9	2	0·8
	100	100	100	23·4	100	24·7

[Source 1976–1981: *Inter-Bank Research Organisation.*]
[Source 1984: *Association for Payment Clearing Services.*]

In this country, the legal obligation to pay a workman in cash had its origin in the Truck Acts (now repealed by the Wages Act 1986, parts of which came into effect on 1 January 1987), principally the Truck Act of 1831. Under that Act, the amount of wages earned by, or payable to, any workman in respect of any labour done by him must be actually paid to him in the 'current coin of the realm'. Any payment made by the employer in respect of wages by the delivery of goods, or otherwise than in current coin of the realm, was illegal. The original Act of 1831 applied only to 'artificers', but over the years the definition was widened to include almost all workers or persons engaged in any manual work under a contract of service. Under the Payment of Wages by Cheque Act, 1960, wages of a workman may be paid into his bank account or be paid by money order, postal order or cheque if the workman so requests and the employer agrees. Despite the enabling provisions of this Act, comparatively little progress has been made in the payment of wages other than in cash. This is partly because of traditional attitudes, but also because of the difficulty of obtaining the consents of those concerned. Any worker who withholds consent is still entitled to be paid in cash. For the most part, trade unions have been opposed to the payment of wages other than in cash, but their attitude has modified considerably over the years. On the whole, employers favour the move towards payment of wages through banking accounts, principally on the grounds of cost and security. There are, however, many problems to be overcome and, in recent times, the banks set up a working party to explore the whole problem of payment of wages. Even if progress can be made in this direction, it does not necessarily follow that employees will wish to have their wages paid direct to bank accounts. Many may prefer to have the transfer made to a building society account. Many workers are not accustomed to the use of cheque books and bank cards, nor to the banking hours of business, whereas payment of wages to a building society account would leave the employee's lifestyle largely unchanged.

As mentioned above only 65 per cent of the adult population of England and Wales have current accounts with *any* bank. This includes the joint stock banks, the Trustee Savings Bank, the Co-operative Bank and Girobank. In the United States, Canada, France, West Germany and the Netherlands, the equivalent figure is over 90 per cent. This is remarkable, bearing in mind the pre-eminence of the British retail banking system. On the other hand, as we have said, other countries do not always have the attractive alternative facilities available in this country.

Some legal aspects

Historically, there have been very few restraints under English law on the seeking of deposits from the public and on the conduct of banking business generally. This may be due to the time-honoured and, for the most part, highly successful tradition of allowing the commercial life of the country to develop organically. Perhaps for the same reason banking as such wanted for any precise definition until the system of recognition introduced in the Banking Act, 1979.

The Protection of Depositors Act, 1963 was the first statutory step to control the soliciting of deposits from the public. Until then, the rule was *caveat emptor* and it was comparatively easy for an institution to advertise for, and obtain, deposits without any indication of the financial standing of the borrowing institution. Under the Protection of Depositors Act, a company wishing to attract deposits was required to comply with regulations laid down by the Board of Trade. Any advertisments for deposits had to be approved by the Board and the accounts of the deposit-taking company had to be made available to the Board and to the depositors. No organisation was allowed to use the word 'bank' or 'bankers', etc. unless they were an exempted bank for accountancy purposes under the Companies Act, 1948, or otherwise accepted by the Board of Trade as being engaged in a *bona fide* banking business. The Act has now been repealed by the Banking Act, 1979 (see below). It did not apply to building societies, friendly societies, savings banks nor the exempted banks under the Companies Act.

The Banking Acts, 1979 and 1987

The Banking Act, 1979 established the criteria by which the Bank of England would recognise an institution as a bank and brought the supervision of banks and deposit-taking institutions into line with the requirements of the European Community.

The principal criteria for the recognition of a deposit-taking institution as a bank were:

1. that the institution enjoyed, and has for a reasonable period of time enjoyed, a high reputation and standing in the financial community; and
2. that the institution provided in the United Kingdom a wide range of banking services, or a 'highly specialised banking service'.

An institution was not to be regarded as providing a wide range of banking services within the meaning of the Act unless it provided all of the following:

(a) Current or deposit account facilities, or the acceptance of funds in the wholesale money markets;
(b) finance in the form of overdraft or loan facilities, or the lending of funds in the wholesale money markets;
(c) foreign exchange services;
(d) finance through the medium of bills of exchange and promissory notes, together with finance for foreign trade; and
(e) financial advice or investment management services and facilities for arranging the purchase and sale of securities.

For the purpose of determining whether an institution is providing 'a wide range of banking services' or a 'highly specialised banking service', the Bank of England could disregard the fact that the institution did not provide one or two of the services listed above.

3. that at least two individuals effectively directed the business of the institution;
4. that the institution had net assets of £5 million if providing a wide range of banking services and £250,000 if providing a highly specialised banking service.

An institution seeking to carry on a deposit-taking business which did not qualify for recognition as a bank could nevertheless be licensed by the Bank of England as a deposit-taking institution. Thus, the Act envisaged two categories of deposit-taking business, viz. a recognised bank as outlined above, or a licensed deposit-taking institution.

The relevant sections of the Banking Act, 1979 came into effect on 1 October 1980.

In 1985, however, a committee appointed by the Treasury and the Bank of England made certain proposals for the revision of the Banking Act, including new minimum capital requirements and the abolition of the distinction between banks and licensed deposit takers. These proposals were embodied in the Banking Act 1987, which repeals for the most part the Banking Act of 1979 and provides a new framework for the regulation of banking businesses whilst re-enacting some of the concepts of the 1979 Act. One of the principal changes is the abolition of the distinction between banks and licensed deposit-takers, but there are still constraints on the use of the word 'bank' or 'banker' and, in particular, no institution with a paid-up capital of less than £5m. will be able to use the title 'bank'.

The principal provisions of the Act are:

1. The Act sets out the functions and duties of the Bank of England in the regulation of deposit-taking businesses in the United Kingdom.

2. The Act provides for the setting-up of a Board of Banking Supervision which is to include six independent members to act in an advisory role to the Bank.

3. There is a provision that no person shall accept a deposit in the course of carrying on a business, which is deemed to be a deposit-taking business, unless that person is an institution for the time being authorised by the Bank.

4. Subject to certain exceptions, a 'deposit' means a sum of money paid on terms (a) under which it will be re-paid, with or without interest or a premium, and either on demand or at a time or in circumstances agreed by or on behalf of the person making the payment and the person receiving it; and (b) which are not referable to the provision of property or services or the giving of security.

5. For the purpose of the Act, a 'deposit-taking business' is one where (a) in the course of the business money received by way of deposit is lent to others or (b) any other activity of the business is financed, wholly or to any material extent, out of the capital of or the interest on money received by way of deposit. It is not a deposit-taking business, however, for the purpose of the Act if (a) the person carrying on the business does not hold himself out as accepting deposits on a day-to-day basis and (b) any deposits which are accepted are accepted only on particular occasions, whether or not involving the issue of debentures or other securities.

6. The Act contains provisions for the Bank to grant, refuse or revoke authorisation as a deposit-taking institution and sets out in Schedule 3 the minimum criteria for authorisation. In brief, these criteria are that (a) every person who is or is to be a director or controller or manager of the institution is a 'fit

and proper person' to hold that position, (b) at least two individuals effectively direct the business of the institution, (c) the Board shall include such non-executive directors as the Bank considers appropriate, (d) the business will be conducted in a prudent manner and (e) the institution has net assets amounting to not less than £1m. (or its equivalent value in other currencies).

7. The Act gives the Bank wide powers to serve directions on an institution requiring it to take such steps or to refrain from such courses of action, etc. as the Bank may consider desirable in the interests of the depositors or potential depositors, such directions to be given in certain defined circumstances, principally on the withdrawing or surrendering of an authorisation under the Act.

8. No person may become a 'controller' of an authorised institution without the approval of the Bank. For this purpose, a controller means any person who alone or with associates controls the exercise of 15 per cent of the voting power of the institution or who is the managing director or chief executive of the institution.

9. The Act prohibits any person carrying on any business in the United Kingdom from using any name to indicate that he is a bank or banker or is carrying on a banking business, unless he is an authorised institution and, inter alia, has issued share capital of not less than £5m.

10. There is provision that the Treasury may, after consultation with the Bank and the Building Societies Commission, make regulations governing the issue, form and content of 'deposit advertisements', meaning any advertisement containing either an invitation to make a deposit or information which is intended or might reasonably be presumed to be intended to lead directly or indirectly to the making of a deposit.

11. Similarly, the Treasury may, after consultation with the Bank and the Building Societies Commission, make regulations governing the making of unsolicited calls with a view to procuring the making of deposits.

12. If the Bank considers that any deposit advertisement is misleading, it may by notice in writing give the institution a

direction under this Section, either prohibiting the advertisement or requiring its modification.

13. As in the case of the 1979 Act, the Act provides for a Deposit Protection Scheme (see below).

14. There are wide powers enabling the Bank to gather information regarding authorised institutions, including power to approach auditors for information.

15. For the first time, there is power (Section 23 of the Act) for the Treasury to direct the Bank to serve a notice of objection on any proposed controller of institution if it appears to the Treasury that such a notice could be served under Section 183 of the Financial Services Act 1986, which provides for the disqualification or restriction of persons connected with overseas countries which do not afford reciprocal facilities for financial business.

Deposit Protection Scheme

The Banking Act, 1979 also contained provisions for the setting-up of the Deposit Protection Scheme for the protection of persons making deposits with recognised banks and licensed institutions. Under the Scheme, which came into effect in February 1982 and for which provision is re-enacted in the 1987 Act, the amount of contribution payable by each institution will be at an overall percentage rate fixed by the Deposit Protection Board in relation to the deposit base of the bank or licensed deposit-taker. There is provision for minimum and maximum contributions of £10,000 and £300,000 respectively and for the Fund to be maintained at a minimum of £5 million and a maximum of £6 million. In the event of a bank or licensed deposit-taking institution becoming insolvent, the Fund guarantees up to 75 per cent of the first £20,000 of a depositor's sterling deposits with the institution concerned.

The banker/customer relationship

There is no statutory definition of a bank customer. There is good legal authority, however, that for a person to be a customer of a bank he or she must have either a deposit or a current account (or some similar account) with the bank. (Great Western Railway v The London & County Banking Company.[7]) There is judicial support for the view that the relationship of banker and customer begins as soon as a cheque or money is paid in and the bank is prepared to accept it and is prepared to open an account. (Ladbroke & Co. v Todd.[8]) Where a banking account has been opened subject to the obtaining of satisfactory references (as would be usual), it seems fairly clear that the customer relationship is not established until a satisfactory reference has been obtained.

It is exceedingly well established that the relationship of banker and customer is that of debtor and creditor. In the case of London Joint Stock Bank Limited v Macmillan & Arthur,[9] the Lord Chancellor said:

> 'The relation between banker and customer is that of debtor and creditor with a superadded obligation on the part of the banker to honour the customer's cheques if the account is in credit'.

In the equally celebrated case of Swiss Bank Corporation v Joachimson,[10] Lord Justice Atkin said:

> 'The bank undertakes to receive money and to collect bills for its customer's account. The proceeds so received are not to be held in trust for the customer, but the bank borrows the proceeds and undertakes to repay them. The promise to repay is to repay at the branch of the bank where the account is kept and during banking hours. It includes a promise to repay any part of the amount due, against the written order of the customer addressed to the bank at the branch, and, as such written orders may be outstanding in the ordinary course of business for two or three days, it is a term of the contract that the bank will not cease to do business with the customer except upon reasonable notice. The customer, on his part, undertakes to exercise a reasonable care in exercising his written orders so as not to mislead the bank or to facilitate forgery. I think it necessarily a term of such contract that the bank is not liable to pay the customer the full amount of his balance until he demands payment from the bank at the branch at which the current account is kept'.

To the obligation stated here we may add that of secrecy. In Tournier v National Provincial & Union Bank of England Limited,[11] it was held that: 'the duty of a banker towards his customer not to disclose his affairs is a legal one arising out of contract . . .' It is a duty which is overridden only by the customer's consent, a legal obligation to disclose, a duty to the public or (in certain narrow circumstances) the interests of the bank.

There have been a number of legal refinements over the years in the relationship of banker and customer, but they are outside the scope of this work and, in some cases, have an unfamiliar sound in this computer age. Nevertheless, it has been a cherished relationship. Customers speak of 'my bank', bank managers speak of 'my customer'. In the final chapter, we refer to some of the newer relationships established in modern banking, such as merchant banker and client, lessor and lessee, insurer and insured. But the basic banker/customer relationship still predominates. The deposit or current account is still the focal point of the relationship. Some customers resent the intrusion from other parts of the banking group, perhaps to sell unit trusts or life assurance, without the mediation of their bank manager. Some bank managers protect their customers almost possessively from such intrusions. The relationship has been the strength of British banking in the past. It might conceivably be a weakness in the future. Bank branches now have so much for sale on their shelves that it would be a pity if only current account 'customers' came into the shop.

So it is that many of the services described in this book stand on their own feet regardless of any underlying banker/customer relationship. There are, however, certain customer services which relate directly to the banker/customer relationship and which would not normally be available to non-customers. Such services are associated only with deposit-banking.

Associated services

Bankers' orders

A banker's order, sometimes known as a standing order, is a written request from a customer to the bank to make a series of payments, usually monthly or annually, either for a limited period or 'until further notice'. The banker is under no obligation to make a payment unless the account is in credit, or within an agreed overdraft facility. Standing order payments are now dealt with through Bankers Automated Clearing Services Limited (BACS). (See Chapter 23.) All payments are processed electronically, each bank preparing each day a magnetic tape for payments to be made to other banks. In 1986, 943 million credit transfers including standing order items were transmitted through this automated clearing system.

Direct debits

Bank customers who *receive* large numbers of payments on a regular basis may do so by banker's orders initiated by the payer. Thus, a large insurance company may receive a very considerable number of payments in this way. The disadvantage of the standing order system is that it takes a long time at the receiving end to reconcile all the payments. Some years ago the banks, therefore, introduced the direct debit system which enables the receiving house to initiate the payments, in effect by claiming on the payer's bank account. This can be done of course only with the bank customer's authority and the banks themselves are indemnified by the receiving organisation in respect of any possible claim or loss. In 1986, direct debits accounted for over 400 million items through BACS.

Safe custody

Most banks provide custody services for their customers' valuables, such as Deeds, Wills, jewellery and sometimes larger items such as silver. Some of the larger branches also provide safe deposit facilities, i.e. private safes or locked boxes to which the customers keep the key. The relationship arising from safe custody is different from that of banker and customer. The transfer of goods to someone for a particular purpose, e.g. for safe-keeping is a bailment and the bank in such a case is a bailee. The relationships are quite separate and a banker does not, for example, have any lien or right over the safe custody property in relation to a customer's overdrawn account. There used to be much debate as to whether or not a bank taking items for safe custody was a gratuitous bailee (not receiving any payment) or a bailee for reward (receiving payment for the service). A gratuitous bailee is obliged to take the same care of the property entrusted to him as a reasonably prudent man would be expected to take of his own property of a like description. A bailee for reward, however, is expected to use the highest degree of care, using all precautions and devices available to him in looking after the deposited property. The distinction seems hardly relevant, however, bearing in mind that a bank, whether paid or not, would keep the articles in its own strongroom with the same care and protection as any valuables belonging to the bank itself. In any case, it is difficult to imagine that the leading banks of today would hide behind the 'gratuitous bailee' principle, if in fact they had displayed some want of care.

Nominee services (see page 118)

Open credits (sometimes known as standing credits)
This is merely a facility by which the customer of a bank may arrange to have cheques cashed up to a stated amount and within a given period at another branch of the bank or at another bank. To avoid the possibility of fraud, it is usual for credits opened with other banks to be passed through their respective Head Offices for confirmation. When a bank has opened a credit at another bank or another branch, it may not refuse to honour cheques within the amount of the credit notwithstanding that funds may not be available in the customer's account.

Travellers' cheques (see page 278)

Cheque cards (see page 216)

Purchase of stocks and shares (see page 119)

Cash dispensers (see page 450)

Banker's opinions
It has been said that 'the giving of opinions by one banker to another was a well established custom among bankers'.[12] The general view appears to be that by opening an account at a bank, a customer agrees by implication that the bank may respond to enquiries from other banks concerning his financial standing, etc. It is an exception to the general rules governing secrecy (see page 50) on the grounds that the information is given with the customer's consent, albeit implied. Bankers' opinions, sometimes known as status enquiries, have given rise to much legal conjecture over the years culminating in the House of Lords case of Hedley Byrne & Company Limited v Heller and Partners Limited.[13] The case had far-reaching consequences well beyond the narrow instance of banker's opinions. For example, in the House of Lords Lord Morris said:

'. . . the giving of opinions by one banker to another . . .'

> 'It must be taken as settled that if someone possessed of a special skill undertakes, quite irrespective of contract, to apply that skill for the assistance of another who relies upon such skill, a duty of care will arise'.

So it is that banks and others may be liable for so-called honest negligence unless a very clear disclaimer of responsibility is given at the time in writing. This was so in the Hedley Byrne case and ever since then it has been the standard practice with banks to issue an express disclaimer, usually in printed form on the status reply form.

Thus, deposit banking has been the platform on which so much else has been built. Not only the 'associated services' listed briefly above, but the entire tide of activity described in these pages springs from that one source. That father of English banking, Sir Thomas Gresham was himself a man of many parts and no doubt he would have approved.

References

1 George Chandler: *Four Centuries of Banking.* Batsford, 1964.
2 *Competition and Credit Control.* Bank of England, 1971.
3 Committee on the Working of the Monetary System (Chairman, The Lord Radcliffe), 1959, HMSO, Cmnd. 827.
4 Committee to Review National Savings, (H.M.S.O., June 1973) (Cmnd. 5273).
5 Price Commission, Banks: Charges for Money Transmission Services (HC 337 (1978)).
6 Section 36, Banking Act, 1979.
7 (1901) A.C. 414.
8 (1914) 111 L.T. 43 per Bailhache J.
9 (1918) A.C. 777.
10 (1921) 37 T.L.R. 534.
11 (1924) 40 T.L.R. 214.
12 Baron Bramwell in Swift v Jewsbury (L.R. 9QB 301).
13 (1963) 2 All E.R. 575.

CHAPTER 3

The Lending Banker

If, as we have said, the taking of deposits is the main spring of the British banking system, with all that that entails in the retail branch network, it may seem surprising to the observer that the technical training of a banker leans heavily towards the business of lending money. Correspondence courses, evening classes, The Chartered Institute of Bankers examinations and the in-house courses are much concerned with matters of lending. To say of a man that he is 'a good banker' usually means that he is a shrewd lender – one who lends money safely and profitably.

It may take a very short time to train a clerk to open a credit account and nowadays the operating of that account will be very much a matter of automation. A good lending banker, however, is the product of years of training and experience. And yet the great majority of bank customers will never avail themselves of those hard-won skills. A comparatively small proportion of bank customers ever borrow from their banks and an even smaller proportion require those negotiated loans which call for the skill of the true lending banker. Most bankers would admit that they meet their borrowing customers quite often, if only for an annual review of their overdraft arrangements, but they meet their credit customers all too seldom and many not at all. The good banker will know his borrowing customers in depth. He is a professional and arguably the best in the world.

It is understandable that the lending banker is the product of much training. He has to deal with a wide category of customers in a risk situation. They may be farmers, produce brokers, professional partnerships or multi-national companies and in each case the parameters are different. He may be lending to husbands and wives, trustees, local authorities, football clubs, nationalised industries or liquidators of companies. In each case, the rules are different. So too with the taking of security – he will be expected to know how to take a valid and effective charge over a half-built house, listed and unlisted securities, produce on the high seas, cattle on the hoof and guarantees from rich uncles.

The development of lending business

If, in modern times, a banker is respected for his expertise as a lender, this was not always so. Throughout the Middle Ages in this country, the lending of money at interest was considered to be unchristian and was forbidden to Englishmen, some of whom were hanged for the offence. The taking of interest was stigmatized with the name of usury and appears to have been based on a rather strict interpretation of the Mosaic Law: 'Thou shalt not lend upon usury to thy brother.'[1] The Jews, however, took a more relaxed and no doubt more accurate view of their law in that 'unto a stranger thou mayst lend upon usury'.[2] And so it was that the lending of money was monopolised by the Jews in this country until their expulsion by Edward I in 1290. The Jews had thrived on moneylending for interest. G. M. Trevelyan tells us that:

> 'The Jews were the King's sponges. They sucked up his subjects' money by putting their own out on usury and were protected from the rage of their debtors solely by the strong arm of the King who, in his turn, drew what he wanted from their ever-accumulating wealth.'[3]

With the expulsion of the Jews, the Lombards became the principal moneylenders. We have already referred to the arrival in England of these Italian merchants and the granting of land by Edward II for them to settle in what is now Lombard Street. They had become the bankers of Europe despite the antagonism of the Church. According to J. W. Gilbart:

> 'The Lombards found themselves engaged in the traffic which was deemed criminal and odious. They were liable to punishment if detected. They were not satisfied, therefore, with that moderate premium which they might have claimed if their trade had been open and authorised by law. They exacted a sum proportional to the danger and infamy of a discovery. Accordingly, we find it

was usual for them to demand 20 per cent for the use of the money in the thirteenth century.'[4]

Whatever stigma may have attached to the business of money-lending and however illegal it may have been, successive monarchs in this country were glad of the services of the Jews and then of the Lombards and were among their principal borrowing customers. The usury laws were partly abolished by Henry VIII in 1545 and the taking of interest on loans was made legal. The rate was fixed at 10 per cent per annum, to be reduced over the next 150 years or so to 8 per cent, then 6 per cent and ultimately 5 per cent.

It was not until 1900 in the Moneylenders Act that legislation was again introduced to regulate the lending of money and the charging of interest. By that time, however, bankers were excluded from the definition of moneylenders. The Act provided *inter alia* that if the rate of interest on a loan exceeded 48 per cent, the Court must presume that the interest is 'excessive' and that the transaction is 'harsh and unconscionable'.

The nature of bank lending

The lending business of the present-day banks is based on the concept of the overdraft, which in itself arose from the development of the current account, the issuing of cheques and the banks' money transfer system.

The overdraft, i.e. a current account with an agreed lending limit, has been and, for the most part, still is the central feature of bank lending in the United Kingdom. As outlined in the previous chapter, bank deposits in Britain have been traditionally short-term, being callable by the public either on demand in the case of current accounts or on seven days' notice on deposit accounts. This obligation to repay on demand or near-demand has conditioned the whole lending scene with the result that bank overdrafts too have been repayable on demand, or at least subject to review within a comparatively short time. From the banker's point of view, an overdraft has the advantage that it is self-liquidating by the normal turnover of the current account. In many cases, this was something of an illusion because there was a tendency for accounts to develop a 'hard-core' of lending, which remained in all weathers, i.e. the account did

'. . . a sum proportional to the danger . . .'

not swing into credit. From the customer's point of view, the overdraft has the advantage that interest is charged on a day-to-day basis and thus, full credit is given for payments into the account. It has been over the years, and still remains, the cheapest form of credit.

Times have changed and the overdraft has been supplemented and, in some cases, supplanted by newer forms of lending. Nevertheless, as recently as 1959 the Radcliffe Committee[5] reported:

> 'Although it is clear that attitudes are changing and that no absolute rigidity limits the range of overdrafts, the banks retain a strong preference for short-term lending of 'self-liquidating' types. This preference has historical roots in awareness of the risk to which a small bank exposed itself if it could not turn its assets quickly into cash to meet sudden demands from its depositors; but the preference still has some sound basis in that it limits the range of judgment required in the lending banker. The great majority of overdraft agreements made by the banks must be based, at least in large part, on the judgment of branch managers, and these managers may reasonably be expected to assess the capacity of a borrower to repay in a short time, though they could have no assurance in estimating long-term profitability. English bankers have therefore traditionally regarded, and continue to regard, themselves as properly engaged in financing working capital, particularly of the "seed-time to harvest" kind, "bridging transactions", and (within cautious limits) the temporary financing of fixed capital development pending the raising of long-term finance through other channels.'

Only 17 years later, the London Clearing Banks in their evidence to the Wilson Committee[6] said:

> 'In addition to the traditional overdraft, a variety of other lending facilities for both corporate and personal customers is now available through the banks' branch networks, although several are provided by subsidiary and affiliated companies. In terms of the range of facilities available, from the very short-term advance to the occasional equity investment, the clearing banks are now much closer than they used to be to the traditionally continental concept of the "universal bank".'

Overdrafts remain the most important part of the British banks' sterling lending activities and are as appropriate as ever to the seasonal, working capital, self-liquidating and 'seed-time to harvest' needs of customers. During the 1970s, however, the banks moved into the business of contractual medium-term loans, principally for industrial and commercial concerns and at times these have represented approximately 40 per cent of lending to the business sector. Unlike an overdraft, such a loan is repayable only at the end of the term or in the event of breach of the arrangements by the borrower. A term loan up to ten years may be agreed, but a more usual period is five to seven years. The rate of interest may be fixed, but more probably it will be expressed by reference to the inter-bank rates in force from time to time. Because of the difficulty of matching interest rates on the liabilities side of the banks' balance sheets, i.e. because of the absence of long-term contractual deposits in this country, the contract for a term loan may contain a 'roll-over' provision which effectively extends the period of the loan at a re-negotiated rate of interest.

The Radcliffe Report quoted above contained recommendations that the clearing banks should offer term-loan facilities as an alternative to overdrafts but, as a matter of bank prudence, the banks are precluded from entering into term-lending commitments on a large scale or for very long periods. The banks were no doubt spurred on not so much by the Radcliffe Report as the competition from overseas banks coming into London in increasing numbers. Those banks were not, for the most part, looking for current accounts, overdrafts and money transmission business (all of which, as we have said, were the hallmarks of the British banking scene), but were offering medium-term loans, quite often unsecured, at a competitive interest rate and had no compunction about knocking on the doors of finance directors to do so. The British banks quickly responded by moving into the medium-term lending business, but in a short space of time a new climate, almost a new era, of banking was introduced. The monogamous British banker/customer relationship began to wear a bit thin. Customers would positively enjoy the 'advances' from other suitors and would sell themselves to the highest bidder. So banking has taken on a polygamous look and an industrial customer may now have a number of bankers, the group current account remaining with one bank and a number of term facilities being taken for varying purposes from other banks. On the whole, the competition has been healthy and salutary.

In addition to the provision of medium-term loans, the extent of which is limited, as we have said, on prudential grounds, the banks provide extensive facilities, some of them of a long-term nature, either under special government schemes, e.g. for export credit and shipbuilding or through specialist corporations such as the Agricultural Mortgage Corporation and Finance for Industry in which the banks are shareholders. Also, through their subsidiaries, the banks provide 'asset finance' in the form of industrial hire purchase, factoring and leasing. All of these matters are dealt with in the relevant sections of this work.

The personal sector has also seen a widening of the lending facilities on offer from the commercial banks. The 'personal loan' was introduced in 1958 and was the banks' first real venture into personal instalment finance. Some bankers in their enthusiasm to sell this new product forgot their basic lending principles and loans were made to people who had no tradition of a banking habit, no record of saving and, in some cases, no means of repaying. Other bank managers, not taking kindly to this innovation, would, when asked for a personal loan by an existing customer, offer an overdraft instead, thus losing a substantial interest differential for the bank. In the first year or two of personal loans the bad debt experience was serious. Personal loans have long since settled down and taken their true place as a very desirable form of consumer instalment finance, providing the customer with a convenience and simplicity not so readily available elsewhere, e.g. with hire purchase, and providing the banks with a formalised and computerised lending facility at a rate of interest which reflects its unsecured nature.

Another major development in the personal lending sector is that of the credit card, which is discussed in Chapter 10 and the offering of hire purchase finance through the banks' subsidiary companies, as discussed in Chapter 11.

Analysis of lending

In their Evidence to the Wilson Committee, the London clearing bankers said:

> 'The pattern of clearing bank lending between the different sectors of the economy is determined largely by the demands of the bank's customers, reflected in the first instance in requests for facilities and then in the use actually made of the facilities agreed.'

And again:

> 'The clearing banks themselves do not set out to strike a particular balance between different sectors of the economy in their lending activities.'

There are times of course when qualitative and quantitative controls imposed by the Treasury through the Bank of England have affected the level of lending to particular sectors of the economy. For example, the banks have been encouraged on some occasions to give priority to export industries and on some occasions not to increase their lending to the property sector. There have been constraints from time to time on lending for speculative purposes and, during times of credit squeezes, the banks have been required to lend to the personal sector for consumer purposes only within the rules appertaining to hire purchase.

At the end of 1986, the analysis of lending to UK residents by the London and Scottish clearing banks was as shown below.

London and Scottish Banks' Group Advances to UK Residents in Sterling and Other Currencies: 1986

£ millions	
1. Agriculture, Forestry and Fishing	**5,778**
of which sterling	5,766
2. Energy and Water Supply Industries	
Oil and extraction of natural gas	789
Other energy industries	511
Water Supply	267
Total item 2	**1,568**
of which sterling	471
3. Manufacturing Industry	
Extraction of minerals and ores	255
Metal manufacturing	454

Continued on next page

Continued from previous page

Manufacture of non-metallic mineral products	575
Chemical industry	845
Mechanical engineering	1,344
Electrical and electronic engineering	1,610
Motor vehicles	455
Other transport equipment	961
Other engineering and metal goods	1,269
Food, drink and tobacco	2,470
Textiles, leather, clothing and footwear	1,064
Other manufacturing	3,094
Total item 3	**14,396**
of which sterling	12,290
4. Construction	**4,332**
of which sterling	4,221
5. Garages, Distribution, Hotels and Catering	
Garages and retail distribution of motor vehicles	1,951
Other retail distribution	4,784
Wholesale distribution	2,964
Hotels and catering	2,928
Total item 5	**12,627**
of which sterling	11,999
6. Transport	
Air transport	236
Other transport	1,710
Total item 6	**1,947**
of which sterling	1,548
7. Postal Services and Telecommunications	**68**
of which sterling	67
8. Financial	
Building societies	139
Investment and unit trusts, etc.	1,409
Insurance companies, pension funds, etc.	1,266
Leasing enterprises	5,096
Other financial	4,650
Securities dealers, etc.	712
Total item 8	**13,272**
of which sterling	10,608
9. Business and Other Services	
Central and local government	490
Property companies	4,917
Hiring of movables	698
Other services	8,533
Total item 9	**14,639**
of which sterling	13,740

Continued from previous page

10. Persons	
Bridging finance for house purchase	871
Other house purchase	21,111
Other advances to persons	18,760
Total item 10	**40,742**
of which sterling	40,699
Total advances to UK Residents	**109,369**
of which sterling	101,411
in foreign currencies	7,959

[Source: CLSB Statistical Unit.]

The figures quoted are the actual amounts of advances outstanding at the particular date. It is a feature of bank lending, however, that an overdraft or loan facility may be agreed, but not 'drawn down' by the customer for some little time or not perhaps used in its entirety. Nevertheless, these overdraft and loan facilities are agreed commitments on behalf of the banks. At any one time, quite a high proportion of the facilities may be unused. For example at the end of 1986, only 77 per cent of total agreed facilities were actually in use.[7] Private persons are more inclined to make full use of the facilities granted to them, so that at that time nearly 90 per cent of personal overdraft facilities had been drawn down, whereas in the manufacturing sector the proportion was less than 44 per cent.

Lending to the business sector

Lending to manufacturing and other productive industries has generally constituted the largest single area of lending by the British banks. There are various reasons for this. There is, for example, in Great Britain a tradition of self-financing among industrial and commercial companies and at any one time as much as 70 per cent of additional funding may come from retained profits rather than from capital or loans raised in the market. This lack of dependence on the capital market for new money, or perhaps merely the reluctance to go to the capital market, almost certainly leads to a greater dependence on bank facilities. Secondly, bank finance by way of overdraft is comparatively cheap and thirdly, at times of high interest rates, there is a natural reluctance on the part of industrial companies to commit themselves to long-term expensive borrowing on the capital market.

It must be said, however, that in recent times the securitisation of debt has become a more common feature of industrial funding in this country. This is the issue of marketable paper sometimes with quite short maturity dates in lieu of bank borrowing – a factor which influenced the UK banks in their decisions to move into the securities business by the acquisition of investment houses.

Lending to small businesses

There has been much attention in recent years to the problems of smaller businesses. This includes the problems of obtaining advice, which we refer to in Chapter 20 and the problems of obtaining equity finance, to which we refer under the heading of Merchant Banking in Chapter 14. One of the areas to which particular reference is made, both in the Bolton Report[10] and in the Wilson Report[11], was the difficulty of obtaining loan finance. The Wilson Committee found that:

> 'Loans are more expensive and security requirements are generally more stringent,'

i.e. for the smaller company. They found no bias against smaller companies as such, but referred to the possibility that:

> 'banks exercise excessive caution in their assessment of the risks presented by lending to small firms, particularly in the case of customers with no capital of their own.'

In their Evidence to the Wilson Committee, the banks had pointed out that they were, in many cases, the only point of contact which the smaller businesses in this country had with the financial system. They concluded that:

> 'One of the most important features of the development of the clearing banks over the past 20 years has been the increasing range of facilities available through their branch outlets to meet the needs of smaller businesses at each successive stage of their development. This, perhaps more than anything else, is what the growth of the concept of "universal banking" has meant in practice.'

The banks referred to the financial help which they gave to certain sections in particular among small businesses, i.e. working capital for the retail trade, building finance for the construction industry and the traditional 'farming advances' for the agricultural industry.

The Wilson Committee made a number of recommendations to assist smaller companies, the principal one of interest to us at this point being that of a publicly underwritten loan guarantee scheme. In June 1981, the government introduced such a scheme known as the Small Firms Loan Guarantee Scheme.

The new scheme was set up for an experimental period of three years. Under the scheme, the government guarantees 80 per cent of a loan up to a maximum of £75,000, the loan to be repayable over a period of two to seven years. Such loans are made through the banks – there are seventeen banks operating the scheme throughout the United Kingdom – but have to be approved in each case by the Department of Industry. In each case, the lending bank must sign a declaration that the loan would not have been made without the guarantee. In other words, the guarantee facility must not be used as a substitute for a loan which the bank would have been willing to make in any case.

The Treasury originally set aside £150m for use under this scheme in the first three years, but the response was considerable and by March 1983, loans totalling approximately £600m had been granted. The government make a charge of 3 per cent per annum for providing the guarantee, which is in addition to the rate of interest charged by the banks in relation to base rate.

More recently the demand for loans under the Scheme has fallen off and reached a record low figure in 1985. At the present time the future of the Scheme is somewhat uncertain.

In addition to participating in the guaranteed loan scheme, a number of banks have introduced schemes for the assistance of smaller businesses. Barclays Bank, for example, had already introduced their own "Business Start" Loans for new or established companies launching a new product. Under this scheme, no repayment of capital is made until the end of the initial period, usually five years, and interest charges are by way of royalties fixed by reference to the level of the company's turnover. Both Barclays and the Co-operative Bank have launched schemes financed by the European Coal and Steel Community to create jobs in those areas where coal mines and steel plants have been closed down.

In November 1985, Barclays introduced a new loan scheme for smaller businesses with provision for loans of between £2,000 and £15,000 to be payable by fixed monthly instalments over one to five years. Most of the banks have similar schemes of one kind or another and by September 1984, National Westminster Bank, for example, had lent £1.2b through 100,000 loans under their Business Development Scheme. In February 1984, Lloyds Bank introduced a flexible business loan scheme with loans available up to 20 years, the main feature being that long-term borrowers could switch every five years from a fixed rate of interest to a rate linked to base rate or vice-versa.

The provision of export finance is discussed in Chapter 22. For smaller companies the financing of exports can be a problem, particularly in the case of those businesses which do not have their own export credit guarantee department insurance. At least one bank, Barclays, launched in 1982 a new scheme to provide smaller companies with export finance through the bank's own ECGD policy. The scheme applies only to customers which have an annual export turnover of less than £500,000 and individual shipments not exceeding £50,000.

Lending to the personal sector

Although the personal sector is the main contributor to bank deposits, (as discussed in Chapter 2), lending to personal customers has traditionally made up a fairly modest part of the total loan portfolios of the banks. There are a number of possible reasons for this. The personal sector always tends to be in financial surplus and indeed, as we have seen, the level of personal savings has increased considerably in recent years. There is also perhaps a lingering emotional reluctance on the part of private individuals to borrow from their banks. The Crowther Committee[8] demonstrated that, in terms of social embarrassment, the idea of a bank overdraft was second only to a visit to a pawnbroker and a more recent survey[9] showed that even among bank customers 21 per cent of those who required consumer credit took it by mail order, and 35 per cent by credit card, whilst only 10 per cent took bank loans as such.

Then again, for the personal borrower there is a considerable range of choice. If he does not wish to go to his bank, he may use hire purchase, various forms of credit sales, credit card, budget accounts in stores and, for house purchase, a building society. Faced with that range of choice and the inconvenience to some people of bank hours of opening, it is not altogether surprising that private individuals have gone elsewhere for personal credit. Surely also there was the reluctance to be exposed to a 'headmaster' interview. There was always the thought that the bank manager was exercising some form of moral judgement – less so nowadays but still a lingering belief.

Bank loans to personal borrowers now account for approximately 40 per cent of total bank advances. This is higher than in past years, partly because of the drive by the joint stock banks to develop their personal banking business but principally because of the move by those banks into the house mortgage market.

The clearing banks were always willing to lend to a limited extent for house purchase, provided the term was reasonably short, say, 7 to 10 years. In addition of course they have lent substantial sums for house purchase purposes to their own staffs. Also, banks would, and still will, assist with bridging finance on the change of house by a customer. Beyond that, the field was left to the building societies and insurance companies and, to a limited extent, local authorities. In fact, until recent times, building societies accounted for approximately 95 per cent of all new mortgage loans. The picture has changed dramatically, however, with the decision by the banks to undertake house mortgage business. At the time of writing, approximately 20 per cent of all new mortgage loans are being granted by the banks and at rates of interest which, at the present time, are very competitive with the building societies. It is business which the banks can undertake in a simple and efficient way. They already have the customer contact, with knowledge, or access to knowledge, of their customers' affairs, they have staff trained in lending disciplines and they are accustomed to taking security. The banks could well have entered this market at a much earlier date had they wished to do so, but it does not of course satisfy the traditional criteria of banking in this country, i.e. it is not short-term or self-liquidating. On the other hand, mortgage lending is not as long-term as normally assumed. Although a mortgage loan may be granted for, say, 30 years, the turnover of houses is such that the average life of a mortgage loan is as low as 5½ to 6 years. Also, of course, the total amount which the banks are prepared to commit to house mortgage business is, and is likely to be, a very modest proportion of their total lending business. Even so, at the end of 1986 mortgage lending accounted for approximately 50 per cent of the banks' net lending to personal customers.

Constraints on lending

There are three basic constraints on the amount and direction of bank lending at any particular time. These are:

1. the level of deposits;
2. capital and liquidity requirements; and
3. government controls.

The first of these, the level of deposits, depends on the overall level of deposits in the economy or, more particularly, that proportion of the total level which the banks are able to attract to themselves. We have already said that historically the joint stock banks were 'deposit-driven', i.e. they took in deposits and then sought to deploy them profitably. This is less true nowadays because, with the development of the money markets, the banks can raise wholesale deposits more or less at will. Some banks without a retail deposit-collecting network conduct a substantial and profitable lending business with funds raised in the wholesale markets. Even so, the total level of deposits, retail and wholesale, must be a constraint on lending. No banker can lend what he has not got. We have already discussed the competitive forces at work in the pursuit of the available deposits in the economy.

The second constraint, that of capital and liquidity ratios, is primarily a matter of prudential management by the banks. There has been much discussion over the years on the capital adequacy of banks, whether in terms of total capital resources in relation to deposits, or, more usually nowadays, in terms of free capital (i.e. excluding fixed assets) in relation to levels of deposits. The Bank of England have issued guidelines on this subject in recent times.

Liquidity ratios, i.e. the ratio of liquid assets including money at call and short notice, treasury bills, etc. to total deposits have over the years been the subject of official control. The liquidity ratio was 28 per cent of each bank's level of deposits and all banks maintained a ratio of 8 per cent between cash in the tills or at the Bank of England and their total deposits. With the introduction of Competition and Credit Control in September 1971, the old liquidity requirements were abandoned and replaced by a Reserve Asset Ratio which was fixed at a minimum of 12½ per cent of eligible liabilities, i.e. sterling deposits other than those with a maturity of over two years. More recently, the system of Reserve Asset Ratios has been abandoned and in its place a system of prudential controls has been introduced by the Bank of England for the guidance of individual banks whose figures are monitored on a regular basis.

The third constraint, that of government control, is no doubt inevitable in a mixed economy, but was the subject of great variation in the days of 'stop-go' controls. As we have already said, these take the form from time to time of quantitative and qualitative controls depending on the Treasury's view of the economy and of course on the overriding political considerations of the day. Such constraints usually take the form of 'guidance' from the Bank of England and the London clearing bankers have always responded to the best of their ability to observe both the letter and the spirit of the Bank's requests.

The principles of lending

The lending of money is one of the oldest and arguably the most important service rendered by the banks. Our purpose here is not to teach anyone to lend money, for there are many excellent books on the subject, but rather to describe the business of lending as part of the total picture of bank services.

To *lend* money is an easy matter. To be sure of repayment of the loan and of making a profit in the process is not so easy. The principal ingredient in appraising a lending transaction is that illusive thing we call 'confidence'. A banker will lend money to a customer only if he has total confidence in the customer's intention and ability to service the loan in terms of regular interest payments and to repay the loan on the due date. That confidence is made up of many components. It is partly the past record of the customer, particularly in financial matters, it is partly the banker's view of the customer's integrity, it is partly an appraisal of the customer's experience and ability in a particular field of business, it is partly an assessment of the customer's resources, both free and fettered, whether it be a small consumer loan or an advance to a large corporation, and all in all it stems from the banker's appraisal of the customer's credit-worthiness.

There are many large companies at the present day whose modest beginnings prospered because their bank managers had confidence in the proprietors. No doubt there are many others which never got off the ground because no bank had that confidence. The art of lending, if art it be, may often lie in the judgement or, indeed, sixth sense of a bank manager – by sheer experience he will acquire a 'nose' for the good or not so good proposition.

In the case of a private loan, the banker's confidence will stem from his knowledge of the customer's financial affairs and general lifestyle and a not too difficult appraisal of the customer's credit-worthiness. In the case of large loans to major corporations, the banker will have to study in depth the balance sheets and profit and loss accounts of the past as well as the forecasts for the future. He will have to have an understanding of the business generally and of the environment in which it is operating. He will have to have some appreciation of stock and debtor control, work in progress, cash flow, inter-company transfers, depreciation, capital allowances and corporation tax liabilities, pending legislation, interest rate movements, and of course the capital resources of the enterprise.

Overall, the banker will look to see the source of repayment of his loan. If this is to be from the profits of the enterprise, then the banker's appraisal of his customer's business prospects is particularly important. If, however, repayment is to come from the sale of a particular asset, e.g. a bridging loan pending the sale of a house, there may be less concern with the customer's overall acumen and the banker's concentration will be directed towards making sure that the proceeds in due time reach the right pocket.

The amount of the loan will itself be important. Obviously, it must always be appropriate to the resources of the borrower and his ability to repay. The loan should, however, be sufficient for the purpose and there are times when to lend too little involves a bank in as much risk as lending too much.

Finally, the banker will wish to know the purpose of the loan. In the past, a customer would not receive a loan from a bank without indicating the purpose and the purpose would have to be such as the bank considered worthy of support. Thus, any customer who sought a loan for the purpose of backing the 'winner' of the 3.30 at Newmarket would get short shrift from his bank. To some extent, therefore, the banks would exercise a moral judgement in a lending transaction and certainly saw themselves as keepers of the public's conscience in these matters. To a degree, this is still true today. A bank will always wish to know the purpose of a loan and will not grant it if it lacks moral substance or if it is for some purpose contrary to the bank's view of the public good. A bank will on occasions advance money for the purchase of stocks and shares to a customer of established means and usually on a short-term basis. Loans for purely speculative purposes, however, are not favoured and in times of credit stringency are unlikely to be granted at all. It is perhaps during such times of constraint that the purpose of a loan becomes particularly relevant. In recent times, the Bank of England has for example asked the commercial banks not to lend money on house mortgage for the purpose of consumer spending. Similarly, from time to time there has been restraint on the making of bank advances for property development purposes.

In the business sector, it is particularly important to know the purpose of any proposed borrowing and to monitor its use. The bank would not expect to find that a loan made for a particular business purpose had been applied in paying off other creditors, or to buy a Rolls Royce for the managing director.

These principles have been breached slightly by the introduction of more formalised loans, e.g. those granted by post on a computerised assessment of the customer's application (see below). It is quite impossible in such cases to monitor whether or not the money is used for the purpose indicated, nor in fact is the lender particularly worried on that score.

Unsecured loans

It is a characteristic of British banking that a very large proportion of loans (certainly the majority by value) are granted without security. This is probably because of the retail network of branches through which most loans are granted and which enables branch managers not only to have face to face contact with their customers, but also to monitor the progress of their customers' borrowing by discussion and review at regular intervals. If a particular proposition does not commend itself to a banker, the availability of security will not change the look of it. There are certain categories of loans, usually of a specialist nature, where repayment is intended to come from the security, e.g. produce loans and bridging loans on property. In general, however, the bank does not lend against security as such, nor in anticipation of repayment being made out of the security. The taking of security is a form of insurance.

Because a banker will approach every lending proposition on its merits (rather than on the strength of any security), he will go through the process of credit appraisal to which we have referred. If it transpires that the customer's capital resources are modest in relation to the required facility or if the profit record or profit forecasts are not wholly encouraging, the banker will seek the insurance of security.

Credit Scoring

This is a statistical method of appraising the credit-worthiness of an applicant for credit. To some extent credit scoring has replaced the traditional interview between bank manager and customer for the more straightforward type of personal and, in some cases, business borrowing. In the case of personal lending, whether by banks or finance houses, a system may be followed of allocating points for various aspects of the applicant's life-style, e.g. age, nature of property occupied, occupation, how long with the present employer and how long at the present address. The previous credit experience of the applicant will also be taken into account. The system of measurement is based on the statistical probability that the credit will be repaid. Most systems of credit scoring are now operated by computer and to some extent the more traditional subjective aspects of lending have been reduced to a fairly basic statistical approach.

Most banks will allow the branch manager on the spot to override the computer's judgement if the manager is aware of circumstances not taken into account statistically. In at least three large banks, credit scoring is now done on computer at some central place, thereby taking away quite a lot of the personal aspect which traditionally applied to branch banking.

Major commercial loans will, of course, continue to be on a negotiated basis, whether the bank is lending unsecured against a company's balance sheet and record of profitability or on a secured basis as discussed below.

Secured loans

In *The Country Banker*, Mr George Rae wrote:

> 'No doubt there is security, of a kind, in honest intention; but honesty itself may be overthrown by unforeseen disaster.'

So it is that no matter how satisfied a banker may be as to the integrity of his customer and the suitability of the proposition, he may wish to reinforce his position by the taking of security. If so, he should do so at the outset – it is always more difficult to obtain security when things are going wrong. In the case of a private loan, security may take the form of a charge over the borrower's house if it is free of mortgage or, indeed, a second charge if that is all that is available. It may take the form of stocks and shares, whether quoted or not, but it is unlikely that the banker would wish to lend more than 80 per cent of the market value. One of the most acceptable forms of security for a private account is a life assurance policy provided the surrender value is sufficient to cover the advance. In some cases, the only security available is the guarantee of a third party. This is perfectly acceptable if the third party is of sufficient means, but any guarantee has the disadvantage that in the event of the customer's default the bank has to look to the guarantor for payment and, if necessary, take proceedings against him. People who give guarantees seldom contemplate the possibility that they may be called upon to pay.

In the case of a company account, security may be available in the form of a mortgage of freehold or leasehold property, but the usual form of security given by a company to its bank is a debenture giving a fixed and floating charge over the assets of the business. This enables the management to conduct the business in the ordinary way, but in the event of default the bank has a charge over the assets of the company at that date and will appoint a Receiver to protect the position. In other cases, it may be appropriate to seek the guarantee of the proprietors of a company. This is particularly so if the assets of a company are only modest and the directors, being also the principal shareholders, have substantial resources of their own outside the business.

Other more specialised forms of security may be taken depending on the nature of the business. These may, for example, take the form of the assignment of debts, the deposit of bills of lading in relation to goods in transit, the mortgage of a ship or of shares in a ship or a documentary bill, i.e. a bill of exchange accompanied by the documents of title to goods.

Interest rates

With the introduction of Competition and Credit Control in 1971, the system of quoting lending rates by reference to the old Bank Rate was abandoned and the banks now determine independently their own base lending rates. These will be determined by the level of interest rates in the economy, but each bank will have regard to both the average cost and the marginal cost of the funds it borrows.

In the great majority of cases, the interest on advances will be quoted by reference to the banks' own base rate and may vary from, say, 1 per cent over base to 5 per cent over base rate. The rate will normally reflect the financial standing of the customer, the nature of the loan and the priority which the bank gives to a particular category of business.

Personal loans and other formalised categories of loan, usually those for a fixed term of, say, two to five years with monthly repayments, are subject to a fixed rate of interest on the total amount of the loan and determined at the time the loan is taken. Because the loan is reducing, the 'true' rate of interest is appreciably more than the rate quoted at the outset. Indeed, it is approximately twice the quoted rate so that, for example, a loan granted at 10 per cent on the amount borrowed, repayable over two years by monthly reductions, would incur a true rate of interest of 19.7 per cent.

A substantial proportion by value of loans granted to industry and other major borrowers is now quoted by reference to London Inter-Bank Offered Rate (LIBOR). This is particularly so where loans are syndicated among a number of banks. Rates quoted by reference to LIBOR will normally remain fixed at that level for an agreed period and 'rolled over' at the end of the period when an adjustment is made in relation to rates then in force.

The banks undertake a degree of 'fixed-rate' lending, but usually in cases where there is some measure of government subsidy, e.g. export credit finance. With such wide fluctuations in interest rates in recent years, any fixed term lending is exposed to market movements in a way which could be detrimental to either borrower or lender.

Unfortunately, we can no longer say with Macaulay that: 'Five per cent is the natural interest of money.'

References

1 Deuteronomy, 23, v.19
2 Deuteronomy, 23, v.20
3 History of England, G. M. Trevelyan, Longman
4 *The History and Principles of Banking,* J. W. Gilbart (1871).
5 Committee on the Working of the Monetary System (Chairman, The Lord Radcliffe), 1959, HMSO, Cmnd. 827.
6 Committee of London Clearing Bankers: 'The London Clearing Banks' – Evidence to the (Wilson) Committee to Review the Functioning of Financial Institutions. Longman, 1978.
7 Ibid.
8 Report of the Committee on Consumer Credit (Chairman: Lord Crowther), Cmnd. 4596, HMSO, 1971.
9 N.O.P. Survey for National Westminster Bank Limited, 1979.

10 Report of the Committee of Inquiry on Small Firms (Chairman: J. E. Bolton), Cmnd. 4811, HMSO, 1971.
11 Committee of London Clearing Bankers: 'The London Clearing Banks' – Evidence to the (Wilson) Committee to Review the Functioning of Financial Institutions, Longman, 1978.

Personal Services

CHAPTERS 4–13

CHAPTER 4

The Administration of Estates

The all-purpose bank is often thought of as providing a cradle-to-the-grave service, and in that context it must seem inappropriate to begin this section on personal services with the subject of death. Nevertheless, as we have said, the trustee services of the banks are the oldest of the extra-banking activities and for that reason, at least, they are a good place to start. Trustee services are not of course all concerned with the dead. For both technical and marketing reasons, trust services fall into the broad categories of (a) private and (b) corporate. For this purpose, private customers can be divided yet again between the living and the dead and so let us begin, as it were, at the end.

The oldest of non-banking functions, that of executor and trustee, is perhaps the most anomalous. It was no doubt thought appropriate that banks who look after the affairs of the living should also look after the affairs of the dead; that the friendly bank manager should become the friendly executor; that those big solid institutions that had seen many a customer through many a storm in life should be the repository for his problems on death. In fact, the leap into trustee work was much greater than with some of the services of recent years and the affinity between banking and the administration of estates is not at all an obvious one. In simple terms, the banker looks after his customer's money but an executor takes over the management of the entire estate; the banker acts as agent for his customer and of course as debtor or creditor, but the executor necessarily acts as a principal. Banks in this country seldom if ever accept the responsibility for dealing with a customer's entire affairs during his or her life, but as executors have shown a willingness to jump in at the deep end on death. Furthermore, the traditional skills and training of bankers as such are not specially related to those of the trust man. One cannot resist the thought that the banks' decision to go into trust business might have been different if they had been confronted with the choice in more recent years.

Historical background

This is not the place to dwell in detail on the history of corporate trustees in the United Kingdom and in any case, the story has been excellently told by D. R. Marsh in a book,[1] now sadly out of print. It was in 1845 that the South Sea Company sought to change the company into a 'Public Trust Company' and to undertake the administration of private trusts on a commission basis. It prompted one commentator to remark that 'instead of its former vocation of fishing in the South Seas, it wished to transfer its operations to fishery of suits in Chancery'.[2] The Charter was granted but apparently owing to some misunderstanding never sealed. In any event, this was the first of a number of Bills laid before Parliament over a period of approximately sixty years, all of which sought to establish companies for the purpose of engaging in trust business and all of which failed. The main reason generally advanced in support of the 'trading' trustee was the alleged unwillingness of private people to undertake the burdens of trusteeship. This was attributed to the decline of the landed aristocracy and the growth of the industrial and commercial classes. The various Bills were opposed not surprisingly by solicitors who saw their business disappearing to banks and insurance companies, but also, more philosophically, by those who could not reconcile limited liability with the concept of a trustee's personal responsibility.

It is a well-known rule of Equity that a trustee may not profit from his trust and only by special agreement or special powers may a trustee benefit, however indirectly, from his trusteeship. Each of the Bills laid before Parliament in the latter half of the nineteenth century on the subject of corporate trustees provided for the payment of remuneration to trust corporations (subject to appropriate safeguards), but Parliament would not have it. This was the more remarkable because in Australia, South Africa, New Zealand and America trustees had the right to charge reasonable remuneration either by statute or the common law. How the trust corporations of later years would have welcomed a Bill similar to Lord Hobhouse's in 1889 when he sought powers for trust companies to administer estates and take on existing trusts even though there was no enabling power in the trust instruments, and to have the right to charge remuneration in those cases on a scale approved by the Board of Trade!

The sense of outrage at the idea of trusteeships becoming a paid business was dramatically summed up by Lord St Leonards in 1858:

> 'that a trustee should be paid for his services is altogether repugnant to our habits and feelings. The office is to be filled by a friend with whom we can communicate freely and confidentially. A paid trustee would stand in a different character. Undoubtedly some would make a trade of the office and endeavour to attract custom to their own mill . . . the trade of a trustee! The business of an executor! Fancy it written over a shop door!'[3]

By the turn of the century only one Act, the Judicial Trustees Act of 1896, had given any sort of recognition to corporate trustees as such, and yet by this time no less than 290 trust companies were in operation in the United States. Here we might reflect on the quite different experience of the United States in the development of trust business. Although it was not until 1853 that the first American company, the United States Trust Company, was formed for the express purpose of administering estates and trusts, there was already by that time a large volume of trust activity in corporate hands in America. The Massachussetts Hospital Insurance Company of Boston had obtained legislative power to administer trusts as early as 1818 and in the following years a number of other insurance and annuity companies obtained similar powers, including in 1836 the Girard Life Insurance, Annuity and Trust Company, now Girard Bank. The later experience was the reverse of that in the United Kingdom in that many of the American banks had their origin in trust company operations – perhaps a more rational development than we saw in this country.

It is strange that England, where the legal concept of the 'trust' had its origin, should have been the last – after the United States and the 'old' Dominions – to give legislative recognition to the management of trusts as a business. Such recognition did not come until the passing of the Public Trustee Act in 1906. It was the culmination of twenty years of tireless campaigning and sponsorship of various Bills by Sir Howard Vincent, MP. The Act created the office of the Public Trustee with power to charge for his services and also empowered banks and insurance companies and the like to act as Custodian Trustees (with power to charge) where the active management remained with private individuals. This latter provision was of limited use as events turned out, but the dam was breached and the concept of the trading trustee was recognised.

It seems there was something of a reaction in official circles and some fear that the Public Trustee might become a monopoly, with the banking balances of thousands of private trusts being swept into the Bank of England. In 1904 the Union of London & Smiths Bank had amended its objects clause to permit 'the undertaking and executing of any trusts', and one by one, before and after the passing of the Public Trustee Act, the other banks followed suit. In the years from 1908 to 1912 the banks and insurance companies set up their trustee departments and arranged for the training of their staff to undertake this new 'non-banking' operation.

Trust business today

Today the trust companies and departments of the clearing banks have on their books over 61,000 cases of all kinds with a total approximate value of over £4 billion. In the course of a recent twelve months' period they accepted the administration of nearly 10,000 new estates with an average value of £65,000. At the present time the total number of will appointments, i.e. for living customers, on the books of the English and Scottish clearing banks exceed one million. The growth of business over seventy years or so has been impressive, but only modest in relation to the development of trust business in the United States.

Trust companies and departments are in the business of asset management. In the course of their activities, they are called upon to deal with almost every kind of asset susceptible to private ownership. Broadly speaking, the business consists of deceased estates, private trusts set up by will or *inter vivos* settlements, trusteeships for pension funds and charities, debenture trusts, unit trust trusteeships and the management of investment portfolios whether for private clients or institutions. The mainstream of that business is the administration of estates.

Executorships and administrations

We need not deal here with the technicalities of estates and trusts for trust administrators. The subject has been dealt with very competently in a number of textbooks over the years, one of the most recent being the excellent book by Mr Sladen.[4] For ease, therefore, we will use the word executor to embrace also the role of the administrator. An executor is the person who administers a deceased's estate, having been named as the executor in the will. An administrator on the other hand is appointed by the Court in those cases where (i) there is no will; or (ii) the will does not name an executor; or (iii) the executor has died before the testator, or does not wish to act. For most practical purposes, the role is the same. A similar function undertaken at times by corporate trustees is that of 'agent' for executors. In such cases, the grant of representation is applied for by the executor or other appropriate person and the bank or insurance company assists with the correspondence and book-keeping, and indeed virtually does all the work for the named executor or administrator. This procedure was occasionally adopted even in the early days of trustee departments in this country and has since been experimented with from time to time, but there are legal and practical difficulties. The service is a little more widespread in the United States.

The work of an executor may be summarised as (i) seeing that the funeral arrangements are dealt with; (ii) collecting the assets; (iii) paying the debts and expenses; (iv) arranging for the assets to be valued so far as may be necessary either for taxation or distribution purposes; (v) discharging any duties and taxes payable on the death; and (vi) accounting for the estate to the beneficiaries entitled.

Where banks are named as executors, they will usually peruse the draft will prior to its execution and offer their assistance, where this is welcomed, to the testator and his solicitor. Quite often, the very considerable experience of trust officials can be useful at this early stage in order to avoid difficulties later on.

Anyone of full age and sound mind may be an executor or administrator and the task is often undertaken by ordinary people with no special financial or legal knowledge. On the first occasion, however, few people know where to start and are utterly dependent on obtaining the right advice and help. To step into the shoes of a deceased person, whether family or friend, is a great responsibility. Few people succeed in managing their own financial affairs adequately and are ill-equipped to take on the affairs of others. In these days of increasing complexity in personal financial matters, executorship is no longer a matter for the amateur, if indeed it ever was. An eminent jurist has described the ideal executor and trustee in the following terms:

> 'The Trustee of my property, my Executor, must be always well and at home; he must never run away and never steal; must have life everlasting; must be rich and stay rich with all his property pledged to the proper performance of his trust; must have no partialities; must be subject to no political or personal influences; must make no mistakes; must never forget; must do what he is told to do, first, last and all the time; must keep a complete record of what he does; must make only reasonable charges, and must have the learning, the experience, the discretion, not only of one man, but of a number of the most successful businessmen of the community.'[5]

The choice of executor

Thus the choice of an executor is not easy. It lies among (i) a relative or friend; (ii) a professional man; (iii) the Public Trustee; or (iv) a corporate trustee such as a bank or insurance company. The banks have always claimed to offer special advantages, notably the continuity of their business, the security which a large bank exemplifies in the conduct of its customers' affairs and the cumulative experience of a highly trained staff, many of whom have spent all or most of their careers in trust work.

Why then do all the world not appoint banks as their executors? In the first place, there are over 20 million adults in this country who do not have accounts with a clearing bank and a few million others who, whilst conducting accounts with their banks, do not come into such a meaningful relationship that they would contemplate the appointment of their bank as executor. Leaving such cases aside on the assumption, for the moment, that they are outside the banks' 'market' for trustee work, we encounter two main reasons why the banks have not swept the board.

The first is the often expressed view that banks are impersonal. Taken as a general proposition, this does not stand up. Banks, like other institutions, can only operate through the human beings they employ. They can be as kind and understanding as the man next door; they can be as unimaginative and as obdurate. A bank's trust department is only as good as the people in it. Over the years one has seen cases administered with a robot-like lack of understanding of the human problems involved and a determination to 'go by the book'. But such cases are not typical: there are many beneficiaries of family trusts who have had cause to appreciate and commend the dedicated attention given to their affairs by trustee department staff. They have gone about their work with sympathy and quiet efficiency and many have become 'friends of the family' in a way which used to be reserved for the clergyman, doctor or solicitor.

For the trustee staff themselves, the work provides one of the most satisfying careers that an institution can offer. To adopt the slogan of a well-known newspaper, 'all human life is there'. Trustee work is a happy combination of professional expertise and a socially desirable objective – never more so than in the administration of an estate on death. It is a task which must be done by someone, usually at a time of family distress and anxiety. It is a task which brings satisfaction not only in its own usefulness, but in the sheer variety of the work. The trust administrator may have to deal in his time with almost every conceivable type of asset – from the post office account to the investment in North Sea oil; from tumbledown cottages to elegant office blocks; from flocks of sheep to fleets of tugs; from the well-worn wedding ring to the glistening tiara.

That is a digression. Let us agree that it is very personal work.

'From flocks of sheep to fleets of tugs.'

The facts remain, however, that at the time a will is made the bank trustee must seem remote and impersonal. It is very seldom that a customer meets the trust official who is going to administer his estate. Some people clearly do not mind. They are comforted by the objectivity and impartiality of the institution which will take over. On the whole, however, most people who give thought to these matters at the time of making a will would prefer to think that family and fortune are in the care of someone they have known in this life. One possible answer lies in the choice of a private executor from among friends or family to act jointly with a corporate trustee, but in practice this can be a cumbersome arrangement. In any case, the corporate trustee should make it his concern to work closely and sympathetically with the family.

We have already dared to suggest that banking in the High Street has to a degree become less personal over the years. Computers have contributed to the situation, at least in the minds of the public. Other factors have been the pressures on managers which make it increasingly difficult for them to meet more than a proportion of their customers: population movements and the uniformity, indeed anonymity, of suburban life, and at times the rapid movement of bank managers themselves. It has become increasingly difficult in modern times for banker and customer to build up a friendly, continuing relationship over a period of years. Whatever the reasons, many customers never meet their bank manager, even less look upon him as a personal friend, and so do not naturally turn to the banks to administer their affairs on death. In sharp contrast, the entry of the banks into trustee work had its origin, at least in part, in the close personal relationship of banker and customer, particularly among the private bankers. We are told that on the death years ago of a partner in Hoare & Co., the well-known private bankers, he was trustee of over 200 trusts, and that the practice of the partners acting as trustee had continued over the 275 years of the firm's existence. The banking relationship was a personal thing started in life and continued after death. Today things are different.

A question of costs

The other deterrent to the appointment of a clearing bank as executor is the comparatively high cost of doing so. The privilege of a bank executorship is not for the poor man. This is a pity because there are many people of modest means who do not have a natural executor to whom to turn. By the nature of things, the less the worldly goods, the less sophisticated the family when it comes to dealing with financial matters. Furthermore, the great mass of people in this country do not have a family solicitor as such, nor any regular contact with a member of the legal profession. In earlier times, the cost of appointing a bank as executor was comparatively small and many people of modest means chose banks as their executors. Not many years ago, nearly 70 per cent of all the estates and trusts in one bank were under £10,000 in value. In recent times, however, banks by force of circumstance have had to price themselves out of the executorship business for Mr Everyman. Strange to say, something of this situation was foreseen in the opposition to the creation of corporate trustees in the long debate towards the end of the nineteenth century, the objecting petitioners pointing out that the charges for maintaining a 'joint stock establishment' would render the administration of an estate as costly as administering it in the Court of Chancery.

To some extent that prophecy has come true. A reasonably well informed clerk can administer an average estate with care and efficiency and everyone will be satisfied. It can be done at a fee which will leave something over as a fair margin of profit. If, however, that clerk has to be trained to a standard where he can deal with a large variety of estates, if for the good name of the organisation his work has to be checked by a senior officer, if a legal department has to be set up as a long-stop, if an inspection team has to be created to keep everyone on the right lines, if a local branch is set up for the convenience of the market, if a manager is appointed to oversee the local business and given the benefit of a car, if all are paid at the present level of bank salaries and adequate transfers made to the pension fund, the cost becomes enormous. The banks have done much to counteract the trend. They have moved cases to low-cost areas and have reduced the number of branches wherever possible. It is significant that the Public Trustee only ever had one country office, at Manchester, and that was closed for reasons of economy many years ago.

Similarly, the banks have done much to rationalise their organisation and methods, but that in itself was an expensive exercise, particularly where the introduction of computers was involved. On the other hand, computers now enable a vast volume of trust work to be done speedily and with economies of scale.

The subject of bank charges for the administration of estates has been commented on from two quarters in recent years. In 1982 the British Legal Association asked the Director of Fair Trading to enquire into the question of these bank services, including the question of charges, but the Director declined to take action on the ground that there was insufficient evidence to merit an enquiry under the Fair Trading Act. The Chairman of the British Legal Association claimed that in some instances the banks were charging 'four times what a solicitor would charge'. The banks pointed out that their customers were made fully aware of the banks' charges because they were the subject of a formal tariff, whereas in the case of solicitors' charges it was not always possible to know in advance what the level would be.

The other quarter from which comment has been made in recent times is the National Consumer Council in their report 'Banking Services and the Consumer'.[6] The Report contained a number of comments which are referred to later in this chapter and suggested that there should be a detailed investigation into the whole area of executor and trustee work. On the subject of charges it was considered that complaints should be dealt with by the (proposed) banking ombudsman, as would indeed complaints on other matters such as maladministration, breach of trust, etc.

The employment of solicitors

There are many matters in connection with the administration of an estate which are of a legal nature and which are properly the concern of a solicitor. There are two areas, however, where duties are reserved for the legal profession which the banks and other corporate executors could well deal with themselves. In the first place, under the rules of the Supreme Court,[7] it is not possible for a corporate body to make a 'personal' application for a Grant of Probate. A private executor can do so, but a corporation must make application through a solicitor. The banks argue that this is an anachronistic rule because today there are hundreds of trained staff in the banks who can prepare the details for a probate application quite as well as those employed in solicitors' offices. The rule is based on the general principle that only a private person or a legally qualified practitioner has the right of audience before the Court and, therefore, a company can only appear through a solicitor or barrister. Thus, a trust corporation has no legal right to apply for a Grant of Probate or Letters of Administration anymore than it would have the right to appear before any other Court other than by its legal representative.

The other rule is that, under Section 23 of the Solicitors' Act, 1974, only a practising solicitor may make a charge for taking instructions for a Grant of Probate or Letters of Administration, or for drawing or preparing papers on which to apply for, or oppose, such a grant.

The effect of these two rules is that in every case where a corporate body is appointed as executor, it is necessary for a solicitor to be appointed with a consequent increase in costs. The Association of Corporate Trustees made representations on both these points to the Royal Commission on Legal Services and, in its Report, the Commission recommended that the Non-contentious Probate Rules and the Solicitor's Act be amended to permit personal applications by trust companies and the preparation by trust companies of the documents leading to an application for Probate. The Commission went on to recommend that, if the Probate Rules and the Solicitors' Act were so amended, the charges made by banks and other executors who are not solicitors should be subject to the same control as applies to solicitors, i.e. that an interested party may require all the charges made by the bank, including all financial advantages arising in the course of the administration, to be taxed by the Court. The application to the Lord Chancellor was opposed by the Law Society, principally on the grounds that the existing regulations were designed for the protection of the public and for the better administration of justice. There the matter rests at the present time.

There is another legal aspect of the banks' trustee business which has caused some heart-searching over the years, that is the drawing up of wills and codicils for customers. Although it is contrary to the Solicitors' Act for anyone but a legally qualified person to prepare legal documents 'in expectation of any fee, gain or reward', this does not apply to wills or other testamentary documents. The banks have not seen it as their business to make wills for people, although some customers may have wished it, and it was the practice (and for the most part still is) to insist that wills appointing a bank as executor be drafted by solicitors. This enabled the solicitor quite properly to advise his client on the legal aspects of the matter and indeed, the preparing of a will has always been an important feature of a solicitor/client relationship. In some cases, solicitors have been known to advise clients against appointing the banks as executors, advice which they are perfectly entitled to give, but which naturally did not please the banks. In other cases, customers have not seen the need to pay for what they regarded as a simple will or codicil to be prepared by a solicitor if, as they thought, the bank would do it instead. In recent times, some of the banks have broken with the past and will now prepare a will for a customer who does not have a solicitor and who does not wish to engage a solicitor. One bank in particular, National Westminster Bank still declines to adopt this practice which, on the whole, will not endear the banks to the legal profession.

Profitability

To return, however, to the banks' own costs, it seems unrealistic to suppose that they will ever fall significantly below their present level. In 1974 some figures produced for the Price Commission in support of proposed increases in fees showed that the administration of an average estate, involving no particular complexities, cost a bank considerably in excess of the fees then chargeable.

Even on the basis of the fee scales now in force, the administration of a comparatively small estate of, say, £20,000 would still produce little or no profit for the corporate executor. This is to some extent the story of trust business in the banks over the years, although it was brought into sharp relief by the inflation of recent times.

At one time, the trust activities of the clearing banks were subsidised to the extent that they were not charged specifically with some overhead charges, such as rent and pensions. Taking all costs into account and taking one year with another, trust business in the United Kingdom has so far not been a very profitable exercise. Naturally, one asks why. The most probable explanation is that the public of this country are not accustomed to the idea of paying for their estates to be wound up. It is accepted that a solicitor is entitled to a certain level of charges for preparing a property conveyance, that an estate agent receives a standard commission for selling a house and that the undertaker be paid at the appropriate level of fees for burying the dead. Indeed very many life policies were taken out with the industrial life companies for the very purpose of ensuring that money was there for the funeral, but traditionally the executor who stepped into the shoes of the deceased was either expected to do it as a labour of love or given a small legacy for his trouble. Certainly, people with assets on paper to a value of, say, £20,000 are unaccustomed in their lifetime to paying a £1,000 fee to anyone for anything and therefore do not take kindly to the thought that their executor should receive such a fee, particularly as it would be in addition to legal charges. On the other hand, the view is sometimes advanced that the testator is not unduly concerned about the burden of costs which falls on his beneficiaries provided he is not asked to pay anything in his lifetime.

The unprofitability of the business is not peculiar to the United Kingdom. Out of the 14,000 or so banks in the United States, large numbers do not undertake trust business because they regard it as unprofitable and, of those who do engage in trust work, only a handful admit to making profits on trust activities as such.

The observer will wonder why the banks continue in this line of business if it be unprofitable. The answer lies partly in the difficulty of extricating themselves from a situation where such vast numbers of living customers have already appointed the bank as executor. To withdraw from this situation would be a mammoth operation, but more particularly would be regarded by many as a breach of faith. The other reason is that executorship services are seen quite properly as part of the concept of total financial management. This is no doubt the better view and it may well be that as the public come to accept more and more the role of the all-purpose bank, they will be readier to pay the costs of winding up their estates.

Some related benefits

In any case, trustee work is not without its related benefits – the 'spin-off' to other services. The most important and most quoted benefit is the level of banking balances generated by trust work. The sad thing is that even allowing for the benefit of executorship balances, the service has not always been profitable; and one must remember that if banks did not undertake the administration of estates, many of those balances would remain with the banks as bankers. Then again, the work provides opportunities for the cross-selling of bank services and many an executorship has led to an investment management portfolio or income tax work or perhaps insurance business. Of less tangible benefit but of equal importance is the goodwill created among beneficiaries and others, and the additional points of contact developed between bank and customers or potential customers. These things are difficult to evaluate, but much money can be lost in the name of 'goodwill' or 'service'. True costs should be balanced against true benefits.

The system of charging

A particular feature of trust companies throughout the world is the *ad valorem* system of charging. It is usual to quote a percentage fee graduated according to the size of the estate. This has always been so and probably will remain so. The responsibility for administering an estate is measurable primarily by reference to the size of the assets: thus the *ad valorem* fee reflects the responsibility involved. The weakness of the system is that it does not reflect the varying degrees of difficulty among different estates. Thus, a large estate can sometimes be quite simple and the fee looks disproportionate, whereas some small estates can be difficult and time consuming and the fee can never recompense for the work involved. The student of these matters might care to consider possible alternative systems. One obvious possibility is to charge on a 'time' basis. This is a professional service and it would be quite in keeping with professional practice in this country to charge on a time-involved basis, allowing a margin for profit. This has the disadvantage of uncertainty and some might argue that the estate would be at the mercy of the executor bank. At least the present system has the advantage of simplicity and certainty.

The market

It is unfortunate that inflation has taken bank executorship services further away from the ordinary man. The market is large and the banks' share of that market after seventy years' experience is not great. The report of the National Consumer Council referred to on page 93 suggested that the banks' share of the market was less than 10 per cent. At first sight, the total market for executorship business is made up of the adult population of Great Britain. This is of the order of 40 million people. For all practical purposes, however, we can limit the number to those 20 million or so who have accounts with the old clearing banks. As we have said, trustee services developed from the banker-customer relationship and the banks in general do not expend their marketing efforts for these services on the unbanked population. There are of course exceptions but they are rare enough to be ignored. The market is further restricted, and very considerably so, by the subtraction of those citizens who have little or no assets to dispose of on death. Out of the 600,000 or so people who die in England and Wales each year, approximately one-half leave 'estates' so small and so simple that no application is necessary for a Grant of Probate or Grant of Letters of Administration. On a recent calculation by the Principal Probate Registry, the number of wills admitted to Probate (i.e. excluding intestacies) in the course of a three month period was just under 41,000.

Marketing methods

So much for the market. Let us turn now to the methods by which that market is attacked. It has been said that bank trustee departments are associated with 'graves and worms and epitaphs'. Certainly the image of death has clouded – or should we say shrouded? – the marketing of these services. In the Bankers Almanack of 1907 the announcement by one bank of its executor and trustee services was in the smallest print and most tentative wording compared with the bold type and forthright announcement of the similar services offered by the Northern Trust Company in Chicago. For decades, the banks contented themselves with the cautious announcement that they would 'undertake' executor and trustee business. Not surprisingly, the word 'undertake' did not help and in one bank in the early days a blackedged counter announcement with the word 'undertake' prominent had to be withdrawn hastily. The general approach to the marketing of trust services was just about as low key as one would expect from 'undertakers'. Most banks were satisfied with an announcement on their counters or bank windows and left the rest to the local manager. In later years, the Midland Bank produced an excellent film entitled 'Why not Uncle Willie?' and some of the banks introduced slightly more graphic advertising, but it was all part of the back-up to the local manager's own efforts. Few if any bank people expected to sell executorship business by advertisements. What then of the bank manager? There is of course no prototype for the 12,500 bank managers in Britain. Some found it easy and natural to offer executorship services to their customers and thus built up a useful volume of business. Others did not wish to risk offence by talking of such delicate matters and potential business went by default. Success tended to be measured by numbers alone, with the result that large numbers of cases of small value were taken on to the banks' books and, with inflation, it became increasingly difficult to administer these without loss. Also, the higher level of fees bore heavily on small estates and thus it became the practice on the part of the banks to offer to renounce, wherever the estate was small. Definitions of 'small' varied from time to time and from bank to bank, but at the present time bank managers are seldom encouraged by their trust departments to go in pursuit of business worth less than £20,000, and on death the banks will normally offer to renounce their appointment if the estate turns out to be less than that sum.

The banks use different methods to encourage their managers to obtain trust business, but over the years the most usual method has been to pay an introductory commission to the branch concerned. There is some variation of practice among the banks, but the aim has always been to give branch managers some extra inducement to introduce business to the trust department.

Nowadays, few managers find it difficult to raise with their customers the delicate subject of executorship, but it would appear that they do encounter a certain resistance to modern fee levels. Part of the difficulty is that the bank managers themselves find it difficult to accept the need for the current level of charges. Nevertheless, the business still flows in as evidenced by the total number of estates taken on to the banks' books, as quoted on page 86.

Over the years, solicitors in general have been antagonistic to the appointment of banks as executors. As we have seen, they resisted the entry of the corporate trustee into what they regarded as their own field and that attitude has continued, at least in some parts of the country, down to the present time. On the whole, particularly in the south of England, trust companies and solicitors work together in a friendly, co-operative way. The Trustee Departments' Committee of the Committee of London Clearing Bankers established a regular liaison at senior level with the Law Society and this has been very helpful in resolving particular problems. The fact remains, however, that many solicitors find it difficult to recommend their clients to appoint banks as trustee at the present level of remuneration, which as we have said is in addition to the legal charges. Generally, the duties will be carried out more cheaply and equally satisfactorily if a member of the family is appointed executor, perhaps under the guidance of the solicitor. However, there are many cases where a testator does not wish a member of the family to act and where he is attracted by the professionalism and independence of the corporate trustee.

In one related area there is a market for bank services which is perhaps not fully explored. A large number of people in this country die without having made a will. Their families quite often do not know which way to turn and the bank manager (who is usually one of the first to hear of the death) can be of help in offering the services of the bank's trust department as administrator. The banks take on many such cases in the course of the year and can be of very real help to customers at what is usually a very difficult time. Indeed, the Committee of London Clearing Bankers, responding to the report of the National Consumer Council mentioned above, agreed that a 'hand-holding' service was often appropriate for those customers who wished to do most of the executorship work themselves.

Some conclusions

In conclusion, we may say this of the administration of estates:

1. It is a service which is here to stay because of the banks' very considerable commitment to hundreds of thousands of customers under existing wills and also because of the substantial deployment of resources on this work, principally in terms of highly qualified staff – resources which could not easily be redeployed, certainly in present conditions, elsewhere in the banks.

2. It is a service which the market regards as expensive, almost elitist, notwithstanding that current fee scales are very much in line with those charges which are permitted by law in other parts of the world.

3. Profits will be hard earned: it is a sophisticated and personal service requiring high-grade staff and, because of the small routine content of the work, there is but limited opportunity for improving productivity.

4. It is valuable as a means of consolidating and developing existing banker/customer relationships and opens up the market for other services.

5. It is very much in keeping with the modern theme of comprehensive financial management – it would be inconsistent for the banks to proffer the solution to virtually every personal financial problem in the customer's lifetime and then quietly withdraw at the graveside.

6. It is a service which meets a very real market need.

References and notes

1 D. R. Marsh: *Corporate Trustees*. Europa, 1952.
2 *Legal Observer*. Volume XLVI, p. 300.

3 *Handy Book on Property Law.* 1858.
4 M. Sladen: *Practical Trust Administration.* Europa, 1977.
5 I am indebted to Mr R. A. M. Coker, of the National Westminster Bank, for this quotation.
6 *Banking Services and the Consumer.* A report by the National Consumer Council. Methuen, 1983.
7 *Non-Contentious Probate Rules 1954.* S.I. 1954, No. 796 R2(2).

CHAPTER 5

Private Trusts

Departing from the 'business of an executor' we come, in the words of Lord St Leonard's alliterative strictures, to the 'trade of a trustee'. Although the distinctions between the two functions have become blurred in the public mind, they have their origins in entirely different corners of the law, the one in the law of succession and the other in our singular and fascinating law of trusts. An executor is not *per se* a trustee, but may become one. For practical purposes and with deliberate over-simplification, we may say that an executor or administrator becomes a trustee at that moment when he holds the estate or any part of it on behalf of the beneficiaries. He does not necessarily hold the capital at their disposal: the funds may be 'settled' for a further specified period and such settled trusts are, as we shall see, the hard core of the trustee business of the clearing banks at the present day.

The origin of the trust

Every student of law knows that the trust is a special creation of the Anglo-Saxon legal system, although not without its points of similarity with the *Fideicommissum* of Roman law which had developed in the last Republic and was given recognition under the Emperor Augustus.[1] The trust had its origin in the thirteenth-century practice of making conveyances ('feoffments') to 'uses'. The word 'use' had its derivation in the latin 'opus', gradually corrupted to 'oes' and 'ues' and ultimately 'use'. Even before the Domesday Book it was not uncommon for a man to make a transfer of property *ad opus* another, but it was not until the year 1230 that we see the first instance of a man holding land permanently to the *use* of another. With this simple device of holding property for the benefit of another person, it became possible (i) to avoid the cumbersome methods of land transfer; (ii) to devise land by will – not otherwise possible in feudal England; (iii) to avoid feudal dues; (iv) to create future interests in land; (v) to avoid forfeiture for felony; (vi) to get round the Mortmain Statutes which forbade the holding of land by corporations, e.g. monasteries; and (vii) in the case of the clergy, to circumvent the vows of poverty because a Papal Bull of 1279 ordained that a 'use' was not 'property'. It was not altogether surprising therefore that King Henry VIII, like many a modern Chancellor of the Exchequer, sought the 'extinguishment of all such subtle practised feoffments' in order to stave off regal poverty and, after a stormy passage, the Statute of Uses was passed in 1535. The purpose of the Statute was to prevent conveyances to uses. The effect of the Statute was that the transfer of property to A for the use of or in trust for B would give B the entire legal ownership, which of course was not the intention of the transferor. If the matter had ended there we would presumably not have had the development of trust law as we know it today in this country. However, with characteristic resilience, the English lawyers found a simple and ingenious device for circumventing the Statute. This was for A to make a transfer of property to the use of B to the use of C. The effect of the Statute was that, where there was such a 'use upon a use', the first use attracted the Statute and gave B the legal estate and the second use was void. It was only a matter of time before the Chancellor in the exercise of his equitable jurisdiction, was found to be upholding such second uses for the benefit of the second named person. In the case of Sambach v Dalston in 1634, such a 'second use' was put to the test for the first time and upheld in the Chancellor's Court. This is believed to be the beginning of the English Law of trusts.

This slight historical excursion serves to illustrate that from the earliest days there was a 'commercial' aspect of uses or trusts to the extent that they were used to mitigate taxes and conserve capital. The whole concept is based on confidence or trust in the wider sense of the word and it has been developed over the years with a flexibility and adaptability which has given the system much of its strength. Today we have a canon of trust law which is the envy of our continental friends.

There is no very satisfactory definition of the trust. One which is often quoted is that of Professor Keeton, viz. 'a trust is the relationship which arises wherever a person called the trustee is compelled in equity to hold property, whether real or personal, and whether by legal or equitable title, for the benefit of some persons (of whom he may be one and who are termed *cestuis que trust*) or for some object permitted by law, in such a way that the real benefit of the property accrues, not to the trustee, but to the beneficiaries or other objects of the trust'.[2]

Within such a definition there is an almost infinite variety of trusts in operation in this country today. For our present purpose, we shall categorise them into (1) private trusts and (2) corporate trusts. The distinction is not clear cut: for example some trusts such as charitable trusts are hybrid in the sense that they fall into either category. In this section we are concerned with trusts set up by private individuals.

Where funds have been 'settled' for someone's benefit, the trust is generally known as a 'settlement' and the person creating the trust is the 'settlor'. Such terminology would be wrong, however in relation to certain non-private trusts such as pension funds.

Private trusts fall into two broad categories – those which arise under a will or on intestacy and those which are made *inter vivos*.

Settled estates

Turning first to will trusts – let us call them 'settled estates' – we encounter the largest category both in numbers and value of trust business in the United Kingdom banks. The great majority of trusts under administration in the banks today are settled estates arising under the wills of testators who died over the last sixty years or so. They are thought to number in total approximately 50,000 cases. In former years, it was more common than it is today to settle all or part of one's estate for the benefit of successive generations in so far as this was permissible within the perpetuity laws. There were a number of reasons for this. First, there was the testator's concern to protect beneficiaries, particularly female beneficiaries, from either themselves or the exploitation of others. Thus, the daughters would be lucky if they received more than a life interest in their part of the estate whereas the sons would take their shares absolutely. With the 'liberation' of women and greater enlightenment all round, this practice has largely disappeared. Secondly, a widow (and sometimes a widower) would be given a life interest in an estate partly for reasons of protection already mentioned, but more particularly because of the relief which this gave from Estate Duty. With the introduction of Capital Transfer Tax[3] (now Inheritance Tax), all transfers between husband and wife became free of tax and thus the old exemption is no longer relevant. Thirdly, it was often the wish of the testators to tie up their fortune in trust for as long as possible in order to give the next generation but one, including those still unborn, a share of the cake. Perhaps this was personal vanity, perhaps a genuine desire to provide for future generations. In any case, swingeing death duties made it increasingly difficult to leave large sums in trust, but more particularly there has been a noticeable change in social attitudes. Testators show diminishing concern about locking up funds for even the next generation, although most parents would rather see their worldly wealth go to their children than evaporate in taxes. The change in attitude over the years probably owes less to egalitarianism than to inflation: people of all financial levels find it difficult enough to maintain standards in this life without worrying too much about future generations.

Are we to conclude therefore that the days of the settled estate are numbered? Certainly it is unlikely that we shall ever again see substantial fortunes locked up for successive generations, but cases will still remain where estates are not immediately distributable on death. One of the largest banks estimates that one in seven of new estates result in a settled trust when the executorship is completed, but this would include minors' legacies and other absolute bequests which, for some reason, could not be immediately distributed. The number of settled estates in the true sense is probably only one in fifteen cases.

Lifetime trusts

Inter vivos settlements are those made by deed in the settlor's lifetime. Traditionally they were made for a variety of reasons. Perhaps the most typical was the marriage settlement, usually following a set pattern and embracing the property brought in by the husband and wife into the 'husband's fund' and 'wife's fund' respectively. New settlements in this form are seldom seen, largely because of the fiscal and social changes to which we have referred. Other trusts would be set up for unmarried daughters or for handicapped children and the so-called protective trusts would be created to guard against the possibility of the beneficiaries' bankruptcy. This could be done by the express terms of the trust or by adopting the statutory terms set out in Section 33 of the Trustee Act 1925. The general desire of a settlor, however, would be to set aside funds for the future benefit of the family and to do it, if possible, in a way which would minimise the impact of taxation and the old Estate Duty. The most convenient and deservedly popular vehicle for this came to be the discretionary trust.

All trusts may be swept into one of two broad categories, viz. 'ministerial' (to use an old word) or 'discretionary'. The former requires no more than the exercise of normal prudence and business judgment in carrying out the express terms of the trust; the latter, as the name implies, requiring the exercise of a discretion by the trustee – sometimes in the choice of beneficiaries, sometimes as to the quantum of the benefit and sometimes as to its timing. In their earlier forms, discretionary trusts were usually to protect beneficiaries from themselves or from a trustee in bankruptcy, and in fact the statutory protective trusts provide for the trustees to exercise discretionary powers in certain circumstances. In more recent years, however, the discretionary trust became almost the standard form of family trust.

Discretionary trusts

A discretionary trust combines those two essential features of English trust law to which we have already made reference – confidence and adaptability. The settlor must have confidence in his trustee as a person or institution of integrity and good sense. The trustee must be prepared to adapt to changing circumstances and exercise his discretion with wisdom and understanding. A discretionary trust has three distinct advantages. First of all, it makes for maximum flexibility because the trustee's discretion will be exercised according to changing circumstances over the years. Even in the best regulated families it is impossible to foresee future hazards whether of a financial or matrimonial nature or worse. Secondly, a discretionary trust allows the settlor to have at least a moral say in the management of the trust. He has surrendered his legal right to control the destination of the funds, but the trustee is entitled to have regard to the settlor's wishes and will normally do so not only during the settlor's life, but as far as practicable after his death, always bearing in mind that he, the trustee, must act in the best interests not of the settlor but of the beneficiaries. Thirdly, the discretionary trust may still be an effective vehicle for reducing taxation notwithstanding the efforts of successive Chancellors to close the gap. It is rather sad that successive fiscal legislation imposed an undue burden of taxation on this most valuable, perfectly legitimate and indeed historic aspect of the English trust. However, the 1982 Finance Act introduced a welcome simplification and rationalisation of capital transfer tax (now Inheritance Tax) in relation to discretionary trusts so that they no longer stand at such a disadvantage in relation to other gifts.

Banks as trustees

During the last seventy years the banks have built up an enormous fund of expertise in the management of settled trusts. They have managed the affairs, sometimes for three generations, of some of the most influential families in the land. They have managed over 100,000 settled trusts in a sensitive and professional way and the proportion of error or oversight has been minute. In at least one bank, the settled estates were referred to over the years as 'automatics'. It arose no doubt from the need to set up arrangements for the automatic collection and distribution of income, but beyond that such cases are far from automatic. The burden of a trusteeship, whether discretionary or not, is considerable and lies heavily on the shoulders of the trustee. He must exercise a wise judgment in such matters as: (i) the advancement of funds to beneficiaries; (ii) the maintenance and education of infant beneficiaries; (iii) the preservation of the trust property; (iv) requests for the partitioning of the trust; (v) applications by the beneficiaries to the Court for varying the terms of a trust under the Variation of Trusts Act 1958. During the life of a trust beneficiaries will die, others will come of age and new ones will be born. It can be more than a lifetime's task and the continuity of the trusteeship is important.

Investment matters

The most important aspect of a trustee's role is his stewardship of the trust property, whether it be investments, land, houses or chattels. The beneficiaries may forgive him for a technical or mathematical error in some apportionment of income or application of a legal rule, but he will not be excused for negligent management of the assets. Very few people today have the knowledge and the technical back-up to manage trust funds over a long period of years. It is a job for corporate trustees, particularly the banks with their concentration of economic and financial knowledge and familiarity with the principal markets throughout the world. Even so, corporate trustees do not always get it right. Perhaps at times they have seen their task as a legal or technical one, or possibly as an accounting process, rather than the stewardship of investments. It would be unfair to criticise some of the investment decisions made years ago because they should be judged against the climate of the times. Even so, many thousands of family trusts have been diminished in value by an undue allegiance to gilt-edged stocks in past years. This applied whether the trustees were private or corporate but, with the passing of the Trustee Investments Act 1961 which gave trustees wider investment powers, the trustee departments of the banks had the resources to move quickly to take advantage of the new legislation. The important point, however, is that nowadays banks hold themselves out as investment experts, for example in the management of pension funds and private portfolios, and thus their management of trusts will be judged increasingly by their performance in the investment field.

Older fee scales

Improved investment performance will lead in many cases to higher fees (because of the *ad valorem* system of remuneration) and this will be a useful contribution to the problem of profitability. Many of the settled trusts administered today by the clearing banks were accepted years ago on the basis of fee scales which are no longer relevant. In one bank, out of approximately 20,000 settled trusts no less than 12,000 were at one time on out-of-date fee scales. As we have said, this country is one of the few which do not have a statutory or common law power to charge fees and thus, in all cases the pattern of remuneration is governed by the terms of the trust instrument. All the banks have made approaches to their beneficiaries from time to time to secure an improvement in fees and these approaches have met with varying success. It is a problem which is fraught with difficulties and for the most part the banks are having to live with an uneconomic commitment into which they entered years ago. Some assistance may be found in a modern case[4] In re the Duke of Norfolk's Trusts where, in the Court of Appeal, Lord Justice Fox said:

> 'I conclude that the Court has an inherent jurisdiction to authorise the payment of remuneration of trustees and that that jurisdiction extends to increasing the remuneration authorised by the trust instrument. In exercising that jurisdiction, the Court has to balance two influences which are to some extent in conflict. The first is that the office of trustee is, as such, gratuitous; the Court will accordingly be careful to protect the interests of the beneficiaries against claims by the trustees. The second is that it is of great importance to the beneficiaries that the trust should be well administered. It is, therefore, open to the Court to conclude, having regard to the nature of the trust, the experience and skill of a particular trustee and to the amounts which he seeks to charge when compared with what other trustees might require to be paid for their services and to all the other circumstances of the case, that it would be in the interests of the beneficiaries to increase the remuneration, and the Court may properly do so.'

To add to the banks' problem, the introduction of Value Added Tax in the 1972 Finance Act required payment by the banks of VAT on the fees in these old cases without any corresponding statutory power to charge the tax to the trust. This was almost certainly an oversight in the drafting of the Bill and representations were made to the Treasury, but no one in government circles felt inclined to amend the Act.

There is a touch of irony in the fact that the banks carry this great incubus of old cases on inadequate fees at a time when the market for new private trusts has declined. If all the old cases were on modern fee scales the profitability of trust business would look very different. In fact, the English banks act in approximately 60,000 settled trusts with a capital value of over £4 billion, but a very large proportion of these are on old and uneconomic fee scales.

Charitable trusts

If the flow of private trust business has diminished, the philanthropic instincts of the English settlor still remain and find expression in trusts of a charitable nature. We mention them here because they are private in origin if set up by an individual, but in law they are public trusts enforceable not by the beneficiaries as such but by the Attorney-General. A charitable trust enjoys the advantages of freedom from taxation, freedom from the perpetuity rules (and thus may continue for an indefinite period) and freedom from the normal trust rules regarding the ascertainment of the beneficiaries – as the lawyers would say, a charitable trust will not fail for uncertainty. Even in these stringent times, people are prepared to set aside part of their personal fortunes for the public good and who shall deny them a touch of immortality for doing so.

Living trusts

There is one aspect of private trust business which has grown widely in the United States, but has little or no counterpart in this country. It is the so-called living trust. In America there are advantages in settling one's assets on named beneficiaries in either revocable or irrevocable form whilst still retaining the use and benefit of the trust fund at the discretion of the trustees. There is no fiscal advantage, any more than there would be in this country, in a revocable trust and Gift Tax is payable if the trust is irrevocable. Citizens in their declining years find it helpful, however, to pass the management of their affairs in this way to a trust company and on death the procedures are simplified and costs saved because title has already passed to the trust company. A living trust offers flexibility because it may be varied according to family circumstances and yet also certainty, in that the settlor can see the deed operating in his

'. . . a touch of immortality.'

lifetime and thus avoid the problems of interpretation and even of legal contest which may arise where property passes under a will. There is also a greater degree of privacy. There may well be a model here for the English market to adopt, particularly now that there are no death duties payable on the passing of property between husband and wife. Is it too fanciful to suggest that if A settles all his assets on himself in a revocable trust with remainder to his wife on his death, there will be nothing for an executor to do because the assets will already be held for the wife's benefit in the trustee's name?

Trust policies

Another area of trust business, although of comparatively minor importance, is the trusteeship for a life policy. The proposer or 'life assured' under a life policy may settle the proceeds by a simple form of trust in favour of his wife or children or other beneficiaries and thereby avoid aggregation of the policy monies on death with the rest of his estate. Such a policy in favour of a wife was normally expressed to be taken out under the Married Women's Property Act 1882 – an Act which removed the disability of married women to dispose of their property by will – but this is not necessary: any disposition of the policy monies by way of a trust deed will be enforceable. The appointment of a corporate trustee for such a policy is not normally favoured as it would incur extra costs, and thus this is not a significant part of the banks' market. However, of more importance and a creature of our times is the off-shore trust. This is essentially the settling of funds in one of the tax havens of the world, usually under one of the schemes approved by tax counsel, in order to put one's fortune beyond the reach of the United Kingdom Treasury. We will come to these matters in Chapter 21 on 'Offshore Services', but they are of diminishing importance in view of recent law cases and tax avoidance legislation. They are of interest primarily to persons of substantial means and normally the bank trust departments and trust companies can be of assistance through their subsidiary companies off-shore.

Such is the private trustee business of the clearing banks. It is substantial for historical reasons, it is of diminishing importance, it is unprofitable overall, but there is still a future for the discretionary type of trust with its built-in flexibility to allow for changing circumstances.

References

1 Justinian ii.23.1.
2 G. W. Keeton and L. A. Sheridan: *The Law of Trusts,* 10th ed. Professional Books, 1974.
3 Finance Act 1975, Part III.
4 In re Duke of Norfolk's Settlement Trusts; Perth (Earl) v Fitzalan-Howard (1981) 3 W.L.R. 455.

CHAPTER 6

Investment Services

It is arguable that nothing has changed so much on the face of British banking as the provision of investment services consequent upon and concurrent with the 'Big Bang' and the 'City Revolution' referred to in Chapter 1.

The clearing banks in Britain have always been rather shy of any activities bearing the name 'investment'. Until comparatively recent years, the banks did not regard themselves as being in the investment business other than for the purpose of managing their own gilt-edged portfolios and their own pension funds. Today the banks are four-square in the investment business and under that heading have probably built up the most comprehensive package of investment services to be found anywhere in the world.

Perhaps the new approach can best be summed up in the words of Sir Timothy Bevan, then Chairman of Barclays Bank, in March 1984,

> 'We are confident that a combination of Wedd Durlacher, one of the largest Stock Exchange jobbing firms with a leading position in the United Kingdom domestic market, and de Zoete & Bevan, a major United Kingdom stockbroker will form the core and basis for development of a powerful new international securities company, supported by Barclays' extensive United Kingdom and worldwide resources and network.'

As mentioned in Chapter 1, at least four of the major banks have moved extensively into the investment field by the acquisition of dealing firms and the other banks, to varying degrees, are developing their investment services from within their own resources.

A straight catalogue of the more traditional investment services of the banks is as boring as a laundry list (particularly compared with the more glamorous developments consequent upon the Big Bang) but they are nevertheless important and we list here a cross-section of the investment services available through the bank branches.

The word 'investment' requires some explanation or definition, particularly as it is often linked almost synonymously with 'savings'. The act of saving is an accumulation of a capital sum: investment, at least for our purpose here, is the putting of the capital sum to work.

We need not take much space over those investment services which are of an administrative or procedural nature. They are:

(a) custody of bearer securities and collection of income

Many bank clerks will have spent time in the strongroom cutting coupons from bearer bonds and sending them for payment. This task of collecting the customer's income goes back well into the last century and is referred to by Bagehot in his book *Lombard Street*, in 1873. In modern times during the operation of the Exchange Control Regulations, it was necessary for foreign securities to be held by the banks, stockbrokers and other authorised agents as 'authorised depositories' and the collection of coupons was a natural corollary of this. It is of advantage to the customer, who does not need to keep a look-out for dividend announcements and other company notices.

(b) nomineeships for shareholders

All the banks operate nominee companies for the convenience of their customers, as do other financial institutions. It has been estimated that over 25 per cent (by value) of ordinary shares in the leading UK companies are held in nominee names.[1] The banks offer this service as a convenience to stockbrokers, charities and other associations, and to customers living abroad. It is a convenience to customers in that it saves a lot of work and other administrative chores. The banks will not knowingly allow nominee services to be used for tax avoidance or other abuse of our fiscal legislation.

(c) **valuation services**
Most of the banks, as an extension of their computer services, will provide customers with valuations of quoted securities for a modest charge.

The next category of investment services is really no more than an extension of the banking function in that it covers alternative avenues for placing liquid funds within the banking group itself, which therefore appear in the bank's balance sheet. They include:

(d) **negotiable certificates of deposit**
The principal United Kingdom banks, whether direct or through their merchant banks or other subsidiaries, issue negotiable certificates of deposit denominated in sterling and usually offering a higher rate of interest than that available on normal deposit accounts. The minimum amount accepted in this way is usually £50,000. These are bearer certificates and are negotiable. Dollar certificates of deposit, usually issued by the international subsidiaries of the London banks are also available.

(e) **market rate deposits**
The London banks will offer market rates for substantial funds placed direct with their Treasurer's Department. Here again, the arrangements are flexible and the rate of interest higher than the normal seven-day bankers' deposit rate. (See Chapter 2.)

(f) **deposit receipts**
Most of the London banks will issue a deposit receipt for a fixed sum on the basis that interest, which will be at current rates, will not be paid until the date agreed with the customer. The scheme is useful for tax planning and income equalisation purposes.

In all the foregoing cases, the banks are acting in their primary role as bankers, but they have been included in this section in order to present a full picture of investment services. In other instances the banks act as intermediaries for their customers and these services include:

(g) **purchase of stock exchange securities**
A survey conducted in 1966[2] showed that 53 per cent of all

owners of stocks and shares made their purchases and sales through their banks. This has been borne out by subsequent surveys and there is no doubt that the clearing banks play a major role in stock market investment on behalf of their customers. The procedures adopted by the banks vary, but the result is the same – the banks buy and sell investments for their customers through stockbrokers, usually of the banks' choice and sometimes nowadays in the banks' ownership. Traditionally this service has been provided free by the banks for their customers, the banks receiving a share of the stockbrokers' commissions. It is a great advantage to the private customer to be relieved of the paperwork in such cases and to have the transaction settled by the bank on his behalf. The service extends to all ordinary stocks and shares, and gilt-edged stocks and bonds, quoted on the principal stock exchanges in this country or abroad.

A notable development in this area was the introduction by Barclays of their 'Shareline' service operated through Barclays de Zoete Wedd. This facility, originally conceived by stockbrokers de Zoete & Bevan as a research service for professional firms, was extended, on an experimental basis at first, to a number of Barclays branches. It provides details of 350 or so selected shares and has resulted in an encouraging flow of orders through the bank branches. A service of this kind is expensive to install, principally because of the cost of introducing computer terminals in the bank branches on-line to the securities house. Nevertheless, it would appear that the future for the purchase of stocks and shares sold through bank branches lies in this direction and the resulting commissions should, in time, make a useful contribution to the costs of the branch network.

Similarly, National Westminster Bank have introduced share dealing services at bank branch level. Their first major move in that direction was the computerised facility for shareholders in British Gas at the time of privatisation. Within six weeks of the launch the bank carried out 140,000 transactions in 120 million shares through 245 branches throughout the country.

In 1986 Lloyds Bank, the only large clearing bank without a stockbroking affiliate, introduced its Sharedeal service available throughout its branches nationwide.

(h) local authority investments
All the banks will place funds with local authorities on behalf of their customers, whether by way of mortgages or bonds, usually for periods of one year upwards.

(i) Treasury bills
The banks will purchase Treasury bills on behalf of their customers – these are bearer instruments issued by the Bank of England for ninety-one days – and usually take a small commission for their trouble. The minimum amount is £5,000 and the bills may be discounted with the Bank of England or negotiated in the market.

(j) insurance contracts
The banks also act as intermediaries in placing investment funds in various forms of insurance contract. These include annuities, single premium policies, income bonds and pension plans. These are discussed in Chapter 8 and have been very much affected by the 'polarisation' rules under the Financial Services Act (see Appendix).

There remain two very considerable areas where the banks demonstrate an investment capability. These are investment advice and investment management.

(k) advice on investments
Various surveys have shown, not surprisingly, that most people regard their bank managers as financial advisors and indeed it is customary for letters of allotment and other documents to contain the suggestion that the investor in need of advice should consult, among others, his bank manager.

In a survey published late in 1983 by the Mintel research company it was shown that 45 per cent of those interviewed regarded their bank managers as the first line of advice in investment matters. It must be noted, however, that only 5 per cent of those interviewed had savings of more than £10,000 and 44 per cent had savings of less than £1,000. It would seem, therefore, that the branch managers' investment role is confined to the less rich and perhaps less sophisticated sector of the community.

Paradoxically it has been a standing instruction in the English banks down the years that their managers must *not* advise on investments. The banks' reluctance to be seen in this role is understandable. It would be unthinkable that 12,000 or so bank managers should hold themselves out as being sufficiently expert in the art of investment to advise their investing customers. We are not a litigious nation, but such a pose by the banks would inevitably lead to a spate of claims for negligence on the part of disappointed customers. Such a claim did in fact reach the Court in the rare and unfortunate case of Woods v Martins Bank (see p. 259).

The Woods case provided a platform on which to rehearse the law on the subject, but it was not a typical case and the decision turned very much on the rather singular facts in question. However, it is reasonably clear that if banks allowed their managers to advise on investments, they would have to do so with that standard of care expected of a clearing bank, which would be a very high standard indeed. It would almost certainly be that same standard of care as the bank exercises in the management of its own investments. In other words, the advice would have to be backed by those processes of research and analysis which are conducted in great depth by the banks, but the results of which are not available, nor would it be feasible to make them available, to the managers in the front line. For that reason and others which we shall discuss, it would be wrong to expect the bank manager in the High Street to be an investment advisor. The present system is that the manager is a channel for investment advice and information to the customer. The manager who is asked for his 'advice' on the investment of a sum of money or on whether or not a particular 'rights' issue should be taken up or whether indeed certain investments should be bought or sold, will obtain the comments of one of the stockbrokers allocated to the branch or the securities firm owned by the bank and pass these on without embellishment to the customer. The system works well enough and keeps everybody happy.

There are occasions however when customers seek not the second-hand advice of a stockbroker, but the opinion of the bank itself. In such cases, the information or advice must come from the centre where in all the banks a degree of investment expertise is concentrated. In fact, there is no formal enquiry service of this kind, partly because the demand is not apparent and partly because the cost of providing such a service would be more than the market would bear. Perhaps the nearest thing of its kind was the Investment Report service introduced by Barclays a few years ago. This provided the customer with a detailed report on, and valuation of, a customer's portfolio at intervals selected by the customer, together with up-to-date comment on the stock market and the economic climate. The management of the investments remained with the customer and there was no continuing service between reports. A fee was charged according to the number of holdings in the portfolio. This was perhaps the nearest approach to an advisory service as such, but it had limited appeal and was discontinued. Most owners of stocks and shares prefer to have the comments of a stockbroker, passed on to them by the local branch manager, no doubt believing that they are receiving some kind of combined opinion which of course is far from the case. Let us conclude by saying that the High Street banks are not *prima facie* in the investment advice business although that may be changing.

(l) **management of investments**

We have already remarked on the reluctance of banks in this country to manage the affairs of their living customers, although willing enough to do so on death. Perhaps the dead are more reasonable to deal with. Certainly, years ago it would have been unthinkable that the banks would undertake the management of customers' investments, but out of the business of administering estates and trusts has grown a very considerable investment management capability.

In discussing private trusts, we have stressed the importance of the investment role but, as we have said, the active management of the trust investments was seldom seen as a matter of primary responsibility. None of the trustee departments conducted any basic investment research but were satisfied with a distillation of stockbrokers' circulars. Each trust had a stockbroker advisor and an investment review would be conducted with the stockbroker at least once a year. The system was not without merit – it was perhaps unimaginative but it worked, although the banks did not regard themselves as investment experts and were slow to take the initiative in investment decisions.

On the winding-up of an estate or trust it would quite often happen that the investments passed into the absolute ownership of a beneficiary, perhaps a widow or daughter, who did not feel able to take on the responsibility of management. In other cases, parents would not wish their children, albeit of full age, to have the control of their inheritance. In these and similar cases, the bank would agree to continue to hold the investments and execute a 'declaration of trust' to the effect that they were held absolutely for the beneficiary who could call for the transfer of the investments at any time. Thus, the banks moved with apparent ease into the business of managing the assets of the living. With very few exceptions the assets of a declaration of trust were always quoted securities, and investment decisions would not normally be taken without the approval of the beneficiary and then only on the recommendation of the stockbroker. It was the beginning of investment management and it was only a matter of time before 'declarations of trust' were entered into for bank customers at large, regardless of any trustee connection already existing.

There were visionaries in all the banks who saw a great future for investment management business, but it was Lloyds Bank from among the English clearing banks who first moved overtly into the investment management business and changed the name of 'declaration of trust' to 'investment management account'. The Scottish banks too, perhaps a little less affected by the constraints of the English 'trust', saw the opportunities for investment management work, and in time all the banks followed suit. Today the investment management business of the English and Scottish banks, including, where relevant, their stockbroking affiliates, is enormous. They manage, on the basis of recent figures, approximately 62,000 portfolios for private clients and the total value is of the order of £5 billion.

To some extent the banks had been hidebound by their own traditional attitudes. On the one hand they could not hold themselves out as investment experts without training or recruiting a team of people for the work, but on the other hand the time-honoured method of managing trust investments did not seem to call for, nor justify in terms of cost, the employment of analysts, accountants and economists. When, in 1964, Martins

Bank (perhaps a little unexpectedly for a provincial bank) set up a small investment research unit, it claimed to be the first of the clearing banks to do so, although there were no doubt varying degrees of research activity in most of the banks by that time. Three years later, Martins Bank Trust Company, the first of the new style trust operations, was devised as an investment-orientated operation. It claimed to be in the business of asset management, for the living and for the dead, for private people and for institutions. On its takeover by Barclays Bank, the combined operation became one of the largest investment houses in Europe in terms of investments managed. Today Barclays de Zoete Wedd and NatWest Investment Bank are almost certainly the largest United Kingdom owned investment operations in London, each employing as they do over 1,300 people.

Discretionary accounts

Even when the banks broke away from their traditional thinking and developed investment management business, they did not readily accept the full responsibility for investment decisions. In most cases, an investment transaction would be put through merely with the approval of the owner. Some customers did not want this. They preferred the bank or trust company to take whatever action they thought necessary and report afterwards. Thus, the discretionary account developed and today one-half or more of new investment accounts undertaken by the banks are of a discretionary nature, i.e. the bank takes a decision and tells the customer afterwards. Indeed the investment specialists prefer it this way and, in one or two of the larger banks, 80–90 per cent of new business is now of a discretionary nature.

Personal Equity Plans

This is perhaps a good place to mention Personal Equity Plans (PEPs) which were introduced by the Chancellor of the Exchequer in his Budget speech in 1986 and came into effect from 1 January 1987.

The essence of the scheme is that an investor is able to contribute up to £200 a month, or £2,400 a year, to an approved investment scheme known as a Personal Equity Plan. Reinvested dividends under the Plan are free of income tax and any capital gains are free of Capital Gains Tax. Ordinary shares quoted on the Stock Exchange qualify under the scheme, as do investments in the Unlisted Securities Market. Investors may also choose unit trusts and investment trusts up to £420 per plan per annum (or 25 per cent of the annual subscription if greater). To qualify for tax relief, investments must be held in the Plan for a qualifying period of between twelve and twenty-four months.

Any investor aged 18 or over may contribute to a PEP and may take out a Plan in each calendar year. If, however, the full allowance is not used in any year, the balance may *not* be carried forward to the following year.

Banks, unit trust groups, stockbrokers, some building societies and other financial institutions are approved by the Inland Revenue as plan managers and many of them have introduced PEP schemes.

Investment policy

The decision-making processes in the field of investment management vary in detail, but follow substantially the same pattern. The amount of time and money spent on research differs from bank to bank and generally reflects the degree of importance attached to investment research. The individual analysts will normally follow the fortunes of particular sectors of the market and as many as possible of the companies in those sectors. This is achieved by day-to-day contact with the market, detailed study of the financial press, distillation of stockbrokers' reports, visits to companies and a continuing awareness of the political and economic climate in which the companies are operating. Depending on how it is used, investment research can be an expensive luxury or the very stuff of which investment decisions are made.

Whatever the quality of research, and whether it be from internal or external sources, it must be fed into the policy-making machine. Investment policy operates functionally at three distinct levels: (a) the degree of liquidity which is considered to be desirable across the board in all the portfolios under management; (b) the balance of the portfolio among the various market sectors, e.g. gilt-edged, equities (UK and overseas) and property; and (c) the designation of individual investments for purchase or sale.

There is little doubt that the first is the most important. Some would say that the only decisions that really matter in portfolio management are those that call for liquidity at the top of the market and full investment at the bottom. Certainly the more graphic performance is achieved by overall timing rather than switching activities within the portfolio, however desirable this may be at times. Judicious switching can of course improve the performance of the portfolio. It can be a mistake to chase the winners in a market where there are only losers. In the tragic 'bear' market of 1972–74 the honours went to those investment managers who took their clients out of the market in good time instead of worrying about which shares would perform best. However, as we know, it is not all that easy. A large bank managing scores of thousands of portfolios (including trust portfolios) cannot readily take such across-the-board decisions. There are always a number of administrative problems to which we refer in the following pages and a great many subjective considerations which have to be interpreted at local level, and it is not always possible to do for one what is done for another.

In the choice of shares for purchase or sale it is the common practice among banks to have a 'shopping list' circulated to their local offices. The list and the grading within the list are usually arrived at by informed debate in the investment department. Such lists are usually intended to be a general guide and are not always expected to be followed slavishly. Nevertheless, a branch office which persisted in buying a stock marked in the list as a 'sale' would do so at its peril.

Ideally, in the interests of scientific management, all the portfolios which a bank has under management should be centred in one place, preferably in one room, where investment decisions may be translated quickly into action and where there would be a uniformity of treatment. This is the normal practice among merchant banks and other investment houses who do not operate through a branch network. On the other hand the management of private portfolios is a very subjective business and many customers attach great value to the facility for discussion at local level. Mr Hoyt Ammidon, former Chairman of the United States Trust Company, is credited with saying that investment management is 10 per cent know-how and 90 per cent public relations – a conscious hyperbole which nevertheless serves to emphasise the personal aspect of the investment business.

Institutional business

Thus far we have looked only at the management of personal portfolios, but the banks are equally in the market for institutional business – the management of portfolios for corporations, pension funds, charities and other institutional investors. Such business is much sought after because the portfolios are usually substantial, the investment guidelines are generally clear cut and devoid of subjective considerations and the work can be centralised in the investment department. Traditionally, much of this work has gone to the merchant banks, largely because of the low profile maintained by the clearing banks in investment matters until recent years. We will look more specifically at pension fund business in Chapter 19, but it is noteworthy that institutional business of all kinds, administered by the clearing banks and their subsidiaries, whether as trustee or investment manager, amounts to approximately £40 billion spread throughout nearly 2,000 portfolios.

In 1985, the Bank of England conducted a survey into the level of investment management business in the United Kingdom, its importance in relation to the economy as a whole and the degree of penetration into international markets since the lifting of exchange control regulations in October 1979.

It was deduced that funds managed by investment houses in this country for United Kingdom residents amounted in volume to over £100 billion. Of this figure approximately one-half was invested in United Kingdom equities and about one-quarter invested in overseas securities.

The survey also revealed that an additional £28.5 billion was managed in the United Kingdom for overseas residents.

As will be seen from the table below, pension funds make up

'90 per cent public relations.'

the largest category of client and the merchant banks are responsible for approximately 40 per cent of the total funds managed. The figures show the position as at the end of 1984.

Funds managed – £ billions

For UK residents

	Accepting houses	UK offices of foreign managers	Other	Total
Analysis by clients				
Government and public sector	2.2	—	1.6	3.8
Pension schemes	28.0	0.6	35.2	63.8
Unit and investment trusts	8.5	0.4	14.3	23.2
Other	5.6	0.1	11.2	16.9
Total	44.3	1.1	62.3	107.7
Analysis of assets				
Equities of UK companies	22.0	0.4	29.8	52.2
UK government and other public sector securities	5.6	0.2	9.4	15.2
Foreign securities	10.2	0.4	21.1	25.5
Other	6.5	—	7.4	13.9

For overseas residents

	Accepting houses	UK offices of foreign managers	Other	Total
Analysis by clients				
Government and public sector	4.7	4.6	2.3	11.6
Pension schemes	3.2	2.8	0.6	6.6
Unit and investment trusts	1.1	0.2	0.4	1.7
Other	4.3	2.1	2.2	8.6
Total	13.3	9.7	5.5	28.5
Analysis of assets				
Equities of UK companies	1.7	0.6	0.8	3.1
UK government and other public sector securities	0.7	0.3	0.6	1.6
Foreign securities	8.9	7.6	3.3	19.8
Other	2.0	1.2	0.5	3.7

[Source: Bank of England]

Some problems of investment management

Not surprisingly, investment management on such a scale has its problems. One of these is the difficulty of dealing with the smaller portfolios. To maintain a sophisticated investment department is an expensive business and it becomes disproportionately expensive when portfolio managers have to be employed to deal with large numbers of small cases. Historically the banks have had more than their share of smaller portfolios. This stemmed from the practice of taking on very small declarations of trust which, as we have seen, were the origin of the present-day investment business. There is also the very real point that the bank in the High Street seeks to provide a service for all-comers – to be all things to all men.

There are two aspects of this problem. The first is the very real difficulty of managing a small portfolio in an economical way. Only a few stocks can be purchased so that the portfolio is not truly representative: just one 'mistake' can be unduly expensive and costs are disproportionately high. If there were no satisfactory alternative one might make a case for portfolio management of amounts of, say, £20,000 and above. In practice, however, there is in this country the very real alternative of unit trust investment which generally is a far better medium for sums up to, say, £50,000 or indeed well above that. This is something we shall consider separately in Chapter 7. There will, however, always be those investors who wish to have their own separately managed portfolio, however small the value.

The second problem is one of costs. The American trust departments will not normally accept the management of portfolios of less than $250,000 and sometimes the minimum size is very much larger. In this country few merchant banks undertake the management of portfolios of less than £100,000. A high proportion of the portfolios administered by the clearing banks today are less than that figure. The banks will have differing views as to the break-even point in terms of portfolio size, but it is improbable that individual portfolios of less than £50,000 can be managed profitably at current fee levels when one takes into account present-day salaries and pension provisions, the cost of a branch network, proper allocation of overheads and some contribution to marketing costs. On a sample costing in one bank, it was found that with comparatively small cases, of which there were a large number, the cost of setting up the records and doing the preparatory work for a new investment management account exceeded the amount of the first year's fee. Taking a typical fee of 75p per £100 on a portfolio of, say, £50,000, the client will be paying £375 per annum for the service. Whilst this is modest for the responsibility of managing a fund of that size, it is large in relation to the net return which the investor will have annually after tax. Unfortunately in this country such charges for the management of assets are not allowable for taxation purposes as they are in other countries, notably the United States. Despite the increase in fees in recent years, however, the banks' charges are still competitive and they have succeeded in increasing their share of the market very substantially.

Another problem area is the multiplicity of holdings. Although we are considering at this point the investment management service for private and institutional customers, the banks have a vast investment business in connection with their estates and trusts. In general these require the same degree of investment management as the investment management accounts. The result is that the total number of portfolios under management might be as many as, say, 30,000 and many of the individual investments in these portfolios would not have been chosen from a select list but 'inherited' from deceaseds' estates and retained for various good reasons. In one bank, on a simultaneous scrutiny of the portfolios, it was found that no fewer than 2,600 separate equity stocks were held, i.e. in separate companies, in addition to large numbers of fixed interest stocks and bonds. It is quite impossible, of course, to monitor adequately such a wide range of holdings. It is doubtful whether a well staffed investment department can follow more than, say, 250 stocks in a meaningful day-to-day fashion and it may well be that the banks will have to limit their investments under management to a more modest number.

If the multiplicity of individual stocks is a problem, so too is the number of portfolios. It is the norm in this country for each estate, each trust, each investment management account and each fund of any kind to have its own separate portfolio which may have a selection of ordinary stocks and a proportion of fixed interest investments. Apart from the investment aspects, this calls for a very considerable administrative operation. If, for example, a bank or trust company administers 30,000 portfolios with an average of only ten investments in each, there are 300,000 separate investments to be recorded and designated, and if on each investment there are two dividend or interest payments per annum, there will be 600,000 separate items of income to be collected and distributed. In some banks, the problem is alleviated by the practice of mandating interest and dividend payments direct to the banking accounts of the beneficiaries. Whatever system is used, the basic pattern of trust business in the United Kingdom remains the same – that each case of whatever size has its own individual portfolio. In recent years, this has been alleviated to some extent by the use of unit trusts, but for legal reasons it has not always been possible to merge portfolios into common funds as is done in the United States. The problems have been (a) that common funds or unit trusts for fixed interest stocks would be at a disadvantage for taxation purposes unless they were authorised unit trusts and even authorised unit trusts were not eligible as narrow range investments under the Trustee Investments Act, 1961 until this was remedied by the Finance Act, 1982 and (b) that a common fund of equities would have to be constituted as an 'authorised' unit trust if it were to qualify as a wider range investment under the Trustee Investments Act 1961. Quite often the authorised unit trusts within each banking group can be used for such purposes, but (i) this is possible only where the trust instrument permits it (otherwise the trustee would be benefiting from his trust to the extent that fees were charged in the unit trust), and (ii) in many cases there might still be a residue of fixed interest investments so that there would be almost as many separate portfolios as before.

Whatever the administrative problems there is also an investment problem, although perhaps of an administrative nature. It is not uncommon for a popular stock to appear across a wide range of portfolios under the management of the same business house. Some years ago, on a sample check in one bank, it was found that a certain leading company was represented in no fewer than 20,000 portfolios under the bank's management. Those portfolios were administered in thirty or so separate offices around the country and total investment was in excess of £20 million. A decision on investment grounds to sell the shares in that company or even to reduce the holdings substantially on a proportionate basis in all cases, would have been quite impossible to execute except over an unacceptable period of time.

The Bank of Scotland have taken a step towards solving the problem not only of smaller portfolios, but of the multiplicity of holdings. They offer their customers what is known as a Managed Portfolio Service, which is in fact a participation in one of two master portfolios, one offering high income, the other offering capital growth with some income. The scheme has some of the merits of a unit trust in that the investor achieves a wide spread of holdings, whilst being relieved of all administrative problems of managing his own investments. From the bank's point of view, there is also the advantage that two major portfolios take the place of a variety of smaller ones. It is not, however, a unit trust as such. Each individual investor owns a cross-section of the master portfolio and, to that extent, has his own list of investments on which he receives regular detailed reports.

The last area of special difficulty is one which is not always recognised or acknowledged. It goes without saying that a bank is *prima facie* in the business of banking and this involves the bank in a very considerable awareness of the financial and economic climate, as well as in a detailed acquaintance with a large number of quoted companies. If then, as has happened, a bank turns its hand to the management of stock exchange investments, to what extent (a) ought it to use or (b) ensure that it does not use, its knowledge as a banker in exercising its role as investment manager? (The author, as a junior bank official, was aware on one occasion of a highly valuable international contract won by a leading company and saw the same day an instruction emanating from the investment department to reduce the shareholdings in that company because of its poor investment prospects: he maintained a proper silence.) The general view in this country has always been that the two functions must be divorced and if the investment side is a separate entity within the group, so much the better. What, however, would be the view where a bank as investment manager last month bought for its client shares in a company and where this month the bank in its role as banker has appointed a Receiver? Is it so improbable? To add to the problem, the research analyst from the investment department might have visited the company and come to the view that it was a good recovery stock! Such conflicts are not necessarily so specific. It may be that a bank in its role as banker may have come to a very firm view on the state of the economy, industrial confidence and investment intentions, whilst the investment subsidiary could well have come to a contrary view and fashioned its investment policy accordingly. Problems of this kind have never been tested in the Courts and the first occasion would be a very interesting one. In the United States it is a very live subject, but there the climate points increasingly to a clear demarcation between the role of banker and that of investment manager or trustee. In the United Kingdom there were times when these problems seemed more apparent than real. In fact, however, the matter has been exacerbated by the development of the banks' merchant banking subsidiaries whose natural and proper role is the giving of corporate advice. There can well be occasions when that advice conflicts with the investment decisions being taken by the investment subsidiaries and trustee departments of the banks. The merchant banking and investment functions are kept separate as we discuss in Chapter 14, but the anomaly remains, i.e. that two customers of the same banking institution may be given quite contrary advice on the investment merits of a situation. All this also goes to the question of insider dealing, which is dealt with more specifically in Chapter 14.

One aspect of conflict which was bound to arise sooner or later, particularly after the acquisition by the banks of stock-broking firms, was the question of comment and advice by the stockbroking subsidiary on the bank's own shares. The issue came to a head in January 1987 when Barclays de Zoete, Wedd advised their clients to sell their shares in the bank because of its deep rooted problems and poor profit prospects. The report by BZW began: "There is something wrong with Barclays . . .". Not surprisingly, this caused a stir in the parent bank. In the case of some of the smaller merchant banks, it is not unusual to forbid the analysts to comment on their own shares. In the case of a large bank such as Barclays, the trading in whose shares accounts for 20 per cent or so of the banking sector, it would be damaging to the standing and morale of the investment arm not to be able to comment on the bank's shares. In the result, Barclays decided to allow BZW to analyse and comment on their shares, particularly as they represent such a major part of a major segment of the market. However, the problem is understandable and it typifies the sort of conflicts which can arise within the banking conglomerates.

The Gower Report

In his discussion document, *Review of Investor Protection*,[3] Professor L. C. B. Gower referred to the need for regulation or supervision of investment management and advisory services as there was already, to a degree, in relation to investment dealing. He considered that:

> 'whatever theoretical arguments there may be for divorcing the activities of dealing and of managing and advising, in practice dealers will inevitably manage and advise as well.'

In his far-ranging proposals for a Securities Act and the setting-up of a number of self-regulatory agencies, he recommended that those engaged in investment management and advice, together with those engaged in investment dealings outside the Stock Exchange, should collaborate in setting up their own regulatory agency. We may note Professor Gower's comments on the growth of investment management and advisory firms, viz:

> 'Fifty years ago there were few firms which specialised in managing and advising on investments for individual investors. In so far as this role was performed, it was as a minor off-shoot of the provision of stockbroking, legal or banking services. Now it is an important service in its own right.'

Professor Gower's report provoked a lively debate which continued for three or four years and culminated in the passing of the Financial Services Act 1986. This is a complex and far-reaching piece of legislation which is discussed in the Appendix to this work and which (at the time of writing) is expected to become law early in 1988. The Act sets out to regulate, among other matters, the conduct of investment business in all its aspects and the impact on bank investment services has been considerable, as discussed in the Appendix.

The market

As we have said, banks are not alone in the business of investment management. Their principal competitors are stockbrokers, merchant banks and a number of investment counselling firms of varying size. For the most part it may be wrong to regard stockbrokers as competitors. Not all stockbroking firms operate an investment management business for private clients on a continuing day-to-day basis. In contrast, some stockbrokers are more than happy to work with a bank as investment manager. Most of the larger stockbroking firms are in any case owned by leading banks or other major financial institutions (see page 15).

The retail outlets of the clearing banks in this as in other matters help to ensure a continuing flow of new business. More and more people with an investment management problem tend to think in the first instance of the High Street bank.

Nevertheless, the market is not unlimited. Although a few years ago there were believed to be over 2 million private shareholders in companies quoted on the London Stock Exchange, many of these shareholdings are quite small and others are in the hands of executors or trustees who cannot readily delegate their responsibility to an investment manager. It is difficult to arrive at accurate statistics for the distribution of personal wealth, but on one estimate a few years ago there were only 320,000 people in Great Britain with net personal resources in excess of £50,000, inclusive of all assets and not merely Stock Exchange investments.[4] Furthermore, among those private individuals who were traditional investors in Stock Exchange companies, there was considerable disinvestment for a number of years. The Wilson Committee[5] reported that:

> 'Over the period between 1957 and 1975, the proportion of ordinary shares beneficially owned by persons fell from 66 per cent to 38 per cent, and it is estimated to have fallen further to 32 per cent by the end of 1978.'

This calculation has to some extent been challenged by the Stock Exchange survey published in September 1981, which suggested that 36 per cent of shares quoted on the Stock Exchange were still owned by private investors.

In recent years there have been various surveys and much conjecture as to the number of equity shareholders in the United Kingdom. In February 1986 the Stock Exchange unveiled plans to boost personal share ownership and those plans are no doubt taking effect. The main factor, however, contributing to the overall increase in the number of shareholders is the privatisation of various national industries. In 1984, for example, the privatisation of British Telecom created two million new shareholders and the pattern was continued with the listing of the Trustee Savings Bank and the privatisation of British Gas, British Aerospace, etc. In March and April 1986 a survey conducted by National Opinion Polls on behalf of the Treasury[6] suggested that 14 per cent of the adult population owned shares, compared with a figure of 7 per cent in 1979. In June that year, however, another poll conducted by Market and Opinion Research International (Mori) suggested that only 8.3 per cent of adults were shareholders. In both surveys the examples excluded unit trust-holders. Also in June that year, a survey conducted by British Market Research Bureau on behalf of the Stock Exchange concluded that 16 per cent of adults owned shares and this was supported by a survey carried out in October by the marketing firm Dewe Rogerson, which suggested that 17 per cent of the adult population, i.e. 7 million people, were shareholders. Whatever the precise figure, two factors emerge quite clearly, viz. that, not surprisingly, the concentration of shareholdings is in the higher age groups and also that a very large number of shareholders are people of modest means having only a few shares in one or two listed companies. In fact, the Dewe Rogerson survey suggests that approximately 4 million people (59 per cent of the total) have shares in only one company.

If the scope for the management of private portfolios is limited (although there is still a worthwhile market to tap), there are two areas where the potential is very considerable. The first is that of pension funds, which we shall look at in Chapter 20, and the second is unit trust investment. The view has been expressed here that for all but the larger investors – probably those with portfolios approaching six figures – unit trust investment is the right answer. This is particularly so for specialist or overseas holdings where there are both administrative and supervisory problems in managing individual portfolios. That is not to say that unit trusts are appropriate for everyone. The first question which every investor must answer is 'is investment in the stock market right for me?' It certainly is not right for persons of modest means to put the whole of their savings into ordinary stocks and shares whether via unit trusts or not; and it is certainly not right for any investor whose resources or temperament are unsuited to the vagaries of the stock market. By the end of 1974 many investors had seen their nest eggs reduced to approximately one-third of their value only eighteen months earlier.

On the other hand, we believe that in our type of mixed economy long-term growth can come only from successful enterprise in industry and commerce. In the long term one expects to see the success of the enterprise reflected in the level of stock market prices, but there are many ups and downs on the way.

We shall look briefly at the history of unit trusts in this country and in Chapter 19 we consider the role of the unit trust trustee. We turn first, however to the part played by the banks in unit trust management.

References

1 Royal Commission on the Distribution of Income and Wealth: Report No. 2, Cmnd 6172. HMSO, 1975.
2 'How does Britain save?' – a survey for the London Stock Exchange by the British Market Research Bureau.
3 HMSO, January 1982.
4 Royal Commission on the Distribution of Income and Wealth: Report No. 1, Cmnd 6171, HMSO, 1975.
5 Committee to Review the Functioning of Financial Institutions (Chairman: Sir Harold Wilson), Cmnd 7937, HMSO, 1980.
6 Economic Progress Report, March–April 1986. H.M. Treasury.

CHAPTER 7

Unit Trusts

We have noted, in the introductory chapter, the movement of the banks, begun by Lloyds Bank in 1966, into the business of unit trust management. In some ways it was a surprising development. As we have seen, the banks were somewhat demure in matters of investment advice and investment management – and it must be admitted that in the minds of the public, banks did not readily come to mind as investment experts.

Furthermore, the fact that the banks were engaged in the trusteeship of unit trusts would be seen by many as a deterrent to their entering the management side of the business. Perhaps for that reason some of the banks set up their unit trust management activities under separate control from that of their trustee departments. In matters of investment policy this could hardly be justified – the same overall view of the market must apply in managing unit trusts as it does in the management of private investment portfolios.

The banks' involvement

The banks entered the unit trust movement by widely differing routes and this is understandable. In new business ventures it is often a matter for deliberation whether to evolve from within or purchase an existing organisation, and whether to 'go it alone' or jointly with another business house. Some developments, as we have already said, are a matter of conscious decision and others arise without being consciously sought. So it was that Lloyds Bank chose to set up their unit trust organisation from their existing resources and this met with immediate success.

The first offer of units in Lloyds First Unit Trust in October 1966 produced £2·3 million – the first time that an English bank had sold its own units over its own counters. Two years later when the Second Unit Trust was launched, the initial offer brought in just under £10 million, then an all-time record for the initial launch of any unit trust.

Westminster Bank chose the 'joint' road with Hambros Bank and they too were pleased with the immediate response. The first trust was launched in July 1967 and six months later the Westminster Bank Chairman, Mr D. A. Stirling, was able to report that the value of the units in issue had grown to over £10 million.

That same year Martins Bank chose the direct acquisition method by its purchase of Unicorn Securities, which gave the bank control of over £40 million worth of unit funds and gave Martins Bank the lead, in terms of size, which it and subsequently Barclays Bank have since maintained over their competitor banks.

In 1968, the Trustee Savings Banks formed their first unit trust and became one of the fastest growing unit trust groups. It is now second in size to Barclays Unicorn among the banks in the United Kingdom and is the seventh in size among all unit trust groups.

To enter the unit trust business was not by any means a natural step for the banks to take, particularly for those banks heavily committed to the trusteeship of unit trusts. Barclays Bank, on the acquisition of Martins Bank, looked hard and long at the lively unit trust baby which had been acquired with its parent. It was some months before Barclays Bank came to terms with what it had bought because it had hitherto taken the view that it wished to be a trustee of unit trusts rather than their manager. If the Barclays approach was a little cautious at first, it was to develop in a short time into almost an excess of enthusiasm as unit trust sales flowed through the branches of the bank and Unicorn's share of new investment in the industry rose as high at one point as 70 per cent. This was not without its consequences, which we shall look at a little later.

It was in fact the Unicorn Group which, under the Rt. Hon. Edward du Cann and Mr Bill Fowler, had led the way in 1957 in the post-war development of unit trusts. The general forms and procedures adopted in the next few years were to become the pattern for unit trust management and have remained so to this day.

The growth of the movement

The following table gives some indication of the growth in the unit trust movement since 1959.

Year	Value of funds (at year end) £m	Sales £m	Re-purchases £m	Net investment £m	Holdings (millions)
1959	200·0	n.a.	n.a.	n.a.	0·52
1960	201·4	26·88	13·37	13·51	0·66
1961	236·6	21·57	14·21	7·36	0·67
1962	272·5	45·01	11·07	33·94	0·82
1963	371·2	77·46	17·78	59·68	1·05
1964	428·9	99·64	22·60	77·04	1·31
1965	521·9	80·80	21·78	59·02	1·42
1966	581·8	129·69	24·26	105·43	1·64
1967	853·6	126·56	42·64	83·91	1·71
1968	1,482·4	328·93	70·45	258·48	2·15
1969	1,411·9	262·70	76·53	186·17	2·39
1970	1,397·7	171·15	73·35	97·80	2·40
1971	1,991·2	204·10	127·45	76·65	2·32
1972	2,647·5	436·86	195·59	241·27	2·29
1973	2,060·4	357·90	171·75	186·15	2·24
1974	1,310·8	194·87	110·17	84·70	2·20
1975	2,512·4	321·21	130·90	191·31	2·20
1976	2,543·0	333·40	165·88	167·52	2·12
1977	3,461·3	372·32	257·90	114·42	1·99
1978	3,873·4	529·68	294·08	235·60	1·95
1979	3,936·7	411·95	353·87	58·08	1·82
1980	4,968·0	531·47	423·90	107·56	1·72
1981	5,902·4	955·60	428·03	527·57	1·79
1982	7,767·8	1,157·51	567·23	590·28	1·80
1983	11,689·4	2,459·75	960·19	1,499·56	2·04
1984	15,099·1	2,918·20	1,476·70	1,441·50	2·20
1985	20,307·5	4,487·70	1,949·10	2,537·60	2·55
1986	32,131·0	8,717·00	3,482·00	5,235·00	3·41

At the end of 1985 there were in existence 806 unit trusts managed by a total of over 120 groups. Of the total unit trust business at the end of 1985 approximately 13½ per cent by value was controlled by the English clearing banks.

The unit trust groups owned by clearing banks in the United Kingdom are listed below with the approximate size of funds under management in 1986:

	(Millions)
Barclays Unicorn	£1,490
TSB	£1,201
Lloyds	£406
Midland	£285
National Westminster (County)	£253

Until early in 1980, the Royal Bank of Scotland also managed two unit trusts, the National and Commercial Income and Capital Funds, but the bank took the decision to sell these to Henderson Administration. In 1985, however, Scottish Unit Managers Limited, in which the Bank of Scotland, through the British Linen Bank, has a 37½ per cent interest, became managers of a range of unit trusts following the unitisation of the Aberdeen Trust PLC, which was a listed investment trust.

In June 1987 the TSB announced the acquisition of the Target Financial Services Group with its substantial unit trust business. In September 1987 National Westminster Bank announced the sale of its unit trust business to facilitate the role of the branches as independent intermediaries under the 'polarisation' rules (see Appendix).

The nature of a unit trust

In considering the basic procedures in the management of unit trusts, it has to be noted that unit trusts are, unfortunately, not easy to define. There are a number of descriptions used for the benefit of the general public which are adequate for that purpose, but are not always technically accurate. It is sometimes said that a unit trust is a joint investment venture. In common parlance it is, but it is not so in any legal sense. Sometimes the expression 'association' of investors is used, but this again would be legally unacceptable. The essential point is that a unit trust is a trust. It is established by a trust deed, the parties to which are the 'managers' who are the promoters of the trust and undertake certain obligations in the trust deed, and the 'trustees' who are responsible for holding the trust assets which are divided into units for the benefit of the 'beneficiaries' or 'unitholders'. Under the trust deed the managers may offer units in the trust fund to potential investors who thereby become unitholders, and the managers are obliged under the trust deed to buy back such units from any unitholders who wish to sell them. Thus we may say that a unit trust is a form of trust where the trust fund is divided into units and held for the benefit of the unitholders, who become unitholders by the purchase of units from the managers of the trust and who at any time may re-sell their units to the managers of the trust, at a price determined in each instance in accordance with the terms of the trust deed.

The unit price

The basic value of a unit is always the value of the trust fund divided by the number of units in issue. Thus, if the trust fund has a current value of £1 million and there are a million units in issue, each unit will be worth £1. The price of a unit for the purpose of purchase or sale will, however, take into account the dealing expenses. A purchaser of units will pay a price calculated according to the underlying value of the units plus dealing costs, on the basis that his investment increases the value of the trust fund and additional securities will therefore be purchased. The seller of units will receive a price based on the underlying value of the units less dealing costs, on the basis that his sale of units results in a reduction of the trust fund and the corresponding sale of securities. Thus there is a margin between the 'offer' and 'bid' prices.

In calculating the offer and bid prices the rules laid down by the Department of Trade must be strictly followed. Under these rules, the maximum price at which units may be offered to the public must be calculated by reference to (a) the lowest price at which the underlying securites may be purchased on the Stock Exchange at that time–*plus* (b) stock exchange commissions, (c) stamp duty, (d) the managers' initial charge of, say, 5 per cent, (e) accrued income in the fund and (f) a 'rounding' adjustment in the final figure in order to avoid fractions (this must be limited to 1 per cent or 1·25p whichever is the lesser amount). Thus the maximum purchase price is arrived at.

On the sale of units by a unitholder to the managers, the minimum price which must be paid by the managers under the Department of Trade rules is calculated by reference to (a) the highest price obtainable at that time on the Stock Exchange for the underlying securities *plus* (b) the accrued income in the fund *less* (c) stock exchange commissions and (d) the permitted 'rounding' figure.

The margin between the maximum purchase price and minimum sale price permitted by the Department of Trade rules will normally be of the order of 13 per cent and such a margin would quite rightly be unacceptable to the investing public. In practice, the managers of unit trusts operate on a dealing margin of 6–7½ per cent, subject to certain exceptions. This is primarily because at any one time the manager will be buying or selling existing units so that some of the costs of creating, or as the case may be liquidating, units can be avoided. The margin would be smaller but for the fact that it includes stamp duty currently at 1 per cent.

When a trust is expanding, i.e. when the managers are selling more units than they are re-purchasing, the offer price will be pitched as high as the Department of Trade regulations permit because that reflects the price which would have to be paid for new securities on the market. When a trust is contracting, i.e. because more units are being sold back by unitholders than new units are being bought, the bid price, i.e. the price which managers will pay for units, will be as low as the Department of Trade regulations permit reflecting the fact that securities will have to be sold on the market. One should visualise, therefore, the managers' buying and selling margin of say, 7 per cent moving up or down the much wider scale of, say, 13 per cent permitted by the regulations. When a trust is expanding, the price will be nudging the top of the scale, usually referred to as being on the offer basis: when a trust is contracting, the price will move to the lower level, i.e. the bid basis. It is thus an advantage to existing unitholders that their trust should be on the offer basis so that if they sell their units (at the bid price of course), the price will be nearer the top of the Department of Trade scale. For the purchaser of units, it would be an advantage to buy when the price is on the 'bid basis' because the price he pays (the offer price) is that much lower.

A large part of the profits of unit trust groups comes from dealing in existing units. Equally it can be a source of losses. A management company must of course have sufficient capital for the purpose of such dealing. It is part of the managers' skill to fix the unit prices at the right level within the permitted range. If, for example, investors are selling back more units than they purchase, a manager who kept the trust on the offer basis, i.e. at the top of the range, would make a loss because he would be paying unitholders at the higher price and having to liquidate units in the market at the ruling bid prices.

Authorisation of trusts

For a unit trust to be 'authorised' by the Department of Trade, it must be invested in 'securities' as defined in the Prevention of Fraud (Investments) Act 1958 (s. 26(1)). The term, for all practical purposes means stocks or shares or government securities. It is impossible therefore for an authorised unit trust to be invested in freehold or leasehold property. Property bonds and similar investments which we shall consider at a later stage are not authorised unit trusts. At the time of writing, however, there are proposals for widening the scope for unit trust investment (see page 164).

Within the definition of 'securities' it is permissible and quite usual to launch unit trusts with a special investment emphasis. Most of the early unit trusts were 'middle of the road' trusts. They sought the kind of performance which would give a mixture of capital growth and a medium level of income. They were designed for the every-day investor. It was the pattern to follow up with a 'growth' trust designed to seek capital gain – if necessary at the expense of income – and an 'income' trust to suit those investors who were looking for as much income as possible from their equity investment. In practice over the years many of the income trusts have had good capital performance and some of the growth trusts have been disappointing. There then followed over the years a variety of 'specialist' trusts with investment policies geared to individual sectors such as financial institutions, small companies, commodities, gold shares, energy shares, recovery shares and so on. The management of unit trusts is very much a marketing operation and many groups launched new funds with popular labels attached to them, but which over the years bore little relation to their investment merit. In more recent years, as anxieties increased over the UK economy, a large number of 'international' funds have been launched designed for overseas investment.

Until 1980 a unit trust investing in fixed interest stocks was at a disadvantage from a taxation standpoint. This anomaly was removed in the 1980 Finance Act and a number of gilt edged and fixed interest funds were introduced. Thus, unit trust investment was no longer exclusively an 'equity' matter and many investors have been attracted to the newer 'gilt' funds.

To obtain Department of Trade authorisation, it is necessary for the trust deed to contain a provision that no investment shall exceed 5 per cent of the total value of the fund with the proviso that this may be increased to 7½ per cent in respect of not more than six separate holdings, provided that the number of separate holdings shall not be less than twenty and the aggregate value of the trust's holdings of investments in any ten separate holdings shall not exceed 55 per cent of the total value.

The normal rule is that investments shall be made only in securities quoted on recognised stock exchanges. Some of the older trust deeds do contain power to invest in unquoted securities, but under the modern deeds a total of no more than 5 per cent of the fund may be invested in this way. Consequent upon the introduction of the Unlisted Securities Market under the umbrella of the Stock Exchange in November 1980, the Department of Trade rules were relaxed to enable up to 25 per cent of the assets of a unit trust to be invested in shares traded on the Unlisted Securities Market. In February 1986, however, the Department of Trade and Industry removed the 25 per cent limit and it thereupon became possible to set up unit trusts for the special purpose of investing in USM stocks.

Since 1980, unit trusts have also been able to invest in the traded options market. In April that year, the Department of

Trade agreed that new trusts may write or purchase call options, provided that they are 'covered', i.e. that the managers can deliver the stocks on which they have written options. Existing unit trusts were empowered to invest in options only if the unitholders agreed and then, only to the extent of 50 per cent of the total market value of the portfolio. There is no such limit for new trusts. Managers may invest only in options traded on recognised stock exchanges and may do so only for legitimate investment purposes, not as speculations.

In October 1985 the Department of Trade and Industry gave approval for a category of unit trust which was not previously permissible. This is a type of vehicle which is similar in some respects to the 'fund of funds' investment schemes launched off-shore in the 1960s but which had a rather chequered career. The new type of unit trust now permitted in the home market is a managed fund, i.e. a unit trust which will in turn invest in other unit trusts in the same management group. Indeed, to obtain Department of Trade authorisation, the managed fund may only invest in the group's own unit trusts. Only one managed fund per group is permitted and the group as a whole must have at least eight underlying unit trusts in which to invest. The fund should invest in at least four unit trusts and not more than 50 per cent of the managed fund may invest in any one of the unit trusts. There must be no element of double charging. In March 1986 Midland Bank became the first of the High Street banks to launch such a managed portfolio of their own unit trusts.

In the unit trust industry there is a great variety of schemes, usually referred to as 'plans', designed to encourage savings and investment in unit trusts. Most of these are available in one form or another among the clearing banks' trusts. They include the following.

Savings plans

We have seen the importance of maintaining a unit trust on an expanding basis and we should also add that the system of charging is such that unit trusts generally depend for their profitability on their ability to sell new units. Thus, from an early stage, most groups recognised the importance of regular savings schemes. The only contractual form of saving permissible in equity shares in the United Kingdom is the life assurance policy. We shall look at life assurance in the next chapter and, in particular, deal with the practice of linking life assurance contracts to unit trusts. It should be noted, however, that this practice has become so important in the unit trust industry in this country that approximately one-quarter of all unit trust sales are now effected through a life assurance link. In the case of the Trustee Savings Bank unit trusts it is understood that approaching 90 per cent of sales are through their life assurance link.

From the management point of view, it is extremely valuable to have a regular and ascertainable flow of new money each month regardless of the state of the stock market at the time.

The ordinary savings account is also very valuable. This enables the investor to contribute so much a month for investment in the unit trust of his choice. No legal obligation rests on the saver and he is free to vary his monthly investment, or cancel or defer it, entirely at will. The great advantage of any regular saving in this way is that it helps to even out any fluctuations in the stock market. There is also the purely arithmetical advantage of 'pound cost averaging': when prices are low the fixed regular investment buys more units – when prices are high fewer units are purchased. The effect is that the average purchase cost of units is less than the average price of the units over the period of regular investment.

Regular savings plans can be used to re-invest unit trust income as well as, if desired, any additional monthly sums. For the re-investment of income, however, it is more economic to use one of the accumulation trusts designed for the purpose. This is because in an accumulation trust the value of the units is increased by the accumulated income and there is no manager's initial charge on the accumulations as there would be if they were treated as new investments.

There is no doubt that for most investors the regular savings plans are attractive in that they reduce the importance of timing and take a lot of anxiety out of stock market fluctuations.

Withdrawal plans

In the ordinary way the income of a unit trust is the amount of interest and dividends on the underlying investments less a deduction for fees and expenses. All the income has to be distributed to the unitholders or re-invested in the ways we have discussed. If the dividend performance of the underlying investments is good, the income distribution to the unitholders is that much greater: if it is poor, the distribution is reduced. To the extent that companies increase their dividends from improved profits over the years, unitholders can see substantial increases in their unit trust distributions and in times of inflation the prospect of seeing an increase in one's income is important and is one of the particular attractions of equity investment.

In some cases, however, investors wish to have a higher 'income' from their unit trust investment than the amount of the annual distribution, and some investors prefer to see that annual distribution expressed as a fixed percentage of their investment. The withdrawal plan (or selective income plan) was devised for that purpose. The investor in a withdrawal scheme can choose, within certain limits, the annual payment he wishes to have, e.g. 8 per cent on the sum invested, and if the annual distribution is less than that, the managers will sell units to make the payment up to the required level. In other words, the investor is receiving a regular annual return made up partly of income from the underlying investments and partly from the sale of capital. This is very satisfactory on a rising market because the investor is merely receiving a part of the capital profits. The danger is that on a falling market the initial investment is already diminishing in value and that process is accelerated by sales of units to make up the annual distributions. Such erosion of capital will usually result in a fall in the annual dividend distributions so that even further sales of units are necessary to make up the required annual payments.

The response to withdrawal plan advertising was considerable. In one group alone, the withdrawal plan sales in two years amounted to approximately £100 million. The dangers we have described were very evident in the 'bear' market of 1973 and the Department of Trade became very concerned on behalf of investors. Unitholders were invited by the management groups to suspend their withdrawals of capital until the market recovered and many investors did this.

Another disadvantage of the withdrawal plan is that many investors, no matter how precisely the advertisements and leaflets are worded, believe they are entering into an investment where they receive a fixed percentage for life. They come to regard it rather as an annuity and are greatly concerned when the true effect of a withdrawal plan in a falling market is made clear to them. Nevertheless, there is a place for withdrawal schemes for investors who understand them and who wish to have a regular source of 'income', partly out of dividends and partly out of capital.

Share exchange schemes

A number of investors with private portfolios have been attracted, with the encouragement of unit trust groups, to the idea of exchanging their portfolios for units in an established trust. This gives them all the advantages of unit trust investment, including a much wider spread than in their own portfolio and complete freedom from problems of management. Most of the leading unit trust groups operate such schemes and will take privately owned shares into their portfolios at a price higher than the bid price which the investor would obtain in the market. Those holdings which the trust managers do not wish to take over will be sold, but some groups pay the stock exchange commission on the sales. In all such schemes, the investor is usually receiving a higher consideration than would be obtainable on the sale of the portfolio in the market.

Unitisation of investment companies

A number of unit trust groups will arrange special schemes whereby the shares in investment companies may be exchanged for unit trust holdings. Whereas the individual shareholdings may not have been readily saleable the units are, of course, marketable and any gain is not taxable until such time as units are sold.

Linked life assurance

By far the most important single development in the unit trust movement has been the introduction over the years of 'linked' life assurance schemes which provide for the investment of life assurance premiums in unit trusts. It is a subject we can deal with more appropriately under the next chapter heading. The London & Edinburgh Insurance Company is usually credited with the introduction of the first equity linked policy because in 1957 that company brought out a scheme whereby life assurance premiums were invested not actually but notionally in the Unicorn Trust (then owned by the London & Edinburgh), and the policies were valued according to the value of the Unicorn units. In the period which followed, unit linked life assurance grew enormously to a point today where investments through linked life assurance account for over one-quarter of all unit trust sales. The special advantages of unit linked life assurance to the managers are fourfold:

1. The contractual nature of most life assurance policies provides a continuing flow of funds for investment, which as we have seen is so important to the unit trust movement.

2. Unit linked life policies could be sold by normal life assurance methods, thereby circumventing the statutory restraints, under the Prevention of Fraud (Investments) Act 1958, on unit trust advertising and marketing methods.

3. The permitted level of unit trust charges can be augmented by fees chargeable in the life office as distinct from the management company.

4. In the case of policies taken out prior to 14 March 1984 the investor receives the benefit of income tax relief on premiums paid under long term life assurance contracts.

Unit trusts for children

Most unit trust groups operate schemes to encourage investment for the benefit of children and this can be done in various ways. In some cases a formal trust deed in standard form is used, normally providing for the invested sums to be set aside for the benefit of the child or children, the income of the fund being accumulated until the beneficiary comes of age. Such trusts tend to be a little inflexible, particularly in times of changing fiscal legislation, and most parents or other benefactors prefer to use the simple device of a designated account until such time as the child can have the units transferred into his or her own name.

Exempt unit trusts

A number of unit trust groups introduced 'exempt' trusts for investment by pension funds and charities because such institutions enjoy complete exemption from Income Tax and Capital Gains Tax. This distinction between exempt trusts and ordinary unit trusts is not now very significant because all authorised unit trusts enjoy exemption from Capital Gains Tax on investment switches within the funds. Among the clearing banks, Barclays, Lloyds and Midland operate exempt trusts at the present time.

So much for the various plans and schemes which are now common in the unit trust business. For the most part they have been designed to appeal to various sectors of the market and, as such, they have met with varying success. In the last analysis, however, a unit trust is judged by the quality of its investment performance.

Investment aspects

We have seen that in an authorised unit trust investment is restricted to quoted securities (with the exception of a limited participation in unquoted stocks and shares), but even within such orthodox limits unit trust investment is not easy. We have said in an earlier chapter that investment success depends very largely on the ability to be liquid, or fully invested as the case may be, at the right time. In the unit trust world, rising stock markets tend to spark off rising sales of units. The investment managers often have substantial new monies coming in each week, which creates a degree of liquidity at a time when they would wish to be fully invested. The reverse is also true: on a falling market when managers would wish to maintain partial liquidity, they are seldom assisted by any new money coming in from unit trust sales other than the contractual premiums under monthly insurance plans.

In any case, it is rare for investment managers to take positive steps to go liquid to any major extent in unit trust portfolios. This is partly because of dealing costs and partly because the

'... positive steps to go liquid.'

risk of being wrong is very considerable. Also some managers have the more philosophical view that they have been given money by the public to invest and not to hold in liquid form. The unit trust manager has a great responsibility. He has a duty to do his best in the management of the investors' money. He has no right to speculate with it nor to take undue risks, but he will be expected to bring an informed judgment to bear, not only as to the quality of individual investments but also in the timing of those investments, both as to entry into and withdrawal from the market. The investment manager is not expected to be a wizard, but he must exercise a very proper judgment, drawing on the best sources of information available to him.

Another area of difficulty for the investment manager is the choice of the number of holdings in the portfolio. There will have to be at least twenty stocks (because of the requirement already mentioned on page 148) and in time the portfolio will probably be built up with between 50 and 100 securities. In very large trusts, the number will be even greater, as it will be in those specialist trusts investing in a wide range of small companies. As the number of holdings increases, so the management problems become greater. Partly for that reason and partly because individual successes or failures have less impact on the larger portfolios, one can normally expect a less volatile performance from the larger trusts. That is not to say that they do not perform so well in the long run. The widely accepted belief that small trusts perform better than larger ones is not easy to substantiate.

Advantages of unit trust investment

We have said in an earlier chapter that investment in unit trusts is suitable mainly for those who wish to commit part of their savings to equity investment and who understand that stock market prices can be very volatile. As a vehicle for investment, unit trusts offer the following very real advantages:

1. It is possible to get a greater spread of risk than is normally available to the private investor.

2. Unit trusts enjoy the advantage of day-to-day management by those who are knowledgeable in investment matters.

3. The annual management charges are effectively allowed for tax within the fund, which would not be possible if an investor paid someone to manage his own portfolio.

4. Dealing costs are proportionately lower.

5. The investor has one investment instead of many and thus the administrative problems of dealing with dividend counterfoils, Income Tax certificates and allotment letters, etc. are reduced.

6. All subjective considerations are removed – the choice of shares and the degree of liquidity is left to the much more objective decision of the investment manager.

7. Authorised unit trusts enjoy exemption from Capital Gains Tax on investment switches within each trust.

The Unit Trust Association

Nowadays most of the unit trust groups are members of the Unit Trust Association, set up in 1959 as the Association of Unit Trust Managers, to monitor standards throughout the movement. The Association was constituted with the following objects:

1. to uphold standards of unit trust practice, to protect the interests of unitholders and to maintain the good name of the unit trust industry;

2. to provide on behalf of its members an agreed channel of communication and representation to government departments and other authorities on matters relating to unit trusts;

3. to act in co-operation with other organisations on matters connected with investment protection.

The Association acted as a watchdog on advertisements by its members and, in particular, stipulated that no advertisements must be allowed to mislead the public. It became a rule of the Association that advertisements by its members must state the aim of the trust as well as contain a warning in precise words that the price of units and the income from them can go down as well as up.

The Association deals with enquiries of a factual nature from the public or the media and is a valuable source of information on the entire unit trust movement. The members of the Unit Trust Association are accountable for over 95 per cent of the total unit trust funds under administration in this country.

Consequent upon the passing of the Financial Services Act 1986, the Self-Regulating Organisations (SROs) for the unit trust management groups became Life Assurance and Unit Trusts Regulatory Organisation (LAUTRO) and Investment Managers Regulatory Organisation (IMRO), which to some extent took over the role of the Unit Trust Association, particularly in relation to such matters as advertising and investor protection. Thus, the Association embarked on a major review of its future role and recommended to its members that the overall objectives of the Association should be:

(a) the achievement of a significant improvement in public awareness and understanding of the investment opportunities provided by unit trusts;
(b) the enhancement of the role of spokesman and lobbyist for unit trusts in dealing with the regulatory bodies in the United Kingdom and in the European Community; and
(c) the provision of a more comprehensive information, advice and support service for members.

The Financial Services legislation provides for most of the regulation of unit trusts to pass from the Department of Trade & Industry to the Securities & Investments Board and thus to the delegated SROs and it is the aim of the Association to continue its role as the recognised link between those engaged in the business of unit trust management and the regulatory organisations.

The market for unit trust sales

The man in the street will be unwise to invest in the purchase of unit trusts until he has first set aside his 'contingency reserve' in bank savings account, National Savings Certificates, building societies or the like. Unit trust investment is mainly equity investment and not everyone's financial situation is strong enough to allow for the hazards of the stock market. This still leaves a very big market for the sale of units. The number of existing unitholders is believed to be approximately 3½ million. This undoubtedly includes some of the 7 million or so private investors who are believed to have invested directly in the stock market in this country. The potential market is very considerable and consists of that part of the adult population who have a few hundred pounds to spare for investment in the industrial and commercial life of the community, having first set aside their safe and accessible nest egg as already proposed. In terms of regular saving out of income, we may say that the market consists of all those people who can afford, say, £10 a month for equity investment for themselves or their children. In recent times, however, economic recession and unemployment have affected many who would otherwise be unit trust investors and in many homes there can be little enough to spare for stock market investment after meeting living costs, mortgage payments and life assurance premiums.

The tendency has been for the clearing banks to regard the market for their unit trusts as being limited to their own customers. This must be so to a considerable degree, but it is not entirely borne out by experience. (In the case of the Unicorn Trusts, which did not have their origin in the banking world, it was quite common to find on a random check of applications long after the group's acquisition by Barclays Bank that 60 per cent or more of cheques received for the purchase of units were drawn on other banks.) For practical purposes, however, we can say that the main market for the clearing bank unit trusts is among the 25 million customers of the clearing banks. The market for unit-linked life assurance is very much wider including as it does quite a proportion of investors who do not have accounts with the clearing banks. We shall look at this more closely in the next chapter.

Like all the unit trusts groups, the bank-controlled groups have recourse to extensive newspaper advertising. It may be thought that the very existence of extensive branch networks is sufficient for the marketing of units without heavy expenditure on advertising, but this is not the case. It is a combination of the two which is most effective, but this can make the whole operation very expensive. We have spoken already of the varying attitudes of bank managers to the question of unit trust investment. We hope never to see again the euphoria of the early

1970s which led to a lot of disappointment for investors generally and for some bank customers. It is a pity that, unlike most products, unit trusts sell best when they are most expensive. Hence the advantage which we have already mentioned of regular systematic investment. Viewed sensibly and with a proper caution by bank managers and customers alike, unit trusts will remain for as long as we can see a highly desirable and commendable form of investment for customers with investable funds.

Unit trust charges

The pricing structure in the United Kingdom unit trust movement was for many years a strange one. It was probably the only area of free enterprise where the level of charges was controlled completely by the government through the Department of Trade. The charges in each unit trust are laid down in the trust deed, but until recent times these could not exceed the maximum level authorised by the Department of Trade rules. Under those rules, the maximum charge exigible by the unit trust management company over a 20 year period was 13¼ per cent of the value of the units in issue. Only two categories of fees were permitted. The first of these, the Initial Charge, could not exceed 5 per cent of the new monies invested in a trust. The other fee, the Annual Charge, could not exceed ½ per cent of the funds under management. Thus, in order not to exceed the permitted maximum of 13¼ per cent over 20 years, the combination of fees was mainly an Initial Fee of 3¼ per cent and Annual Fees of ½ per cent or, alternatively, an Initial Fee of 5 per cent and Annual Fees of ⅜ per cent. Out of those fees, the managers had to pay all costs including the charges of the trustees and the auditors.

In December 1979, the Department of Trade relinquished its control over the level of unit trust managers' charges, leaving the management companies to fix their own level of fees. This meant that, in the case of all new trusts, the level of fees inserted in the trust deeds need no longer conform to the old regulations and, in the case of old trusts, the fees could be increased provided the unitholders agreed. The basic system of charges, i.e. an Initial Fee and an Annual Fee still remains and the fees of the trustees, auditors, registrars, etc. are still payable by the management company, not out of the trust fund itself. The relaxation of the rules was in response to representations by the Unit Trust Association who, in return, gave an assurance to the government that it would not attempt to replace the Department of Trade regulations by any price fixing agreement within the movement.

Profitability

In the 'bull' market in the early 1970s some of the unit trust groups made handsome profits. New money was pouring into unit trusts and at one point in 1972 the Unicorn Group, the largest of the bank unit trust groups, was receiving new money for investment at a sustained level of approximately £2 million per week. The stock market was high and this in itself meant that unit trust fees, which are on an *ad valorem* basis, were also high. In the following years, the position was quite different. Not only were market levels much lower, but potential unit trust investors were more conscious of the perils of falling markets and net investment in the industry diminished for a while. In fact, during 1978 unit trust sales rose by 42 per cent on the previous year to a record figure of £530 million, but fell away again in 1979 and 1980. Sales improved again dramatically in the better investment climate of 1981 and, in that year, gross sales amounted to £955 million and net new investment to £528 million. Since then unit trust sales have improved steadily and in 1985 gross sales mounted to £4·5 billion (nearly double the figure for 1984) and net sales, i.e. after repurchases, reached £2·54 billion. In October 1986 gross sales reached a monthly level of £1 billion for the first time and the total of net sales, after repurchases, for that year amounted to just over £5 billion. At the time of writing the level of sales continues to go from strength to strength reflecting the 'bull' market of present times.

The costs of administering unit trusts rose astronomically in the 1970s. The business is labour-intensive even with the aid of computers and salary costs, particularly in the banking groups, are high. Unit trust managers have also been hit by the considerable rise in stationery and postage costs. Some very attractive profits were made in the heady days of 1972 when the market was buoyant, sales as we have said were running at very high levels and the industry had not yet been hit by the inflation of the middle and late '70s. A degree of profitability returned in the following years with the improvement in the stock market and rise in unit trust sales. The bull market of the mid 1980s resulted in a return to substantial levels of profit throughout the industry. The ability to increase charges helped considerably. Other factors were the removal of Exchange Control which greatly simplified the development of trusts for investment overseas and the ability to launch trusts investing in gilt-edged stocks with the removal of the tax disadvantage which, in the past, had applied to such trusts.

The management of unit trusts must be seen as a legitimate and logical extension of the asset management function. Mr F. W. Holder wrote in 1969 of the entry of Lloyds Bank into the unit trust movement:

> '... there are many thousands of bank customers of moderate means who would be prepared to entrust a few hundreds or a few thousands of pounds to their bank for investment in stocks and shares and wish to be relieved of the task of selection and the paperwork involved in owning a number of separate securities in their own names'.[1]

That is still true today. It is a natural role for the all-purpose bank – to help their customers to put their money to work.

Unauthorised trusts

Only trusts which satisfy the Department of Trade regulations will receive their authorisation. If for example a unit trust did not have an independent trustee, authorisation would not be possible. Equally, if the system of charging did not conform to the rules, or if the portfolio was to include assets outside the statutory definition of 'securities', no authorisation would be possible. There is nothing unlawful or reprehensible about unauthorised trusts as such. They exist in a number of insurance companies as part of the life fund and have also been set up internally in one or two other investment houses. They suffer from the disability that, being unauthorised, they do not satisfy the Prevention of Fraud (Investments) Act 1958 and so it would be an offence under the Act to invite public subscription for the units or to issue circulars or even to hold circulars calculated to induce investment in the unit trust. In the ordinary way, therefore, property unit trusts can be offered to the public only via the vehicle of a property bond, i.e. a life assurance policy. One bank, Barclays Bank, operates an unauthorised unit trust investing in property for the benefit of the bank's private investment clients, but this is possible only under an exempting clause in the Act which permits circulars as between trustee and beneficiary.

A more important exception to the general rule is that of property unit trusts for pension funds and charities. Over the years, a number of unit trusts have been set up with the express purpose of enabling pension funds and to a lesser degree, charities, to invest in property and, under their discretionary powers, the Department of Trade have permitted the issue of prospectuses to approved pension funds and registered charities. This exception was no doubt thought to be socially desirable, but more particularly it was possible because the managing bodies of such institutions are deemed to be experienced business people. There are now 17 pension fund property unit trusts in existence, managing portfolios to a total value of approximately £2,500 million. In most instances, these have been promoted by merchant banks in co-operation with leading firms of surveyors, but in one or two cases the clearing banks have played a leading role as trustee, or even as managing trustee.

Unit trusts designed for more esoteric forms of investment, such as antiques, works of art, wine, gold coins or whatever, are not likely to receive authorisation even for a sophisticated market such as pension funds. It is possible for such trusts to be set up off-shore but for that reason alone, whatever the content of the portfolio, authorisation in this country would be impossible and as the law stands at present the marketing of the fund would be proscribed by the very stringent provisions of the Act.

The Financial Services Legislation

As already mentioned, it is proposed that under the provisions of the Financial Services Act 1986 the regulation of unit trusts will pass for the most part from the Department of Trade to the Securities & Investments Board. In anticipation of the new legislation (which is not yet in force) the Department issued a consultative document in August 1986[2] proposing quite far-reaching changes in the regulatory structure including such proposals as were necessary to bring unit trusts in the U.K. into line with the European Community Directive on collective investment schemes.

Some of the main proposals outlined in the consultative document were:

(i) increased powers and responsibilities of the trustees of unit trust schemes (see page 377),

(ii) simplification of trust deeds,

(iii) changes in trust deeds to be authorised only with approval of 75 per cent of participants who vote,

(iv) schemes falling below £1 million in value to be terminated,

(v) unit trust investment powers to include:

(a) money market instruments,
(b) property and property-related securities,
(c) commodities and
(d) financial futures

(vi) alternative methods of calculating unit prices,

(vii) power for unit trust managers to borrow up to 10 per cent of the fund's value,

(viii) the charging of certain additional expenses, e.g. the audit fees and trustees' remuneration, to the funds managed.

At the time of writing, these and various other proposals in the consultative document are the subject of discussion with the industry.

Reference

1 F. W. Holder: 'The Banks and the Unit Trusts.' *The Banker,* April 1969.
2 The Regulation of Authorised Unit Trust Schemes: Department of Trade and Industry, HMSO (1986).

CHAPTER 8

Life Assurance

At first sight, this must seem an unusual chapter heading in any book on bank services. Years ago it would have been unthinkable that the clearing banks should become involved in the business of insurance, or that the big insurance companies would move into banking. And yet, to a modest degree, that is what has happened. A number of clearing banks are now involved in life assurance activities and some insurance companies have either banking or licensed deposit-taking subsidiaries. Here we must distinguish between the provision of life assurance cover – the underwriting process – and the business of insurance broking. The British banks are engaged in both activities, but first let us look at the extent to which they are involved as writers of life assurance, leaving the broking role to a later chapter.

A second distinction we must make is between life assurance and general insurance. The terminological distinction betweeen the two words 'assurance' and 'insurance' is a feature of the United Kingdom market, but has become somewhat blurred over the years and is probably no longer material. The theory was that one 'assured' against things which were bound to happen and 'insured' against contingencies or possibilities. Hence one assured against death, but insured against fire, theft and accident. However, the words do not matter: the essential point is that the banks are engaged in life assurance, but not at this point of time in the business of underwriting general insurance risks. As brokers, however, they are engaged in life and general business across-the-board.

The banks and life assurance

None of the banks entered the life assurance field because they necessarily wished to be involved in the provision of life assurance *per se*. The writing of life contracts developed directly out of the banks' unit trust business in the form of linked life assurance, such as we have described.

The first move lay with Martins Bank, who on the acquisition of the Unicorn Group in 1967 also acquired control of Griffin Life Assurance Company, a newly created subsidiary of the London and Edinburgh Insurance Company designed for the purpose of issuing unit linked life policies. Shortly afterwards, Lloyds Bank announced that they would issue unit linked life policies through a newly formed subsidiary of the Royal Insurance Company. On 1 September 1967, the Westminster Hambro Unit Trust Group introduced a linked life policy, the insurance being provided by the Commercial Union Assurance Company and in 1971 Williams & Glyn's Bank launched their 'Nest Egg Plan' – a ten-year life assurance policy with Provident Mutual Life Assurance Association, linked to a deposit in Williams & Glyn's Bank. Thus, at one stage, only Martins Bank and then Barclays Bank were engaged as principals in life assurance business, but a few years later, in October 1975, Lloyds Bank introduced its own unit linked bonds through its own captive subsidiary, Beehive Life Assurance Company. Beehive is now re-named Black Horse Life Assurance Company Limited and offers a wide range of insurance contracts linked to Lloyds Bank unit trusts. It is also the vehicle through which the Lloyds Bank Endowment Mortgage Scheme is offered. In February 1976, Midland Bank announced its ten-year savings plan – to be sold over the bank counters – an insured savings scheme with Greville Insurance. In more recent years Canada Life Assurance Company have offered a range of policies linked to Midland Bank Unit Trusts.

The Trustee Savings Banks also have their own life assurance subsidiary through which most of their very successful unit trust contracts are written, as mentioned in the previous chapter.

Linked life assurance

So it is that the banks are to a degree engaged in the business of 'linked' life assurance. The Scott Committee, which published its Report in April 1973, defined linked life assurance as:

> 'All life assurance and annuity contracts, the benefits of which are calculated in whole or in part by reference to the value of, or the income from, specified assets or groups of assets or by reference to movements in a share price or other index, whether or not subject to deductions in respect of tax or expenses.'[1]

Such policies were originally linked to authorised unit trusts so that on maturity or surrender of the policy, the value would be the value of the underlying units. It is equally possible, however, for the policy to be linked to units in a separate fund in the insurance company's life fund or, as the definition allows, linked to some other assets or index. The essential thing is that the value of the policy at any one time is calculable by reference to a formula and the amount payable under the policy whether on death, maturity or surrender, is ascertainable by reference to that formula. In contrast, the amount payable by a life office on a conventional 'with profits' policy would be a pre-determined fixed sum (the sum assured) plus any bonus or bonuses declared by the directors of the company at their discretion.

We may summarise the main differences between conventional 'with profits' policies and linked policies as follows:

1. In the case of a linked policy, its value at any one time will depend on the value of the underlying assets: the value of a conventional policy will depend on the proportion of profits allocated to the policy by the company from time to time.

2. The value of a linked policy, whether on surrender, maturity or death, may thus be subject to very wide fluctuations depending on the values of the shares or property or other assets to which the policy is linked: the benefits under a conventional 'with profits' policy will always be a fixed pre-determined sum (or in the case of surrender, a sum calculated according to a pre-determined formula) plus bonuses which have been declared.

3. Holders of linked policies will receive details of the assets to which their policies are linked, including current valuations at least once a year: holders of conventional policies receive no such details because their policies are not related to specific,

identifiable assets (although they will of course receive details of bonuses added to their policies).

There will no doubt be differing opinions for many years as to the relative merits of 'conventional' and 'linked' life assurance. When the first linked life policies were introduced in 1957, by the London and Edinburgh Insurance Company in cooperation with the Unicorn Group, they were regarded by many as a matter of passing interest, but today approximately one-quarter of all new life assurance annual premiums for new sums assured are related to policies which are linked in one way or another. There is no doubt a section of the public who like to know that their policies are linked to particular assets and indeed to have some say in the choice of those assets. Equally, they count it a benefit to receive regular reports on the underlying assets. Some people like to know that the values of their policies are linked directly to the long-term performance of the economy and therefore of the stock markets or other markets, and to have the opportunity if they so wish of cashing in on their policies when market levels are high. To put it at its lowest, a linked life policy provides the investor with the opportunity of participating in the growth of definable assets, frequently through unit trusts, with the benefit (at one time) of tax relief on his contributions (subject to certain statutory requirements) and with a measure of life assurance for extra protection. These considerations are important to the bank manager and others in the front line, and it would not be appropriate, for example, to sell a customer a linked life assurance product when a conventional policy, and perhaps a particular type of conventional policy, is more suited to the customer's needs.

There are those who consider that linked life assurance is merely an extension of unit trust investment (as indeed it was in its original concept) and that it should not be governed by insurance law, but brought very firmly under the investment law of this country which would have meant the Companies Act and more particularly the Prevention of Fraud (Investments) Act. With one dissenting voice, the Scott Committee came to the very clear view that 'there is no fundamental difference between linked and other policies: the distinction in the method used to calculate the benefits payable seems to us to be a matter more of form than of substance'. In his discussion document on 'Review of Investor Protection',[2] Professor Gower questions whether this view was tenable. It is his impression that the Scott view 'is now generally regarded as a mistake' (see also page 183).

The matter is now brought within the regulatory framework under the Financial Services Act (see Appendix).

Some historical aspects

This is perhaps a good point to consider the nature of life assurance business generally. As far as is known, the earliest form of life assurance was that practised by the Greeks in connection with their burial societies. The Romans too had a system of payment on death for the benefit of dependants and they are also credited with the development of marine insurance. (Other forms of commercial insurance had in fact existed from Babylonian days.) It seems that life assurance had its origins not so much in the desire to provide for dependants, but more in two other areas of human concern – the fear of not having a decent burial and the wish to protect personal fortunes. The desire to provide for burial found expression in the mutual societies of the mediaeval guilds and it is significant that even in modern times it was the fear of ending up in a pauper's grave which probably more than anything led to the massive growth of industrial insurance in this country. The commercial insurance of life – the real beginning of our life assurance business – had its origin in the golden age of exploration when the life of a ship's captain would be insured along with the ship and its cargo. The policy would last for the period of the voyage and seldom for more than a year. Thus our first life assurance policies were what we would call today term assurance – cover against the eventuality of death during a stated period. By the end of the seventeenth century a number of societies had developed life cover and annuity schemes but, as every lawyer knows, life assurance was looked upon as something of a gamble and it was difficult to distinguish between the life contract and an outright wager, as the punters of the day placed their bets on the expectation of life of leading soldiers and politicians. It was the Life Assurance Act of 1774 which required the proposer to have an 'insurable interest' in the life of the assured. From that point on, life assurance developed alongside the more traditional forms of insurance and throughout the nineteenth century in the aftermath of the Industrial Revolution, the insurance societies mushroomed. In 1854 the Prudential Assurance Company was formed to meet the increasing need for industrial assurance and in time became the largest life office not only in this country but in the world in terms of sums assured. By the end of 1985, the total premium income of the life offices in this country including pensions business was approximately £7¼ billion, representing a very substantial proportion of personal savings. During 1986, new annual premiums for life assurance in the United Kingdom, including annuity business but excluding pension plans, rose to £1,560 million. New single premiums in 1985 amounted to £3,500 million.

Categories of life assurance

There are various categories of life assurance and they may be summarised as follows:

1. Whole life assurance – the sum assured is payable only on the death of the life assured.

2. Endowment assurance – the sum assured is payable only on death or at the end of an agreed term, whichever comes first. (Both these types of assurance may be (a) 'with profits', which means that in return for a higher premium the benefits will include a share of the profits of the company over and above the pre-determined sum or (b) 'without profits', which means that the benefits under the policy are as stated without further additions. Also, either category of life policy, i.e. whole life or endowment, may be 'conventional' or 'linked' as we have already described.)

3. Term assurance – the sum assured is payable only in the event of death during a specified period.

4. Convertible term assurance – this is similar to term assurance, but carries the option to convert to an endowment policy or possibly whole of life assurance or a further term assurance at any time during the term without further medical examination.

'Golden age of exploration.'

5. Mortgage protection assurance – this covers the life of a mortgage loan and the sum assured reduces in line with the capital sum outstanding on the mortgage over the years.

6. Children's assurance – this may be on the life of the parent or an endowment policy on the child's life.

7. Personal accident and sickness insurance – there is a great variety of such schemes available.

8. Immediate annuity – a regular annual or other periodic payment commencing forthwith in return for a capital sum.

9. Deferred annuity – an annuity starting at some date in the future.

10. Annuity certain – an annuity scheme which provides a specific number of payments to be made regardless of the death of the annuitant.

11. Reversionary annuity – normally an annuity payable to the survivor of two persons, e.g. husband and wife.

12. Personal pension plan – a form of saving with special tax benefits to secure a pension (deferred annuity on retirement, with or without a lump sum benefit).

13. Pension schemes – in addition to individual retirement schemes, there are group schemes for employees of particular companies, the premiums being paid by way of contribution by the employers and possibly employees over the years to provide individual pensions on retirement.

At the present time, none of the banks is involved as underwriter in such a wide range of insurance contracts, but as we shall see the banks as insurance brokers deal with the whole field of insurance, so that even at local branch level some understanding of the terminology and nature of the various contracts is necessary.

The purpose of life assurance

In its traditional form, life assurance is a matter of protection – protection against (or provision for) the costs of death (as in the case of burial policies) or the financial losses occasioned by death (as for example the need to provide for a family on the death of the bread-winner). For the most part, the life offices still emphasise the element of 'cover' in life assurance. In the last fifty years or so, however, life assurance has become additionally a method of saving and investment. This has been encouraged in the advertisements of the life offices and the public have been quick to respond. It was a natural and commendable development. If a sum of money is to be payable on the death of the insured, it is a small step for him to contract that it shall be paid to him at the end of a fixed period of years if he is still alive. As a means of building up a nest egg for the future, life assurance imposes a discipline on the saver which in most cases is reasonably painless. The opportunity to save in this way accounts on average for approximately 3 per cent of gross national product in the United Kingdom, i.e. at a higher level than in any other EEC country and higher than in the United States, Canada or Japan. In terms of personal saving, life assurance remains the largest single force in the country.

If life assurance has become a vehicle for savings and investment, so unit funds have become, for reasons we have mentioned, vehicles for life assurance. We have said that the banks did not seek to go into life assurance for its own sake, but they are very much there, albeit by force of circumstance. Although the banks' life assurance business is almost entirely linked life assurance, they are nevertheless in life business. That is the name of the game and the banks are bound by the rules of the game. They are governed by the Insurance Acts in all matters, including for example the capital structure of their subsidiary life companies, the methods of selling, the solvency rules and the appointment of actuaries. The selling of life assurance business is now covered by the regulatory framework under the Financial Services Act 1986 (see page 210 and Appendix).

We have referred to the distinctions between conventional life policies and linked policies, the principal distinguishing feature of a linked policy being that it is related to identifiable assets in the life fund. Thus, an equity linked life policy would be related to a particular unit trust and a property policy, usually called a property bond, would be related or linked to a particular portfolio of properties in the life fund. In the late 1960s, however, 'managed' bonds were introduced by the unit trust groups and the conventional life offices. The essence of such a bond is that the nature of the underlying assets may be changed, usually at the discretion of the life company, so that there may be switching among ordinary stocks, gilt-edged securities, properties and certain other securities. So it is that in the case of a managed bond the underlying assets are as amorphous as the life fund behind a conventional policy, blurring still further the differences between the two types of life assurance.

Categories of linked life assurance

The linked life assurance products sold by the banks from, as it were, their own shelves fall into the following broad categories:

Policies linked to equity funds (including specific unit trusts);
Policies linked to property funds;
Policies linked to gilt-edged and other fixed interest stocks, usually known as gilt bonds;
Policies linked to building society shares or deposits;
Policies linked to deposits in the money market, usually known as money bonds;
Policies linked to a mixed fund of varying assets, usually referred to as managed bonds.

In all these several categories of policies there will usually be: (a) single premium policies (or bonds) where the premium will be a single lump sum. In such cases the life assurance cover will be little if any more than the amount of the investment. It is essentially an investment product – not sold for life assurance as such.

(b) multiple premium policies where the premiums are normally paid monthly as with conventional life assurance and the policies are sold on their merits for life assurance purposes. These policies may be either:

(i) whole of life – the proceeds are payable only on death or earlier surrender, there will be a minimum sum payable on death (the sum assured), but beyond that the proceeds will depend on the performance of the underlying assets; or
(ii) endowment – as with conventional policies already described, with the difference that the fixed sum assured will usually be smaller, the proceeds depending on the performance of the underlying assets in the market.

The linked life offices also provide personal pension plans as described below.

Personal pension plans

Nowadays, an important part of life assurance business is the provision of personal pension plans for private individuals. These are dealt with here rather than in Chapter 19 because this is a service to the private individual. In Chapter 19 we deal more particularly with those services which the banks provide in a 'corporate' way to pension funds as such.

There are approximately 2½ million self-employed people in the United Kingdom. They do not qualify for an earnings-related pension under the State Scheme, but are entitled only to the basic State Retirement Pension. Since the passing of the Finance Act, 1956, however, self-employed persons have been able to obtain tax relief on amounts put aside for pension purposes and, in recent years, the relief has been increased quite substantially.

A personal pension plan, may be taken out by:

1. any person engaged in a trade or profession on his own account or in partnership;

2. a director or employee of a company who, for any reason, is in non-pensionable employment: this includes persons contracted into the State Pension Scheme (see Chapter 19), but for whom the employer has provided no additional scheme or who has chosen not to join such an additional scheme;

3. an employed person who has other earnings: a person who is a member of an occupational pension scheme may have earnings from an independent source of employment. For example, a medical consultant may have private fees in addition to his pensionable earnings under the National Health Service. Such a person may contribute to a personal pension plan to the extent of those non pensionable earnings.

4. an employed person who under the Social Security Act 1986 elects to take out a personal pension plan rather than join, or remain in, his employer's occupational scheme (see below).

The essence of a personal pension plan is that the earner may set aside a proportion of his earnings each year to be paid as a premium to an insurance company in return for the provision of a pension at the date of the earner's retirement. The benefit may be taken partly as a capital sum, but mostly as an annuity payable for life.

As the law stands at present, a self-employed person may set aside up to 17½ per cent (indeed up to 32 per cent for persons born in or before 1907) of net relevant earnings before tax under a personal pension plan with the benefit of full tax relief at his or her marginal rate.

Principal features

The main features of personal pension plans are as follows:

The retirement pension may be payable at any time from age 60 to 75 regardless of the actual date of retirement. In exceptional circumstances, e.g. ill health or specialist occupation, the Inland Revenue may allow a pension to be payable at an earlier age than 60, but it may not commence at an age later than 75.

Part of the retirement pension may be commuted for a cash sum payable free of tax, but this sum may not exceed three times the amount of the retirement pension which remains thereafter.

Provision may be made for a widow or widower, or other dependant.

The personal pension plan may include life assurance, provided that the premium for the life cover does not exceed 5 per cent of earnings, i.e. out of the total of 17½ per cent as mentioned above.

Part of the pension may be taken as a guaranteed annuity for a period of five or ten years, i.e. with a residual payment to the annuitant's estate in the event of death during that period.

When the annuity is due for payment, the annuitant may apply the capital value of the annuity in purchase of an annuity from any life company in the market, in order to obtain the best terms. But he cannot receive the total capital sum for his own use, i.e. over and above any commutation as referred to above.

Not only does the self-employed person (or person in non-pensionable employment) receive tax relief on the premiums, but these in turn are invested by the insurance company in an exempt fund so that no further tax is payable.

When the pension is payable, this is treated as earned income for tax purposes, not investment income.

Types of personal pension plan

Plans of this nature may be taken out as part of a conventional with-profits endowment scheme, or as a 'linked' life contract as already described. There are three main types of personal pension schemes. These are:

Pension funded contracts: Under this type of scheme, the premiums are applied in the purchase of a guaranteed amount of pension. This is the minimum amount which will be payable, but to which will be added any bonuses declared by the life office over the period of the plan, (as with a normal with-profits endowment scheme). Although the amount of bonuses will reflect the investment performance of the life office, the amount of pension will not vary with the state of the stock market at the date of payment, nor will it vary with the level of interest rates at that date.

Money purchase contracts: This type of scheme instead of providing a guaranteed amount of pension, guarantees a minimum amount of cash available for the purchase of a pension at the retirement date. As with a 'pension funded contract' mentioned above, bonuses will be added during the term of the contract and will, therefore, increase the total cash sum available. The amount of pension which the cash sum will buy will depend on annuity rates available in the market at that time, which in turn will reflect the ruling level of interest rates. If it so happens that interest rates are then at a low level, the amount of annuity may be considerably less than that which was expected.

Unit-linked contracts: This is similar to a 'Money purchase contract', but the premiums are applied in the purchase of a number of units in one of the insurance company's pension funds. It may be a fund chosen by the policy-holder, e.g. a property fund or a gilt fund, or it may be a managed fund, i.e.

one managed at the discretion of the insurance company. When the pension becomes payable, an annuity is purchased with the value of the units then allocated to the contract. Thus, the amount of the annuity will depend not only on the levels of interest rates at the time, but also the level of the stock market or property market in which the units have been invested. On the other hand, the contributor can see at any time how his investment is proceeding and, within limits, he may time his retirement to take advantage of a high level in the stock market and high interest rates (although clearly the two do not necessarily go together). As his retirement approaches, he may have the advantage if he so wishes of protecting the growth achieved in his policy by switching to a money fund or a gilt fund for the remaining period. During 1981, linked contracts accounted for over 40 per cent of 'regular premium' personal pension plan business.

Within these basic types of contract there are many variations and the contributor will often seek maximum flexibility, perhaps by arranging separate contracts with a number of life offices. Pension policies cannot be surrendered, nor can the pension benefits be assigned. A number of life offices do, however, provide loan facilities to policyholders against personal pension plans.

The number of persons eligible to take out a personal pension plan, i.e. not only the self-employed but all others who do not have the benefit of an occupational scheme, is believed to be very considerable, probably of the order of 10 million, and a large part of this market still remains untapped. The banks offer a number of personal pension plans through their own life assurance subsidiaries and even more so through their insurance broking companies, as discussed in the next chapter.

At the time of writing a new category of person is about to be brought into the market for personal pension plans. This is because under the Social Security Act, 1986, employees may choose not to belong to their employers' occupational pension schemes, or the State Earnings-Related Pension Scheme, and instead take out a personal pension plan. It seems probable that this new concept will add significantly to the market for this type of pensions cover.

Selling methods

The life assurance products of the clearing banks are sold (a) over the bank counters; (b) by sales representatives; (c) by insurance brokers; and (d) by direct advertisement. Let us consider these in turn.

(a) *Counter sales:* The branch network of the clearing banks is usually the subject of envy on the part of other business houses. Well spread and well situated throughout the country, the branches are obviously a major force in the marketing of bank services. At the same time, however, they are costly to maintain and a good many branches do not earn their keep from banking business as such. The selling of many of the services described in these pages can make a useful contribution to branch profits, not merely because of the physical location of the branch, which is obviously important, but because of the captive market which every branch manager has amongst his customers. This applies particularly to the selling of life assurance and indeed many branch managers are familiar with the art from the days when they were allowed to sell insurance as agents for their own account. Here, however, we have a problem. All the British banks are engaged in insurance broking, whether through subsidiary companies or departments, as we shall discuss in the next chapter, and all the bank branches act as agents for those broking activities.

In previous editions of this work we said:

> *It is the duty of an insurance broker to survey the market in relation to the needs of his client and to offer the insurance contract which is most suitable for the purpose. Those banks which additionally have their own subsidiary life offices are, therefore, acting in a dual role. They are both underwriters* and *brokers in the life assurance business. This is an anomalous situation and one which is not easily resolved. Indeed, it may not be possible to resolve it. Although the broking and underwriting activities of the major banks are conducted in separate parts of the group structure and, as it were, go their own ways without conflict, there is a confluence of the separate streams at branch level. How does the branch manager fulfil the role of broker if there is an overriding consideration to sell the products from his own shelf? Equally, how does the bank develop its life assurance business if on each occasion of a 'sale' the manager*

> *has to fulfil the role of broker and test the market for the best product? Some of the banks pursue only a passive role in the marketing of their own life assurance contracts and to that extent the problem is eased, although the risk of conflict still remains. Others take the view that they have products available for customers who seek them, but beyond that as brokers they are willing to research the market to meet their customers' needs. One or two banks take the view that these linked life assurance products are no more than a vehicle for equity or property savings and investment and that if a customer needs life assurance for its own sake, it is a matter for the broking department. The problem will remain, however, so long as the banks are acting as both principal and agent in relation to the same merchandise in the same market.*

We did not realise at the time that this subject was to become an exceedingly contentious one from the standpoint of investor protection under the Rules of the Securities & Investments Board. Under the rules of 'polarisation', it is no longer possible for bank branches to act in an advisory role to customers on investment matters as well as acting as a representative of the bank in selling the various products from the bank's shelf. For this purpose, life assurance contracts, unit trusts and pension plans are all deemed to be investment business. The impact of 'polarisation' on bank branches is such that they can no longer be all things to all men – they cannot purport to give independent advice on investment matters on the one hand and sell their own investment products on the other. Thus, banks have had to choose whether their branches should be 'independent advisors' or 'company representatives'. The subject is discussed at greater length in the next chapter on insurance broking and again in the Appendix on the financial services legislation.

(b) *Sales representatives:* One hesitates to mention the exceedingly trite and rather boring dictum that insurance is not bought but sold. Certainly it is true of life assurance. Proposers for life assurance do not beat a path to the doors of the life offices, possibly because life assurance, rather like making a will, has been associated in people's minds with death. Perhaps people need the friendly if sometimes persuasive help of the salesman in order to concentrate their minds and come to a point of decision. Whatever the reason, the development of life assurance business has depended for the most part in this country, as well as in the United States and probably in all countries, on active selling by agents and representatives.

Although linked life assurance is sold widely by direct selling methods, only two clearing banks, viz. Barclays and Trustee Savings Bank have a separate sales organisation for the purpose. Apart from the early months of training, the representatives are paid entirely on a commission basis and the more successful ones achieve a handsome level of remuneration. In such a situation there must be risks of abuse, hard-selling, undue influence or misrepresentation or, at its lowest, the risk of giving offence to a reluctant audience. But this is true of all selling organisations and it is inevitably the over-zealous or the unconscientious who bring the rest in disrepute. In this country there is a tendency to disparage the role of the salesman. In some vague way he is regarded as surplus to requirements, a kind of parasite living on the backs of more legitimate occupations and existing by the unworthy pastime of selling people things they do not want. Traditionally, commercial travellers were second only to mothers-in-law as fodder for music hall comedians. But this is unfair. Selling is a worthy occupation – and indeed for many it is a vocation. We are all engaged in selling: parsons and politicians, barristers and bankers, doctors and dentists, we are all engaged in purveying ideas or ideals, theories or solutions or, in the nicest way of course, ourselves. If an insurance representative does not have a good product to sell, he and his company will soon know. If he has a good product to sell he may take a pride in it, knowing as he does that insurance, and life assurance in particular, has brought more help and comfort to people than many of the tangible things of life and very often at a time when it was most needed.

If at times there be abuse, the life offices are their own best critics and the best guardians of their own standards. Bad selling methods only rebound on the company. Hard-selling and over-selling result in an undue level of forfeitures, which are not necessarily profitable to the insurer and in any case, in time, operate against the company's good name. The discontinuance rates in the field of linked life assurance are in fact lower than in the area of industrial assurance. It is perhaps not surprising that the Scott Report considered that the responsible salesman is performing a socially valuable function and that 'we received no evidence of widespread malpractice in the selling of life assurance, but we recognise that opportunities for it exist'.[3]

The sales representatives, numbering over 500 in one clearing bank subsidiary, are highly trained and highly disciplined. After an early spell of criticisms and misunderstandings, not least from the bank managers themselves, occasioned in part by the over-enthusiasm of some of the representatives, the organisation settled down into a highly elite team and complaints from any source dwindled almost to nothing. No cold canvassing is allowed on domestic premises, a 'cold' call being one made without any previous arrangement or introduction. Indeed, such calls when they were allowed years ago were usually unproductive. The salesman likes to have an introduction to his 'prospect'. Nowadays, introductions flow steadily from bank branches to the insurance representatives (subject to the rules on 'polarisation' mentioned above and discussed in the Appendix). This results in a sharing of commission between the bank branch and the representative, but in the long run it makes better use of the representative's time. The experience in the past was that more than half of the total business taken on to their books by the sales force was on the introduction of the bank branches.

In the early days of in-house insurance selling, bankers and customers alike found it difficult to accept that the business should be 'sold' so directly, on the basis that the representative was rewarded wholly in commission. Nowadays, that view has mellowed, partly because all banks are having to go out and sell their services in one way or another and partly because it is recognised and remembered that life assurance has traditionally been sold on a commission basis. In fact, who more than the bank managers of earlier years had occasion to be grateful that it was so?

Recognising the dangers of over-selling, the Scott Committee made a number of recommendations which were subsequently reflected in the Insurance Companies (Amendment) Act 1973 (later consolidated in The Insurance Companies Regulations issued under the Insurance Companies Acts of 1974 and 1982).

In 1981, the Office of Fair Trading had occasion to consider possible abuses arising from the selling of insurance in all its forms by representatives and other intermediaries and, in particular, the practice of making unsolicited calls. No new legislation was proposed, but the British Insurance Association undertook to issue a Code of Conduct to be observed by all intermediaries acting on their behalf. It did not apply to insurance brokers, who came to be governed by their own Code of Practice.

Professor Gower[9] in his discussion document on investor protection asks:

> 'Is it really still necessary and desirable that life policies should be hawked from door to door?'

Even if the practice can be justified in relation to whole life or endowment policies, can it be so

> 'in relation to bonds masquerading as life policies'.

He further questions:

> 'Is it possible adequately to control what the intermediary says in the course of door to door selling?'

and:

> 'Is a cooling-off period any real protection?'

In his provisional conclusions, Professor Gower considers that:

> 'if (which I doubt) door to door sales of life policies should continue to be allowed, the practice should be restricted to straightforward life policies and not permitted in the case of bonds (and certainly not be extended to sales of other securities).'

Professor Gower's 'Discussion Document' was concerned of course not only with life assurance but with the whole field of investor protection. It prompted some lively discussion and led in time to a complete re-structuring of the regulatory machinery for the financial services industry and the passing of the Financial Services Act of 1986. The subjects of 'cold calling' and 'cooling off periods' are now dealt with under the Rules of the Securities and Investments Board (see Appendix).

(c) *Sales through brokers:* There are believed to be approximately 9,000 insurance brokers in the United Kingdom operating throughout the entire spectrum of insurance business. Traditionally, however, brokers have not been a major force in the sale of life business nor indeed of personal assurance in general, but they account for the lion's share of the market for commercial business and a very large proportion, probably 90 per cent, of pensions business. It was perhaps appropriate that insurance brokers should apply their skills at the more sophisticated end of the market, but, be that as it may, most life assurance (including all industrial life assurance) is sold direct by the companies concerned, either by mail order or to a much greater degree by their own selling organisations of representatives and agents.

Against that traditional background it is perhaps not surprising that the banks have made little impact on insurance brokers with the life business of the banking subsidiaries. In any case, there are many brokers who did not welcome the entry of the banks into insurance broking, as is discussed in the next chapter, and they see no reason why they should assist in the development of the banks' underwriting business. Futhermore, the fee structure of the life policies from the banks' subsidiaries do not permit of substantial commissions and in many instances it is possible for brokers to obtain higher commissions for selling the life contracts of other companies. There is also the point that insurance brokers in the life field are usually, but not always, conditioned by the nature of their training to conventional life assurance. Whatever the reasons, efforts to sell bank life policies through insurance brokers have not been successful and, so far as one can tell, are unlikely to be.

(d) *Sales by advertisement:* Advertising is not in general a cost-effective method of selling life assurance. It is not a subject fit for 'instant' selling and a television advertisement today will not produce a queue at the local life office tomorrow. People like to think about life assurance, they like to talk about it and they probably like to be seduced into buying it. It is not a case of love at first sight, certainly not a marriage by proxy – the overtures have to be face-to-face. Nevertheless, advertising, whether press or television, is usually necessary to establish the name and image of a company and its products. A representative standing on the doorstep with a well-known name in his bag is probably half way to a sale. Probably the success of the Prudential Assurance Company will never be matched – 'the man from the Prudential', as familiar in placard and press as on the doorstep. A perfect combination. However, it may be argued that good wine needs no bush and that bank subsidiaries do not need to build up their own separate image or identity. The parent's name is all that matters. Indeed, it ought to be so, but there is a credibility gap, the diverse nature of many bank services and the extent of their departure from traditional banking calls for an educational process, in which advertising can help. If a clearing bank moves into life assurance, it is a short-cut to tell the world by press publicity. It is also quite a good way of reminding the managers and staff.

So-called 'coupon' advertising has its place in life assurance. It enables the 'prospect' to indicate his or her interest and provides a lead to be followed up by the representative. In other cases, an application form may be appropriate, but usually this would apply only to the more modest sums assured where medical examination could be dispensed with and where the underwriters can condense the necessary requirements into a few well-chosen questions in the confined space of a newspaper application. A lengthy application form, particularly for life assurance, would be counter-productive.

The advertising of linked life assurance is often similar in form and content (with obvious differences) to unit trust advertising. To the investor, a single premium life policy, usually referred to as a bond, is (quite rightly) an investment with life assurance attached. So it is that during times of stock market optimism, advertisements for life assurance bonds can be as productive as those for unit trusts. They can produce the same 'cash with order' type of response. They can be monitored for immediate cost effectiveness and when confidence is high, the weekend takings can be considerable. However, it is not a good example of life assurance advertising and in any case, it may be a long time before unit trust and bond advertising rides as high as during the euphoric months of 1972.

Despite the special place which life assurance has enjoyed in the saving habits of this country (something to which we have already made reference) there is still a massive, largely untapped market for life assurance throughout the United Kingdom. It was estimated a few years ago that only two people out of five had life assurance cover and even now, despite the high-powered selling of recent years, it is understood that one in four people have no life assurance of any kind and less than one-third have life assurance taken out for protection purposes (as distinct from investment policies). In an article published in 1986, it was estimated that the amount paid out by all-British life companies on death in 1984 was less, on average, than £5,000, and that the amount currently insured under existing policies is only around £11,000. In the same article the writer estimates that less than one in nine British people have life cover sufficient to maintain average living standards in the event of the death of the bread-winner. The market for new life assurance and for increasing existing cover is therefore immense, and indeed nowadays a very substantial part of that market is among women who, on average, have only half the life cover of men.

We have already referred to the growing market for personal pension plans, something which will increase substantially when the proposed legislation comes into force enabling members of occupational schemes to arrange instead their own personal pensions.

Profitability

We have said that to the extent that the banks are involved in life assurance business, it was as a corollary to their unit trust investment business and they almost certainly did not regard life assurance as a profitable venture in itself. Used as a simple vehicle for selling unit trusts, a life company is barely profitable; but in those cases where a variety of linked contracts are being sold, including managed bonds and policies linked to internal funds, there is more profit potential than there is at present in direct unit trust business. It is a truism that in the first ten years or so of a life office's activity, there is little if any profit for the shareholders. During the years of relatively fast growth a life office experiences what is usually called 'new business strain' – this is a reflection of the high initial costs of writing life policies involving the training of staff, advertising and the payment of commissions to representatives and agents. The principal source of growth of a life company stems from surpluses in the life fund. They in turn arise for the most part from favourable mortality experience and more particularly good investment performance. In the case of linked life assurance, however, the benefit of the investment performance accrues to the policy-holders so that the sources of profit to the shareholders are virtually (a) favourable mortality experience, (b) certain taxation benefits and (c) any surplus of fixed fees over expenses. (Indeed the control of expenses in times of inflation can be one of the major items in determining a life company's results.) On the annual valuation of the life fund's assets and liabilities by the company's actuary, a surplus or deficiency will be disclosed. Only when any surplus has grown to a size when it can with safety be transferred to the general fund of the company, is it available for distribution to policy-holders by way of bonuses or to the shareholders as profit. In the long run the rewards can be considerable, but it is a long haul.

'Spin off' business

In the case of the banking groups, the advantage of being in the life assurance business, even to a limited degree, are not entirely those of direct profit. As we have seen, linked life assurance provides a source of investment into the bank unit trust groups, but also makes its contribution to the concept of total financial management. Approximately 70 per cent of all life assurance in this country is taken out by what is sometimes patronisingly called the artisan class. In a later chapter we shall consider the importance of the so-called socio-economic groupings in relation to bank marketing. The point at the moment is that a very large proportion of persons seeking, or being persuaded to accept, life assurance are not among the 25 million or so customers of the clearing banks. In many cases, therefore, on the sale of life assurance the banks have the opportunity of insisting on the payment of premiums by bankers' order which in turn usually results in the opening of a new account with their own bank. It is not necessarily profitable banking. It widens the net of the bank and perhaps there is something in the character of a proposer for life assurance that marks him out as a careful, prudent chap who over the years ought to make a responsible bank customer. There is also the point that if banks seek ways and means of consolidating customer relationships, there is much to be said for a life policy taken out with the banking group. By its nature, it fits well with the 'cradle to the grave' concept of bank services. It does not follow that 'where my life assurance is, there shall my bank account be also', but like executorship business, life assurance has that long-term quality which tends to keep the customer in the family.

The risks

What then are the risks to bank or customer? The normal 'risk' of life assurance, that is to say premature death, is oddly enough hardly a risk at all. So carefully and cautiously are the risks balanced by the actuary and so reliable is the record of human experience as expressed in the expectation of life tables that so-called mortality risk is more of a certainty than a risk. Not necessarily so, however, is the matter of investment risks. Even if all the lives assured come to an end obligingly in accordance with the tables, the amount payable on death (the sum assured) depends upon whether the investment performance of the invested premiums over the years has come up to the arithmetical expectations of the actuary. In times of catastrophic stock market performance, as in 1929 and 1973–74, the calculations are upset and in general the longer the life office has been established and the greater its reserves, the better it will be able to weather the storm. A well-managed life office will match its assets and liabilities and not enter into guarantees which it cannot keep.

The failure of a number of life assurance companies in the early 1970s arose not so much from disappointing investment performance, but from the failure of the companies to match their assets to their liabilities, both as to the quantum of those liabilities and the time scale. The sad story of guaranteed income bonds is outside the scope of this book, but it flowed almost entirely from the failure to match liabilities.

From a banker's point of view, there is also the risk of damage to customer relations if a policy taken out for investment purposes, and particularly a single premium policy, fails to come up to the customer's expectations. However cautious the advertisements and explanatory leaflets, if a customer has taken out a single premium policy with a bank group in expectation of a particular investment return and finds when he or she has to 'surrender' the policy for some particular purpose that their nest egg has diminished by two-thirds of its original value (which was in fact the case with some of the single premium policies taken out when the stock market was high in 1972), the cherished banker/customer relationship begins to look a bit dented. On balance, however, life assurance customers are satisfied customers. They have acquired a degree of security and protection and embarked on a worthwhile programme of saving. They may also have the consolation that although the insurance company or bank cannot be responsible for the vagaries of the stock market, it is extremely unlikely that any large banking group would stand aside, or be able to stand aside, and see its subsidiary life office fail to meet its obligations.

Banking and insurance

The two industries of banking and insurance are to a degree in competition with each other for personal savings. To the extent that banks were the traditional custodians of personal savings, we may say that the insurance companies have challenged the banks rather than the other way round. As we have seen, the banks' share of personal savings has decreased noticeably over the last twenty-five years, a period in which there has been a marked increase in the insurance companies' share of the savings market.

We may say that the points of similarity between banks and insurance companies are:

(a) They are both in the market for personal savings although, as we have said, insurance companies are in the longer-term savings market, whereas bank deposits are traditionally the home of short-term savings.

(b) In both cases those savings are 'invested' in government, industry or commerce whether through the traditional markets or, in the case of the banks, by way of overdrafts and loans.

(c) Both act as channels to direct personal savings into the commercial sector.

(d) The marketing skills and commercial judgments are similar, but not of course identical.

There are, however, essential differences between the functions of banks and insurance companies, viz:

(a) Life assurance saving is contractual: bank saving is *ad hoc*.

(b) Insurance contracts are long-term: bank deposits are repayable on demand or short notice.

(c) Insurance companies *invest* their premiums whereas banks *lend* a proportion of their deposits, the skill of the investor being different from that of the lender.

(d) The risk-taking decisions of insurance companies tend to be centralised: the risk-taking decisions of bankers are widely diffused.

We may care to reflect on the probability and desirability, or otherwise, of a major coming together of banking and insurance. Indeed this happened to a degree when in 1984 Standard Life Assurance Company acquired the significant shareholding, previously held by Barclays Bank in the Bank of Scotland. It is something which, at least in theory, could have happened during the bank merger period of the 1960s. It would still be legally possible in this country, but quite impossible under the antitrust laws in the United States. In fact, such a merger in this country could lead to difficulties for the associates in the United States of the merging bank and insurance company. Would it be politically acceptable in this country? Would such a merger be seen as such a concentration of financial power as to invoke political opposition, at least in some quarters? On the other hand, might the coming together of the banking and insurance functions help to simplify and rationalise the marketing of financial services in the High Street? Might it not also produce a better use of management resources? Might the concentration of financial resources facilitate both the investment and lending function in the development of capital projects at home and abroad? In a few words, might it conceivably lead to an integration of financial services in the market, an availability of resources for industry and, for the shareholder, a better return on resources employed? The questions are purely rhetorical.

References

1 'Linked Life Assurance': Report of the Committee on Property Bonds and Equity Linked Life Assurance (Chairman: Sir Hilary Scott), Cmnd 5281. HMSO, 1973.

2 HMSO, January 1982.
3 'Linked Life Assurance': Report of the Committee on Property Bonds and Equity Linked Life Assurance (Chairman: Sir Hilary Scott), Cmnd 5281. HMSO, 1973.
4 Insurance Companies Act 1974, s. 62(1).
5 Ibid, s. 63.
6 Ibid, s. 65.
7 Ibid, s. 66 and s. 67.
8 Ibid, s. 68.
9 'Review of Investor Protection': A Discussion Document by Professor L. C. B. Gower, HMSO, January 1982.
10 Michael Hepher, Money Observer, February 1986.

CHAPTER 9

Insurance Broking

In an article in the *Financial Times* on 15 March 1976, the insurance correspondent, Eric Short, wrote, 'Over the past few years insurance has come out of the shadows of several centuries. The public is now much better aware of how the industry functions. The insurance brokers – the middle men – are no longer the faceless men of old.'

We have already said that there are 9,000 or so insurance brokers in the United Kingdom. Whether or not they are 'faceless', as Mr Short says, is perhaps not very important. What is important is that the public are becoming more aware of insurance brokers and beginning to appreciate a little of the role they play in the business world. Insurance broking is not difficult to define. The broker's task is to meet the insurance needs of his client by obtaining cover in the market, having first researched the market to ascertain the most appropriate contract for the purpose. The 'most appropriate' is not necessarily the cheapest, although cost may well be a major factor. The good broker will look for the best all-round solution to his client's insurance needs and the answer may well lie in a combination of cost, the standing of the insurance company, past performance, flexibility and the customer's own subjective considerations.

It is perhaps anomalous that although the broker speaks of 'his client' and he is deemed to act for 'his client', he is paid by the insurance company with whom he does the business. There have been one or two attempts to change this situation, but it is a time-honoured custom in this country and one which is not likely to be changed easily.

The professional bodies

Until 1976 there were four insurance broking bodies in the United Kingdom – the Association of Insurance Brokers, the Corporation of Insurance Brokers, the Federation of Insurance Brokers and Lloyd's Insurance Brokers Association. Approximately 3,000 brokers were members of one or other of these associations, the remaining 6,000 not being members of any broking association. The insurance broking bodies were concerned in recent years about the ease with which anyone could profess to be an insurance broker, the carelessness of some brokers in dealing with the administrative aspects of insurance, certain unacceptable methods of selling insurance, the tendency of some brokers to place insurance where commission rates are highest and the general difficulty of applying any test of quality which the public could learn to understand and accept. In 1975 the Secretary of State for Trade invited the four principal insurance broking bodies to put forward proposals for supervision of the profession and this was done. The four bodies formed the British Insurance Brokers' Council (now the British Insurance Brokers' Association) as a step towards the formation of a professional institute, and the Council developed a dialogue with the Government, resulting in a number of developments to which we will refer in a moment.

We have said that it is easy to define an insurance broker, but it is not so easy to arrive at a definition which separates the men from the boys or the sheep from the goats. The European Economic Commission defines insurance brokers (in language characteristic of the Commission's directives) as:

> 'Persons who, acting with complete freedom as to their choice of undertaking, bring together, with a view to the insurance or re-insurance of risks, persons seeking insurance or re-insurance and insurance and re-insurance undertakings, carry out work preparatory to the conclusion of contracts of insurance or re-insurance and, where appropriate, assist in the administration and performance of such contracts, in particular in the event of a claim.'

Although the British Insurance Brokers' Council accepted this definition, it is difficult to see that it throws much light on the situation. One of the problems is that throughout insurance business there are a number of 'intermediaries' who place insurance on behalf of a client, but would not pass the test as a 'broker' because they would not have, nor claim to have, the skill of a broker; they would not in many cases have conducted any research in the market for the particular insurance in question and they would not undertake any administrative or negotiating responsibility on behalf of the client. In many cases, they would not have the 'freedom as to their choice of undertaking' mentioned in the EEC definition.

In the consultative document issued by the British Insurance Broker's Council in August 1976, the tripartite division of the insurance broking profession was described. The three broad areas are:

1. international insurance broking where brokers play a leading part in maintaining London's importance as the largest international insurance centre;

2. commercial insurance broking which consists mainly of servicing the insurance needs of industry and commerce in this country, a sophisticated area requiring great expertise; and

3. personal insurance broking—the great majority of smaller insurance broking firms or one-man businesses throughout the country seeking to meet the insurance needs of private individuals.

These broad areas are not mutually exclusive, nor is it always a matter of size. It is a loose functional division reflecting the historical development and varying skills of the different firms.

Lloyd's of London

There is another line of demarcation in the insurance broking profession. This is the one which is drawn very clearly between Lloyd's brokers and the rest. It is no doubt a matter of general knowledge that the world famous corporation of Lloyd's had its origin in Mr Lloyd's coffee house in 1688, and from that modest beginning over a period of 300 years Lloyd's has become the world centre for shipping insurance. It is often said that anything can be insured through Lloyds and although this is not true, it is very nearly so. The essential feature of Lloyd's is that, as in its earliest days, the insurance risk still rests on the individual underwriters personally. Membership of Lloyd's includes the

'From a modest beginning . . .'

underwriters who, as we have said, carry the insurance risk and the brokers who make the market. There are also brokers who are not members as such, but are subscribers. The underwriters cannot do business in the market place themselves. They rely entirely on the brokers who bring to them the insurance needs of their clients. The underwriters operate in syndicates specialising in one or other sector of the insurance market. A close understanding is developed between brokers and underwriters, the brokers with their world-wide network placing their clients' business with the underwriters depending on the nature of the risk. The risks covered at Lloyd's comprise virtually every type of insurance except life. All the major insurance brokers in this country are represented at Lloyd's.

Out of the 9,000 or so insurance brokers in this country, some 280 are Lloyd's brokers, i.e. they are members of the Lloyd's Insurance Brokers' Association. A Lloyd's broker does not place business exclusively with Lloyd's. It is his duty to his client to place the business on best terms in the market and a Lloyd's broker will often place business with insurance companies in this country or overseas.

A widespread business

The top two dozen or so insurance broking companies account for nearly 60 per cent of the total broking market, but the remaining business is well spread. Insurance brokers as a whole deal with approximately one-half of all non-life insurance business in the United Kingdom, between 30 per cent and 50 per cent of life business and up to 90 per cent of pensions business. On a rough approximation, it is thought that the value of premium income of all the insurers in this country, including Lloyd's is approximately £33,000 million, of which insurance brokers produce over one half.[1] Insurance broking in total is big business.

One may say also that insurance broking is a socially desirable business. If insurance brokers did not exist, they would have to be created. How else could the uninitiated seeking to cover an insurable risk find his way through the maze of insurance possibilities on the market or indeed, in many cases, know where to start. Of course there are the good and the bad. A major

London broker placing a multi-million pound insurance contract with underwriters throughout the world displays a professionalism unsurpassed in other walks of life. At the other end of the scale, there are those whose main concern is a quick commission, who are not qualified even by experience and who are no more than intermediaries between one or two insurance companies and the public.

The banks' involvement

Let us come then to the involvement of the clearing banks in the business of insurance broking. As with many other services described here, insurance broking has little if anything to do with banking. However generous one might be in the definition of the banking function, it would not include the placing of insurance business. Like most of the newer services it was a banking appendage. The move of the clearing banks into insurance broking is a feature of the last twenty years or so. Nevertheless, it was not unknown before that. If one looks outside the United Kingdom, the placing of insurance for customers was probably one of the oldest of the banking-related services. For example, many years ago some of the constituent banks of Barclays DCO had their own insurance departments; the National Bank of South Africa placed insurance business with Bray Gibb & Co. (now Stewart Wrightson), the Colonial Bank placed business with Sedgwick Forbes and the Anglo Egyptian Bank placed customers' insurance through the Marine Insurance Company (subsequently part of the Royal Insurance Group). When the three banks amalgamated to form Barclays Bank (Dominion, Colonial & Overseas) in 1925, an insurance department was set up under the head office inspector, later to become the insurance manager. The department was not a broker as we know the term today, but was an intermediary for the placing of insurance in connection with financial operations conducted by the bank on behalf of customers. Marine insurance would include rice, wheat and grain cargoes and apparently the 'ship of the desert' was not excluded because insurance was taken out regularly for approximately £1½ million of silver which crossed the Sudan every month on the backs of camels. It was the proud boast in those days that the bank 'never lost a shilling', which means no doubt that the insurers also lost nothing. Other contracts also placed with the Marine Insurance Company included the entire tin ore production of West Africa from the moment of its mining until its arrival at Liverpool. Insurance contracts for gold, diamonds, ground nuts, growing crops and wool on sheeps' backs were all placed by the old insurance department.

Coming nearer home it was the National Westminster Bank which first moved in a major way into insurance broking in this country. Before the merger, the Westminster Bank had been operating a small insurance department since 1928, which was expanded in 1961/62 when the decision was taken to discontinue managers' agencies. Thereafter, this department developed rapidly and acquired corporate status in 1973 with the formation of the present insurance broking company, National Westminster Insurance Services.

In February 1970, Barclays Bank, which had not hitherto had an insurance department in this country, announced the formation of Barclays Insurance Services Company to 'act as brokers to the Group for all classes of insurance business'. Six years later Barclays Bank formed an additional company, a Lloyd's broking subsidiary, Barclays Insurance Brokers International, in order to place business for their customers with Lloyd's.

In 1971, Lloyds Bank set up its own centralised insurance department to provide 'a comprehensive insurance advisory service for its customers', but a few years later, in December 1977, followed the pattern of the other clearers in establishing a separate company, Lloyds Bank Insurance Services.

In 1971, Williams & Glyn's Bank (now Royal Bank Group) incorporated a new wholly owned subsidiary, Williams & Glyn's Insurance Consultants, 'to provide insurance consultancy services and insurance broking' and in November 1972 the Midland Bank entered the field with its subsidiary, Midland Bank Insurance Services. In Scotland, the three clearing banks, Bank of Scotland, Royal Bank of Scotland and Clydesdale Bank all now have insurance broking operations.

In December 1979, Midland Bank announced the extension of its insurance broking services through a new subsidiary company catering for the bank's corporate customers. This company, Midland Bank Insurance Brokers Limited became a Lloyd's broker.

Although the banks' share of total insurance broking business is still small, it has become increasingly significant. In terms of brokerage income earned, the total figure for the English and Scottish banks is now believed to be of the order of £100 million per annum. Through their retail banking outlets, the banks have considerable opportunity for the development of personal insurance business and this has applied particularly to the life side. In 1980, the *Financial Times* estimated that National Westminster Bank Insurance Services Limited handled more life assurance business than any other single broking firm.

The reasons why

It is interesting to reflect on the reasons advanced at the time for the banks' entry into the broking field. Those who know the ways of the British banks will not be surprised that it was not a quick, greedy decision to snatch a profit from some new enterprise to the detriment of others in the field. The prospect of a direct and overt profit seems to have been low down in the banks' thinking and in at least one bank the tentative suggestion of 'profit' was described as 'the cream on the cake'. Not surprisingly, however, the banks were thinking along similar lines and there were one or two common themes running through the deliberations of the time which together made up the rationale of the banks' decisions.

First, it was generally accepted that to set up a broking department or subsidiary company was a natural extension of the existing arrangements whereby bank managers placed insurance on behalf of customers.

Secondly, in most banks the branch managers were accustomed to retaining all or part of the commissions earned on customer insurances and the opportunity was seen for dispensing with this custom. It no doubt had its origin in country banking of former days when a local solicitor or other professional man would be the 'Agent' for the bank and agent for various insurance companies, as well as attending to his professional duties. Whatever the history of the matter, it was certainly an anomalous situation. It was perhaps the only instance where the bank manager, in the bank's time and in some cases using bank staff, could conduct what amounted to his own private business – and in a number of cases, particularly in the North of England, the annual commissions received by the manager exceeded his bank salary. It made it difficult to promote a man to another area and resulted in wide disparities of total remuneration quite unrelated to the purely banking duties. When the new departments or subsidiaries were set up, the agencies of the managers were acquired on the basis of one year's purchase of the annual commissions or some similar arrangement.

Thirdly, it was realised that to the extent that managers were selling insurance, they were acting in a professional field without having the necessary professional knowledge. No doubt in Westminster Bank the setting up of their insurance department helped to remedy this situation by providing a central source of advice and information. As financial life became more complicated, it must have been increasingly difficult for managers without central guidance to exercise a proper advisory role in matters of insurance.

Fourthly, there was perhaps an undefined awareness that the selling of insurance fitted in nicely with the marketing of other bank services. Mr Randle Manwaring, former Vice-Chairman, Midland Bank Insurance Services, has said that apart from a man's income 'the two most basic financial requirements of the individual are a bank account and some form of insurance cover'.[2] Certainly from a marketing point of view the two go nicely together. The bank manager is accustomed to talking with his customers about their personal financial affairs and the subject of insurance is a natural one to be raised, whether by customer or manager. In any case it is, as we have said above, a service which most managers were already accustomed to selling.

There were those, of course, who saw insurance broking as part of the concept of total financial management – another item on the shelf of the financial supermarket. (The author recalls that the corporate plan for the formation of Martins Bank Trust Company, designed to be a financial services conglomerate, included provision for insurance broking.) Perhaps, therefore, it does the banks an injustice to suggest that they did not necessarily see themselves embarking on the full-blooded business of insurance broking in all its aspects. In 1974, speaking at the World Insurance Conference, the author referred to the situation by saying that 'the banks espoused the business of broking partly in order to rationalise what was already happening and partly to augment their very comprehensive range of financial services. There was no particular wish to become "the biggest", no thought of putting anybody out of business, no desire to corner the market or to do other than take their place in a modest way in a highly respected profession.' These words which others have been kind enough to quote were probably an over-statement of the banks' intentions. It is doubtful whether they saw themselves as entering a new profession as such. But that in fact is what has happened. The banks are now in the business of broking in a big way and are well on the road to becoming among 'the biggest'.

All this could not easily have been foreseen at the time the decisions were taken. Barclays Bank, for example, in setting up Barclays Insurance Services Company for the domestic market, did not necessarily contemplate that within a few years they would be initiating their own firm of Lloyd's brokers, Barclays Insurance Brokers International, taking their group broking activities into a new dimension both at home and abroad. Even less could Midland Bank have realised in setting up their broking company that in due time, through the acquisition of Samuel Montagu, they would acquire the very large broking firm of Bland Payne. In January 1979, Midland Bank announced the sale of its interests in Bland Payne to Sedgwick Forbes, a merger which resulted in the Sedgwick Forbes Group becoming the largest insurance broking operation in the UK.

Some criticisms

The entry of the banks into insurance broking was not received with general acclaim. Although the larger broking companies did not see it as any sort of threat to their business, the smaller and medium-sized firms naturally expressed concern at this new competition. The banks have facilities which smaller and more local organisations can never have. They have vast branch networks, occupy prime positions in the towns, they have central resources for research and information and, at local level, an unequalled opportunity for meeting the public for discussion of financial matters. Nevertheless, there is one aspect which could well favour the smaller professional broker. We have said that personal insurance, as distinct from commercial insurance, has not traditionally been placed to a large extent through brokers. Personal insurance has been sold predominantly through the insurance companies' own branch offices and their sales representatives. It has also been sold through intermediaries, including solicitors, accountants, garages, estate agents and building societies, and the industrial life companies have sold most of their business through their 'home service' agents. Banks, too, of course, were among the intermediaries selling personal insurance, particularly life assurance. The change on the banks' part from 'intermediary' to 'broker' merely switches the statistics from one column to another, but the very considerable increase in insurance broking business among the banks does mean that far more personal insurance is now coming through the broking sector and, perhaps more important, the public are becoming more aware of the role of insurance brokers, which in turn should lead to increased business all round.

Criticism of the banks came in one or two unexpected ways. One anonymous writer in the *Policyholder Insurance Journal* suggested that 'The trouble seems to be that they (the banks) were not able or willing to equip themselves with strong enough-false teeth to chew what they hoped to bite off!'[3] The complaint was that the service from the banks was inefficient and that in many cases the banks were leaving it to the insurance companies to handle many of the details which in the ordinary way would be done by the broker. There may have been grounds for this type of criticism and inevitably in the early days of the banks' broking activities there were teething troubles. Today, however, the banks pride themselves on having very substantial broking organisations with extensive facilities, management in depth and the ability to provide a speedy and efficient service throughout the country.

Another, at first surprising, criticism of the banks was that they would use their knowledge of their customers' affairs to attract business from existing broking connections. One suggestion was that the banks examined the standing orders of their customers to identify existing insurance contracts so as to offer alternative policies, or at least a switch of the existing ones to the banks' agencies. There may have been such cases of over-enthusiasm on the part of individual managers, but in general it was made clear by the banks that their branches were not to take advantage of their special position to the detriment of other brokers, many of whom were in any case good friends and customers of the banks.

Another criticism was that banks would make the granting of overdraft facilities conditional on the taking out of life assurance, and indeed other insurances, through the bank. No such pressure would be permitted. The question of insurance may often arise in the course of negotiations for a banking facility, but the customer is absolutely free to place his insurance business as he pleases. Fortunately, most bank managers cherish the traditional banker/customer relationship too much to risk offence by an over-weaning ambition to build up their insurance book.

These last two criticisms and the suggestion that bank insurance salesmen had access to customers' confidential records were brought to the notice of the Director of Fair Trading, who had discussions with the banks on the subject. The banks confirmed that they did not approve of their staff making the granting of a loan or overdraft conditional on the placing of related insurance business and they repudiated the suggestion that customers' standing orders relating to insurance business were withheld in the hope of switching the business to the banks' insurance subsidiary. The banks also confirmed that they had given instructions to the effect that their salesmen must not have access to privileged financial information in customers' records. The Director of Fair Trading emphasised that any such instances of unfair practice appeared to have been very few and largely inadvertent.

Customer attitudes

As for the customers of the banks, they appear to have welcomed the new broking services in so far as they have noticed at all this further extension of banking activity. They may not know what an insurance broker does and they may not think of the banks in that role, but if they have an insurance problem they no doubt find it convenient to raise it on the occasion of the next visit to the local branch. If customers see their banks as solvers of financial problems, the banks no doubt like it that way. Nevertheless, as recently as 1984 it was estimated that only between 5 per cent and 10 per cent of bank customers used their banks' insurance services.

In varying degrees, the banks are now engaged in virtually every aspect of insurance broking. On the personal side, life business has tended to predominate partly because branch managers were accustomed to selling life assurance and partly no doubt because, as a vehicle for savings and investment, it is a kindred activity to the banks' more traditional roles. In the section on life assurance, we have listed the various forms of life contract and all these are undertaken by the banks' broking departments or companies.

The leading banks claim that there is no insurance that they will not place, including marine, aviation, fire, theft, motor, fidelity, public liability, livestock, insurance against the weather and insurance against the birth of twins.

Some of the major commercial contracts, particularly those of a specialist nature or involving an international spread of insurance, might be placed through the banks' Lloyd's broking subsidiaries. The rest will be handled in the centralised insurance departments, on the introduction of the local bank branches. Some of the simpler everyday insurance arrangements are handled on the spot at the bank branch. In this category a number of 'pad' schemes (so called because the branch will have a pad of application forms) are arranged by individual banks with particular insurance companies, or for such purposes as travel insurance and household insurance. Such package schemes cannot necessarily provide the best terms available on the market at a given time. The essence of the schemes is their simplicity and accessibility. On the whole, such schemes have not been popular and may not in all cases be continued. It must be acknowledged that the banks have everything in their favour when negotiating group schemes in matters of everyday insurance. Like any other broker, they can find the best rates available, but then can usually negotiate attractive discounts for particular schemes because of a very considerable market of customers which the banks command.

The market

The market for insurance is considerable. In the previous chapter we have referred to the life assurance market and now for a moment we can look at the total market for insurance in all its forms. In one sense, of course, it is unlimited because as life goes on new ventures are undertaken, new possessions acquired, new risks arise and new lives come into being. The British insurance market also enjoys the special position that the world is its market. The domestic market consists of every home and every business in the country. It is often said that most people are underinsured and, taking all insurance needs into account, this is probably true. The number of life policies in force in the United Kingdom at the end of 1986 was:

	m.
ordinary life assurance	24·5
industrial life assurance	61·2
linked life assurance	9·5
	95·2

[Source: The Association of British Insurers]

Just over half the householders in the United Kingdom are owner-ocupiers, the great majority buying their houses on building society or bank mortgages for which insurance would be compulsory, but it is estimated that one-tenth of all owners do not have any insurance on the fabric of their properties. Even more remarkable is the fact that approximately 40 per cent of householders do not have any insurance on the contents of their properties.

The market for motor insurance has grown with the increased number of cars on the road – the average number of new vehicle registrations is over 1½ million each year.

The market for insurance broking is *ipso facto* the market for insurance, with the proviso that the market for each individual broker is that part of the whole for which he has the expertise to give advice and the facilities to provide service. For the most part, it is an uninformed market. People do not know much about insurance, they are not always aware of the risks against which they may insure, they are not familiar with the choices open to them and they do not understand the small print. None of this will be remedied by high-pressure selling. What is needed is education (as indeed in most financial matters) and the insurance broking profession can play a valuable part in that. The broker has a responsiblity to the insurance companies whose products he sells, because if he sells the wrong policy or fails in some way to service his client's needs it is usually the insurance company which comes into disrepute in the eyes of the client. The broker also has very clearly a responsibility to his client in the quality of the advice he gives, in the administration of the contract and the handling of any claim.

The market for the banks' insurance broking activities is primarily, as with many bank services, the existing customers of each bank. Again, as with most services, the focal point of the marketing effort is the local branch. The marketing methods include the distribution of explanatory leaflets, displays and presentations in the bank branches, discussions with customers as opportunity permits, and in support of all that a certain amount of advertising. The successful marketing effort that has been made along these lines is reflected in the considerable growth of the banks' broking business in only a few years.

Profitability

The remuneration of an insurance broker comes primarily from commissions on the policies he sells. Lloyd's brokers also receive management fees from the syndicates for whom they act. The large broking companies also have substantial investment income and fees from sources outside their main broking activities. The profits from broking vary enormously from the one-man broker who ekes out a modest living to the very considerable profits of the big companies. Even the very large companies suffered from the difficult climate of the 1970s and profits were badly affected, partly because of exchange rate losses, partly because of rising costs, and perhaps most of all from the overcapacity which leads to intense competition in the international insurance markets. In more recent years however, there has been an improvement in profitability and the banks' insurance broking subsidiaries have made satisfactory but not dramatic contributions to group profits.

Overall, the growth in life business has continued and after a slightly sluggish period in 1977, new annual life assurance business in terms of premium income has continued to show a renewed upsurge. This trend has been augmented in recent times by the boom in pensions business. The banks' involvement in pensions services is discussed in Chapters 8 and 19. Suffice to say here that after a period of some years when pensions were a political football, the Social Security Pensions Act reached the Statute Book in 1975. The main effect of the Act is that with effect from April 1978 all employees were covered automatically by the government pension schemes unless they had been contracted out and covered by the occupational pension scheme of their own employer. It has been estimated that approximately two-thirds of all the pension schemes in the country are insurance based, which means that the contributions paid by employer and employees are paid to an insurance company as premiums to provide pensions and a degree of life cover for the employees of that company. The remaining one-third of pension schemes are self-administered, funded schemes usually run by the companies themselves, the investments being held by trustees. It was perhaps natural that some of the life offices and specialist insurance brokers developed an expertise in pensions matters and some life offices, apart from offering insured schemes, also operate funded schemes for their company clients. The new legislation required careful examination of the pros and cons of contracting out of the government scheme. This resulted in an enormous demand for the consultancy services of life assurance brokers with a considerable upsurge in new business. To some extent the bank broking subsidiaries shared in this. Now, with the passing of the Social Security Act 1986 there will be increased opportunities for the sale of pension plans to those who prefer personal pensions to occupational schemes.

Recent years have been a time of great change for the insurance broking profession, partly because of the advent of the banks as competitors, partly because of the new commission structure, partly because of the flurry of pensions business and partly because of the emphasis on consumerism and 'fair trading' throughout the whole of business life. We have already referred to the Consultative Document issued by the British Insurance Brokers' Council in 1976 in response to an invitation from the Secretary of State for Trade who asked the four insurance brokers' organisations to consider possible arrangements for a self-regulatory body to determine standards for brokers, to draw up a code of conduct and consider arrangements for controlling admission to the profession and maintaining discipline. The subsequent discussions culminated in the Insurance Brokers (Registration) Bill introduced by Mr John Page, MP, and supported by the government. The Bill became law on 29 July 1977. In broad outline the Act provides for the establishment of self-regulatory arrangements within the profession under the Insurance Brokers' Registration Council which was set up on 1 December 1977. Under the Act, the Council is required to maintain a register of insurance brokers and lays down the broad qualifications which the Council shall accept for registration. The Council is charged with the task of drawing up a code of conduct for insurance brokers and laying down the financial requirements to be met by registered brokers. The Council is also required to set up a disciplinary committee to regulate the conduct of registered members and to have powers of erasing names from or restoring names to the register. Perhaps the most sweeping provision is that the Act provides for legal penalties against anyone who, not being registered under the Act, or any corporation which, not being enrolled under the Act, uses the style, title or description of 'insurance broker' or other related description.[4] Although the Act also confers powers on the Council to regulate the educational requirements and qualifying examinations of insurance brokers, it makes wide provision for the registration of those who are qualified by experience.

As mentioned on page 194, the British Insurance Brokers' Council became the British Insurance Brokers' Association, which is now the regulatory body for insurance brokers in the

United Kingdom. Under their aegis, the new regulations required by the Act came into force on 1st December 1981.

Thus in a swift and comparatively painless way, the profession of insurance broker moved into a new dimension. The coming together of the four professional bodies in the compilation of the Consultative Document and the excellent presentation of that document won the confidence of the Government and Parliament, and secured for the profession the right to regulate its own affairs with what would appear to be just enough statutory backing.

Nevertheless there were problems. The Act provides for two levels of registration, viz. insurance brokers as individuals and insurance brokers as businesses. Any person of the right experience and integrity may register as a broker and by 1985 the British Insurance Brokers Association represented over 3,700 companies and offices employing some 55,000 staff. Registration does little more, however, than confer a professional status on the person registered. For a business to be registered, it must be run by a registered broker or brokers, it must satisfy the capital requirements of the Act, it must separate the firm's money from clients' money and it must take out the statutory minimum professional indemnity insurance, viz. a minimum of £250,000 or three times the commission income of the business in the last accounting period (up to a maximum of £7·5 million), whichever is the greater. So far, a large number of smaller firms and sole proprietorships have not registered their businesses as insurance brokers, either because they cannot satisfy the requirements of the Act or, more probably, they prefer to remain independent. In that case, they may not describe their business as 'insurance brokers' and thus the term 'insurance consultants' came into wider use.

The Financial Services Act 1986

The Financial Services Act and the Regulations under that Act are dealt with in broad outline in the Appendix. Under Section 22 of the Act, any body which is authorised under Sections 3 or 4 of the Insurance Companies Act 1982 to carry on insurance business which is deemed to be investment business is an authorised person for the purpose of the Act in relation to that investment business. The Act defines investment business in wide terms and includes those life assurance policies which are written for investment purposes as distinct from those policies which are issued to cover specific risks, e.g. whole life policies, certain term insurances, accident and sickness policies. Insurance companies remain subject to the prudential supervision of the Department of Trade & Industry, but they come within the Financial Services Act in relation to the marketing of their policies and the management and marketing of pension funds. The appropriate self-regulating organisation is the Life Assurance & Unit Trust Regulatory Organisation (LAUTRO).

For insurance brokers the appropriate self-regulating organisation is the Financial Intermediaries, Managers & Brokers Regulatory Association (FIMBRA) in relation to those categories of insurance which fall within the definition of investment business. As regards the broad range of general insurance business, the British Insurance Brokers' Association remains the regulatory body for insurance brokers in the United Kingdom under The Insurance Brokers (Registration) Act of 1977. As regards, however, insurance business of an investment nature, brokers must conform to the requirements of the Securities & Investments Board as delegated to their self-regulating organisation LAUTRO.

A particular problem area for banks and building societies arose from what came to be known as 'polarisation'. The Rules of the Securities & Investments Board require that any person engaged in the marketing of unit trusts and life assurance policies must do so in one of two capacities, i.e. as an independent advisor or as a representative of a particular company or group. The Board considered that if persons engaged in investment business could act in both capacities, the investor would be confused as to the true nature of the service offered. The impact of this rule has been considerable for banks, building societies, brokers and intermediaries. It has meant, for example, that a bank branch cannot act in the role of advisor to a customer whilst being a representative of the bank for the purpose of selling in-house products. The matter is discussed in more detail in the Appendix. One particular effect of this dichotomy is that the insurance broking role of banks in relation to life assurance and pension business is divorced more sharply from the branch role of company representative in those banks which have chosen to go along the company representative route. There the matter rests.

References

1 Evidence of The British Insurance Brokers' Association to the Wilson Committee and Association of British Insurers.
2 R. Manwaring: 'Insurance and Banking: two sides of the same coin'. *The Banker*, March 1977.
3 *Policyholder Insurance Journal* 4, February 1977.
4 Insurance Brokers (Registration) Act 1977, s. 22.

CHAPTER 10

Credit Cards

If an American shopping in Harrods presents a Visa credit card for a substantial purchase the store will telephone Barclaycard at Northampton who will in turn contact the Visa Centre in California by means of a permanent transatlantic link. A computer in San Mateo will, if necessary, check the customer's credit rating with the bank that issued the card, which could for example be in Chicago. It is the proud claim of the Visa Group that the entire process, whilst Harrods wait on the line for an answer, takes but seven seconds. It is a telling commentary, not only on the universality of the modern credit card system but on the advanced electronic network which supports it.

The development of the credit card is probably the most significant phenomenon of the modern banking scene. It embodies two essential aspects of a basic banking function – the transmission of payments and the granting of credit. It is such a departure, however, from traditional banking that it merits a separate place in any survey of banking services.

Early developments

Mr Frank Snushall, the former Head of Barclaycard, has pointed out that the first credit card of a kind was introduced by the Provident Clothing Group in this country in the 1880s.[1] It was the earliest 'check trading' scheme – customers were issued with vouchers which they could use at shops on the approved list and payment for the vouchers was made on a weekly instalment basis to the Provident Clothing representative who called at the customer's home. It was the forerunner of credit cards in two

'. . . an American shopping in Harrods.'

respects, in that payment was made by a voucher and the customer enjoyed the benefit of revolving credit.

It was in the United States, however, that the credit card as we know it today was developed. In the early days of the century some of the American department stores issued credit coins or tokens which enabled customers to pay for goods, and the oil companies introduced 'courtesy cards' to be honoured at their gasoline stations. To this day, the largest issuers of credit cards are the retail stores in North America. A few years ago, it was estimated that out of 600 million credit cards in use in the United States, 85 per cent were issued by non-banking groups. Indeed Sears, Roebuck are believed to have issued no less than 60 million of their own cards. These cards differ from the bank cards in that their use is usually limited to purchases from the store issuing the card and associated stores. Mr John Biggins of the Flatbush National Bank, New York, is credited with introducing the bank credit card. Under his 'Charge-It' plan, the credit for retail purchases was provided by the bank. That was in 1946 and in the next few years cards were introduced by The Diner's Club, American Express and Carte Blanche. These were primarily for travel and entertainment purposes and became known as 'T and E' cards. They were a method of payment rather than a source of credit and did not provide a credit limit as such.

The first bank credit card as we know it today was issued by Franklin National Bank in 1952 and numerous bank cards were issued in the following years. The Bank of America issued Bank Americard in 1958 and eight years later, in 1966, the banks comprising the Western States Bankcard Association issued the Mastercharge Card. Bank Americard and Mastercharge became the focal points for the eventual groupings of all bank cards throughout the world. Today, the Visa card is issued by approximately 9,000 banks throughout the world and a slightly larger number of banks issue the Mastercard. There are now about 250 million cardholders from these two groups.

In the United Kingdom, there are three categories of cards associated with the clearing banks. These are (a) travel and entertainment cards, (b) cheque cards and (c) credit cards. (Cash dispenser cards are in a different category, being *debit* cards rather than credit cards. There is an increasing tendency for one card to serve as a cheque guarantee card and a cash dispenser card. This is discussed in more detail in Chapter 23.)

Travel and entertainment cards

In the first category, as aready mentioned, The Diner's Club card was the first to appear in America and was introduced to Great Britain in 1951, a year after its launch in America. In 1965, the then Westminster Bank took a minority shareholding in The Diner's Club in the UK, increasing this holding to 47·8 per cent of the equity in the following year. Thus, Westminster Bank, now National Westminster Bank, became the only British bank with a significant interest in a travel and entertainment card as such. Ultimately, it held 49·7 per cent of the UK based operations of The Diner's Club. The American parent, Diner's Club Inc., is now owned by Citicorp.

American Express opened offices in England in 1963 and a few years later entered into an arrangement for the promotion of its cards through Lloyds Bank and Martins Bank, but this move was overtaken by and overshadowed by the subsequent development of card business among the clearing banks. It is interesting that ten years later American Express had 4·8 million cardholders around the world generating over $4,000 million of business per annum. The number of cardholders was doubling every two years or so, but nevertheless the 'T and E' cards were not destined to grow at the rate of bank credit cards as such in this country, and at the time of writing The Diner's Club has approximately 250,000 UK cardholders and American Express has approximately 1 million. A charge is normally made for travel and entertainment cards.

Cheque cards

The second category of card is the cheque card. The purpose of a bank cheque card is, in effect, to guarantee payment of a cheque within prescribed limits, whether presented for cash at a branch of the paying bank or to a trader for goods or services. The first cheque card was introduced by National Provincial Bank in October 1965, guaranteeing payment of cheques up to £30. In March the following year Midland Bank introduced their cheque card, and in the following month Lloyds Bank,

Martins Bank, Williams Deacon's Bank, National Bank, Yorkshire Bank, Glyn Mills & Co., Lewis's Bank, Bank of Scotland, Royal Bank of Scotland, National Commercial Bank of Scotland, Bank of Ireland and Hibernian Bank, representing in all 4,600 branches, issued their joint 'Bankers' Card', similarly guaranteeing payment of cheques up to £30. In 1969, it was estimated that 1 million cheque cards were in use in Great Britain. With the merger of Barclays Bank and Martins Bank that year, the Bankers' Card was withdrawn from the former Martins Bank customers (Barclays Bank having already issued their Barclaycard, although at that stage this was not a cheque card).

An inevitable corollary of the cheque card's arrival was the reluctance of traders to accept cheques without a supporting card. To many this seemed a backward step, particularly as in pre-merger days there had been only eleven clearing banks all of whose cheques were familiar pieces of paper in the UK, and whose 10 million or so customers operated their accounts very satisfactorily. It was suggested in *The Banker* that:

> 'The decline in the cheque's acceptability is in part connected with the growing number of people with bank accounts. Until fairly recently, banks served a rather privileged section of the community – the same section as, rightly or wrongly, shopkeepers deferentially expected to be honest. The extension of the market has been accompanied by an increase of dud cheques and a greater degree of suspicion on the part of shopkeepers.'[2]

For a few years after the re-alignment of the banks in the post-merger period, only Barclays Bank operated without a cheque card as such. This led to the strange but perhaps predictable result that some traders refused to accept Barclays Bank cheques. As a result, Barclays Bank arranged for Barclaycards to serve the dual role of credit card and cheque card, and thus nowadays cheque cards are available in support of cheques issued by all the British clearing banks. The limit of the 'guarantee' is £100 for cash withdrawals from Barclays branches and £50 for cash withdrawals at other banks or for the purchase of goods and services. By the end of 1976, there were nearly 9,500,000 cheque cards in issue in the United Kingdom, including Barclaycards. In more recent times, Barclaycard announced the introduction of a cash advance service, which enables cardholders to draw cash up to £100 a day at any one of the approximately 70,000 branches of banks belonging to the Visa International scheme, and Access banks have introduced similar arrangements.

Credit cards

The third category of card, and our main subject of discussion in this chapter, is the credit card. The first bank credit card issued in Great Britain was Barclaycard, launched in 1966 in co-operation with Bank Americard. Commenting on the development, as Chairman of Barclays Bank that year, Sir John Thomson said of Barclaycard:

> 'We look upon this as a natural extension of ordinary banking facilities. For a long time we have had the cheque; more recently the credit transfer; and now we have the Barclaycard as a convenient and easy way for the everyday shopper to make his payments for all kinds of goods and services without the use of cash. We particularly want the use of the Card to be widespread throughout all sections of the community.'

By 1972, six years later, Barclaycard had over 1·7 million cardholders and 52,000 merchant outlets. That same year the other leading banks announced the introduction of the Access Card. The original sponsors were National Westminster Bank, Midland Bank and Lloyds Bank. Together the three banks promoted the Joint Credit Card Company, in which they share the equity. Before the launch, Williams and Glyn's Bank, Clydesdale Bank, Northern Bank, Ulster Bank and Royal Bank of Scotland joined in the scheme. Within the first year, Access had 3·3 million cardholders and 65,000 merchant outlets. The following year, 1973, the group negotiated an agreement with Eurocard (a travel and entertainment card) which gave a link with a further 60,000 shops, hotels and restaurants throughout Europe. The truly international nature of the card was established with effect from March 1975 when Access became a member of the Interbank Card Association (now Mastercard) with, then, 32 million cardholders around the world.

At the present time, there are just over 5 million Barclaycard holders (including those who use Barclaycard as a cheque card only) and nearly 5·5 million Access cardholders.

There are three quite distinct parties to a credit card operation and it may help if we consider these in turn. They are the cardholder, the merchant and the bank or other card-issuing organisation.

Credit cardholders

Any credit-worthy adult may be a credit cardholder. In Britain, he or she will tend to be a middle class person who probably, but not necessarily, has a banking account already. In fact, between 70 per cent and 80 per cent of Access and Barclaycard holders are believed to be in the A B and C1 socio-economic groups.[3] Over 80 per cent of the adult population do not possess a credit card and among people with incomes of £5,000 or over, approximately half of them possess a credit card. Approximately 70 per cent of all Access and Barclaycard holders are between twenty-five and fifty-five years of age and in each case, over half of the cardholders live in London or the south-east of England.[4]

When a person applies for a credit card, he will be asked to supply details of his financial circumstances and, subject to satisfactory references, he will be given a card with an appropriate credit limit. Some limits, for example in the case of student cardholders, are very small, but very substantial limits may be allowed for cardholders of considerable personal means. Many cardholders will have applied for a card not in order to obtain credit as such, as a means of postponing payment for goods, but in order to have the convenience of a card as a method of payment as an alternative to cash or cheques. In the early days of credit cards in this country one of the major banks reported that the majority of cardholders 'continue to settle their accounts monthly' and were not availing themselves of continuing credit. In more recent times, however, another major group has estimated that about 70 per cent of its cardholders use their cards as a means of obtaining instalment credit.

There is in any case an element of free credit granted to cardholders because (a) accounts are sent out monthly covering purchases of goods or services since the last monthly statement and (b) the cardholder is allowed twenty-five days from the date of his monthly statement in which to settle the outstanding amount. It follows that if a cardholder's statement is normally sent out on, say, the 15th of the month, any purchases he makes on the 16th of the month could carry the benefit of fifty-five days' free credit.

The advantages to a cardholder under the credit card system may be summarised thus:

1. A card is a convenient method of payment as an alternative to cash or cheques. It is simple to operate, convenient to carry and reasonably immune to financial loss compared with losing cash or a cheque book.

2. It is a convenient source of credit if desired, involving no formalities and no 'headmaster' type meeting with the bank manager. Owing to the revolving nature of the credit, the customer can take advantage of it as and when he pleases within, of course, the overall limit.

3. Because all monthly purchases are covered by one payment, the activity on the customer's banking account is considerably reduced with possible savings in commission charges.

4. It is an aid to budgeting because the cardholder can pay a fixed amount each month according to his circumstances, and plan accordingly.

5. The monthly statements in narrative form are a great help to domestic and even business bookkeeping.

6. The acceptability of the leading cards in so many countries of the world is an aid to business and holiday travel.

7. Under the Consumer Credit Act 1974 (s. 75) the credit card companies may be held jointly and severally liable with the supplier in respect of defects in goods purchased on credit cards where the purchase price exceeds £30 and is not more than £15,000. This added protection is available to those who became cardholders after the relevant section of the Act came into force on 1 July 1977.

Notwithstanding these very real advantages of the credit card system and the fact that cards are widely held, it has been estimated that only about 4 per cent of retail sales in this country are financed by the use of credit cards. The typical credit cardholder uses his card on average about fourteen times a year and the average purchase is still believed to be quite small. i.e. approximately £25 per transaction. Thus there continues to be great scope for the credit card issuing houses to encourage the greater use of the cards already in issue.

It is no doubt inevitable that a large number of cards get lost and some stolen. If the finder or thief uses the card fraudulently, the cardholder may be held responsible for the first £25 of loss up to the time that he reports the circumstances to the card company. The machinery within the card companies for dealing with the fraudulent use of cards is very impressive, but the risks are considerable, as discussed below.

The merchants

The second 'party' to the credit card transaction is the merchant. There are approximately 250,000 merchant outlets in the United Kingdom who accept credit cards in payment for their goods or services. From the merchants' point of view, there are a number of advantages in operating a credit card system:

1. By accepting a credit card, the merchant has a guarantee of payment and his account is immediately credited with the cleared funds on payment of the vouchers into his bank.

2. He can use the card system as an alternative to other means of allowing credit and thus avoid bad debts.

3. The acceptance of a card in lieu of cash reduces the security risk.

4. A merchant who accepts credit cards may expect to increase his turnover, as more and more people accept the practical advantages of credit cards and turn to those traders who will accept cards in settlement.

5. A credit card system permits the merchant to offer his customers the facility of taking credit without involving himself in the expense, administration or risk of setting up his own credit arrangements.

6. The merchant is able to expand his business to include overseas visitors.

7. He will also have the support of the credit card company in advertising campaigns and other promotional activities.

8. The credit card record of purchases is a convenience for bookkeeping.

Each retailer will be given by the card company an agreed 'floor limit' up to which he may accept customers' cards at his own discretion. Beyond that, he must telephone one of the principal card centres where a twenty-four-hour service is operated, to confirm whether or not a card may be accepted for a particular purchase.

The cardholder does not pay a fee for his card, but the merchant will pay a service charge of up to 5 per cent on his credit card turnover. The average charge is about 2½ per cent.

The level of charge will vary according to the nature of the business. In general, goods sold on a small margin with a rapid turnover will suffer a lower service charge than, say, luxury items with a wider margin of profit.

The card companies

Finally, let us return to the third party in the triangle, the card companies themselves. In recent times, the two principal card schemes in the United Kingdom have been able to report a trading profit on their operations. This was not always the case, however, and in the early years the administrative developments, and to a considerable extent the credit regulations imposed by the Government, caused substantial losses in the card companies.

The service charge paid by merchants provides some income towards meeting the costs of running a credit card scheme, but the real source of profit to a card company lies in the interest charge made to customers who use their cards to take extended credit. If all cardholders paid their monthly accounts within the stipulated period, there would be little profit to the companies and indeed they would probably operate at a loss. It is estimated that the average period of credit taken by cardholders is between four and six months, and it is certainly in the interests of the card companies to encourage cardholders not only to make more use of their cards but to avail themselves of the revolving credit facility.

The introduction of credit cards into Britain was a major marketing operation and despite the enormous initial costs it may be rated as a highly successful exercise in terms of the market penetration which was achieved and the ultimate profitability. In broad terms, the marketing effort of the credit card industry is pointed in three directions. There is the market among merchants, there is the market among potential cardholders and there is the marketing drive to encourage existing cardholders to make greater use of their cards.

The market

Taking first the market among merchants, the view has been advanced that this market is approaching saturation point. With a few notable exceptions, virtually all the major retail trading groups in the United Kingdom accept payment by credit card. In most cases, these retailers will accept the cards of either of the two main card-issuing groups in the UK. There may still be scope for expansion of the market into, for example, the food trade and certain non-trading areas such as local authorities for the payment of rates; and there are also a large number of small shops and other retail houses which do not accept credit cards, but for the most part their turnover is so small or their margins so narrow that they are outside the credit card market. There are believed to be approximately 400,000 retail outlets in the United Kingdom, over one half of which now accept credit cards from the two principal groups. At peak shopping times and particularly, for example, at Christmas, the activity is very considerable and both Access and Barclaycard may have as many as 100,000 calls from merchants in the course of a day. The main marketing thrust so far as the merchants are concerned lies in servicing and developing the existing merchanting outlets. Each of the major card groups has a team of salesmen who pay regular visits to the merchants in order to assist with administrative problems and the training of staff. The card companies also take a close interest in the marketing of the trader's merchandise and will assist with advertising campaigns or displays in order to improve the merchant's turnover and thus enhance the return to the card company.

As for the market among cardholders, there is no question of having reached saturation point, but the number of cardholders may well have reached a plateau for the time being. Something over 20 million cardholders is approximately one-half of the total adult population in the UK and it amounts to a high proportion of those who have developed a banking habit. Whilst it is not necessary to have a banking account before possessing a credit card, the main market for cardholders so far as the banking groups are concerned is among their own customers. Although the card groups will no doubt contine to encourage as many people as possible to carry credit cards, there could well be a diminishing return in relation to the marketing costs involved. There is still a fair amount of misunderstanding and indeed prejudice in relation to credit cards. Even some well-informed people fail to recognise that a credit card is a convenient, safe and efficient method of payment as an alternative to a cheque. Instead it is too often regarded as merely a means of consumer credit and shunned by those who regard a credit facility as an undesirable temptation, whether to themselves or their fellow men.

The potential number of cardholders in the United Kingdom was given a significant boost when the Trustee Savings Banks came into the Visa family in 1978. Their 'Trustcard' was very actively promoted and, at the time of writing, accounts for approximately 14 per cent of credit cardholders in this country. The Trustee Savings Bank now operates its 'Trustcard' as an independent member of the Visa group instead of having the card processed by Barclaycard. In fact, in April 1984, the Co-operative Bank had taken a similar step and became the first British bank to operate its own credit card independently of the two main Access and Barclaycard groupings.

Although the development of credit cards in this country has been fairly rapid since the first introduction of Barclaycard, we have a long way to go before cards are accepted as a way of life, as they are in the United States. In that country, there are over 600 million credit cards in existence representing over 4 cards per adult person. Nevertheless, the issue of credit cards in the United Kingdom is gaining pace, at the present time each of the two main groups, Access and Barclaycard, are enrolling new cardholders at the rate of approximately half a million per annum.

Probably the main growth area for the card companies, however, lies in the increased use of cards by the existing cardholders, which in turn would lead to an increase in the amount of credit taken. Even if the average use of credit cards merely doubled from, say, one purchase per person per month to an average of two purchases per month, with a doubling in the value of the credit taken, the effect on the profits of the credit card companies would be dramatic. Administrative costs would not increase proportionately and even if the average credit period did not increase beyond the present figure of four to six months, the increase in interest earnings would double. It is very much in the interests of the card companies, therefore, to encourage greater activity among their cardholders.

Another sector of the market which has grown significantly in recent years is that of company cards, i.e. the issue of cards to companies for use by their employees for expenses etc. Over 25,000 companies are members of the Company Barclaycard scheme and it is believed that a comparable number belong to the Access scheme. Barclaycard alone have issued 96,000 company cards. Nowadays Personal Identification Numbers (PIN) are issued with company cards so that the holders may obtain cash from automated teller machines and also use Pinpoint machines at railway stations and petrol pumps (see page 235). From the standpoint of the employer company these cards provide more effective control of expense accounts and obviate the need for cash advances or the use of imprest accounts

In-house cards

There is yet another main growth area which, at this point in time, has achieved only modest proportions. It is the development of credit card schemes among retailers, i.e. the introduction of in-house cards. We have already said that the largest issuer of cards in America are the department stores, whereas in the U.K. it has been a predominantly bank-dominated industry. Debenhams was one of the first stores to introduce a credit card, followed in 1978 by Marks & Spencer who introduced a credit card scheme financed by Citibank. In more recent times

Marks & Spencer have actively developed their credit card to a point where they now have approximately 1 million cardholders. The first national supermarket to adopt their own credit card was International Stores, whose scheme was administered by Barclays. On the whole, such schemes have been administered and financed by the clearing bank groups, e.g. Marley Homecare by Lloyds Bank, Associated Dairies and Boots by National Westminster Bank, Tesco by Midland and Burtons by Lloyds & Scottish. In 1978, Barclays launched a special service for this purpose under the name Barclaycare, but this scheme was terminated in June 1981 because it had not developed as anticipated. It administered credit card schemes for 24 stores and the Handycard for Co-operative Bank, but the total of all cards issued under the Barclaycare schemes was only 90,000.

The most active credit card group in the development of in-house schemes is Unicredit, a subsidiary of the Provident Financial Group who, as we have already mentioned, were one of the pioneers of credit trading in this country. They operate a credit card scheme for Woolworths and a large number of retail groups.

In September 1985 National Girobank (now Girobank plc), introduced its own card, thereby enabling Girobank customers to obtain cash from Girobank's automated teller machines (as part of the LINK organisation) or from the counters of any bank belonging to Visa International.

At the end of this chapter the table shows the level of business of the two main credit card groups operating in the UK.

Some risk aspects

The credit card business is not without its risks. The original risk was that the conservative British public might not respond to the vastly expensive campaigns launched to introduce credit cards into this country. In the event, the confidence of the pioneer promoters in the United Kingdom, notably Barclays Bank, was well repaid. It was a major business decision and the risks were considerable, but the operation was well timed and well executed. The hazards which remain are those which are inherent in this type of business, viz. legislative controls, fraud and bad debts.

To the extent that the card companies are in the credit business, they are inevitably exposed to the varying monetary controls introduced from time to time by successive Chancellors of the Exchequer. Any major restraints on credit or on credit repayment terms (such as have been a recurring feature of the UK economy) can be a burden to the credit card business, both in terms of administrative costs and the impact on interest earnings. It is a hazard which must be accepted as part of the environment in which the companies operate. Other legislative hurdles are the Consumer Credit Act 1974, with the already mentioned attendant liability on credit card companies for defects in goods purchased by cardholders, and the provisions of the Fair Trading Act 1973 under which the major card companies were the subject of a reference to the Monopolies and Mergers Commission, as mentioned below. It is noteworthy that, under the United States anti-trust laws, the member banks of the two major card groups in the US may now issue each other's cards if they so wish, thus introducing a degree of 'duality' in the card business in America. The major credit card groupings are now multi-national businesses (although dedicated only to serving the interests of their member banks) and as they develop they may well be faced increasingly with local hazards in one country or another, whether it be in terms of credit control, consumerism, anti-monopoly rules, exchange control or a variety of other local requirements and attitudes.

A more truly operational risk is that of fraud. In this we can include theft, forgery and general misuse of credit cards or of the credit card system. The risks are considerable and must inevitably become greater with the international growth of credit card business. Readers of Arthur Hailey's *The Moneychangers*[5] will recall the bank losses occasioned by mammoth-sized credit card forgeries, but such risks are not confined to the pages of novels. In 1985 losses through credit card fraud in the US was estimated to be $300 million. The scope for the fraudulent use of cards is considerable, but the anti-fraud organisations of the major British card companies are very impressive and have been highly successful in keeping losses of this nature to an acceptable level. Each year a considerable number of cards are either lost or stolen and used fraudulently. About 50 per cent of these are recovered, but the loss through fraud in Barclaycard alone runs at a level of about £10 million a year. This must be viewed, however, against their total turnover of approximately £3·75b in the course of a year. Access and Barclaycard have expert teams of investigators and in recent times some new and highly sophisticated methods have been introduced to defeat credit card fraud.

Of even greater concern is not the fraudulent use of credit cards as such, but the fraudulent use of cheque books and cheque cards. At the end of 1981, there were approximately 16 million cheque cards in issue in the United Kingdom. It is believed that in that year the loss to the British clearing banks through the fraudulent use of cheque cards was of the order of £12 million. A high proportion of fraud arises from the use of cheque cards outside the United Kingdom and it came as no great surprise when in April 1982 the clearing banks announced that the use of cheque guarantee cards would be restricted to the British Isles from May 1983. Even though the cheque card limit has been retained at £50 for purchases over the counter, a stolen book of 30 cheques is worth potentially £1,500 to a thief with the aid of a stolen or faked cheque card. Approximately 70 per cent of all card frauds take place over retail counters, not in the banks themselves.

The last risk area is fundamental to the business – the risk of bad debts. Here again, the experience of the major card companies in the United Kingdom is very encouraging. The two large groups lend on credit card transactions in the course of a year sums in excess of £3,000 million. That money is lent to complete strangers who are unknown in any personal sense to the credit card companies and with whom, unlike traditional banking, no continuing business relationship will necessarily have been established. The money is lent without security and without guarantees, and it says much for the integrity of the great majority of cardholders on the one hand and the efficiency of the card companies' debt-collecting procedures on the other that the bad debt experience is so modest and is, in fact, significantly below that sometimes encountered in other forms of consumer credit. It has been said that losses occasioned by fraud in the case of American card companies can be as high as

4 per cent of the sums outstanding at any one time. In the United Kingdom, the combined losses from both fraud and bad debts is significantly below that percentage.

At the time of writing, there is a certain amount of concern in the United Kingdom about the upsurge in consumer credit and there has been some suggestion that for some people credit card finance has been, as it were, too easy. In June 1987, the Visa Group in the UK adopted a code of practice to re-state and reinforce their existing procedures regarding the issue of credit cards and the granting of credit. The institutions issuing Visa cards agreed that:

1. they will check that applicants have the means to repay the amount of credit applied for, and in all cases a banker's reference and/or a credit bureau check will be made and the applicant's address verified.
2. application forms will request enough information to enable the card issuer to make a proper credit assessment and credit limits will prudently reflect the applicant's financial standing.
3. card issuers will abide by the Consumer Credit Act and the Data Protection Act, and where credit scoring is used card issuers will comply with guidelines laid down by the Office of Fair Trading.
4. early warning will always be given to customers overdue with repayment and customers in genuine financial difficulty will be allowed longer repayment periods.

Barclaycard, in particular, have emphasised that cards are issued only to people who 'are able to handle them properly' and in 1986, as many as 30 per cent of applications were refused. Barclaycard have said that only around one per cent of cardholders have long-term problems with repayment.

The monopoly aspect

It is a term of the contract between a credit card company and a merchant that a credit card customer will be charged the same price for goods or services as a cash customer. In other words, a merchant may not add a surcharge to a credit card sale. In

1977, a number of garages complained to the Office of Fair Trading that this constituted an unfair practice on the part of the leading credit card companies. The matter was referred to the Monopolies and Mergers Commission, which reported in September 1980. The Commission concluded:

> '. . . that it is against the public interest for a credit card company to exclude or restrict a trader's freedom to charge for goods and services, on presentation of a credit card, prices different from those charged in the case of other means of payment. This practice has the effect of preventing a trader from competing with other traders by offering different prices to credit card users and other customers, so depriving the customer of an important choice in purchasing goods or services, and in some cases possibly leading to increased prices generally to all a trader's customers, whether or not they are cardholders.'

The Commission went on to recommend that any exclusion or restriction on the ability of a trader to charge different prices should be unenforceable and that it should be illegal to include such terms in any new contracts.

The Commission also criticised Barclaycard and the Joint Credit Card Company (Access) for exchanging information on charges made to particular traders and rates of interest to be paid by cardholders. The Commission considered:

> '. . . that such discusssion about policy, or arrangements with particular traders or groups of traders, are intended to maintain or exploit the monopoly situation in favour of Barclaycard and the Joint Credit Card Company by restricting such competition as exists between them.'

The leading credit card companies had in fact undertaken to the Commission that it was not now their policy to discuss with their rivals matters affecting competition and that dealings between the leading companies would in future be limited to procedural methods, such as technological developments and the training of the staff of traders.

So it was that the policy of 'dual pricing', i.e. the surcharging of credit card customers appeared to have official blessing and it became the practice among garages and, to a degree, among other retailers to add a surcharge, usually up to 25p per transaction, to credit card sales, in breach of their 'no-discrimination' clause with the credit card companies.

Over a year later, in December 1981 the government Minister for Consumer Affairs announced that the government was not going to act on the Monopolies and Mergers Commission's recommendation because:

> '. . . the absence of surcharges makes for general convenience.'

After a period of some confusion, the credit card companies made it clear that traders were expected to observe the terms of their contracts if they wished to retain their credit card franchises and the system of dual charging has now disappeared.

In May 1987 the Office of Fair Trading asked the Monopolies and Mergers Commission to look again at the credit card operations of the banks in the belief that the banks were charging too high a level of interest rates and making monopoly profits from credit cards. The Commission is expected to report within two years. The particular points referred to the Commission were:

1. Are credit card companies making monopoly profits?
2. Are they charging their customers too high a rate of interest?
3. Is the period of interest-free credit offered to cardholders fair or is it cross-subsidising those people who pay their bills in full on the monthly statement?
4. Is the credit card market sufficiently open to new competitors, e.g. building societies?
5. Are retailers, particularly the smaller ones with little bargaining power, being charged too much?
6. Should retailers continue to pay credit card companies a percentage fee or should this be a flat fee?
7. Is the 'no discrimination' clause in credit card agreements anti-competitive?

Some legal aspects

It is characteristic of mercantile law in the United Kingdom that a substantial commercial practice may develop without the introduction of any new legal framework and, indeed, without any new canon of law emerging other than that derived from the *de facto* practice of those engaged in the business. So it is that since credit cards were first introduced in this country in 1966, there has been the minimum of legal problems and certainly no new 'law of credit cards' has emerged nor been thought necessary. We have referred on page 220 to the effect of the Consumer Credit Act, 1974 on the liability of credit card companies where defective goods are purchased by cardholders and we have mentioned above the strictures of the Monopolies and Mergers Commission on the subject of restrictive practices.

There was, however, one particular case which came before the House of Lords in June 1981 and it concerned the dishonest use of a credit card (R. v Lambie (1981) 3 W.L.R. 88). The case involved the purchase of goods by a young woman with a credit card when her credit limit was £200 and she was already overdrawn with the credit card company in excess of £800. The prosecution had been brought under Section 16 of the Theft Act, 1968 on the grounds that the accused had obtained a pecuniary advantage by deception. The House of Lords, allowing the Appeal from the Court of Appeal, had no difficulty in concluding that the presentation of the credit card was a representation of authority to make a contract on the bank's behalf that the bank would honour the voucher. The only remaining question was whether the shop was induced by that representation to complete the transaction. Would the shop have allowed the transaction to go through if it had been known that the accused was acting dishonestly, and the jury had been perfectly entitled to conclude that the answer was: 'No'. In the Court of Appeal, the case had been distinguished from that of R. v Charles (1977) A.C. 177, which concerned the dishonest use of a *cheque* card. That too was a House of Lords case, in which their Lordships concluded that the manager of a gaming club, in accepting cheques backed by a cheque card, believed that the accused was entitled to use the card but, in the result, the amounts of the cheques greatly exceeded the accused's overdraft facility at his bank. In the Lambie Case, the main question before the House of Lords was whether or not there was any essential difference between a cheque card transaction (as in R. v Charles) and a credit card transaction. It is no doubt a comfort to the credit card companies and, indeed, to the public that the House of Lords took the same view of both cases. It is a pity, however, that such an important case should have been established on such a slender base. It must be very doubtful whether cheque cards and credit cards are accepted in an essential belief that the customer has sufficient funds at the bank. The cheque and/or card is no doubt accepted because the shopkeeper knows that it will be paid by the bank or card company (assuming the customer is not on the 'stop' list). It must be doubtful whether we have heard the last of this subject and it may be necessary one day for Parliament to clarify the position.

Another matter of some interest arose in the case of *Re Charge Card Services Limited* before Mr. Justice Millett in June 1986. Charge Card Services Limited was a credit card company promoted by the Motor Agents' Association and the Scottish Motor Trades Association which went into creditors' voluntary liquidation with an estimated deficiency of nearly £2 million. Some of the garages which had not been paid by the credit card company sought to claim against the cardholders for petrol which had been supplied on credit card. It was argued on behalf of the garages that payment by credit card, like payment by cheque, operated only as conditional payment, i.e. someone who chose to pay for goods or services by credit card was not thereby unconditionally discharged from his liability to pay. His Lordship held, however, that payment by credit card was not conditional and that the customer must be discharged at the latest when the supplier's account with the credit card company was credited on receipt of the voucher, not when the garage was paid. Payment by card was absolute and not conditional and the process did not depend on the card company's continued solvency. Whilst it must be unlikely that any of the major credit card companies will become insolvent, the case is nonetheless important in determining that payment by credit card is not like a cheque – it is absolute and not conditional

Profitability

When credit cards were first introduced in this country, the promotional costs were very heavy. The public were not accustomed to this method of payment and in some cases, cards were sent unsolicited to people who did not want them and, in some cases, to people whose financial standing did not merit a credit card. Progress was inevitably slow and profits were hard-earned. For some years the credit card companies made very little contribution to their group profits. 1974 was a particularly bad year, partly because the credit card companies were slow to bring their interest rates in line with the very high rates of interest in that year, and partly because the Government imposed stringent credit controls on credit card companies, which were designed to operate retrospectively to existing credit transactions. In that year substantial losses were made. For the past decade, however, profitability has improved considerably and now most major credit card operations make substantial contributions to their parent groupings. This has been due mostly to the increased volume of credit card transactions without, for the most part, any corresponding increase in operating costs. Also there has been an increased awareness of the convenience of credit cards, not only as a means of payment but as a method of obtaining credit. At the time of writing, credit cards account for nearly one-quarter of consumer credit transactions in this country, second only to bank lending as a source of credit.

Some recent developments

In the world of credit cards there have been a number of developments in recent years, some of which are cosmetic but others may well point the way for the future. Some of the newer features are listed below.

Premium cards

In 1981 American Express introduced their Gold Card designed for persons of fairly substantial means, e.g. £20,000 or above annual income. The main features of the Gold Card are the availability of unsecured overdraft facilities through Lloyds Bank at 2½ per cent per annum over base rate; £150,000 travel accident insurance when travel tickets are purchased with the Gold Card; the facility for drawing up to £1,000 per week in travellers' cheques against a personal cheque at any American

Express office throughout the world; the facility to cash personal cheques up to £300 a day at any branch of Lloyds Bank in Great Britain, and the use of a Lloyds Bank Cashpoint card.

More or less identical facilities were subsequently introduced by American Express in co-operation with Royal Bank of Scotland, Bank of Ireland and Grindlays.

In November 1981 Midland Bank introduced a 'Gold' Mastercard offering similar facilities to the American Express Gold Card and in October 1982 Barclays introduced their Premier Card entitling the holder to similar facilities plus free financial planning consultations with Barclays and 24-hour message services through Barclays branches worldwide.

Smart cards
The smart card was invented and developed in France but is now being used experimentally in the USA and trials are also taking place in Japan, Norway, Germany, Italy and latterly in England. The so-called 'smart card' is like a credit card in that it may be used for the purchase of goods and services and with the use of a Personal Identification Number (PIN) may also be used for obtaining cash from automated teller machines. The card contains an in-built micro-processor and memory, i.e. a microchip. The chip is pre-programmed with the customer's credit limit. It may be used to make a remote financial transaction as well as other electronic functions such as making telephone calls and opening security doors. Its main advantage is that it makes fraud much more difficult. At the time of writing it seems quite possible that some kind of smart card will one day have worldwide application. The card has to be paid for however, perhaps £2/£3 per card, and thus may not be welcome at first in this country where bank credit cards are issued free.

Pinpoint machines
These were introduced by Barclaycard in May 1984. They are believed to be the first machines anywhere in the world by which credit cards could be used for the automated purchase of rail tickets. The first Pinpoint machine was installed in Euston Station where a traveller with a Barclaycard may key in his Personal Identification Number (PIN) and obtain a ticket

to any one of 27 selected destinations. Similar machines have subsequently been introduced in other main line stations.

Petrol cards

In similar vein, Barclaycard have introduced automated machines for the purchase of petrol in certain areas of the country. When a Barclaycard is inserted for payment of petrol the transaction is recorded on magnetic tape which is then communicated on a Post Office line to the Barclaycard centre at Northampton. As with the Pinpoint service mentioned above, this obviates the need for paper vouchers.

Cardlink

In 1984 the principal card companies introduced a joint company for authorising credit card purchases by telephone. Under this scheme, known as Cardlink, retailers contribute to the installation of a telephone link to the joint company, On Line Card Services Limited, so that card transactions for the principal groups may be dealt with in a uniform way. The card is passed through a magnetic strip reader on the telephone and the amount of the transaction is relayed via Cardlink to the appropriate card company. The card company then flashes a response on the display panel on the user terminal. This eliminates the need for the merchants to dial an authorisation centre quoting the merchant number and the card number. Also there is no need for the merchant to refer to warning notices regarding lost and stolen cards because the transaction is automatically checked by the card-issuing company.

Credit interest

In November 1986, the Co-operative Bank announced a new and possibly far-reaching development in connection with its Visa credit card operations. The Bank became reputedly the first in Europe to allow cardholders to build up credit balances on their credit card accounts with interest paid on those balances at a competitive rate. This development will no doubt be watched with interest because it provides customers for the first time with a combined interest-bearing current account/credit card facility.

Debit cards
These by definition are not credit cards. They are a method of debiting the cardholder's account with a bank or building society, more or less instantaneously by electronic means on the insertion of a piece of plastic in a machine. Arguably, the earliest form of debit card was the cash card (known by various names) enabling the holder to obtain cash from an automated teller machine. In 1987, however, Barclays introduced Connect, a debit card available to current account customers as a means of payment as well as a means of obtaining cash. Such cards belong more appropriately to the subject of Money Transfer discussed in Chapter 23.

The future
What of the future? Here we may pose a number of questions, but the card industry is a fast-moving business and the questions we ask today will give way to others tomorrow. Some have called in question, for example, the practice by which credit cards (as distinct from the travel and entertainment cards) are issued free, with free credit being allowed to cardholders, as we have seen, for up to nearly two months. This is only possible, so the argument goes, if those who take extended credit are charged a high rate of interest. In other words, the borrowers subsidise the remainder of the cardholders. An opposing argument is that by issuing cards free and not charging for short-term credit, the card companies are able to operate on a larger scale with lower administrative costs and therefore greater efficiency in everyone's interests. Nevertheless, it is a matter which may well remain the subject of debate, and it could be that cardholders will at least be required to pay for the privilege of holding a card and thus contribute to the cost of the otherwise free credit. Indeed, cardholders may be encouraged to make greater use of their cards if they were required to pay for them in the first instance.

One may also question whether the development of the credit card is consistent with the introduction of cheque cards. There are those who regret the introduction of cheque cards because in the United Kingdom cheques on the clearing banks used to be widely accepted in payment for goods and services, whereas today a cheque is seldom accepted without a supporting cheque card. Is there in fact any good reason why a bank should guarantee payment of its cheques by means of a cheque card? Why should the bank accept the risk of loss on the transaction between customer and merchant when there is no other direct benefit to the bank itself? Admittedly, the wider use of cheques encourages current account banking with valuable free balances, but it must be doubtful whether the introduction of cheque cards as such encourages the banking habit. The need for cheque cards is perhaps even more questionable in an age when the major banks issue credit cards to creditworthy customers. Is it not possible that without the introduction of cheque cards, the two leading credit cards – Access and Barclaycard – would have come even more into their own as acceptable methods of payment for goods, quite regardless of the credit aspect? Might this not have been desirable? It would presumably have diminished the volume of cheques in circulation and helped to pave the way for the next stage in payment transmission, the linking of credit cards to electronic data systems.

This last subject must in itself be one of the major issues for the bank credit card industry. Already the combined use of credit card and telephone (e.g. the ordering of theatre seats) has become an acceptable feature of our society. Much more exciting is the possibility of using the plastic credit cards as a means of instruction to computer terminals in shops, airports, hotels, travel agencies and the like, virtually dispensing with all paperwork. As illustrated above. All this has been perfectly possible for some years and is now coming into effect. In some respects, the linking-up of credit card companies internationally has resulted in electronic equipment of a sophistication which exceeded that in normal banking. The international settlement of card liabilities is already achieved to a large extent by electronic means. In the case of Barclaycard, for instance, transactions generated by overseas cards in this country or by domestic Barclaycards used overseas are settled not by the despatch of paper around the world, but by electronic data transmission. The San Mateo computer provides the Barclaycard organisation with daily settlement in dollars, notwithstanding that the original transactions may be made in any of fifty or more currencies.

Credit Card Statistics
Access and Visa

End-December	*1975*	*1976*	*1977*	*1978*	*1979*	*1980*	*1981*	*1982*	*1983*	*1984*	*1985*	*1986*
ACCESS (a)												
Credit outstanding (£ millions)	112	153	190	318	449	564	760	984	1,258	1,504	1,901	2,346
Number of cards in issue (thousands)	3,100	2,700	3,255	3,700	4,321	4,863	5,418	6,056	6,823	7,589	8,515	9,846
Number of accounts (thousands)	2,800	2,300	2,765	3,100	3,590	4,010	4,423	4,924	5,529	6,133	6,923	8,067
Number of UK outlets (thousands)	97	100	107	123	142	158	175	190	205	218	236	260
During the year:												
Value of turnover (£ millions)	302·1	409·7	541·5	767·1	1,021·1	1,390·3	1,833·4	2,384·2	3,152·6	3,955·0	5,031·8	6,287·1
of which cash advances	62·4	78·5	92·3	120·5	120·8	131·5	177·0	205·0	274·3	351·3	445·7	581·8
Volume of turnover (millions of transactions)	24·6	30·4	38·3	47·7	55·1	68·8	80·9	102·6	128·8	155·8	184·4	212·5
of which cash advances	3·4	4·0	4·6	4·5	3·7	3·6	4·1	4·3	5·6	7·0	8·0	8·9
VISA (b)												
Credit outstanding (£ millions)	114	175	214	330	485	622	811	1,037	1,335	1,694	2,146	2,539
Number of cards issued (thousands)	3,310	3,542	3,874	4,417	5,526	6,810	7,683	8,499	8,994	9,942	11,080	12,121
Number of accounts (thousands)	3,008	3,148	3,437	3,729	4,628	5,647	6,442	7,062	7,465	8,191	9,240	9,948
Number of UK outlets (thousands)	87	92	100	115	131	153	177	192	202	216	235	258
During the year:												
Value of turnover (£ millions)	336·2	451·5	581·9	773·7	1,072·1	1,493·0	1,892·6	2,514·2	3,243·6	4,088·0	5,472·3	6,927·3
of which cash advances	49·0	67·9	83·9	102·5	117·3	158·7	232·7	320·5	388·5	462·1	593·6	755·6
Volume of turnover (millions of transactions)	34·3	40·6	48·8	56·1	64·9	81·6	93·7	114·7	138·5	165·8	204·0	238·7
of which cash advances	3·0	3·8	4·4	4·1	3·9	4·4	6·0	7·9	8·9	9·6	11·1	12·8

(a) Access card issuers include: Clydesdale, Lloyds, Midland, National Westminster, The Royal Bank of Scotland and the Bank of Ireland (UK branches only).

(b) Visa card issuers include: Barclays Bank, Yorkshire Bank (figures included in Barclaycard), Girobank, Bank of Scotland, TSB group, Co-operative Bank, Standard Chartered, Robert Fleming (through Save and Prosper Group) and Allied Dunbar & Co.

Source: CLSE Statistical Unit.

Whether by accident or design the credit card business has usurped some of the older and more routine functions of traditional banking. As Mr D. V. Weyer has written:

> 'Customers, helped by external cash dispensers and by credit cards can get along surprisingly well without often visiting their bank.'[6]

This was not entirely unforeseen and, in particular, the architects of Barclaycard emphasised its merits as a convenient method of payment and foresaw its contribution to the 'cashless society' (although a 'chequeless society' is the more likely).

In the earlier editions of this book, we made some tentative prophecies regarding the development of plastic card banking. In a comparatively short space of time, many of those possibilities have come to pass and are dealt with under the heading of Money Transfer in Chapter 23. So-called plastic card banking will almost certainly replace banking by cheque and will have had its origins in the quite phenomenal development of credit cards. The two major groupings, Mastercard and Visa have achieved throughout the world a degree of co-operation and harmonisation which has been exciting to observe. They have probably set the pattern for retail banking for the future.

We began with the illustration of a shopper in Harrods. Our visitor might equally have called at Fortnum & Mason. He or she might there have seen the first of the DARTS machines in use. (DARTS is derived from Data Capture Authorisation Transmission Service.) DARTS was introduced by Barclaycard with the co-operation of the other credit card companies. It enables the credit card of any of the user companies to be inserted in a machine kept by the retailer and which is on-line to the credit card companies. The card and the credit limit is verified immediately and the transaction automatically logged with the credit card company. No paper, no telephone call, no delay, no signature, no check against a blacklist – surely the shape of things to come.

References

1 F. Snushall: Credit Cards in *Credit Management Handbook,* 1975.
2 The Decline of the Cheque. *The Banker,* November 1973, p. 1411.

3 Target Group Index, 1976.
4 Ibid.
5 A. Hailey: *The Moneychangers*. Michael Joseph, 1975.
6 D. Vander Weyer: 'Clearing Bank Marketing: the Practical Issues Today'. *The Banker*, October 1970.

CHAPTER 11

Hire Purchase and Consumer Credit

The system of hire purchase, according to the Report of the Crowther Committee on Consumer Credit, 'has been one of the chief contributory causes of the great rise in the material standard of living of the British people in the last generation'.[1] The same Report expressed the belief that 'the first principle of social policy should be to treat the users of consumer credit as adults who are fully capable of managing their own financial affairs and not to restrict their freedom of access to it in order to protect the relatively small minority who get into difficulties'.[2] Thus hire purchase, which had been viewed with mistrust and suspicion for over 100 years in this country, received the accolade of an official Committee of Inquiry and the majority of those who might default in their hire purchase commitments were categorised as 'inadequate people who never quite face up to reality, are incapable of managing their own affairs and never seem to be able to predict the consequences of what they are doing' whilst others 'have become overwhelmed by a burden of debt through illness, unemployment or other misfortune and some over-commit themselves through not budgeting'.[3]

The nature of hire purchase

Hire purchase is a particular aspect of instalment credit. This is the provision of finance to be repaid by instalments over a period in accordance with a contractual arrangement. Thus occasional credit granted by a local shopkeeper is not instalment credit as such, nor is the allowing of 'time to pay' in the case of a debt which is overdue. Using the language of the same

'A transaction was deemed to be harsh and unconscionable.'

Crowther Report, consumer credit like all credit may be classified as 'lender' or 'vendor' credit. The former is the lending of money, usually for a particular purpose, such as a bank overdraft or personal loan. The latter is an arrangement made with the vendor of goods or property whereby the purchase price is to remain outstanding over a period and repaid on an agreed basis. Hire purchase was historically the largest single category of instalment credit in this country and is a perfect example of vendor credit, although the distinction has become blurred in modern times when the finance for a hire purchase sale has in fact come from an outside source. (In fact, the distinction introduced in the Consumer Credit Act 1974 is between 'debtor-creditor' agreements and 'debtor-creditor-supplier' agreements.)

Historical note

Whilst the lending of money or chattels goes back to the beginning of mankind and has never been the subject of any great moral strictures, the charging of interest, i.e. usury, finds a degree of condemnation in the codes of Judaism, early Christianity and Islam. Down the ages, however, various devices and fictions were adopted to avoid the usury laws and throughout Europe over the years various statutory constraints were imposed on the rate of interest which might be charged. Interest could not legally be charged in England until it was permitted by an Act of 1545, and then could not exceed 10 per cent. There were many variations over the next 400 years or so, culminating in the comparatively permissive Moneylenders Act 1927, by which a transaction was presumed to be 'harsh and unconscionable', if the interest rate exceeded 48 per cent per annum.

Primitive communities are preoccupied with the production rather than the purchase of goods and it is only in the more developed communities that consumer credit as such has any meaning. In the UK it appears to have been in the sixteenth century that the lending of money, and indeed the lending of goods, became common, usually on a personal basis, between the more well-to-do members of society, such as farmers, tailors, grocers, mercers and parsons, for the benefit of the less well-to-do. What we do not often appreciate nowadays is that during the seventeenth and eighteenth centuries goods were almost invariably sold on credit, a practice which led to endless entanglements and an ascendancy of trader over customer often manifested in short weight, excessive charging, the ultimate impoverishment of the consumer and his imprisonment for debt. We are told that:

> 'It was no uncommon thing for a family to be in debt to an unscrupulous chandler who allowed increasingly short weight at increasingly extortionate prices, so that while they dare not desert his shop, they worked only to enrich him and drive themselves even more hopelessly into his power.'[4]

Indeed, in 1780, a London bookseller, James Lackington, was ridiculed for attempting to run his business on a cash sale basis.

The term hire purchase has its origin in the 'hire and purchase' of goods and it was introduced into England in the 1840s, principally for the sale of pianos and subsequently of sewing machines. It appears that the practice had its origin in the hiring of furniture in France and the United States on a temporary basis – perhaps to equip a town house during the 'season' – a practice which is more akin to our modern leasing contracts than hire purchase as such. The essence of 'hire and purchase' was that the hirer had the option to purchase the goods at the end of the hiring period. Because the hirer did not have title to the goods, he could not pass a good title even to a purchaser in good faith – a principle established in the leading case of Helby v Matthews,[5] which virtually set the pattern for hire purchase contracts right down to the present day.

The hiring of railway wagons

In the early days of hire purchase, each transaction was financed by the supplier or manufacturer of the goods in question. If that had remained the situation there could never have been the tremendous growth in hire purchase to the level which exists today, because makers and suppliers of goods would not have had the resources to finance consumer demand on such a scale. It was the arrival on the scene of the third party financier which set the pattern for future hire purchase development in Britain, and the massive finance house industry of the present day has its origins in the entrepreneurial instincts of a small group of Victorian businessmen in the North of England. It was in 1861 that the North Central Wagon Company was formed in Rotherham. The objects of the company were 'the purchasing, hiring and manufacturing of railway wagons and (sic) Railway Companies, Coal Proprietors and other persons'. Such was the insatiable demand for coal, both for domestic and industrial purposes, in the late nineteenth century that neither the railway companies nor the colliery companies could afford to provide the necessary wagons and a number of wagon companies were formed to manufacture or purchase wagons and hire them to the railway companies and collieries. In its concept, this arrangement was similar to our modern leasing contracts. The wagons bore the name of the wagon company and remained in their ownership, but this soon developed into a 'hire and purchase' arrangement and thus was the beginning of our modern industrial hire purchase business.

By 1900, North Central Wagon Company had 25,000 railway wagons on hire to its customers. Not surprisingly, it took its house symbol from coal, the 'black diamond'. As we have seen (see p. 8) the company was acquired in 1958 by National Provincial Bank and in 1971 merged with Lombard Banking as part of the National Westminster Bank Group under the name Lombard North Central. It is believed to be the oldest hire purchase company in the world and in its crest under the L (or £ sign) for Lombard, still retains the black diamond of the past. With the nationalisation of the railways in 1948 all rolling stock on the railways became vested in the Transport Commission and thus ended a highly successful, and indeed romantic, chapter in British financial history.

It was in 1934 that the Southern Counties Finance Corporation (following its acquisition by North Central Wagon and Finance Company) 'noted with concern' a proposal to undertake the hire purchase of motor cars. It suggested that any such transactions should be limited to business cars. The comment was perhaps prophetic in relation to the vast business of financing the purchase of car fleets for business purposes in more recent years, but more particularly it was symbolic of the transfer of interest from the railway wagons to the motor car. It is believed that the first instance of a motor car being bought on hire purchase was in 1912, but it was not until the 1930s that car hire purchase developed rapidly. Nowadays, out of the 1·5 million new cars registered each year, 25 per cent are sold on credit.

The finance houses

There were two other factors contributing to the growth of finance house business in this country. The one was the arrival of American companies for the purpose of financing consumer credit and the other, the setting up by the larger manufacturing companies of their own finance companies. The Finance Houses Association was formed in 1945 and now consists of forty-six members who together account for 90 per cent of the instalment credit business undertaken by finance houses in the United Kingdom. The aims of the Association are to promote the interests of the members; to act as a channel of communication between members and government departments, local and other public authorities, trade associations and the press; to establish and maintain good relations with the public; and to promote good business practice among members of the Association and disseminate information of interest to the credit industry.

There is no legal definition of a finance house. Historically they have been associated with hire purchase, but nowadays the larger finance houses not only conduct hire purchase business in all its forms, but a wide range of other credit operations including, as discussed later, leasing and factoring. Some of the larger ones are statutory banks and most of them engage in deposit-taking activities to finance their lending business. A number of them grant personal loans as part of their consumer credit operations, even though this may be seen by some as being in competition with a parent bank.

It was estimated by the Crowther Committee that there were as many as 1,900 finance houses in the United Kingdom, but of these only 1,000 or so were thought to be in active operation. Apart from those finance houses which grew up independently as financial institutions, there are those which were established as subsidiaries of manufacturing companies and retail stores.

Hire purchase debt has been traditionally the major part of consumer credit finance in this country, but in recent times consumer lending by the banks has become an increasing part of the total instalment credit debt.

Categories of instalment credit

Hire purchase in the broad sense of the term covers a number of different instalment credit arrangements, of which there are three in common use:

1. Hire purchase in the strict sense of the term where goods are hired to the customer over a period and, as we have seen, no title passes until he is deemed to purchase the goods at the end of the hire period.

2. Credit sale agreements, which are strictly an arrangement by which the purchase price of goods is paid by instalments. It is 'vendor' credit rather than 'lender' credit in that there is not a loan as such, but an agreement for deferred payment over a period.

3. Conditional sale, which is an arrangement by which the vendor agrees to sell goods to the customer, the title to the goods to pass on payment of the last instalment of the price. Under this arrangement the finance house lends the price of the goods and the credit charge is interest on the loan. Until the change in the taxation laws introduced by the Finance Act 1969, the interest thus paid by the consumer was allowed for tax purposes. Although this relief was withdrawn, a large part of instalment credit business is still conducted in this way.

For most practical and legal purposes, these differences in consumer credit arrangements are no longer significant. Both credit sale agreements and conditional sale agreements were brought within the scope of the Hire Purchase Act 1965. Similarly, the distinction is no longer material for the purpose of the Consumer Credit Act 1974. A more important distinction to be drawn in hire purchase business is that between consumer hire purchase and what is usually called industrial hire purchase. In broad terms, the first is instalment credit for the private individual: the latter is instalment credit for businesses. In 1969, for example, some 65 per cent of all instalment credit provided by finance houses was for private consumers but nowadays, as we shall see, the comparative figures have been more or less reversed.

Consumer hire purchase

When a finance house provides the finance for consumer business, it often does so through an umbrella agreement with the manufacturer or supplier of the goods. The purchaser acquiring goods on hire purchase may be under the impression at the outset that the agreement is with the supplier, but this is rarely so: normally it will be a triangular arrangement bringing in a finance house – which will be either a captive finance house set up by the manufacturer or supplier of the goods or an independent financial institution. The hire purchase agreement will be between the finance house and the purchaser. In some cases a supplier will deal with two or more finance companies, but this is an inconvenience to the supplier because it means that he must be familiar with two or more sets of forms and with the varying special requirements of different houses.

Although the hire purchase contract is between the finance house and the purchaser, great reliance must be placed by the finance house on the good sense and experience of the supplier and the quality of his business generally. Although the normal enquiries will be made by the finance house on the creditworthiness of the purchaser and the finance house will have the security of the goods, the strength of the finance house's loan portfolio will depend very much on the standing and integrity of the suppliers with whom they deal.

It is a feature of consumer hire purchase that the finance houses hardly, if ever, meet the consumers with whom they do business. It is not the personal, subjective lending of a clearing bank, but a detached, clinical and even mathematical assessment of facts and figures set out on a piece of paper. Because of this, the security aspect is important and the interest costs can be relatively high. Although the legal relationship with the customer continues during the currency of the hire purchase agreement, there is not usually a continuing customer relationship as such, nor would this always be possible. In practice, the finance house 'customer' is often the dealer.

Business credit

Turning to industrial hire purchase and business credit generally, we have already noted the growth in this side of the business as a component of the finance houses instalment credit activity. It has outstripped the growth of consumer credit to a point where the industrial or business side (including leasing) now accounts for approximately 60 per cent of all finance house business and in one or two of the larger institutions the proportion is very much greater. The distinction between business credit and consumer credit is somewhat blurred because of the high proportion of private motor cars, approximately 60 per cent, which are purchased for business use.

The subject of industrial credit is dealt with more particularly in Chapter 16.

From the standpoint of the finance houses both consumer and industrial finance have been areas of considerable growth, but this has not been achieved without some problems. During the secondary bank crises of the early 1970s some of the finance companies went through a difficult time and in some cases recovery was a long, slow process. The changed climate of today brings its own difficulties, not least the difficulty of funding a major hire purchase operation in the face of intense competition for medium-term finance. Among the finance houses themselves competition for consumer and industrial business is keen and, on the whole, there is no particular loyalty among suppliers to one or other finance house. At first sight the rates earned by finance houses seem generous in relation to traditional rates for, say, bank credit. At the time of high interest rates, a hire purchase contract will yield a very high return on a day-to-day basis, but against this one must take into account (a) the comparatively high present-day costs of a labour-intensive business; (b) the commissions paid to dealers which amount on average to approximately 15 per cent of the finance houses charges and may on occasions be as high as 25 per cent; (c) the comparatively high cost of maintaining a marketing-orientated business; and (d) the bad debts experience which, although not high, is above the level for bank finance.

Profitability

The profits of the finance houses stem not only from hire purchase business, but from leasing and, in some cases, factoring. With instalment credit business generally, however, there tends to be a strain on profitability during periods of rising interest rates. This is because contracts are written in some cases at fixed rates over fixed periods, but the cost of financing those contracts may rise considerably. This applies less so to commercial instalment credit, which is increasingly on a variable rate basis, but most consumer credit is at a fixed rate. At times of falling interest rates, the reverse is true as the finance houses are able to fund their fixed term lending (at high rates) at lowering rates of interest. The pattern of profits, therefore, tends to be the reverse of that in the clearing banks where, for the most part, high interest rates mean high profits. The banks and their subsidiary finance houses tend, therefore, to have a complementary effect on each other throughout the interest rate cycle.

Finance houses have traditionally looked for about a 3 per cent margin on their outstanding contracts, but this is difficult to maintain during periods of high interest rates. Apart from the problem of matching rates on fixed contracts, as mentioned above, the high rates themselves meet market resistance, more so than is the case with traditional borrowing from banks. In the high interest rate period of 1979/1981, the effective rate of interest on instalment finance was around the 30 per cent mark. Such high rates and of course the overall business recession, coupled with an above average bad debt experience, all brought finance house profits under strain.

The major finance houses are outward-looking organisations which know that they must work hard to maintain their share of the market. The branches throughout the country are primarily marketing outlets, and in its branches or regional control office a large finance house may have 500 or more sales people. They are pensionable staff paid on a salary basis, and are separately recruited and highly trained for their work. As one senior official remarked: ‘Our people are selling and it’s hard work’.

The market for hire purchase business

Let us turn now to the market for hire purchase business in the United Kingdom. Here we must differentiate again between personal consumer credit and industrial hire purchase, meaning in the latter case hire purchase lending for industrial and commercial purposes to companies or private firms.

The motives which prompt an individual to resort to consumer credit were categorised in the Crowther Report:

> 'First, it enables him to achieve great practical convenience in paying for the purchase of goods and services. Secondly, it enables him to bridge the gap between income and spending in the intervals between the receipt of income, be it a week, a month or longer. Thirdly, it enables him to purchase goods and services for current consumption over a period longer than the normal interval between income receipts. Fourthly, it enables him to purchase real and financial assets in excess of the amount permitted by his own savings.'

The first three of these needs are met by *account* credit in its various forms, e.g. bank overdrafts, personal loans, budget accounts and credit cards. The fourth need or motive – the acquisition of assets in excess of current savings (or because of a desire not to disturb current savings) – constitutes the main *raison d'être* of the consumer credit movement.

Any understanding of the consumer credit market involves a consideration of some deeply entrenched social attitudes. It is, for example, widely accepted that a householder will buy his home on mortgage (usually justified on the grounds that this is an appreciating asset, although it was not always so), but conventionally it would not be so widely accepted that he should furnish his home with capital assets also acquired on credit. The NOP Market Research survey, commissioned by the Crowther Committee, showed that up to 1969 only 49 per cent of the population had ever used hire purchase. The profile of the typical hire purchase customer was not very precisely defined. Not surprisingly, the twenty-five to forty-four age group had the highest proportion of credit, and among the various income groups the highest percentage of borrowers was among those who were above the subsistence level but whose incomes did not exceed £1,500. In fact, however, the percentage of credit customers above that level was not significantly lower. Only half of those making use of hire purchase had banking accounts.

After hire purchase (used by 49 per cent of the population, as mentioned above) there was a sharp drop in the proportion which had ever used other forms of consumer credit. About 37 per cent had, at some time, rented their television sets; 28 per cent had made use of mail order on credit; and 12 per cent had bought goods by means of check trading, mostly in the North of England. It is interesting that the same survey revealed bank borrowing as high on the list (second only to borrowing from a moneylender) of sources of credit thought to be undesirable by the public. It was regarded as socially embarrassing for it to be known that one had a bank overdraft, compared with, say, hire purchase credit.

Apart from such social attitudes, the survey showed a remarkable degree of ignorance on the subject of consumer finance generally. Although all the people interviewed had heard of hire purchase, television rental and house mortgages, about half of the sample had little or no knowledge on the subject of second mortgages, approximately a third had not heard of credit sales and a tenth did not know of the existence of bank overdrafts. It is perhaps not surprising that about 20 per cent of those questioned had little or no knowledge of the basic nature of the various credit contracts, and it is well known, of course, that a considerable number of credit customers are unaware of the true rate of interest being paid.

It was another conclusion of the Crowther Report that 'consumers display a considerable amount of inertia in their buying habits and, even if they are aware of differences in the cost of credit, prefer the convenience of dealing with familiar suppliers'. The Report goes on to say that 'many consumers, through a failure to shop around, are simply unaware of existing variations in the cost and availability of various forms of credit'.

The result of such attitudes, whether due to social inhibitions, ignorance or an unwillingness to 'shop around', is a very imperfect market. There was, and to a degree still is, a wide disparity in interest rates quoted for comparable forms of credit. For example, the Crowther Report, quoting the Consumers' Association, showed that in a specimen year, interest rates at electrical showrooms varied from 6·3 per cent to 17 per cent and in furniture shops from 3·3 per cent to 110·9 per cent! It is not surprising that the Committee concluded that 'competitive forces are weak'. The Finance Houses Association has done much to improve consumer education in matters of instalment credit and the Consumer Credit Act 1974, itself a result of the Crowther Report, now requires the licensing of credit brokers, i.e. those engaged at any time in advising members of the public on credit facilities. (In other words, all dealers who offer finance house facilities have to be licensed as credit brokers.)

Despite the increase in hire purchase and instalment credit debt, the level of personal consumer credit has probably no more than kept up with inflation until recent years, notwithstanding the increased strength of the finance houses following the alignment of some of the larger ones with the major banks. Successive government controls and, more particularly, the years of recession and high interest rates have kept in check what would otherwise almost certainly have been a period of boom in consumer credit.

There is an acknowledged difficulty in assessing the actual amount of consumer credit at any one time. The figures published by the Government Statistical Service for consumer credit include banks, credit card companies, finance houses, retailers and insurance companies. The total amount outstanding under these headings at the end of 1986 was over £30 billion. This does not include that part of building society lending which is applied for consumer purposes. In March 1985, the Bank of England estimated that a little over 50 per cent of new building society lending had gone into consumer spending. A certain amount of concern has been expressed by the authorities at the rise in consumer credit in recent times and indeed, the availability of credit could well be increased with the new powers of the building societies to grant unsecured personal loans.

The Clearing Banks

It remains only to summarise the involvement of the British clearing banks in the finance house field. Differing reasons have been advanced for the banks' entry into hire purchase and it is probably fair to say that at the outset it was not so much a desire to engage in the business as such, but rather to broaden the lending base during periods of credit control and, more particularly, to be able to lend through subsidiary or associated companies at rates of interest outside the clearing bank cartel.

Reference has already been made in Chapter 1 to the initial investment by the major banks in hire purchase companies by way of minority shareholdings and it was very largely the subsequent mergers and the desire to tidy up some anomalous situations that led to the present-day position. Each of the major banks in the United Kingdom came to own a finance house subsidiary, as shown below:

Bank of Scotland	North West Securities
Barclays Bank	Mercantile Credit Company
Co-operative Bank	First Co-operative Finance
Lloyds Bank	Lloyds & Scottish (60·7%) and Bowmaker
Midland Bank	Forward Trust
National Westminster Bank	Lombard North Central
Royal Bank of Scotland	Lloyds & Scottish (39·3%)
Trustee Savings Bank	United Dominions Trust
Williams & Glyn's Bank	St. Margaret's Trust
Yorkshire Bank	North British Securities

Thus, by varying routes the banks augmented their traditional skills to include a new competence in the field of instalment credit. Whilst to many it must seem a natural extension of the clearing banks' role, it is nevertheless an area with which the banks had little acquaintance until recent years. The market, the marketing approach, the lending skills and even the accounting systems differ from those of the traditional banks, but by their acquisition of finance houses the banks have been able to move into this new dimension in an effective and profitable way. Through their associated finance companies, the banks now reach out to a market which they might not otherwise have entered and are able, at one remove, to lend considerable sums of money, fully secured, at higher rates of interest than might have been possible through the traditional banking outlets. Indeed, as much as 60 per cent of the total business of the Finance Houses Association is accounted for by those members which are owned by banks.

As for the finance companies which are now part of the banking groups, they are rightly proud of their history and they have retained a considerable degree of autonomy and perhaps, more than any other single enterprise, have brought a whole new dimension of activity to the clearing banks in Great Britain.

References

1 Report of the Committee on Consumer Credit (Chairman: Lord Crowther), Cmnd. 4596. HMSO, 1971. p. 69.
2 Ibid, p. 153.
3 Ibid, p. 145.
4 Dorothy Davis: *A History of Shopping.* Routledge, 1966.
5 Helby v Matthews (1895) A.C. 471; (1895–1899) All E. Rep. 821.

CHAPTER 12

Personal Advisory and Agency Services

'I have found,' said Mr Justice Salmon in the case Woods v Martins Bank Limited,[1] 'that it is part of the defendant's business to advise customers and potential customers on financial matters of all kinds.' His lordship reached this conclusion having quoted at length from the bank's published literature, which included such statements as 'You may consult your bank manager freely and seek his advice on all matters affecting your financial welfare' and 'We shall be delighted . . . to help you with your finances in every possible way . . .'. It was part of the bank's defence in that case that it was no part of their business as bankers to advise on the particular type of transaction on which the claim for negligent advice was based, but his lordship found as a matter of fact rather than one of law that it was within the scope of the bank's business, on the evidence of its own publications, to give advice on all financial matters.

To some extent the line taken by the bank in that case typifies the slightly ambivalent attitude of the clearing banks over the years in the matter of giving advice. On the one hand, it is widely claimed in advertisements and elsewhere that bank managers will assist their customers and potential customers with advice on financial matters. On the other hand, the banks have been reluctant to formalise their role as advisors, and in some specific instances the bank is no more than a channel for the purpose of obtaining advice. This is well illustrated in the matter of investment advice, which we have already discussed in Chapter 6.

Even where banks adopted a clear advisory role, they were reluctant to charge for the advice given. This was no doubt partly because of the known unwillingness of the British public to pay for advice (it being a commodity which is given freely on all sides) and partly because of the assumption, almost certainly erroneous, that gratuitous advice was less likely to give rise to legal responsibility than advice given for a fee. On one occasion, National Westminster Bank caused a slight furore in the press by suggesting to their managers in a circular that in appropriate cases customers should be charged at the rate of so much per hour for interviews. This, of course, had nothing to do with payment for advice. It was no more than a rationalising of the managers' time and an indication of a greater profit consciousness at a time when the true earnings of banks were newly exposed to the public.

In more recent years, any bashfulness on the subject of advice has faded and in a number of areas clearing banks overtly and for reward offer highly developed advisory services. In almost all these areas, however, it is not the bank manager who gives the advice, although it may come through him. It may even be arguable that the bank manager in person gives less advice today than in former years because of the increase in the number of specialist departments which now assume the advisory role.

Advice to customers falls into two main categories – personal advice to the individual, and business advice whether to an individual or to a corporate body. In this chapter we are concerned with personal advice to the private individual. There is considerable overlapping in the areas of advice, but for simplicity's sake we can list the main advisory services as follows:

Investment advice
Insurance advice
Taxation advice
Personal financial planning
Special categories of customer.
Agency services.

We have discussed investment advice in Chapter 6 and insurance advice by the banks as insurance brokers in Chapter 9. We come now to the role of the banks as taxation advisors.

Taxation services

The taxation service of a bank is something more than 'advisory'. It is a full agency service under which the bank, as agent for a customer, completes the taxation return for the year, computes the tax liability or repayment and settles the position with the Inland Revenue. In most cases, but not always, it is a continuing service and the bank will advise the customer on any aspect of his taxation affairs as the occasion arises throughout the year.

In the United Kingdom at the present time personal taxes may be payable under the following headings:

Income Tax, which, subject to the statutory allowances, is payable on all incomes earned and unearned;

Higher rate Income Tax, which is payable on higher incomes, on a graduated scale;

National Insurance Contributions, payable by employed persons and their employers and by self-employed people;

Capital Gains Tax, payable on the disposal of capital assets (with some exceptions) with annual relief for smaller gains;

Inheritance Tax (replacing Capital Transfer Tax), payable, subject to certain reliefs and exceptions, on the transfer of assets to another party on death or within the previous seven years.

Despite attempts at simplification, the taxation structure has become increasingly complicated over the years and people from all walks of life require help in the settlement of their tax positions. Even those who have the time and basic knowledge to deal with their own tax do not necessarily have sufficient acquaintance with the quirks of revenue law and practice. Most difficult of all is the task of keeping up to date with the system of rules which seldom remain the same for more than two years.

There are approximately 25 million tax payers (counting a married couple as one tax payer) in the United Kingdom. The great majority deal with their own tax affairs and never know whether with the right advice they might have achieved a worthwhile saving. Taxation advice is not cheap and

> 'Wise men affirm it is the English way
> Never to grumble till they come pay.'[2]

As taxation has become more complicated and the need for advice has grown, so the training of tax experts has become more costly and the price of advice has increased. There are three main sources of taxation advice. First, there is the accountancy profession who have a natural and leading role in the provision of taxation services for their clients. Secondly, and a little less obvious, there are a large number of solicitors who deal with their clients' taxation affairs, taxation being very much a matter of law although the resultant computation of tax liabilities and the application of the rules is more particularly a financial matter. Thirdly, there are the banks. They have been in the business of taxation advice for over sixty years. It is a matter over which there has always been an uneasy relationship between the banks and the accountancy profession. As long ago as 1936 the Committee of London Clearing Bankers agreed with the Institute of Chartered Accountants in England and Wales that they, the banks, would not advertise their taxation services other than to their customers and potential new customers. The banks stated that 'it was not their practice to solicit income tax work from those who are not their customers, although they occasionally agree to do such work upon request as the result of recommendation by a satisfied customer'.

The agreement is still honoured in its spirit, with perhaps occasional departures by the banks in their advertising. In general, however, the banks advertise their tax services only to their existing customers or as part of their more general advertising of services, and even when offering taxation help to an existing customer of the bank it is customary to say 'If you do not already have professional advice in connection with your tax affairs, we shall be pleased, etc. . . .'. Whatever the reason, the growth of the banks' taxation services has been very modest. Out of the 25 million or so tax payers in the country, the clearing banks act for only 140,000.

The banks have not in general sought the taxation work of business customers. The argument is that if an individual is in business, it is necessary for accounts of his business to be prepared and this is properly the work of an accountant. There has been a departure from this to the extent that at least one bank has set up in recent times a special service to deal with the taxation affairs of business customers, including the preparation of accounts.

The susceptibilities of the accountancy profession are understandable. For many years they were precluded by their own professional rules from advertising and it must have been irritating to see the banks openly seeking taxation business on all fronts. On the other hand, in this over-taxed country there is enough business for everyone and the problem is not that of competition, but the fact that neither the banks nor the accountants can afford to provide taxation services except at a level of remuneration which at present the market will not bear. It is doubtful whether any of the banks make any profit from their taxation services, after allowing for a full allocation of overhead costs.

Most of the banks will offer an *ad hoc* advisory service where a customer needs immediate help but does not necessarily require a continuing service. In Barclays Bank this is known as the Tax Aid Service as distinct from the more comprehensive service. It has the advantage that costs can be kept to the minimum and a customer can be interviewed at a local branch, given assistance (for example with the completion of his income tax return), and charged an on-the-spot fee on an hourly basis.

In some instances, the banks provide a tax service to their customers without charge, provided that an interest-free deposit is maintained with the bank. This practice was taken up a few years ago by the Institute of Chartered Accountants who were given an assurance by the Committee of London Clearing Bankers that it is not the policy of the member banks to advertise, or otherwise offer, such a facility to customers who are professionally advised elsewhere.

To help a citizen with his taxation problems is a socially desirable thing. It is a sad commentary on our society that taxation has become so complicated that the ordinary man in the street cannot hope to understand it. It is particularly sad that the cost of paying for professional help is sometimes prohibitive. One possible solution would lie in the allowing of tax fees as a deduction for income tax purposes, as is done in the United States. In the UK such fees are allowed as accountancy charges for the purposes of business expenses, but the same relief is not allowed to the private individual.

From the standpoint of the banks, taxation work – even if it brings no profit – makes a very real contribution to the consolidation of banking business. It provides another point of contact with the customer and it is another area where lasting goodwill can be built up. It is a common cry of bank managers that they do not have as much time to meet their customers as they would like, particularly those who maintain credit accounts and do not therefore see their bank manager in connection with overdraft facilities. In such cases the contact maintained through the taxation service will be stronger than through the local banking branch. In many cases the taxation branch will know more about the customer's affairs than will the banking branch and thus will be able to advise him in some of the wider aspects of finance. In fact, contact with customers through the taxation departments is often one of the most successful in terms of the cross-selling of other bank services.

Personal financial planning

Over 30 years ago the distinguished banker Mr L. C. Mather wrote in the *Journal of The Institute of Bankers:*

> 'From time to time the wealthier type of private customer complains to his bank manager concerning the heavy burden of estate duty, and may seek advice in friendly manner as to what means are legally available to limit the likely liability of his estate in this respect for the benefit of his dependants. Let there be no doubt at the outset; it would be foolish of the manager to attempt to advise on such a complicated and delicate subject. To deal adequately with serious enquiries of this kind demands deep knowledge of an extensive and specialised branch of the law and it is no part of the duty of a bank manager to pretend to guide the customer through the complicated maze of estate duty, replete with legal pitfalls. But, before recommending the customer to discuss the problem with his solicitor, it is always helpful to have a general chat, carefully avoiding any suggestion of advice, nevertheless displaying a working knowledge of the salient principles at stake. To profess ignorance or disinterest would be contrary to the tenets of our business, particularly in view of the publicity accorded in recent years to several aspects of the matter in the financial press.'[3]

Mr Mather's words illustrate yet again the nature of the tightrope walked by bank managers in the matter of giving advice. 'Display a working knowledge', says Mr Mather, but avoid 'any suggestion of advice'. At branch level, those words are still valid. The difference is that nowadays the bank manager can refer his customer to some other part of the group where the most detailed financial planning advice will be available.

Financial planning for wealthier customers is often referred to as estate planning. (The author first came across this term in the United States in 1966, when the best-seller among non-fiction for the month of June was a massive tome with the improbable title of *How to Avoid Probate*, selling at $15.) It is the organisation of one's financial affairs to the best advantage according to one's personal philosophy. Generally, estate planning is concerned with the conservation of capital by minimising taxation.

In former years, the trustee departments of the banks would quite often prepare 'estate duty savings schemes' for beneficiaries of trusts or, on occasions, for customers of the bank. They helped a lot of families to save a lot of money in estate duty. The amounts involved in such schemes were usually considerable and those giving the advice were conscious of the risks involved. Always the advice was hedged in by provisos and disclaimers, but in at least one case the accidental ommission of a few words led to a very substantial claim in later years. The first bank to introduce a formal estate planning service was Martins Bank. This was subsequently adopted by Barclays Bank and all the clearing banks in varying ways will now assist customers with advice on the arrangement of their affairs.

The true estate plan must be comprehensive. It must take account of the basic thinking and needs of the customer and must take into account all aspects of his financial circumstances. It is usually a very impressive document running perhaps to twenty or thirty pages and setting out in fine detail the customer's present position with the various alternative courses open to him. It is a rich man's service. The fees can be substantial, often running into four figures, but the costs are high and there is no direct profit. There is some spin-off to other services and, here again, an opportunity for creating goodwill.

It is a platform for displaying the professionalism of the trustee departments: a person who is impressed with the quality of the advice in his lifetime will be more inclined to entrust the bank with the management of his affairs on death.

The banks' principal competitors in this field are life assurance brokers and a small number of highly specialised financial counsellors. Some large insurance brokers were in fact the forerunners in this field, but not surprisingly their schemes often tended to be insurance orientated whereas the banks would claim that their planning services embrace the wider aspects of finance, including taxation planning and investment planning. Perhaps only the banks can draw together such a cross-section of financial expertise under one roof and perhaps only the banks can afford to maintain what is very much a luxury service.

What then of financial planning for the man of modest means? Barclays Bank were the first to attempt a comprehensive report service for the middle classes and this, 'Money Doctor Service', received almost universal acclaim in the press. The applicant for the service is invited to complete a questionnaire about his financial affairs and in due time he receives a comprehensive survey of his finances with recommendations for improvement. The financial affairs of most people fall into a limited number of defined categories. They are, for example:

(a) savings and investment;
(b) provision for contingencies, e.g. insurance;
(c) provision for the family, e.g. education, family trusts;
(d) pension arrangements and provision for retirement; and
(e) testamentary arrangements.

These are matters on which everyone needs help and advice at some time, and the Money Doctor Service seeks to provide the answer. That there was a need for such a service was borne out by the initial flood of applications, but it transpired that many of these came from people of substantial means who really needed more expensive estate planning advice. The main problem with any service of this nature is the cost of providing it. As we have said elsewhere, the effect of inflation in the 1970s on bank salaries was dramatic and so today it is difficult to

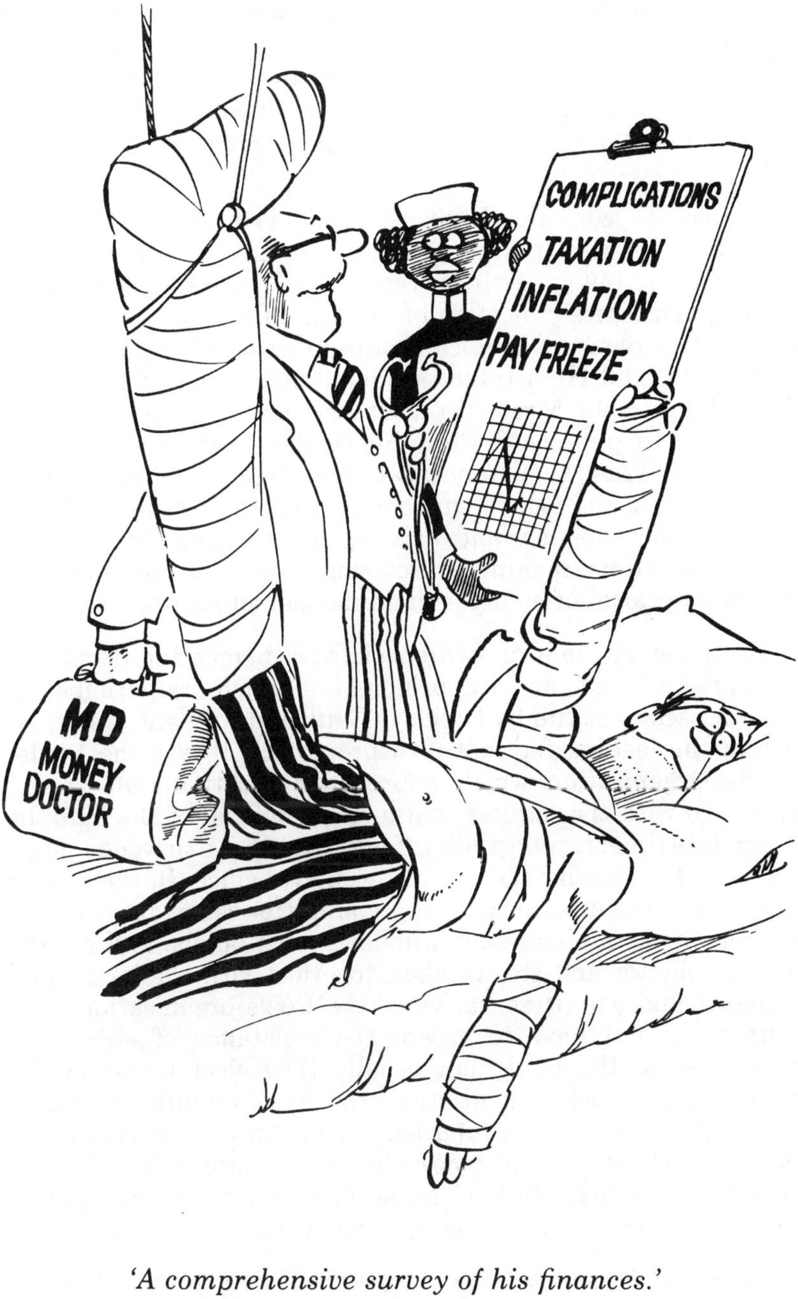

'A comprehensive survey of his finances.'

provide a middle-of-the-road planning service on the lines of Money Doctor at an acceptable level of fee. Although one may point out that the fee is no more than the cost of having a car serviced or carrying out some modest repairs to one's house, the same obstacle is there – that people are generally reluctant to pay for advice.

For some years the Midland Bank Trust Company have offered a financial planning service to individuals, whatever their means, but no written report was prepared, the advice being given entirely by word of mouth. Subsequently, Midland offered free personal financial counselling to retired customers with a Midland High Interest Cheque Account and to holders of Midland Gold Mastercard. Other customers were charged £30 per hour plus VAT. From September 1985 however, Midland Bank Trust Company has offered free personal financial counselling to all Midland customers. This service covers advice and guidance on new and existing investments, income and capital taxation, making or revising a will, or providing an overall appraisal of a customer's financial situation.

There remain one or two specialist schemes for particular categories of customer, the principal of which are perhaps the advisory schemes run by Barclays Bank and Midland Bank, for two of the leading football pool promoters. It was the Littlewoods Organisation which approached Martins Bank many years ago with the request that a senior official of the bank be given full-time responsibility for advising Littlewoods prize winners. The scheme has worked well ever since. In the case of the larger amounts, an advisory committee is set up for each winner, the committee consisting of a trust official and a nominated solicitor and stockbroker, together with the local bank manager and a representative of the Pools organisation. The winners do not have to accept the assistance of either the committee or the bank, but usually they elect to do so. On behalf of the pools organisation, the bank maintains contact with the winners on a regular basis over the years and at times the financial service becomes almost a pastoral function. In more recent years, Midland Bank Trust Company established a similar service on behalf of Vernons Pools.

There are of course other categories of people for whom the

banks' advisory services are particularly appropriate. There are those in receipt of substantial inheritances, those who receive large capital sums on the sale of a business and others who find themselves in possession of unaccustomed wealth, perhaps as the result of a court order or a compensation award. In many ways such cases are straightforward. The greater difficulty lies in providing a continuing, economic, advisory service for the man in the street. Most people will no doubt continue to obtain financial advice in pub or club, or from their banker or broker on an *ad hoc* basis. Perhaps this is good enough. On the other hand, it seems a pity that there is no comprehensive source of information and advice on personal financial matters to which people of all walks of life can turn, knowing that they will receive reliable, comprehensive and up-to-date answers at a price they can afford.

As we have written elsewhere:[4]

> Personal finance is an ever-changing scene. It changes partly because of the fiscal variations introduced at least once a year by successive Chancellors, partly because of moods and fashion in the financial markets, partly because of overall changes in the economy and partly because of the steady flow of new products marketed by financial institutions. It is also a moving scene because individual financial problems differ from person to person and from time to time. Not only do the problems differ, but there are variations in the solutions. What is right for one person, is wrong for another; what is right today is wrong tomorrow. Money is arguably the most complicated and most changeable aspect of modern life.

The financial services legislation

The Financial Services Act 1986 and the consequential Rules of the Securities & Investments Board have greatly affected the advisory services of the banks. For the most part, the discrete services described in this chapter are provided by departments or subsidiary companies of the banks and not by the bank branches direct to the customer. Nevertheless, as we have said, bank customers have traditionally seen their bank managers as the first port of call for financial advice and it is that relationship which has been disturbed by 'polarisation' to which we have already referred and which is dealt with also in the Appendix.

In broad terms, it is no longer possible for a branch bank to act as 'independent advisor' to customers on investment matters as well as being 'company representative' for the purpose of selling the bank's own unit trusts, life assurance or pension products. The Securities & Investments Board considered it confusing to customers that a branch should act in both roles. Thus, for the most part, the banks have chosen to make their branches 'company representatives' for the purpose of selling their own investment services, whilst offering their advisory services in investment and insurance matters through separate parts of the group.

Over the years, various surveys have shown that many people seeking financial advice go in the first place to their bank managers. This was borne out yet again by a MORI Poll commissioned by National Mutual Life in 1987. The survey suggested that 18 per cent (the highest category) would seek advice in the first place from their bank managers whilst only 8 per cent would go to an independent intermediary. Apparently, only 4 per cent said they would seek financial advice from an insurance company.

Agency services

It has been said many times that the relationship of banker and customer is that of debtor and creditor. In connection, however, with many of the services described in this book quite different relationships are established between the banks and their customers and these are referred to in the closing chapter. One relationship which arises in a number of circumstances is that of principal and agent, i.e. where a bank acts as agent for a customer. This may arise where a bank collects a cheque for a customer (see page 453), or where a bank sends coupons from bearer bonds for collection on behalf of a customer, or where a bank buys stocks and shares on behalf of a customer (see page 119). A bank acts as agent for a customer when it engages in insurance broking (see Chapter 9), although rather anomalously the insurance broker receives payment from the insurance company not from his client. A bank may also act as agent for a customer in the course of managing investments, making travel arrangements or submitting an Income Tax Return to the Revenue on behalf of a customer. A bank is not an agent for its customer, however, where it acts as executor or trustee, nor when it acts as an insurer under a life policy, nor when it pays a cheque or leases plant and equipment.

Perhaps the most dramatic example of a bank moving into an agency field was the announcement by Lloyds Bank in May 1982 that it was entering the estate agency business. A new subsidiary of the bank known as Black Horse Agencies was set up with a view to taking over 'a number of high-calibre practices of chartered surveyors'. Since the original announcement a number of such practices have been acquired by Lloyds Bank. The main *raison d'être* advanced for this development was the banks' entry into the home loan market and, in fact, by the end of 1986 Lloyds were able to say that they were providing mortgage finance for one in three of all houses sold through Black Horse Agencies.

This is a most interesting step forward into a new dimension and, if we may say so, one which we advocated in our early days as part of the overall concept of the universal bank. It may of course be argued that the buying and selling of houses is not a financial matter, but to most people it is the money aspect which matters most rather than the woodworm or the dry rot. It is trite to observe that the buying of a house is the biggest financial decision which most people ever take. The financing of a house purchase is a legitimate bank function – the bringing together of a buyer and seller can but be a convenient and agreeable corollary to that function.

Perhaps one of the most challenging aspects of this development is the additional use which can be made of the branch network in offering yet another 'retail' service to the public. Houses are bought and sold in the high streets of this country and the banks once again are well placed, partly from their physical location and partly because of their enormous customer lists, to offer this service. Indeed Lloyds Bank already use their branch network to display details of houses available through Black Horse agencies. An interesting development within Black Horse agencies was the acquisition of Anchor Relocation Services, a service designed for companies and their executive employees to facilitate the movement of key personnel.

For the most part, this is not the business of 'surveying' nor the business of fine art auctioneering (although Lloyds Bank find themselves in that area by reason of their purchase). It is primarily a marketing operation – the matching of buyers and sellers over a wide area with the use of computerised systems.

Although Lloyds Bank was the first to take this step in this country, it is not uncommon among the trust companies or so-called 'near banks' in Canada where some years ago at least one such North American institution had a sales force of 1,700 or so representatives who dealt exclusively with the buying and selling of domestic property. It was (and is?) not unusual for a salesman to make himself known to a house owner, offering to sell the property for a good price, find the owner another even more desirable property and provide the finance for the transaction! It seems unlikely that the British banks will pursue estate agency activities so aggressively. Nevertheless, estate agency work is becoming an integral part of the concept of the financial conglomerate discussed in Chapter 1. At the time of writing, the Trustee Savings Bank in Scotland has acquired one of Scotland's largest residential estate agencies, Midland Bank have taken a 35 per cent stake in an estate agency in the North and Midlands, National Westminster Bank has formed a link with the Team Association, which acts for a chain of independent estate agents, Hambros Bank have acquired Bairstow Eves, which is one of the largest estate agents in the United Kingdom and Barclays Bank have arranged to sell their financial services through a group of independent estate agencies. Similarly, the giant Prudential Assurance has to some extent entered the estate agency field. It will be interesting to see how this trend develops, particularly as the building societies now have statutory powers to move into estate agency business. Indeed, in September 1986 the largest society, the Halifax, announced plans to establish a countrywide estate agency service and have now acquired a number of leading firms in local areas. Similarly, a number of insurance companies are moving into this field. The attraction seems to be, as we have indicated above, not merely the commissions available on house sales, but the acquisition of additional high street outlets and the opportunity to sell a range of related financial services.

References

1 Woods v Martins Bank Ltd and Another (1958) 3 All.E.R. at page 174.
2 D. Defoe: 'Britannia'.
3 L. C. Mather: 'A Practical Approach to the Problem of Saving Estate Duty'. *Journal of The Institute of Bankers,* March 1954.
4 *Moneyguide: the handbook of personal finance,* D. G. Hanson, Kluwer Publishing, 1981.

'Money and travel go nicely hand in hand.'

CHAPTER 13

Money and Travel

'Much have I travel'd', wrote the poet Keats, 'in the realms of gold'. Certainly nowadays he would not have travelled very far without gold or its modern equivalent. Travel and money are like intersecting circles which overlap very considerably, for it is almost impossible to contemplate modern travel without both the provision of money and the problems of money. The traveller abroad must pay for his tickets, he requires currency for the journey, he needs the wherewithal to pay hotels and restaurants and personal shopping bills, perhaps in a succession of countries, he needs (or should have) baggage and health insurance, he must know the rules of the game and he should have a lifeline in case of need.

The banks respond to these needs of the traveller by issuing him with currency and travellers' cheques at his local branch, advising on exchange control regulations in the countries concerned and marking his passport appropriately, opening credits with foreign banks, supplying credit cards with almost world-wide acceptance, providing airport branches and *bureaux de change* en route and generally instructing, counselling and sometimes rescuing the traveller in all the financial aspects of his visit. For the business traveller, one may add the supply of economic data, advice on local markets and in all probability some worthwhile local introductions. Thus, money and travel go nicely hand-in-hand.

Foreign Currency
All the principal banks in the United Kingdom provide foreign currency for overseas visits, either at all their branches or at

selected branches. Most foreign countries will allow unlimited amounts of their own currency to be taken in, but there is usually a limit on the amount which can be brought out. In a few countries, notably U.S.S.R., the local currency cannot be purchased until arrival in that country. The banks charge a small commission, in most cases around ½ per cent per transaction, for the sale of foreign currency to a customer and will usually buy it back without any further commission charge within six months from the date of purchase at the then current buying rate.

Since the removal of Exchange Control restrictions in the United Kingdom, residents of this country have been able to open accounts in foreign currency with most of the UK banks, usually subject to a minimum sterling equivalent, e.g. £500 or £1,000.

Open Credits Abroad

We have discussed the system of open credits in Chapter 2 and, in broad terms, the same facilities are available in countries overseas. The facility will normally only be available in a particular town at a particular branch of a bank and will be arranged by the customer's bank in the United Kingdom. There will be a commission charge, usually of the order of £2.50 plus postages and other out-of-pocket expenses. This is in addition to any charge made by the overseas bank. Open credit arrangements are not normally necessary or appropriate for short overseas visits owing to the widely accepted use of travellers' cheques and credit cards.

Overseas Payments

Money may be remitted overseas by International Money Orders (IMOs), which are appropriate for smaller transactions, i.e. up to £500 or US $1,000 and thus are appropriate for remitting the cost of hotel bills and car hire, etc.

Larger amounts may be remitted by International Payment Orders (IPOs), whether in sterling or other currencies. Whereas an IMO (see above) is in the nature of a pre-signed draft obtained from the customer's bank in this country for him to send abroad, an IPO payment is made through the banking system, i.e. the customer's bank makes the payment to the overseas bank for the benefit of the beneficiary concerned.

Telegraphic Transfers (TTs)
This is a cable authority to an overseas bank to make payment to the beneficiary concerned. It is thus the fastest means of making an overseas payment and it may be made in any currency. The commission charge for IPOs and TTs is currently around 25p per £100.

Postcheques
Customers of Girobank cannot use their cheque books overseas, but may obtain a free book of postcheques for use overseas. In most countries a postcheque can be used to draw any amount up to the local currency equivalent of £100. Up to ten cheques a day may be used if desired. They may be used at approximately 90,000 Post Offices in approximately 34 countries. A single fee of £5 is charged when each book of postcheques is issued.

Eurocheques
Most of the English banks are members of the Eurocheques scheme, which enables customers to draw cash in European countries at banks displaying the Eurocheque symbol. Cheques can also be issued in the currency of the country concerned and each cheque is guranteed up to the equivalent value of £100. Eurocheques may be issued for higher amounts but these are not guaranteed. They are acceptable in over 4½ million retail outlets in 20 countries as well as nearly 200,000 branches of 15,000 banks in 39 countries. As mentioned on page 228, the British clearing banks withdrew the facility to use their cheque cards for payments overseas with effect from May 1983.

Credit Cards
This subject has been dealt with at length in Chapter 10. The principal credit cards, i.e. Mastercard, Visa, American Express and Diner's Club are accepted in most countries of the world. The two principal British cards, Access and Barclaycard, through their respective Mastercard and Visa groups each claim to be accepted by about three million retail outlets in other countries. Diner's Club and American Express also claim that their cards are accepted in 750,000 retail outlets respectively throughout the world.

In 1978 the European Council for Payment Systems was formed to improve technical co-operation among European banks. The Council announced in January 1985 that banks from

17 countries had agreed to work together to achieve technological compatibility so that a single plastic card could be used to obtain cash from bank machines throughout Europe. The intention would be that the three major credit card groups, Visa, Eurocard (Access and Mastercard) and Eurocheque should set up reciprocal facilities so that their cards would become virtually interchangeable for the purpose of obtaining cash and ultimately for electronic shopping.

Travellers' Cheques

Travellers' cheques are almost certainly the most universally accepted method of payment for overseas travellers and indeed, for payments in the UK. They may be obtained from branches of most of the banks in Britain and may be issued in sterling, dollars or other overseas currencies. The normal charge for the issue of travellers' cheques is 1 per cent of the amount of the cheques, plus a further 1 per cent when the cheques are encashed. In the case of the loss or theft of travellers' cheques, the issuing bank will arrange a refund or replacement provided the cheques were signed in the correct place at the time of issue and not signed a second time, as would be done on encashment.

For many years, the travellers' cheques business of the banking system was regarded as unexciting and unprofitable. It was dominated by American Express who still have approximately 36 per cent of the worldwide travellers' cheques business and by the larger American banks. Historically, the travellers' cheque has been more popular in America than in other countries, largely because of the absence of inter-State banking. Whereas a cheque drawn on a London clearing bank would be acceptable in any part of Britain, a cheque drawn on any one of the 14,000 banks in America would probably not be acceptable even in a contiguous State.

The events of recent years have, however, given a boost to the worldwide travellers' cheques business. One major factor has been the development of credit cards with their highly automated international network. This led to the announcement by Visa in 1979 that it was to undertake the marketing of travellers' cheques for member banks. This move was followed in March 1980 by Mastercard, who introduced the Master's Travellers' Cheque. The other aspect is the consequence of high interest rates, which have made travellers' cheque business increasingly profitable, particularly as quite a large proportion of travellers' cheques are paid for by customers and not used for a considerable length of time.

The entry of the credit card companies into the travellers' cheque business has led to a concentration on the three main groups, Visa, Mastercard and American Express. In 1981, it was expected that a new consortium of European banks known as Euro Travellers' Cheques International (ETCI) would become a new major factor in the European scene. This would have been based on the United Kingdom Thomas Cook operation, which the European consortium was to buy. This was to have been in association with the American-based Mastercard, but was to function independently and would include the development of Eurocard, a travel and entertainment card introduced alongside Eurocheque. These proposals were abandoned, however, because the West German Savings Banks were unhappy about the arrangement and had in fact agreed to sell American Express travellers' cheques. The influence of the German Savings Banks is considerable: they have 17,000 branches and more than 50 per cent of the personal banking business in West Germany. In August 1981, Thomas Cook announced a joint venture with Mastercard to issue sterling and dollar travellers' cheques and agreed to explore with ETCI the possibility of developing a multi-currency European cheque.

At the present time, the annual world sales of travellers' cheques are believed to be in the region of $40 billion and are understood to be growing at the rate of approximately 15 per cent per annum. As mentioned above, approximately 36 per cent of the business is with American Express and the rest is fairly widely spread among Visa (18 per cent), Thomas Cook (16 per cent), and Bank of America and Citicorp (12 per cent each).

In this country, Barclays Bank travellers' cheque business is of course with the Visa Group, Midland Bank with Cooks, National Westminster Bank with Mastercard and Lloyds Bank have formed a joint venture with American Express. The Trustee Savings Bank travellers' cheques are issued through the Visa Group: the Co-operative Bank issues Citibank travellers' cheques.

The pattern of travellers' cheque business on the continent of Europe has not yet been finally resolved. It remains to be seen what emerges from the link between Thomas Cook and Euro Travellers' Cheques International. Some of the Europeans, particularly the West Germans, view with some suspicion the possible intrusion of the major credit card companies, largely because of the difficulty of controlling a domestic economy with inter-state payments being made so freely by credit card and partly because of the inflationary effects of credit cards. There is some preference in Europe, therefore, for the Eurocard concept which, as we have said, is a travel and entertainment card and not a credit card as such.

The travellers' cheque 'war' is all part of the worldwide competition for retail banking business, particularly at current levels of interest rates and also because of the advent of plastic card banking which we discuss in Chapter 23.

The travel business

All the foregoing services are essentially of a banking nature, but they are inextricably mixed with travel. It was no doubt this relationship which prompted the debate over many years as to whether or not the British banks should engage directly in travel business. For long enough the Australian banks had conducted their own travel departments; in some respects they were among the first to appreciate the needs of the traveller and to provide lounges for the comfort of foreign visitors in some of the principal cities around the world. A number of American banks have travel departments or travel agencies and perhaps one need look no further than Wells Fargo for an historic link between travel and money. Some of the German banks have direct interests in travel agencies and in Scandinavia, the Netherlands and France the banks allow facilities in their branches for tour operators and travel agents.

Although no one doubts the financial needs of the traveller, one must question the philosophy of banks in the travel business. To provide travellers' cheques, currency, credit cards and to advise generally on the financial arrangements may be seen as part of the total financial service of the commercial bank. To book rail tickets, air tickets, hotel rooms and the like is essentially a different business. It is not of course banking and it is not strictly a financial service at all. It stands alone in the gallery of services described in this book as a non-financial operation. Perhaps such a nice distinction is unfair and even irrelevant. After all, two of the principal operators in the travel business, Thomas Cook and Son and American Express, have for long been bankers in their own right. Nevertheless, as a matter of pedantry if nothing more, perhaps we may be allowed the proposition that travel business is not banking business.

Whatever the philosophy may be, the fact remains that many banks around the world have found it convenient and profitable to engage directly or indirectly in the provision of travel facilities. It was not surprising, therefore, that the clearing banks in this country showed interest when, in 1972, the government announced its proposals for selling off Thomas Cook and Son from the government-owned transport holding company. At the conclusion of the tendering process, the company was aquired by a consortium of Midland Bank, Trust Houses Forte and the Automobile Association. Thus the Midland Bank acquired a direct interest in one of the best known and oldest established travel businesses in the world. In 1977, Midland Bank bought out the minority shareholdings of the other members of the consortium. When, however, in 1981 the U.S. Federal Reserve Board gave approval to the acquisition by Midland Bank of a majority interest in Crocker National Corporation, it required the bank to divest itself of the ownership of the Thomas Cook travel agency activities in the United States within a period of 2 years. The attractions of Thomas Cook to a bank buyer were no doubt its name, its worldwide outlets, its banking and travellers' cheque business and the expertise of its staff.

Of the other clearing banks, Barclays Bank also had a direct interest in the travel business through its wholly-owned subsidiary, Travel Enterprises. Originally developed as a captive travel agency to deal with the very considerable travel requirements of the Barclays group, its services were nevertheless available to business customers through the bank's branches. It was of course a modest sized operation in relation to the giant Thomas Cook and was in fact sold by Barclays in January, 1981.

The Co-operative Bank too has a link with the travel business through its associated Co-op Travel, which is a travel agency with 38 branches.

Some advantages

From a bank's point of view there are a number of advantages to be gained from involvement in the travel business. The first and principal benefit must be that of profits and it is generally accepted that there are good profits to be made among travel operators, although in the past there have been some very lean years and some failures. The combination of a well-established travel group with an international bank must, it is thought, have a very worthwhile profit potential. Secondly, a bank like any business house must be on the lookout for valid opportunities of extending its influence and the travel business offers a very real way of doing this. The tourist industry is very big business indeed and now constitutes the largest single item in the analysis of world trade. Thirdly, the close contact between a travel agency and its travelling customers provides considerable opportunity for gaining new accounts for the associated bank. Fourthly, the same extensive connections present cross-selling opportunities for a wide range of the bank's other services.

Disadvantages

On the other side of the coin, there are of course some possible disadvantages. We have already said that the travel business has had its troubles and can, at times, be particularly exposed to extraneous factors, such as bad weather, strikes, unemployment, credit and exchange control restrictions and to some extent also to changes in fashion. In addition, there is the danger of some unfortunate travel experience 'rubbing off' on the operator or agent who made the arrangements and if this happened to be a bank, some unfavourable publicity could result. From a bank's point of view, there is also the disadvantage that the travel business tends to be labour-intensive with the administrative organisation which that entails and the consequential high costs. Lastly, it could perhaps be said that for a bank to obtain the full benefit from an affiliated travel business, the services of the latter should be available in the bank's branches – something which is difficult, but not impossible to organise, within the framework of banking hours in the United Kingdom.

In a speech in 1973 to the Financial Times Conference on World Tourism and Travel,[1] Mr Malcolm Wilcox, then Assistant Chief General Manager of Midland Bank and Deputy Chairman of Thomas Cook, outlined with great lucidity the three fundamental aspects of travel busines, viz. the 'originating sector' (the travel agents and tour operators who book the trains, flights and hotels, put together the packages and sell the tickets); the transportation sector (the air and shipping lines and railways); and the accommodation sector (the hotels, holiday villages, etc.). At the front end of the total operation, i.e. the travel agency section, it is not difficult to see the affinity between banks and the travel people. They have reciprocal, or at least complementary, marketing strengths, and as we have already mentioned there is much common ground between them. In the middle section, that of transportation, the banks are already involved, as Mr Wilcox points out, in the leasing of ships and aircraft (although it must be acknowledged that this is a far cry from being involved in the transportation business at first hand). In the final category, at the accomodation end, the banks are already accustomed to financing hotels and similar leisure complexes.

It must remain very doubtful, however, whether the banks would ever wish to become involved at first hand in either the transportation or accommodation business. They are both highly specialised activities and both areas have suffered serious setbacks over the years. It may be that the banks will participate to a degree in the provision of hotels and aircraft, but this must surely, at its most, be no more than a trade investment and one would expect any significant involvement by the banks to be at the originating end of the operation, as agents for the operators, if there is going to be any direct involvement in travel business.

Bureaux de change

One particular aspect of travel business has experienced a boom in this country in recent years, that is the provision of *bureau de change* facilities. The growth of tourism in London during the past few years (and no doubt the closing of the banks on Saturday mornings) led to the development of independent *bureaux de change* in London and, to a lesser degree, in the provinces. According to one recent estimate, there were approximately 170 shops, stores and hotels offering *bureaux de change* facilities in London and other centres in the UK. Naturally enough, the banks have not stood aside from this development. Barclays Bank opened its first bureau at Marble Arch in September 1977 to provide a six-day service from 8 a.m. until 6 p.m. in the winter months and from 8 a.m. until 8 p.m. in the summer months. Lloyds Bank, through their subsidiary Lewis's Bank, offer *bureau de change* facilities at fourteen of the Lewis's Group stores and Midland Bank, of course, offer exchange facilities through Thomas Cook. Apart from these 'separate' *bureaux de change,* the banks have made a move to extend banking branch opening hours to provide exchange facilities. In March 1978, National Westminster Bank extended the opening hours of its Shaftesbury Avenue Branch and later in the year, Barclays Bank reached agreement with the staff side for the opening of four branches on Saturday mornings to provide bureau services with the intention, subject to demand, of developing a small network of exchange bureaux operating from bank branches on Saturday mornings. These are in addition to branches at Heathrow, Luton and Stanstead Airports. This development was of course well in advance of the wider opening of branches on Saturday mornings, as discussed on page 475. Midland Bank too, augmented its existing Thomas Cook outlets by opening a Thomas Cook bureau in the bank's Leicester Square Branch. It is a self-contained unit within the branch and is open six days a week until 10 p.m. and also open for most of Sunday.

The provision of travel services through the banks is a subject of continuing interest and one in which some major developments might well be seen in the coming years. A particular attraction of travel business for banks is that it provides an extra product to sell through the banking branches. As the traditional banking services have become more formalised and, in some cases, centralised, it has become increasingly important for other, profitable, services to be provided across the bank counters. To some extent that is a continuing theme of this book and the subject is discussed again in the closing chapter. Travel services may well have a special place in the increased catholicity of banking business. On the other hand, it must be recognised that this is a different type of business, requiring different skills and different knowledge. It may be some time therefore, before many bank branches are open for travel business.

Reference

1 M. G. Wilcox: Banks and the Travel Business, *Journal of The Institute of Bankers,* October 1973.

Business Services

CHAPTERS 14–22

CHAPTER 14

Merchant Banking

Lord Denning's dictum that banks are easier to recognise than to define (see p. 1) might have been applied with even greater force to merchant banks. Merchant banks and merchant banking are almost impossible to define. Indeed, to quote the late Sir Edward Reid, the term merchant bank 'is sometimes applied to banks who are not merchants, sometimes to merchants who are not banks and sometimes to houses who are neither merchants nor banks'.[1] There is no doubt that the title 'merchant banker' still has glamorous overtones. It conjures visions of power and influence, giving advice to kings and being in the confidence of governments. Even in these down-to-earth days the name has a cachet and a mystique which is uncommon in other professions. The merchant bankers are the princes of the financial world. Nor is this reputation undeserved. The history of the old merchant banks makes fascinating reading. Not without good reason were the six Great Powers of Europe in the late nineteenth century listed as England, France, Russia, Austria, Prussia and Baring Brothers.[2] Nor is it all in the past. Among the modern merchant banks, it has been said of the rise of S. G. Warburg & Co. that 'there has been nothing like it this century'.[3] The student who wishes to know more of merchant banking history will find pleasure in Richard Kellett's entertaining and well-researched book *The Merchant Banking Arena,* but here we must concern ourselves with more functional matters.

The Accepting House

What then is merchant banking? The term has its origin in the merchanting activities of the late eighteenth and early nine-

'. . . giving advice to kings.'

teenth centuries when trade between countries would be financed by bills of exchange drawn on the principal merchanting houses. At that point, the merchants were merely financing their own trading activities. As international trade grew and other lesser-known names wished to import goods from abroad, the established merchants 'lent their names' to the newcomers by agreeing to accept bills of exchange on their behalf. The 'accepting house' would charge a commission for this service and thus there grew up the business of accepting bills to finance the trade not merely of themselves, but of others. Acceptance business thus became and to a degree always has been the hallmark of the true merchant bank. The acceptance 'credit' was primarily a means of financing international trade until the 1930s, but the use of acceptance credits for domestic business was given an impetus by the Macmillan Report in 1931. The Macmillan Committee recommended that commercial bills be used more widely as a means of financing domestic trade and either for this reason or because of the falling-off in foreign trade and the difficulties of a number of countries, bills of exchange became more widely used as a means of financing domestic trade. Although bank overdrafts were comparatively cheap by present-day standards, it was cheaper still to finance current transactions by means of acceptance credits. Thus bill finance became and still remains a valuable alternative source of finance for the shorter term transactions of industry in this country. Sixteen of the leading merchant banks constitute the Accepting Houses Committee, which acts as the regulatory and disciplinary body and also the principal mouthpiece of the merchant banks in this country.

Capital issues

The second historical characteristic of the merchant banks was the raising of capital for foreign governments. In many cases, the merchants had been trading in the countries concerned and had gained the confidence of the governments and other authorities in those countries. So it was that they were entrusted with the issuing of bonds in the London market. Originally the interest on such bond issues would be payable in foreign currency, but in 1818 Nathan Rothschild, the founder of N. M. Rothschild & Sons, floated the first foreign loans carrying interest in sterling and as Mr Kellett tells us, within two years of the Battle of Waterloo, Rothschild 'had floated £7 million of loans in London for four Continental governments, the Austrian, Prussian, Russian and the defeated French'.[4] In the next 100 years or so, despite the interruption of the First World War, loan after loan was to be raised in London for foreign governments. Hambros Bank made thirteen issues of loans for continental governments in the three years 1926–28; Morgan Grenfell & Co. handled six issues in those years; and Barings dealt with twelve, all of them for various countries around the world.

As with acceptance credits, it was international business which preceded the developments in the domestic market. During the spate of foreign government loans, there had been very few issues for industry in this country. The foreign bond business ceased with the failure of international currencies and the lack of international confidence. Those years – the 1930s – were to see the gradual move of British industry into a new dimension partly from growth within and partly from mergers. New capital was required and the merchant banks with their vast experience were on hand, both with expert advice and the machinery for capital issues. Thus the second principal ingredient of merchant banking became and still is the raising of capital through the issue of stock or bonds. This business, however, was not by any means the preserve of the merchant banks. Some of the leading stockbrokers have a long tradition of issuing work, and there are many firms with no tradition of commercial credit business which have undertaken capital issues. The regulatory body is The Issuing Houses Association, with 56 members.

Diversity of business

Thus there are accepting houses and issuing houses, and most of the leading merchant banks are in both categories. Together they make up the merchant banking scene. That is not nearly, however, the sum total of their business. Some retain their original merchanting activities and all have moved into new financial activities. The scope of those activities was well summed up in the evidence of the Accepting Houses Committee to the Radcliffe Committee,[5] which may be paraphrased as follows:

The granting of acceptance credits is a business which all have in common.

Many of the members act as issuing houses.

All conduct banking accounts in one form or another for customers at home and abroad.

All handle stock exchange business on their customers' behalf.

Most of them manage investments for private customers, pension funds, colleges and charities.

Several members have an active trustee business.

Several conduct registration work for companies.

Three are prominent in the bullion market.

Several are active dealers in foreign exchange.

Several handle insurance business.

Two run merchanting companies.

One owns subsidiary companies in the production and marketing of timber and one trades in rubber.

One is prominent in the London Coffee Market.

We may also add that accepting houses and issuing houses manage investment trust companies, unit trusts, life assurance companies, pensions consultancy services and almost every other legitimate form of financial activity.

Two particular characteristics are usually attributed to merchant bankers. They are (a) their entrepreneurial instinct, which is borne out in many ways – at one time by their merchanting activities and their handling of government loans, which in the early days they would take on to their own books in full before placing them with the public, usually at a large profit; and (b) their adaptability, borne out not only by the catholic nature of their present-day activities, but by their ability to adjust to changing circumstances over the years. The perfect example is their invention of the eurodollar (or eurocurrency) – the making of a market which enabled the principal currencies of the world to be used outside their countries of origin.

Good times and bad

It has not all been plain sailing for the merchant banks and not all have survived. Perhaps the most dramatic moment was the weekend of November 1890 when the great house of Barings could not meet its commitments and the governor of the Bank of England swiftly and secretly mounted a rescue operation with the aid of the joint stock banks and the private banks, and with some help from Russia and France – surely the first 'lifeboat' operation the City had seen. For all the merchant banks there were good times and bad and for the most part they have survived by virtue of their own great resilience. Out of the thirty largest merchant banks, no less than twenty-five were incorporated before the end of the last century. Barings, the oldest, goes back over 200 years to 1772, and Rothschilds and Schröders can look back on over 170 years of history. Perhaps their greatest growth period was in the late 1950s and early 1960s, with the enormous increase in public issues and the growth of the eurodollar markets. In March 1963, Mr C. Gordon Tether, the Lombard columnist of the *Financial Times,* was able to write, 'The past five to ten years have seen the merchant banks fully restored to their glory'.

Corporate advice

It is in the last twenty years or so that the merchant banks and issuing houses, and others who enjoy neither title, have moved into the field of corporate advice and with it the attendant business of 'bids and deals'. This is something of a 'chicken and egg' development, but for the most part these services grew out of the issuing side of the business which in itself, as we have already noted, was dominated in earlier years by stockbrokers. The issuing of capital on behalf of a company which is quoted or to be quoted calls for a combination of functions, principally (a) advice, (b) investigation, (c) documentation and (d) financial muscle or placing power. The accountants to the issue will carry out the necessary investigations in their field and the solicitors will attend to the documentation. The advice on the issue and the underwriting of it – indeed the whole responsibility for the issue – rests on the issuing house, which may be a stockbroker or merchant banker or other type of issuing house, or a combination of these. The advisory and issuing role are inseparable and as more and more companies have turned to merchant banks to handle their capital issues, largely because of their placing power, merchant banks have in turn developed their corporate advice departments. It was natural that those companies which were not seeking new capital but seeking advice on the development of their business, or a merger, or an acquisition or defence to a bid, should turn to the merchant banks for advice. Ideally, the advisory relationship should be a continuing one, but this has not always been the case in this country. This is partly because industrial companies turn to their advisors on an *ad hoc* basis in the kind of situations we have mentioned and the merchant banks in many cases have been less interested in a continuing advisory role than in handling the first public flotation and subsequent capital issues for their client. In some instances, particularly contested takeover bids, companies would choose their merchant banks rather as one might choose defence counsel, and some banks acquired reputations not unlike those of eminent defence lawyers of former days. Some companies would change their merchant banker advisors at intervals and this inhibited the creation of a continuing advisory relationship. Nevertheless, there are many merchant banks who have had a number of their clients for very many years and have a close working knowledge of their clients' affairs.

The clearing banks

It was the traditional view of the clearing banks that merchant banking was a role apart from the mainstream of domestic banking. This view was partly in recognition of the entrepreneurial nature of merchant banking; partly because of the equity participation by some merchant banks which did not seem to fit in comfortably with the lending function of the clearers; and partly because of the advisory function of the merchant banks – a role which was thought to be better exercised objectively, aside from the everyday banker-customer relationship, particularly in contested and possibly contentious situations. On the other hand, there were those in the clearing banks who disagreed with this view. It seemed to them that for many years they would nurse a particular account, giving help in good times and bad, only to find that when the fledgling company left the comparative seclusion of its unquoted status to seek a stock exchange listing, the pickings in the form of large fees and a certain amount of financial kudos would go to a merchant bank. In fact, long before that stage was reached many companies would be seeking an institutional investor, perhaps to relieve the death duty position, and the clearing bank would have no alternative but to introduce its customer to a merchant bank that could place the shares. It seemed at times that the clearing banks were losing not only the opportunity of equity participation, with its anticipated growth, but also the prospect of substantial fees for the issuing work (fees which could exceed the net banking profit on the account over many years) and the opportunity of a continuing advisory relationship.

In the event, in a comparatively short period of time, all the clearing banks moved into the business of merchant banking and it is the extent of their involvement which we must now consider. Out of the long list of merchant banking activities which we have mentioned there are many which the clearing banks already traditionally undertook, e.g. acceptance credits, export finance, investment management, share registration and foreign exchange dealing. Some 'newer' activities which overlapped with those of merchant banks included unit trust management, insurance broking, pensions advice and linked life assurance. When, therefore, we speak of the clearing banks' entry into merchant banking we are contemplating a mere handful of non-traditional activities, viz:

medium-term lending (and here it is a matter of emphasis or degree, because medium-term loans were not unknown to the banks in bygone years);

new issues;

equity participation in developing companies; and

corporate finance advice.

It is generally accepted that the first move towards merchant banking came when, in 1965, Westminster Bank issued a debenture stock for Tecalemit Limited, the first occasion in modern times on which a clearing bank had brought an issue to the market. This was seen by Westminster Bank as a natural development of their banker-customer relationship, but it was the subject of a certain amount of criticism at the time. Nevertheless, by 1969 some six companies were brought to the market by Westminster Bank. In 1967 Midland Bank acquired a one-third interest in Samuel Montagu & Co. 'to give Midland's customers immediate access to Samuel Montagu's skills'. It was a major step for a clearing bank to take and the then Governor of the Bank of England made it clear that the further acquisition of accepting houses by the clearing banks would not have the approval of the authorities. Thus, in this twilight period, the banks moved tentatively into merchant banking activities by the development of their own subsidiaries.

In the same year, 1967, Glyn Mills entered the issuing house field with the handling of an issue on behalf of Beatson Clark & Co., indicating that more issues were in the pipeline and that they had built up a team of ex-merchant bankers for the purpose.

Perhaps the most energetic move into merchant banking was that of the National Westminster Group which in 1969 announced that one of their small subsidiaries, County Bank (a subsidiary of the District Bank and thus part of the National Westminster Group), would undertake merchant banking. Over the next seven years, County Bank was to become twelfth in the batting order of merchant banks in terms of the number of clients, and towards the end of that period they were to achieve a client growth rate greater than that of any other merchant bank.

Barclays approached merchant banking rather more diffidently. Their subsidiary, Barclays Bank (London & International), was developed as a deposit-taking and medium-term lending institution and gradually over a period of a few years a merchant banking team was built up. In the early 1970s Barclays Bank Trust Company handled three issues through their investment department, but it was primarily a caretaker operation until such time as the merchant banking side had been established. In the Chairman's address to stockholders for 1972 it was stated that Barclays Bank (London & International) 'has also entered into the field of merchant banking' – a modest way to describe such an important decision. It was not until 1975 that the new name, Barclays Merchant Bank, was adopted.

Meanwhile, following a change of attitude on the part of the Bank of England, Midland Bank had acquired the remainder of the equity of Samuel Montagu and thus became the first clearing bank – and still remains the only clearing bank – to own one of the old-established merchant banking houses. (In July 1982, Midland Bank announced the sale of a 40 per cent interest in Samuel Montagu to Aetna Life, a major insurance company in the United States. In July 1985, however, Midland re-acquired the Aetna Life stake in Samuel Montagu, which is thus a wholly owned subsidiary again of Midland Bank.)

Lloyds Bank, like Barclays Bank and National Westminster Bank, chose to develop 'from within' and in December 1972 set up a special corporate services operation to develop its merchant banking activities. In July 1985 Lloyds Bank formally incorporated its merchant banking business in Lloyds Merchant Bank.

The merchant banking activities of the Bank of Scotland were centred on the Bank of Scotland Finance Company set up in 1968. Although this originated as a deposit-taking institution, similar to the finance house subsidiaries of the English banks, it moved into the business of commercial lending and, through its subsidiary companies, engaged in leasing, investment banking and related operations. As the corporate advice side was developed, the bank moved more positively into a merchant banking role and became the largest of the Scottish 'merchant banks'. In 1977 the business of the finance company was transferred to the British Linen Bank, which has thus become the merchant banking arm of the group. The British Linen Bank, which was merged with the Bank of Scotland in 1971, holds a Royal Charter going back to 1746 and its entrepreneurial traditions of those days fit in well with its modern role of merchant banking. The merchant banking business of the Royal Bank of Scotland was developed for a while through its subsidiary, National, Commercial and Glyn's, but in January 1985 the bank acquired the Charterhouse Group, which was merged with National, Commercial & Glyn's to become Charterhouse Development.

Thus the banks came by varying routes to the business of

merchant banking and their choice of vehicles was perhaps typical of the empirical approach of the British banks.

The bidding subsidiaries

In the late 1960s all the banks had set up or made use of existing subsidiary companies in order to compete for larger deposits and also operate in the eurocurrency markets. Because of the official liquidity constraints and the agreement on interest rates, it was not possible to operate in this way through the parent banks. Thus, these 'bidding subsidiaries' competed for the deposits of large customers, deploying the funds in the market and moving gradually into the business of medium-term lending. A few years later, with the new freedom to compete, the subsidiaries were no longer necessary for the original purpose as outlined by the banks in their evidence to the Wilson Committee:

> 'After the introduction of Competition and Credit Control in 1971, the clearing bank parents were free to bid for deposits and the original rationale for the bidding subsidiaries disappeared. The function of bidding for deposits from branch customers was in most cases transferred to the parent bank, and eurocurrency business for the most part either to the parent or to an international subsidiary. But given the specialist expertise that had been built up in sterling medium-term lending and sterling "wholesale" money market dealing, the banks found it convenient to keep the bidding subsidiaries in being for one or both of these purposes.'[6]

It was natural to use these subsidiaries for the wider range of merchant banking activities which the banks embraced, but there was little uniformity in the pattern which emerged. Barclays Bank, for example, linked together the functions of medium-term lending, corporate advice and the role of an issuing house, but deliberately kept portfolio management separate from their merchant banking function. Lloyds Bank retained investment work and corporate finance in the parent bank, but continued to use its subsidiary, Lloyds Associated Banking Company, in a deposit-taking and term lending role. In the case of the National Westminster Group, County Bank set up three divisions, viz. corporate advice, finance and investment, the last division having responsibility for the unit trusts of the group as well as pension fund management. In the case of the Midland Bank Group, their merchant banking subsidiary, Samuel Montagu & Co., embraced not only the traditional merchant banking business but investment and unit trust management (through Drayton Montagu Portfolio Management).

That was approximately the position until the run up to the Big Bang and the City revolution to which we have referred in Chapters 1 and 6. Barclays announced in March 1984 their intention to bring together Barclays Merchant Bank, the jobbing business of Wedd Durlacher Mordaunt & Co., the stockbroking business of De Zoete and Bevan and Barclays Investment Management Limited, to form a new investment bank under the name Barclays De Zoete Wedd. In July 1984 National Westminster Bank announced the formation of an integrated securities house based on County Bank and incorporating the bank's interests in stockbrokers Fielding Newson-Smith and jobbers, Bisgood, Bishop. In September 1985, this grouping of activities became Natwest Investment Bank and the bank indicated its intention to acquire 100 per cent of the stockbroking and jobbing affiliates.

As mentioned in Chapter 6, Midland Bank, through Samuel Montagu, acquired an interest in stockbrokers, Greenwell & Co. and Royal Bank of Scotland, in association with the Charterhouse Group acquired stockbrokers, Tilney & Co. Thus most of the banks have grouped together under one umbrella, some of the traditional aspects of merchant banking plus capital issues, corporate advice and investment management as well as acting as market makers in the gilt market and broker-dealers in equities.

We have already said that if one leaves aside those various activities which were already undertaken by the clearing banks in varying degrees, the only new functions which they assumed under the heading of merchant banking were corporate advice, company issues and equity participation. Although the first two are inseparable in everyday life, we shall deal here only with the work of an issuing house, leaving the wider aspects of corporate advice to be dealt with in Chapter 13 on business advice generally.

The issuing houses

The work of an issuing house is to supervise the issue of a company's stock or shares. This may be the first public issue of a hitherto 'private' company which is seeking a stock exchange quotation or it may be a further issue of stock (a 'rights' issue) to existing shareholders. It may be an issue of ordinary stock or of loan stock, or a variation of either. It may be a public issue or a private placing.

The issuing house which brings a company to the market has a great responsibility. It must be satisfied that the company is one for which a public quotation would be appropriate. This is partly a matter of assets size, turnover, past profitability and profit forecasts, but it is more than that. The issuing house is putting its name to a venture in which the public at large are being invited to participate. The issuing house must therefore satisfy itself as to the standing and business integrity of the company, the nature and value of its contracts, the quality of the management, the adequacy of its records, its labour relations record, its marketing strength and virtually every aspect of the business relevant to its long-term stability. For a stock exchange quotation is a long-term matter – it is not for birds of passage. In all this the issuing house will work closely with the firm of accountants – usually known as the reporting accountants, whose report will accompany the offer documents – and with the firm of solicitors responsible for the documentation of the issue. The issuing house will also work closely with the stockbrokers to the issue and one of the major decisions will be that of the issue price. This will be fixed at the last moment and will reflect the general state of, and expectation in, the market, and indeed the economy at large; the size and standing of the company in question; the market view of that particular sector; the level of interest rates; dividend expectations and the dividend cover of the company concerned; and every factor large or small which may affect the price of the shares when issued. Then there are the imponderables, including the public awareness of a company before it comes to the market. Companies like Pilkingtons and Christie's were household names before they became public companies. In the case of Penguin Books, the remarkable over-subscription was attributed to the success of *Lady Chatterley's Lover*. In more recent times, the very considerable over-subscription of most of the privatisation issues may be attributed partly to the public awareness of such names as British Telecom, British Gas, Rolls-Royce, etc., but not least to the massive public relations exercise which preceded each issue.

The issuing house has a responsibility to the proprietors of the company, as much as to the new shareholders, to pitch the price at or around the right level. The new shareholders will not wish to see the share price sinking to a serious discount within a few weeks of the issue. Conversely, if the shares move to a substantial premium, no matter how much this may please the 'stags', the proprietors will suspect that their shares were introduced to the market at too low a value.

There was a time when smaller, thrusting businesses considered that they had 'arrived' when they were ready for, and accepted for, a stock exchange quotation. That is probably less so today and perhaps some of the smaller and medium sized companies, usually family businesses, are more inclined to cling to the comparative seclusion of having a small number of shareholders, notwithstanding that there is no exemption nowadays from publication of the accounts. There will always be cases, however, where a market quotation will be desirable, assuming a company satisfies all the criteria. In some cases, large shareholdings in a family company will be in private hands and to 'go public' may be the most satisfactory way of exchanging a proportion of the shares for cash as well as ensuring the future marketability of the shares which are retained. Perhaps even more typical is the successful company which needs resources for expansion on a scale which would only be obtainable if it widened its shareholder base by going public.

'Rights' issues

Traditionally, British companies have sought to finance expansion from their own resources backed by bank lending. At one time, up to 70 per cent of industry's additional capital needs in the course of a year would be met from retained profits. In more recent years, the pressure on profits from taxation and recession has reduced the availability of profits for expansion. There has been a steady flow, however, of 'rights' issues – so called because the shareholders are given the right to subscribe for new shares and in 1986, new capital raised in this way amounted to £5,790 million (an increase of nearly 50 per cent on the previous year). It is part of the issuing house's role to assist with the raising of capital in this way and to handle the 'rights' issue.

Capital issues

The flow of new money less redemptions raised in the United Kingdom by the issue of marketable securities over the years 1982 to 1986 is shown in the table below. These figures include ordinary and preference capital, loan capital, issues by local authorities, but not government stocks.

	UK £m	Overseas £m	Total £m
1982	993	563	1,556
1983	2,746	582	3,328
1984	1,463	875	2,338
1985	4,500	675	5,175
1986	8,612	535	9,148

[Source: Bank of England]

Over the years, the merchant banking affiliates of the clearing banks have strengthened their position in the business of corporate finance, but for the most part it is the old accepting houses which have continued to lead the field. In the business of mergers and acquisitions, only Samuel Montagu appeared in the 'top ten' by value, i.e. in the number 10 position in 1986. That same year, Montagus occupied the fifth position, again by value, in capital flotations with County Bank coming into the list at number 10. In the matter of rights issues, however, County Bank led the field in 1986 both in number and value of issues underwritten. Neither Barclays de Zoete Wedd nor Lloyds Merchant Bank appears among the leaders, but both continue to move up rapidly in the league table and in 1987 BZW acted in a number of major mergers and acquisitions.

Management buy-outs

In recent years, nearly 1,500 smaller and medium-size businesses with a total value of approximately £3½ billion have been purchased by the managers from the former shareholders. In many cases, this has been the purchase of a subsidiary company from a parent. This is normally done with the assistance of a financial institution, which puts up some of the money in the form of loan capital and some of the equity capital, the rest of the equity coming from the management team. One of the reasons for this development is the recession of recent years which has caused a number of larger companies to slim down and they have sold off subsidiaries, either to third parties or to the executive management. Apart from having a streamlining effect on the business, this produced a cashflow which was extremely valuable during the recent times of high interest rates. The hiving-off of subsidiary companies has been facilitated by changes in taxation legislation. To some extent, it has been part of the move towards smaller units of private enterprise and many managers have welcomed the opportunity of owning for the first time a stake in their businesses. All the clearing banks have indicated their willingness to assist in attractive buy-out situations, either with loan finance or equity capital and whether alone or as part of a consortium. Indeed all the major clearers have featured in management buy-out situations, either direct or through their merchant banking subsidiaries.

The unlisted securities market

It was, and to some extent still is, a matter of criticism that smaller companies and newer companies could not readily achieve a Stock Exchange listing, partly because of the stringent requirements of the Stock Exchange and partly because of the costs involved. Indeed, the Wilson Committee[7] took the view that there was an equity gap for the small to medium size company and expressed the hope that the organised securities markets 'should be made available to as wide a range of companies as possible' and that:

> 'Companies should not be excluded because the market in the shares is narrow or because their prospects are no better than average.'

Under Rule 163(2) of the Stock Exchange, it was possible for stockbrokers with the permission of the Council of the Stock Exchange to carry out transactions in shares, notwithstanding that they were not listed in the market, but with effect from 10 November 1980 the Unlisted Securities Market (USM) was introduced. The USM offers smaller and newer companies many of the advantages of a full listing with less onerous requirements and lower costs. In general, a company may be admitted to the USM provided:

1. a minimum of 10 per cent of the company's capital is made available to the public;

2. the company has been trading for 3 years (although not necessarily profitably), for which audited accounts are available;

3. certain financial statistics are available in a prescribed form for the previous 5 years, or such lesser period for which the company has been trading; and

4. there are jobbers who are prepared to act as market-makers in the shares of the company.

By the end of 1986 as many as 529 companies had been admitted to the USM.

It is not necessary that shares quoted on the USM should become the subject of a full listing in due course. Indeed, the Wilson Committee saw:

> 'no reason why companies should not opt to have their shares traded permanently as unlisted securities.'

The receiving banker

Wherever there is a cash subscription for shares, it is necessary for a bank to receive the applications and the accompanying cheques. This is the role of the 'receiving banker': usually part of a clearing bank group because of the need to deal with large volumes of cheques through the clearing system. In the case of a popular public issue where the offer is heavily over-subscribed, the volume of funds handled by the receiving banker may be very large indeed and the value to the bank of these balances, albeit short term, may be very substantial.

Some special characteristics

All the merchant banks have their differing traditions and philosophies and have tended to specialise in particular fields.

Some have concentrated on corporate advice, others on equity participation, others on international issues, notably of eurobonds, and others have made their name in mergers or 'bids and deals'. What then is the particular characteristic of the merchant banking affiliates of the clearing banks? Like all merchant banks, they handle capital issues, they conduct marriage bureaux for companies seeking merger situations, they act in mergers and acquisitions and defend companies from takeover bids, but principally they are involved in corporate advice, as discussed in Chapter 20.

Perhaps the two features which characterise the merchant banking arms of the clearing banks are (i) the links with company customers, many of whom at one time or another will be eligible for the corporate advisory services and (ii) the vast resources of the banks which enable the merchant bank subsidiaries to back up their advisory services with financial help, particularly in the area of medium-term loans.

Equity participation

It would probably be generally agreed that there is little or no profit in corporate advice as such. Where this leads, however, either to equity participation or loan financing, or both, the rewards can be very considerable. In their Evidence to the Wilson Committee, the London Clearing Banks stressed:

> 'that companies themselves frequently show a marked, but understandable, reluctance to release equity to outsiders.'

To participate in the equity of their clients is something to which the banks came slowly and a little reluctantly. It required different skills, or at least a different approach, from the normal lending processes, it was essentially a long-term process and for the most part the amounts involved were likely to be small. It is well known that the German banks have substantial stakes in the industrial life of their country, but this arose from the special situation after the First World War when the support of the banks was needed to get industry going again. In fact, it has been suggested that the extent of this investment tends to be exaggerated and that the German banks exercise a far greater influence through share proxies held for their customers. There is little, if any, counterpart of that situation in this country, and no apparent inclination on the part of the clearing banks to have anything but fairly modest equity participation in their company customers. Indeed, some bankers would argue that the roles of lender and shareholder are not always compatible and that, in any case, the functions should be kept apart.

Nevertheless, the British banks have become increasingly inclined to participate in the equity of their clients, sometimes with quite modest stakes of perhaps 5 per cent, sometimes with options to take additional equity and sometimes with an initial participation of perhaps 25 per cent/40 per cent.

In similar vein, it would have been quite unusual in former years for a bank to appoint a nominee director to one of its customer companies. This is still the exception rather than the rule, but it is an increasing tendency. Apart from anything else, this policy accords well with the increasing call for the release of executive officials to serve as non-executives on other boards, again a recommendation of the Wilson Committee.

Most of the major clearing banks have now established subsidiary companies for the express purpose of participating either in established companies in need of equity finance, or in newer or emergent companies where there is a need for so-called 'venture' capital.

Some possible conflicts

The converging roles of clearing banker and merchant banker caused a certain amount of speculation on the possibility of conflict. For example, the role of an issuing house does not fit comfortably with that of investment manager if there is any temptation or persuasion to support an issue from the portfolios under the bank's management. Even greater is the risk of conflict if the merchant bank is dealing for its own account in shares held in a fiduciary role in its portfolio department, or again, if in a contested bid situation the merchant bank can command blocks of votes through its fiduciary portfolios. In fact, all merchant banks have sought to resolve this problem by segregating their investment management activities from the corporate advice area – and even where, in a leading clearing bank group, the two activities are under one roof, strict separation is maintained and there is no question of disclosure or discussion in these areas of possible conflict.

We have referred in Chapter 6 to the possible conflicts which can arise where a bank in the role of investment manager might also be in possession of price-sensitive information *qua* banker. The problem is accentuated, however, where the banker acts in a merchant banking role as well as being an investment manager. In 'bid' situations the general principles are laid down in the *City Code on Takeovers and Mergers* first published in 1968 and revised from time to time. In the case of dealings by directors of companies, the Stock Exchange published in 1977 a *Model Code for Securities Transactions by Directors of Listed Companies*. There was, however, much concern about so-called 'insider' dealing by those in possession of price-sensitive information with the result that new rules were introduced in the Companies Act, 1980 and insider dealing became a criminal offence. The subject is now governed by the Company Securities (Insider Dealing) Act 1985 as amended by the Financial Services Act 1986 (see Appendix). Insider dealing means dealing in the securities of a company whilst in possession of unpublished price-sensitive information. For this purpose the following are deemed to be 'connected with a company':

(i) Individuals who are, or at any time in the preceding six months have been, knowingly connected with a company.

(ii) Individuals who are contemplating, or have contemplated, making a takeover offer for a company in a particular capacity.

(iii) Individuals who have knowingly obtained, either directly or indirectly, certain information from an individual in one of the first two categories above.

Thus, connected persons not only include directors and senior officials of companies, but also their auditors, solicitors, merchant bankers and other professional persons acting on the companies' behalf. Whilst a bank acting as a merchant bank is certainly in the first category above, it is perfectly possible that a banker acting as banker could be in that same category. In any case, the banker could certainly be in the third category, i.e. that of receiving information from another person such as one of the company officials. One of the apparent anomalies of the legislation is that a 'connected' person is free to deal in the securities concerned six months after his connection has terminated (although normally the price-sensitivity of his information would have passed by that time), whereas someone who receives information from a connected person appears to remain disqualified for so long as the information remains price-sensitive. The meaning of 'unpublished price-sensitive information' is defined in the Act. It must relate to *specific* matters concerning the company whose securities are in question, it must not be generally known to those persons who are accustomed to, or are likely to, deal in those securities and it must be such that, if it were generally known, it would be likely materially to affect the price.

Insider dealing does not necessarily, therefore, have anything to do with bids and mergers. The three ingredients are (a) the dealing in the securities in question, (b) by a connected person (or someone receiving information from a connected person) when (c) in possession of price-sensitive information. There are times when bankers, merchant bankers and their colleague investment managers hardly dare speak to each other or be seen together. What at one time might have been an unfortunate indiscretion would now be a criminal offence.

Another field of possible conflict among the clearing banks is the contested takeover where the in-house merchant bank might be opposing, strongly and publicly, a bid by a customer of its parent bank for the customer of another bank. Thus Natwest Investment Bank might be defending, say, a Lloyds Bank customer against a bid from a National Westminster Bank customer. When one recalls the bitterness of some public takeover battles, one can appreciate the risk of some lasting resentment. However, the merchant bankers among the clearers affirm that they see their role as doing the best for their client, of whatever bank, and that all concerned, winners or losers, respect their special position.

Yet another kind of conflict is the competition between the merchant bank and other parts of the banking group for customer business. This may apply to a degree where the domestic bank and the merchant bank are offering comparable services, for example, medium-term loans. It may also arise in another way. The merchant banks pride themselves on high-level personal contact with their clients and indeed, this is essential if they are to maintain a proper advisory role. As that contact is strengthened, it is possible that the link with the domestic bank, whether it be at local manager, regional director or general manager level, may be weakened. With the modern tendency for account executives in the clearing banks to deal with the business of the larger companies, this could possibly conflict with the merchant banker's idea of being *the* corporate advisor. However, if it be a problem, the banks will no doubt resolve it with their customary resilience.

It must be accepted that the scope for possible conflict is considerable, bearing in mind the diversity of roles now undertaken by our major banking conglomerates. Nowadays a large bank and its subsidiaries may be engaged simultaneously in:

commercial banking,
market-making (in the stocks of listed companies, whether customers of the bank or not, and thus at times holding a position as principal in those companies),
stock-broking (advising on and dealing in the shares of public companies including the bank and its customers),
investment management (for private clients and institutions),
investment research and analysis,
corporate advice (including merger and takeover situations, whether contested or not and whether on behalf of bank customers or not), and
acting as trustee or in other fiduciary relationships (often in relation to substantial shareholdings in companies for which some other part of the group acts in one or other of the foregoing capacities).

For the most part, the legislature, the Stock Exchange and the Takeover Panel leave it to the good sense and integrity of financial conglomerates to build up barriers of confidentiality, 'Chinese walls', around these areas of possible conflict, subject to the law on insider dealing and subject to the rules of the Takeover Panel that where a corporate finance arm of a financial group is advising a bidder, the stock-broking or market-making associate may not advise the defending company.

Such possibilities of conflict inevitably arose from the day the clearing banks moved into merchant banking and the risk was accentuated by the subsequent acquisition of market-making and stock-broking subsidiaries. When one considers that any one bank in relation to any one corporate customer might be acting as lending banker, market-maker, stockbroker, pension fund trustee and investment manager, all acting within barriers of confidentiality, the risks and temptations are obvious – it is quite remarkable that it succeeds at all.

References

1 Sir Edward Reid: 'The Role of the Merchant Banks Today' – being the Presidential Address to The Institute of Bankers, 15 May 1963.
2 P. H. Emden: *Money Powers of Europe in the Nineteenth and Twentieth Centuries*. Sampson Low, 1946.
3 R. Kellett: *The Merchant Banking Arena*. Macmillan, 1967.
4 Op. cit.
5 Report of the Committee on the Working of the Monetary System [Chairman: Lord Radcliffe], Cmnd. 827 HMSO, 1959.
6 Committee of London Clearing Bankers: *The London Clearing Banks – Evidence to the (Wilson) Committee to review the Functioning of Financial Institutions*. Longman, 1978.
7 Ibid.

'. . . reproduced in a legible form . . .'

CHAPTER 15

Share Registration and Computer Services

One of the comparatively 'backroom' services of the commercial banks has assumed considerable proportions in recent years. It is share registration work or, more correctly, the function exercised by banks and others as company registrars.

It is a requirement of company law[1] that every company shall keep a register of its members and that the register will contain the names and addresses of the members, a statement of the shares held by each member, distinguishing each share by its number so long as it has one and the amount paid or agreed to be considered as paid on the shares of each member. The register must also show the date on which each person was entered as a member and the date on which any person ceases to be a member.

The Companies Act also requires the register of a company to be kept either in a bound book or in such other form as may be adequate to guard against falsification.[2] Under the Act there is provision for company registers to be kept 'otherwise than in a legible form so long as the recording is capable of being reproduced in a legible form'. The purpose of the Act was to permit company registers to be stored on computers.

The term 'Registrar' has no legal definition, nor are there any precise duties of a registrar laid down in the Companies Acts. It is the person or institution appointed by the directors to maintain the register of the company and to see that the company's legal obligations in that respect are fulfilled. In practical terms, the registrar of a company maintains the list of stockholders and shareholders with their addresses and individual stock and share holdings, he issues certificates, registers transfers, attends to the payment of dividends and, in effect, supervises the mailing list of shareholders for the purpose of despatching notices and reports to members.

There are approximately 2,400 companies whose shares are quoted on the London Stock Exchange. Many of these are small companies with, say, a few hundred shareholders, and the secretary or other official of the company will normally deal with the company registration work. For larger companies however, the duties of a registrar can be an immense chore and it becomes a matter of decision whether or not the company maintains its own registration department or contracts the work out to a professional registrar.

The London and Scottish clearing banks act as registrars for approximately 1,700 companies and handle about 17 million individual shareholder accounts. The number has increased considerably with the privatization of national industries and indeed only the large banks have the resources to cope with the enormous registers of some of the de-nationalised concerns. There are believed to be 900 or so company registrars (including companies which maintain their own registers) acting for companies listed on the London Stock Exchange, but a very large proportion of these registrarships are now with the seven banks which offer such a service, viz. Bank of Scotland, Barclays, Clydesdale, Lloyds, Nat. West., Royal Bank and Yorkshire.

Although company registrarships may seem to be among the banks' less glamorous activities, it is in fact a highly professional service involving minute attention to detail. There is a high routine content in the work associated with the maintenance of company registers which in the past required the employment of large numbers of staff, but as the operation lends itself to computer applications, it is now far less labour intensive. In the past, it was not unknown for some of the smaller registration companies to run into difficulties because of the sheer weight of administrative routine. It is a service which the large financial organisations, such as the banks, are well equipped to provide. The work involved may be summarised as follows:

The maintenance of the register of members

The number of shareholders in the privatised industries now runs into millions but even a more typical, large company may have over 100,000 shareholders, and others would have in the region of 30,000–60,000 shareholders. The majority of companies, however, have fewer than 5,000 shareholders and may have even less than 2,000. As shares are bought and sold, the transfer forms are registered and in the case of partial sales, the transfer forms have to be 'certified'. A few years ago it was established that approximately 50 per cent (by volume) of all share transfers on the London Stock Exchange were handled by the ten largest registrars, including the Bank of England and ICI who keep their own registers.

Apart from such voluntary transfers, there are transfers on death involving the registration of death certificates and grants of probate. Changes of name on marriage have to be registered, as do other documents affecting the transfer of and title to shares, for example powers of attorney and court orders.

On average, there is some activity each year in connection with 25 per cent or so of total shareholdings. Even before the privatisation issues a large bank would have an average of 3,000 share transfers to deal with each day. In a typical day, they would deal also with over 150 deaths of shareholders, 600 or more changes of address and 700 or so new dividend mandates.

Preparation of share certificates

Share certificates in the United Kingdom come in all shapes and sizes and traditionally have been completed by manual means. In more recent times, a process has been developed for the printing out of share certificates by computer. These must bear the company seal, but the majority of companies' articles of association permit the affixing of the seal without signatures or with signatures affixed by mechanical means. In many cases a facsimile of the common seal is held by the service registrar for this purpose but, as opinion is divided over the legality of such an operation, the opportunity was taken in the Stock Exchange (Completion of Bargains) Act 1976 (Section 2) to authorise companies to use a separate seal for the purpose of sealing certificates. This is a facsimile of the common seal with the addition of the word 'securities'.

Enquiries from shareholders, stockbrokers and others

A considerable amount of time is involved in dealing with written enquiries concerning a register. For example, a major bank may deal with over 4,000 enquiries a week relating to the registers of over 500 listed companies, unit trusts and local authorities. These may be received either in the form of correspondence or by telephone and largely relate to the current and historical holdings of shareholders and to matters associated with the payment of dividends, e.g. regarding tax credit figures and requests for duplicate dividend tax vouchers.

Dividend and interest payments

The registrarship service includes the preparation and despatch of all dividend and interest payments on behalf of the company or authority for which the registrar acts. In the case of the bank registrars, the usual procedure is for the bank to open dividend accounts for payment of the warrants, the total cost of the dividend being covered in one payment from the company. Dividends may also be paid by means of the mandated dividends system which routes dividends direct to the shareholders' banking accounts. Considerable savings in postage costs can be obtained by the use of this system. Thus it is that a registrar handling, say, 500,000 shareholder accounts might operate at any one time as many as 300–350 current banking accounts, to deal with the dividend and interest payments for various companies and various classes of share.

Company communications

The statutory requirements relating to the maintenance of a company's register must of necessity include the addresses of members to facilitate the despatching of notices of meetings, annual reports and accounts and other documents of title to the shareholders concerned.

Statutory returns

It is a duty of the company secretary to make the statutory returns, but it often falls to the registrar to provide the necessary information. In particular, the registrar will prepare the annual return required under Sections 363 and 365 of the Companies Act 1985, which is a list of past and present members of the company with addresses and certain other statutory information regarding transactions in the shares. In other cases, the registrar will assist the secretary in the preparation of such returns as 'Notice of change of directors or secretaries in their particulars', pursuant to Section 228 of the Companies Act 1985 and 'Notice of change of situation of registered office', pursuant to Section 287 of the Companies Act 1985.

Company meetings

The registrar frequently deals with assessing the proxy votes returned through the post for annual or extraordinary general meetings. At meetings of companies, the registrar will often be required to assist the company secretary in checking the names of shareholders against the attendance sheets and in the conduct of a poll.

Transfer audit

It is usual in the case of the registrar services provided by the clearing banks to provide a continuing internal audit, in some cases through the Inspection Department of the bank, thus avoiding the time and expense of a transfer audit by the company's accountants.

Profitability

So much for the role of the registrar. From the standpoint of the client companies, there are considerable advantages in having this large volume of work taken over by a bank or other registrar company. The charges made by the banks, however, have seldom if ever caught up with rising costs and for the most part company registration work has been for the banks a loss-making activity. In earlier times, the level of charges was almost certainly fixed too low as the banks sought to compete for this type of business. It was and presumably still is a matter of prestige to have the bank's name on virtually every communication sent out to scores of thousands of shareholders by a large company. It was also considered, as with many bank services, that the registrar service would consolidate the existing banking connection.

These assumptions need examination and perhaps qualification. It is not untypical for the registrar's department of a clearing bank to run at a substantial loss. At no time have there been adequate compensating profits. The prestige value of an administrative service of this kind is probably minimal. In terms of its advertising value, the level of losses can make it very expensive. Furthermore, it must be doubtful whether the provision of a registrar service for a particular company is very material in relation to the obtaining, retaining or losing of that company's account. Admittedly as with many bank services, it is another point of contact with the bank's customers. It is another way in which a bank can extend its influence. If a bank registration department handles, say, 1 million accounts, 3 or 4 million communications are going out each year bearing the bank's name. Each bank must evaluate these intangible benefits for itself. Even if registration services were to break even after a full allocation of costs, there are risks and responsibilities which remain unquantified and the resources employed in these services are very considerable.

Among the banks, the charges for registration work vary quite a lot, depending on the size of register and the number of transfers handled. There is normally a fee per shareholder account and an additional charge if the volume of transfers processed is abnormally high. The charge per account for the smaller company is normally substantially higher than that for the larger company where economies in volumes may be obtained – the tariff is also influenced by the overall size of the individual bank registration business, and the relationship of a particular company with its banker may also have a bearing on the tariff.

A number of companies, including some very large ones, still maintain their own registers because they prefer to keep these under their own control. The banks would suggest, however, that there are savings to be made even for the largest companies by transferring the registration work to a bank, and that all relevant information from the registers is still readily available to the directors and officers of the company. This was apparently acknowledged in recent times by a company with 140,000 or so shareholders, which was pleased with the economies achieved by transferring the register to a clearing bank. From the banks' point of view, profitability remains a problem, although the position is better if one takes into account the earnings from handling new issues.

Work of this nature, largely done nowadays with the aid of computers, can well be based in low-cost areas and some years ago the four major banks moved their registration departments out of London – Barclays Bank to Knutsford, Lloyds Bank to Goring-by-Sea, Midland Bank to Sheffield and National Westminster Bank to Bristol. In September 1981, Barclays Bank and Midland Bank announced that they had embarked on a feasibility study with a view to operating a joint share registration organisation at Knutsford, but in March 1982 decided not to proceed with the proposal as the benefits were not sufficient to justify disbanding the existing arrangements. The following year Midland Bank announced the closing of their Registrar's Department and Midland does not now provide a company registration service.

Although by this means it is possible to stem the tide of rising costs, there was the additional problem that company registers were getting smaller in numbers of shareholders. Apart from the privatisation issues the proportion of private shareholders diminished considerably in recent years and, in a few cases, companies had been known to encourage holders of small numbers of shares to sell their holdings. In some companies the numbers of shareholders on the register diminished quite substantially. From a profitability point of view, with fees on a per account basis, a high volume of work is essential to achieve maximum economies, although where market conditions are favourable, contributions from capital issues augment the earnings. Although the combined effect of rising costs and diminishing registers will be passed on to the companies concerned, it will inevitably be a continuing struggle. Nevertheless some of the banks will no doubt continue to provide this most valuable service. In recent times a proposal was considered by the Stock Exchange for the elimination of share certificates for those who are prepared to dispense with them. The suggestion was that a Central Stock Office of the Stock Exchange would record all dealings on behalf of the scheme's members who would be stockbrokers, banks and large institutions. The system would be entirely computerised and was designed to eliminate much of the paperwork involved in share dealings. A private investor would join the scheme only through an agent who would be a member of the Central Stock Office and who would act as the investor's nominee rather as the banks use their nominee companies now. So far this proposal has not been implemented.

Computer services

The keeping of company share registers is an example of a 'quill-pen' activity which lent itself naturally to computerisation. There are many services, however, which owe their existence to the advent of computers. They fall under a number of broad headings such as book-keeping and accounting, management information, other aspects of business administration and research. These are not strictly financial services. They are more correctly technical services and they are offered by a wide range of businesses in addition to the banks.

Some of the fairly basic computer services are akin to the work of share registration. These include, for example, the subscription lists for charities and the membership lists of large organisations. The function is similar to that of recording shareholdings in public companies. Similarly, payroll billing, one of the earliest of computerised services, is a basic use of computerisation to speed up and simplify the work of repetitive payments of a routine nature.

It was no doubt to be expected that the increased sophistication of the banks' own computer applications, i.e. for their own accounting purposes, would lead to the offering of comparable computer facilities to the banks' customers. Perhaps an obvious example of this is the exchange of tapes for money transmission purposes (see Chapter 23). It is probably true to say, however, that considering the enormous investment by the banks in computers, the development of related services to customers has been comparatively modest. This may be because, as we have said, automation in all its forms is a matter of technology rather than one of finance. More probably, it may be said that the computerisation of the banks' own recording systems was the subject of a good many ups and downs in the early years and a considerable amount of development and refinement in the later years. It has not been a very static subject and it is not surprising that the emphasis has been on the developments for the banks' own uses rather than for customer services in the broader sense.

Nevertheless, most of the banks offer, at least to a degree, technical computer services to the public and in some cases these have achieved a very advanced level of technology and sophistication. The following are some examples of the services offered.

Payroll services

As we have said, this is one of the older forms of computer application to routine purposes. The essence of the service is the computerisation of salary and wage payments, whether made monthly or weekly and whether made in cash, by cheque or credit transfer or a combination of methods. The computer calculates the hours worked, the wages or salaries due, PAYE tax, national insurance and any other deductions. The computer prints out the appropriate pay slip and indicates the cash break-down for those employees who are to be paid in cash. Credits to employees' bank accounts are made the same day as the debit to the employer's account through the Bankers' Automated Clearing Service (BACS) (as described in Chapter 23). The computer also produces any statutory forms or certificates required for income tax or social security purposes. Where desired, the service includes the maintenance of personal record cards for all employees which are thus readily available for management information purposes.

Stock control

The use of computers for the efficient control of stock levels is now widely accepted and the leading computer houses offer a number of integrated systems embracing stock control with the accounting function. Typical stock control systems provide up-to-date information on stock levels and requirements, coupled with price details and current valuations.

Accounting systems

There is a wide range of accounting systems offered by the banks and other computer houses. These usually involve the recording of the nominal ledger, the sales and purchase ledgers and the provision of a full invoicing system linked to stock control. These are normally complete systems, for which the computer house provides the hardware and software and all necessary advice and back-up facilities.

Industrial and professional services
Some of the banks or their subsidiaries have specialised in a number of customer-related services including portfolio valuation and bookkeeping services for stockbrokers; mortgage accounting and other bookkeeping services for building societies; instalment credit accounting systems for retailers and finance houses; time-recording systems for solicitors and accountants; the taking out of bills of quantity for the construction industry; and specialist book-keeping and invoicing systems for publishers and printers.

It may be argued that the provision of technical computer services is not strictly part of the total concept of the universal bank. As we have said, these are not financial services as such. On the other hand, if it is acceptable that the banks should engage in the work of company registration and the distribution of dividends to shareholders, it is a natural step to undertake the calculation and payment of wages. Then again, if the banks are in the business of providing advice to business customers, as is now the case, there is a certain logic in being able to offer the services of the banks' subsidiary or associated company in the provision of stock control, ledger control and invoicing systems. Clearly, anything which enhances business efficiency has a financial significance and not unnaturally the banks have a very real interest in the financial well-being of their customers.

The banks do not by any means dominate the field of computer services as they do some of the other services discussed in these pages. This is partly because of the large number of computer services companies in this country and partly no doubt because of the development of micro 'do-it-yourself' computers which can deal with a large range of everyday business accounting requirements.

Cash management services

This is one of the newer services available to company customers of banks in this country. We refer in Chapter 21 to the development of cash management services from an off-shore base for the benefit of multi-national companies. It is not necessary of course that such an operation should be off-shore and quite a number of banks are now providing cash management services for their customers in this country and in Europe and the United States. The essence of the service is that companies with a worldwide operation (or indeed a widely based operation in any one country) may obtain more or less instantaneous information on the cash balances held in those operations around the world and thus, can monitor their worldwide cashflow on, for example, a daily basis. In June 1982 Midland Bank became the first UK bank to introduce such a service on a multi-currency basis in this country. Nowadays most of the larger banks offer cash management services to their corporate customers.

References

1 Companies Act 1985, s. 352.
2 Ibid, s. 722.
3 Ibid, s. 723.

CHAPTER 16

Leasing and Industrial Hire Purchase

In English law, the word 'leasing' is historically associated with land, i.e. freehold and leasehold property. Thus, a freeholder may grant a 'term of years' to a lessee and a lessee or leaseholder may grant a shorter term of years (or sub-lease) to his lessee. Until comparatively recent times, the terminology of leasing was not applied to movable property. One's goods and chattels could be hired, loaned, bailed, chartered or borrowed – but not leased. Even the Oxford English Dictionary does not contemplate the possibility of anything but land being leased, apart from the occasional exception such as the wartime expedient of 'lease-lend', which was in any case an Americanism.

Some history

Here, however, we are concerned with the modern use of the word in relation to the leasing of goods and equipment. In fact it is not all that new. Whatever terminology may have been used, we are told that the leasing or lending of one's goods for the benefit of other people goes back at least 5,000 years. In the Sumerian cities of Southern Mesopotamia, where all land was deemed to be owned by the local deity, the ruler-priest would 'lease out' seed to the villagers for the next year's crop. Indeed, all down the ages there have been instances of the goods of one person being used by arrangement in the business of another. Perhaps the chartering of ships is as good an example as any. More particularly, we might mention the hiring of railway wagons in the last century – the origin of much of our hire purchase business in this country (see p. 246), but nevertheless more akin to leasing in its concept.

The business of leasing as it is in the United Kingdom today had its impetus in the United States in the post-war years. The opening up of subsidiaries of American companies in this country brought with it an awareness of leasing facilities and leasing transactions were entered into by the merchant banks and finance houses. This applied particularly in the late 1960s when the more traditional methods of finance were restricted by government policy. Although there were some difficult years to follow, particularly during the liquidity crisis of the early 1970s, the eventual development of leasing activities among the subsidiaries of the clearing banks brought a great upsurge in business and an awareness of the advantages of leasing contracts.

The nature of leasing

What is leasing? In its simplest form it is the use of an asset which belongs to somebody else. In more precise terms, it is a contractual arrangement under which one party, in return for an agreed rent, uses a capital asset owned by another party. Such capital assets are usually business plant and machinery or other forms of equipment and, as we shall see, embrace a great variety of items.

Leasing is based on the quite fundamental concept that one does not have to own an asset in order to enjoy the benefit of it. This has been accepted readily enough over the years in such matters as the renting of houses and more recently the hiring of television sets, but only recently has it been applied on a large scale to business activity. There are obvious examples, of course, of businesses which have benefited from their investment in fixed assets over the years. Some businesses have made substantial capital profits from the sale of assets, or have been able to improve the look of their balance sheets by the revaluation of assets. In countless instances, a strong asset base has enabled businesses to borrow for working capital and development purposes. But the reverse is also true. Some businesses would have traded more profitably if their capital had not been locked up in fixed assets and in many cases the proprietors have seen their capital assets, often of a specialist or purpose-designed nature, depreciate over the years. In the main, the profitability of a business lies in the use to which the resources are put. It is the use, not necessarily the ownership, which matters. Once a business decision, i.e. the investment appraisal, has been made on some new venture, the choice of purchasing or leasing is partly a matter of arithmetic, partly a question of the availability of capital and partly a question of whether or not there is a case for taking finance outside the balance sheet.

It follows that to run an airline one does not need to own the aircraft, to carry oil one does not need to own a tanker, to computerise a business one may lease the hardware, to equip an office one may lease the desks and chairs. The same applies, albeit for different reasons, to non-profit making bodies. To equip a school a local authority may lease the furniture; a hospital may lease its beds.

There are psychological barriers to leasing. The successful business man likes to feel that he owns the plant and machinery around him and even in large companies there is a pride in the possession of assets. To quote from one survey: 'Perhaps we are old fashioned, but we prefer to own what we use.'[1] The same survey showed that the usual method of acquisition of assets by British industry was still by purchase; 83 per cent of companies had bought more than two-thirds of their assets outright. Perhaps more significant was the fact that, in the short space of time that leasing had then been available in the United Kingdom, 45 per cent of companies had made use of financial leasing arrangements and the figure would be in excess of this if one included operating leases (which we shall come to in a moment) and various forms of hire purchase. At the time of writing it is estimated that approximately 16 per cent of all industrial investment in the United Kingdom is undertaken by leasing contracts.

Taxation aspects

It must be doubtful whether leasing would have gained ground in this country so rapidly were it not for the special taxation provisions relating to the purchase of business assets. Certainly the capital allowances introduced by the 1971 Finance Act gave

'. . . psychological barriers to leasing.'

a considerable impetus to leasing in the United Kingdom. Exponents of leasing argue with some justification that the advantages of leasing do not depend on the special tax concessions. The same generous benefits have not been available in most other European countries and yet leasing in those countries continues to flourish.

Until 1971, the taxation allowances on the purchase of capital assets were roughly in line with the standard methods of annual depreciation. Under the 1971 Finance Act, however, 60 per cent of the cost of acquisition of a business asset was treated as a 'capital allowance', deductible for tax purposes in the year of acquisition or carried forward at the discretion of the tax payer, in whole or in part, against future profits. In the following year, the taxation relief was extended to 100 per cent of the acquisition costs of business assets. Different rules applied to motor cars. In many cases, however, companies did not have in the year of acquisition sufficient taxable profits to take advantage of the full capital allowances. They could not be sufficiently sure of future profits to take advantage of capital allowances carried forward, and in any case in times of inflation, the real value of those allowances would diminish. In the case of non-commercial corporations such as local authorities and charities, the capital allowances were meaningless because there were no taxable profits as such. Nevertheless, in all such cases there was benefit to be gained by the leasing of assets. The leasing company became the purchaser and became entitled to the capital allowances. Assuming that the leasing company had taxable profits to take advantage of the capital allowances, the benefit of the allowances would be passed on to the lessee company in the rental terms. Thus the lessee obtained indirectly the benefit of capital allowances which might not otherwise have been available in that year or indeed at all.

In certain parts of the country, development grants became available in addition to the full capital allowances and the leasing company could obtain the benefit of these provided that they were to be used by the lessee company in the designated area. The benefit of the grants would be passed on to the lessee in the rental terms.

In 1984 the Chancellor of the Exchequer announced new

regulations affecting first year allowances on plant and equipment. These were reduced from 100 per cent to 75 per cent for the fiscal year 1984/85, to 50 per cent for the year 1985/86, and replaced by a 'writing down allowance' of 25 per cent from April 1986 onwards. This phasing out of the first year's allowances was accompanied by a parallel reduction in corporation tax down to a level of 35 per cent from 1986 onwards. Thus, one of the major advantages of leasing for British companies, i.e. the taxation benefit, was removed. The gradual reduction in the capital allowances gave an impetus to leasing contracts in order to take advantage of the relief before it expired. Nowadays leasing must be viewed, as it were, on its own merits as a valuable alternative source of finance and so far it seems that the level of leasing business has been well maintained despite the changes in the tax rules.

We have already said that, for a leasing company to secure the capital allowances and pass these on by way of reduction in the rental costs to the lessee, the leasing company had to have sufficient taxable profits. This meant that for the most part only large groups with taxable profits from other activities could undertake major leasing transactions on competitive terms. As we shall see, this is one of the reasons why the major banks were well equipped to enter the leasing field.

Although the tax allowances were a legitimate feature of the leasing business, the Inland Revenue would not permit a capital allowance to be claimed if the contract was not a bona fide leasing transaction and had been entered into merely for the purpose of securing allowances which would not otherwise be obtained. This applied also if the vendor and the purchaser were connected with each other.[2] Also, with effect from 1979, leasing companies were unable to claim capital allowances on equipment leased to local authorities and others who had no liability for corporation tax. In such cases, the leasing companies are still able to obtain the normal 'writing-down' allowance so that such contracts can still be entered into profitably. On the other hand, in the case of local authorities, special regulations were introduced from April 1981 to categorise leasing contracts as capital expenditure and thus bring them within the statutory constraints on capital spending by local authorities.

A source of finance

So much for the taxation aspects. Despite the importance of the tax allowances, leasing should not be regarded purely as a means of securing a taxation advantage. It is a legitimate and important method of financing the purchase of capital assets and should be regarded as an alternative, or indeed additional, source of finance. A company in a growth situation may well be short of working capital and the position could be aggravated by the additional purchase of fixed assets. The leasing of those assets will leave the working capital position unimpaired and if indeed it is a question of replacing existing assets, the working capital position can be improved by the sale of the old ones and the leasing of the new ones. In any case, the cash outflow on the purchase of assets can be an unwelcome burden and leasing provides a means of spreading the cost over a number of years. If the investment appraisal has been worked correctly, the additional income earned by the new assets should outweigh the leasing rental and, to that extent, a leasing contract may be regarded as self-liquidating.

Another important feature of leasing as a source of finance is that it covers the full cost of the equipment to be purchased. Most forms of finance would require a margin of security in favour of the lender, particularly in the case of depreciating assets. In the case of a leasing operation, however, ownership remains with the lessor whose 'security' is automatically increased as each rental payment is made but, as mentioned below, the depreciation of an asset may exceed the rental payments, particularly in the early stages of a contract.

Another way in which leasing contrasts with the more traditional forms of finance is that it 'stands on its own feet'. A leasing contract can be viewed as a single transaction outside the normal balance sheet situation of the company. Other forms of finance, for example equity financing, long-term debt, medium-term loans and bank overdrafts, are all absorbed in the overall financial situation of the company and are only as safe as the overall performance of the company permits. A leasing contract, however, is an independent transaction outside the asset and liability structure of the company. The leased assets belong to the lessor and are not, for example, available to the general creditors of the company, and the 'liability' is not of a capital nature but rather a revenue obligation to meet rentals as they fall due. Thus, a company in a strained capital situation but with a good cash flow and good growth prospects might, with advantage, turn to a leasing situation to finance further developments.

The fact that a leasing transaction does not appear in a company's balance sheet became the subject of criticism and debate. The Companies Act 1985 (Schedule 4) requires a company to show in its profit and loss account 'the amount charged to revenue in respect of sums payable in respect of the hire of plant and machinery'. Some accountants maintained that obligations under leases should be 'capitalised' and shown in a company's balance sheet. Purists argued, however, that the leased assets belong to the lessor and that the rental outgoings are no different from any other annual revenue item. In August 1984 the Accounting Standards Committee introduced a new Accounting Standard (SSAP 21) based on their E.D. (Exposure Draft) 29 published in October 1981. The Standard is primarily concerned with finance leases (see below) and its principal requirement is that such leases should be capitalised in the balance sheets of the lessee company. This means reflecting in the balance sheet the leased asset and the obligation to pay future rentals. It is also a requirement of the Standard that lessor companies will be required to record the amount due from a lessee as a debt in their balance sheets.

Apart from these characteristics of leasing as an additional source of finance, there is the advantage that it facilitates the budgeting process. Capital costs are spread evenly over the years, uncertainties are removed, peaks of expenditure smoothed out and all in all there is introduced into the budgeting process a degree of certainty and stability, which smaller companies in particular will welcome.

Lastly, leasing arrangements are exceedingly flexible and contracts are increasingly tailor-made to suit the needs of the client company. The leading leasing companies will usually structure the rental arrangements to suit the anticipated cash flow of the lessee and, wherever possible, the terms of the agreement will take into account the characteristics of the industry and the special situation of the lessee.

Types of contract

There are two broad categories of leasing situations. These are (a) finance leases and (b) operating leases. It is the first of these, finance leasing, with which we are principally concerned here. It is the essence of a finance lease that the lessor has no commercial interest in the transaction other than as a supplier of finance. The lessor pays for the equipment and thereafter remains throughout the owner of it. The rental paid by the lessee will cover the capital cost of the equipment, the lessor's expenses, interest on the money and the lessor's margin of profit. Under the leasing contract, there will normally be a primary period, possibly up to five years except for very big contracts when the period may be longer, within which the entire costs of the lessor will be recovered. There will then be provision for the contract to be continued into the secondary and sometimes indefinite period at a nominal rental level. Under such a contract, the lessor is not concerned with the servicing of the equipment nor, after the primary period, is he so interested in its value or in problems of obsolescence. He will be concerned, however, to ensure that the primary period does not exceed the useful life of the asset. The primary period is the period of risk. It is during that time that the lessor still has substantial funds outstanding under the contract and in the event of the failure of the lessee, the lessor must look to the sale value of the asset to recoup his losses.

A typical finance lease will include:

(a) a schedule of the equipment to be leased;

(b) an undertaking by the lessee to pay when due the rent provided for in the agreement;

(c) undertakings by the lessee to keep the equipment in good repair, to keep it insured to its full replacement value and to allow the lessor access for inspection of the equipment;

(d) provision for termination of the agreement in the event of default;

(e) provision that the equipment shall remain movable property in the ownership of the lessor, notwithstanding that it may be affixed to any land or buildings; and

(f) an indemnity in favour of the lessor against any claim by a third party arising out of the condition or use of the equipment.

Although a lessor owns the leased equipment and to that extent may be looked upon as a secured lender, there are financial risks attaching to leasing. The day after new equipment has been purchased it has only a secondhand value. It has been installed in the lessee's business, perhaps adapted to his use, and if subjected to even the minimum wear and tear the saleable value may be considerably less than the purchase price. The leasing arrangement will normally have started on the payment of the first month's rent and it is quite likely that the depreciation of the asset will exceed the rental paid for the early part of the primary period. In the case of very large contracts, the shortfall could be considerable. The lessee is concerned, therefore, not so much with the value of the leased assets, but with the credit-worthiness of the lessee. He will not normally enter into a leasing contract with a company which is not well-established and which does not have a good record of credit-worthiness and a cash flow forecast which will support the rental payments.

The other main category, known as operating leasing, is undertaken mainly by manufacturers and suppliers, or agents on their behalf, as a means of developing the market for their equipment. It is a form of contract particularly suitable to specialised or highly technical equipment and differs from a finance lease in that the cost of the asset is not wholly amortised during the obligatory or primary period of the lease. It is a convenience to the lessee to be relieved of such problems as maintenance and servicing, the risks of obsolescence and occasional needs for upgrading the equipment. On the replacement of the leased equipment, the lessor will where appropriate make some allowance for the value of the replaced items. As we have said, this is not strictly a financing operation, but in some cases the leasing houses will finance the manufacturer on a sale and leaseback basis, the manufacturer then sub-leasing the equipment to his customer on an operating lease basis.

The clearing banks

As already mentioned, leasing was not developed in the United

Kingdom until the early 1960s and only gained momentum with the period of credit restriction in 1967–69. A number of the leading finance houses set up leasing operations as an alternative to the more traditional forms of finance and it was, as it were, through the back door of the finance houses that the clearing banks entered the field. In 1958, the then National Provincial Bank had acquired the North Central Wagon and Finance Company, the oldest surviving hire purchase business in the country (see p. 247). In the same year, Westminster Bank had acquired a 20 per cent interest in the Mercantile Credit Company as had Martins Bank. In his Annual Statement for that year, Lord Aldenham, Chairman of Westminster Bank, referred to the purchase of the interest in Mercantile Credit 'after careful consideration of the desirability of obtaining a participation in the field of hire purchase finance, about which we are wholly satisfied'. In May 1958, Barclays acquired a 25 per cent interest in the largest finance house, United Dominions Trust. The interest of Midland Bank in Forward Trust and the joint venture of Lloyds Bank and the Royal Bank of Scotland in Lloyds and Scottish completed the involvement of the clearing banks in finance company business.

Thus, the banks were into instalment finance (as we discussed in Chapter 11), but not necessarily into leasing as such. Barclays Bank developed its own leasing activities using the re-structured Barclays Export & Finance Company for the purpose; Midland became involved in leasing through Forward Leasing, Midland Bank Finance Corporation and Samuel Montagu & Company; Lloyds Bank formed a new subsidiary in 1973, Lloyds Leasing, notwithstanding its interest in Lloyds & Scottish; National Westminster Group, having disposed of its interest in Mercantile Credit in 1972, concentrated its leasing activities in Lombard North Central, itself an amalgamation of North Central Finance and Lombard Banking. When Barclays Bank disposed of their interest in United Dominions Trust (ultimately acquired by the Trustee Savings Bank) and acquired the entire share capital of Mercantile Credit, the combined leasing activities of Barclays Bank and Mercantile Credit were concentrated in Barclays Mercantile Industrial Finance, which is now the largest leasing house in the country. At present, nine of the ten largest leasing companies are owned, or controlled, by the principal banks.

The main leasing activities of the clearing banks are now undertaken through the subsidiary companies as shown below:

Bank of Scotland	North/West Securities Ltd.
Barclays Bank	Barclays Mercantile Industrial Finance Ltd.
Co-operative Bank	First Co-operative Finance
Lloyds Bank	Lloyds Leasing
Midland Bank	Forward Trust Group
National Westminster Bank	Lombard North Central
Royal Bank of Scotland	Royal Bank Leasing Ltd.
Trustee Savings Bank	United Dominions Leasing Ltd.

With the increased popularity of leasing, a number of 'big-ticket' contracts were entered into by consortia and partnerships and a number of the banks combined to form Airlease International to finance the re-equipping of the world's airlines and shipping lines, and set up Omnium Leasing for the purpose of leasing a complete oil refinery. Lloyds Bank (in conjunction with British Aerospace) operate Lloyds Associated Air Leasing for the purchase of British aircraft for leasing to airline operators. Midland Bank also has a joint venture with I.C.L. for leasing computers. One of the largest leasing contracts entered into by a single leasing company is believed to be the financing by Barclays Bank at a cost of over £50 million of a support vessel for Shell and Esso in the North Sea.

In the business of leasing, the commercial banks took a little time to sort themselves out, but that does not detract from the impressive progress which has been made. Once again it was an empirical approach and it is doubtful whether anyone sat down with a blueprint or strategic design for the ultimate pattern of a clearing bank's involvement in leasing.

Successive credit squeezes had led the banks and finance houses to look for alternative means to finance their customers' requirements, but it was the publication of the Bank of England discussion paper, 'Competition and Credit Control' in 1971 which led to greater competition among the banks both in terms of their freedom to compete for deposits and the removal of the rigid structure of interest rates. New and profitable outlets for bank finance and banking skills were needed. If leasing had not existed, it would perhaps have had to be invented.

For the clearing banks the benefits of leasing were:

(a) the means (until recent years) of obtaining taxation relief by way of capital allowances against the very substantial profits earned by banks;

(b) the convenience and comparative safety of fixed contracts with built-in security and a regular rental cash flow;

(c) the opportunity for using funds which, for one reason or another, from time to time may not be applied through the more conventional banking channels;

(d) the facility for offering customers an attractive alternative source of finance;

(e) the fact that leasing can be done for non-customers of a bank – it does not depend on a continuing banking relationship and contracts may be won on a competitive basis regardless of existing connections.

The lease-buy decision

From the lessee's point of view, we have already listed some of the main advantages of leasing. Some of those benefits do not apply, however, in relation to large companies with access to substantial financial resources and possibly a steady flow of taxable profits enabling them to secure for themselves (until recent years) the capital allowances. The decision whether to lease or buy is a matter of calculation. The finance department will have to take into account such factors as:

(a) the opportunity cost of capital, i.e. what the purchase price of the equipment would earn if used elsewhere in the company's business; or

(b) the current cost of borrowing elsewhere, discounted over the period in question; and

(c) the current (discounted) value of future tax allowances; and

(d) the discounted cost of meeting the annual or quarterly rental payments over the period of the lease.

In a situation where the capital allowances would be available equally to either the lessor or the company client and where there would be equal access to finance at equivalent rates, leasing would be more costly than buying. The difference is the premium which one pays the lessor by way of his profit and administrative costs. Whether that premium is acceptable would be a matter of business judgment depending on the overall position of the company, other foreseeable calls on its resources, budgeting convenience, balance sheet considerations and even differing views of movements in interest and tax rates.

Growth of business

The growth in the use of leasing by British industry for equipment financing purposes has been remarkable. It is understood that in 1967 new leasing contracts were being written at the rate of approximately £20 million per annum. By 1976, that figure had increased to £420 million and the following tables show the value of new leasing contracts entered into each year from 1977 to 1986 and the breakdown by types of asset in 1986.

Assets Acquired in 1986 by Type of Asset

	1985 £m	1986 £m
Plant, machinery and equipment		
Plant and machinery	1,858	1,406
Computer and office equipment	1,305	1,597
Oil exploration and extraction equipment	152	88
Cars and commercial vehicles		
Cars	583	814
Commercial vehicles	609	579
Aircraft and ships		
Aircraft	561	329
Ships	247	81
Industrial and commercial buildings	145	128
Other	297	160
Total	5,757	5,182

[Source: Equipment Leasing Association]

Value of New Leasing Contracts

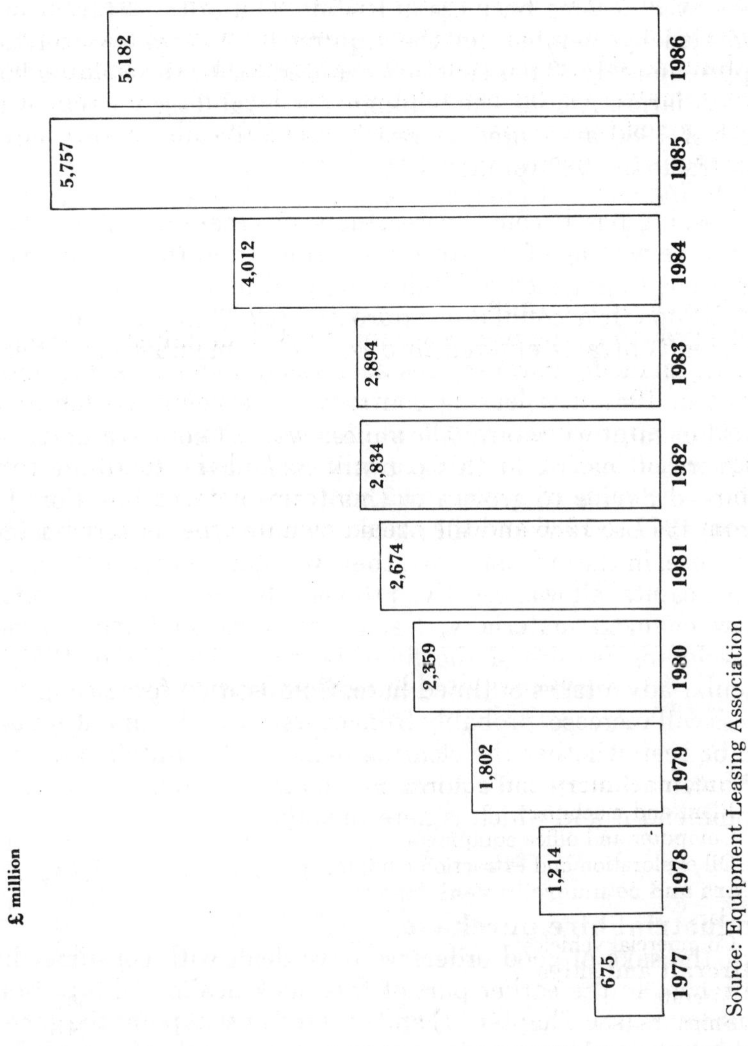

The total value of leased assets in the United Kingdom at the end of 1986 is estimated at £24 billion.

Most of the leasing companies operating in the United Kingdom are members of the Equipment Leasing Association, who have approximately 60 members and account for about 90 per cent of all leasing business in Britain. Out of the total business handled by members of the Equipment Leasing Association, approximately 80 per cent is accounted for by the clearing bank subsidiaries. Among the bank groups total leased assets at the end of 1986 amounted to nearly £14 billion and new leasing contracts in 1985 totalled £3¾ billion.

Leasing has become increasingly international, particularly with the writing of 'big-ticket' contracts and the United Kingdom has established a dominating lead in the leasing business in Europe. It accounts for approximately 30 per cent of all the leasing contracts entered into by the 15 member countries of Leaseurope.

The statutory capital allowances were of course a particular feature of leasing in this country and have contributed to a marked degree to growth in this form of financing. For their part, the banks were well placed to enter the leasing business because, in the ordinary way, they would have very little benefit from capital allowances. Even though the taxation situation has now changed materially, leasing remains an important and developing feature of the financial scene because of the particular advantages outlined here. Competition for leasing business will increase, probably from overseas banks, and it remains to be seen whether the clearing banks will maintain their very substantial share of a form of financing which has much to commend it and which is here to stay.

Industrial hire purchase

For the sake of good order, we have dealt with consumer hire purchase in the earlier part of this book dealing with personal customers (see Chapter 11) and covered at that point the general background to hire purchase in this country. We have said there that industrial or business hire purchase now accounts for approximately 63 per cent of all finance house business and, in the case of one or two of the major finance houses, it represents between 70 and 80 per cent of their total business.

To an industrial or commercial concern hire purchase is another source of possible finance. It is in many ways akin to leasing with the important difference that under a hire purchase contract the customer company becomes in due time the owner of the goods and thus, was able to claim the capital allowances for corporation tax purposes. A company with sufficient taxable profits could, therefore, be more attracted to hire purchase finance than to leasing.

A company seeking to renew its car fleet or install or replace equipment of a reasonably movable nature might well find it an advantage to do so by hire purchase. The particular benefits may be summarised briefly as follows:

1. Until recent years capital allowances were obtainable, as mentioned above.

2. The company's working capital will not be strained, nor its existing overdraft arrangements disturbed.

3. Budgeting will be facilitated by the fixed and regular nature of the instalments and, if desired, by a fixed rate of interest.

4. Individual assets can be seen to earn their keep.

5. Hire purchase contracts have the advantage of simplicity and a degree of flexibility.

Industrial hire purchase is now commonly available for the purchase of industrial and agricultural equipment, plant and machinery, and business assets generally. As with consumer finance, the equipment in question is purchased by the finance house and hired to the customer to whom ownership of the equipment passes on payment of the last instalment.

Although it has in the past been a feature of hire purchase finance that the rate of interest is fixed at the outset and remains constant throughout the term of the contract (and this is still generally so with consumer hire purchase), it has become increasingly the custom in the case of industrial and commercial contracts to quote a variable rate of interest, usually by reference to the Finance House Base Rate (FHBR), which is in itself an arithmetical calculation of the last 8 weeks' rates in the 3 month inter-bank market.

The motor industry
Over two-thirds of new motor cars are purchased for business purposes and thus the motor industry is the largest single category of customer among the finance houses. The customer may be a private individual buying his car for business purposes or, more probably, the employer will have a fleet purchase arrangement. Most of the major car distributors in the United Kingdom have an established link with one of the leading finance houses for 'point of sale' financing of their cars. For example, Lloyds and Scottish have a link with Datsun and V.W./Audi, Mercantile Credit with Talbot and Peugeot, U.D.T. with Volvo and Forward Trust with Fiat. The major finance house link, however, is between Lombard North Central and British Leyland for the provision of retail finance for approximately 250,000 cars a year. The Ford Motor Company have their own finance company and thus have no formal link with an outside finance house.

Block discounting
A service offered by both banks and finance houses to traders who are in turn entering into hire purchase or credit sale agreements with their customers is that of block discounting. This is in effect the purchase by the finance house of the debts due by the customer to the trader in return for the purchase consideration which reflects a discount on the total amount of the debts. A 'block' or batch of agreements is thus purchased by the finance house and the trader is put in funds to enable him to finance further transactions. In a modern case,[3] it was sought to show that such a block discounting arrangement was not a purchase of debts as such, but a loan by the finance house to the trader in which case, being unregistered as a charge under the Companies Act, it would not have been enforceable against a liquidator. The House of Lords held that such an agreement was an assignment of debt and not the taking of security for a loan, although the circumstances might have been different if the whole transaction had been a sham to cover up a loan.

The market
The market for business instalment credit is virtually the entire business community embracing sole proprietors, partnerships

and all sizes of companies. The finance houses make contact with the market through their existing branch network and through the branches of their parent banks. Most of them have agents or representatives operating throughout the country and they run seminars and assist with sales aids for their merchant contacts. Depending on the customer's needs, they are able to offer hire purchase finance, leasing, factoring, block discounting or secured loan facilities.

As it was said in the Evidence of the London Clearing Banks to the Wilson Committee:

> 'the old idea that banks and finance houses served quite different types of customers is now obsolete'.

References and notes

1 'The Lease-Buy Decision'. British Institute of Management, 1976.
2 Refer to the Finance Acts 1971–1973.
3 Lloyds and Scottish Finance v Cyril Lord Carpet Sales.

CHAPTER 17

Factoring

Not for the first time in these pages we come to a subject which has no precise definition in this country. So far as the word is known to English law it means an agent who is employed to sell goods on behalf of his principal. The title is enshrined in the Factors Act 1889 although it is almost lost in the wider definition of 'mercantile agent', defined in the Act as 'having in the customary course of his business as such agent, authority to sell goods or to consign goods for the purpose of sale or to buy goods or to raise money on the security of goods'. In that sense the word has almost disappeared from our law and from our language except to the extent that it lives on in some parts of the country to indicate a specialist wholesaler, e.g. a cheese factor.

Some history

Factoring, as we know it today, is something quite different. It is the management and in some cases the purchase of business debts which, in the words of Mr Justice Mocatta, is 'the business nowadays somewhat confusingly called factoring'.[1] The word in its modern form came to us from the United States, but almost certainly had its origin in the older concept of a factor as an agent. The word may owe something to the agency contracts *facio ut facias* of the later Roman Empire. Certainly the Romans employed agents to manage businesses, including the recovery of debts due under contracts, and to take charge of trading ships for the purpose of managing contracts entered into on the voyage. In parts of Europe in the thirteenth and fourteenth centuries, agents were employed on a commission basis to sell goods and in some cases undertook responsibility for the credit-worthiness of the buyer. This became the origin of the 'del credere' agent who would receive an extra commission from his principal for guaranteeing the solvency of the customer to whom the goods were sold on credit.

Attempts have been made to show that modern factoring is related, perhaps a little tenuously, to the trading and financing operations of the Pilgrim Fathers on their arrival in America. What seems more certain is that with the upsurge of the textile industry in the United States at the turn of the century, the trading aspect of factoring diminished and the term was applied to the method of financing some of the newer industries, particularly that of textiles. Henceforth the factor would be more concerned with assessing the credit-worthiness of the buyer and in some cases would buy outright the debts receivable. In one of the few authoritative works on factoring in this country, Melvyn Westlake describes admirably the growth of factoring in America. He writes:

> 'Thus, the factor came into being with three distinctive functions: he assessed the credit-worthiness of the customers from whom orders had been received and in most cases he cashed the sales – that is bought these receivables outright without recourse; he made cash advances to textile mills, selling agents and converters against finished merchandise as security; in some cases he performed a group of special services such as providing space for display and storage of merchandise, handling insurance, billings, packaging, shipping and making city deliveries."[2]

So it was that modern factoring was developed, but it remained a feature of the textile industry alone right through the years up to the Great Depression in the 1930s, and it was not until after the Second World War that factoring in America was extended to other industries.

Going back over 100 years or more, a number of American factoring companies provided factoring services for sales to the United States by a number of British companies in the Yorkshire woollen trade. This was, it seems, the first acquaintance with modern factoring in this country and it was not until 1960 that locally based factoring operations were set up here. In that year, Tozer Kemsley & Millbourn set up a factoring operation under the name of Towergate Securities, later to become International

'. . . the trading . . . operations of the Pilgrim Fathers.'

Factors (see p. 358). In the same year, Meinhard & Co., one of the factoring houses in New York, commenced a factoring operation in the UK which, although not greatly successful in itself, sparked off considerable interest among other institutions. The National Provincial Bank, as it then was, became the first of the English clearing banks to enter the factoring field in 1968 and it was followed in turn by all the other major banks.

The nature of factoring

What then is factoring? There are three main aspects of the factoring function. They are:

1. An administrative service, under which the factor manages the trade debts of the client company. The factor will keep the sales ledger, issue the invoices, collect payment when due and generally relieve the client of the administrative burden of this side of his business.

2. A system of credit protection, by which the factor assumes responsibility for the trade debts due to the client company and thereby relieves the client of the risk of loss. This is the central, but not essential, aspect of factoring. In effect, the factor purchases the debts from the client company so that in the client's books one debt due from the factor takes the place of all the various trade debts due from the company's customers.

3. A method of financing in that the factor who takes over the client's trade debts will, in certain circumstances, advance a proportion of the their value immediately and the balance on maturity of the debts. The client's liquidity is thus improved to the extent that a cash balance has been substituted for book debts.

There are other related aspects of factoring which are less important in the present context. They are:

(a) *Invoice discounting:* this is the purchase of a debt or a number of debts from a client, usually in order to improve the client's cash flow, and under the title of 'receivables financing' it is a service which has existed in the United States alongside factoring for a long time. Strictly speaking, it is not a factoring operation in the accepted sense because (i) the factor does not control the client company's sales ledger and (ii) invoice discounting is usually a 'one off' operation on a confidential basis and does not involve the purchase by the factor of the entire sales turnover of the client. It has certain attributes of factoring in that the client is put in funds and there is a degree of credit insurance. (At least one major factoring company undertakes invoice discounting on a 'total turnover' basis on the assumption that this gives the factor a stronger legal position than with individual transactions.)

(b) *'With recourse' factoring:* although a full factoring service will usually include the full underwriting of the client's trade debts, the factor may in exceptional circumstances wish to retain recourse against the client in the event of the failure of a debtor to meet his obligations. Such 'with recourse' arrangements may apply to particular transactions, e.g. above an agreed level, or to certain customers where the credit risk is not acceptable to the factor.

(c) *'Non-notification' factoring:* it is doubtful whether this is strictly factoring at all because the client's debtors are not informed of the arrangement and the client continues to collect the debts himself, having sold them to the factor. It is similar to invoice discounting with the difference that it would normally apply to the entire sales turnover. Although it may have its usefulness in certain cases, it is not a form of factoring adopted by the clearing banks in this country. If a client company particularly wishes to conceal the factor's presence, an arrangement can be made for a company to be set up, owned by the factor, with a name similar to that of the client company. This is not 'non-notification' factoring, but a normal full factoring service with a company interposed for cosmetic reasons.

Let us return, therefore, to the three basic functions of factoring which for ease of reference we will call debt administration, credit insurance and factor financing.

Debt administration

This is something more than the typical customer-billing service which a company might arrange through a computer bureau. Under a factoring contract the sales ledger of the client company will be managed by the factor. Thus the client will be saved the administrative costs of bookkeeping, invoicing, credit control and debt collection. The factoring company can usually handle these matters more economically because it will be organised on a large scale, it will be able to make more efficient use of computers and it will be trained in credit control. Depending on the size of the operation, the extent of the factor's risk and all other relevant aspects, a typical charge might be somewhere between ½ per cent and 2½ per cent of the annual turnover in the sales ledger. If the turnover is small, the charges may be disproportionately high, but, in general, factoring services are not suitable for companies with less than, say, £250,000 annual turnover although there would be exceptions below that figure. At that level of turnover, the client company might incur a fee of, say, £3,750 but would save the cost of the bookkeeping clerk (including social security contributions and pension) and the not inconsiderable cost of stationery, postage and telephone charges. More particularly, management time would be saved, the company would be seen to have an efficient invoicing service and there could be substantial savings from the more speedy collection of debts. All in all, the small to medium sized company is able, at a very modest cost, to import a degree of professionalism in the management of its debts far beyond what it might otherwise achieve from its own resources.

Credit protection

Just as the large factoring companies have the resources to manage sales ledgers in an efficient, large-scale operation, so they have the facilities for credit intelligence to enable them to assess credit risks and advise their clients accordingly. Indeed, debt protection is now an essential feature of factoring because, as we have said, it involves the purchase by the factor of the client's entire turnover of trade debts. In the comparatively rare instances of 'with recourse' factoring, the risk of bad debts remains with the client, but in a more typical 'without recourse' relationship the factor assumes the credit risk and therefore the entire responsibility for credit control. The extent of credit allowed by the client to individual customers will be approved by the factor and the monitoring of that customer's account will become part of the factor's day-to-day operations. The pursuit of outstanding debts may require careful handling, particularly if the customer is an important supplier of the factor's client. The factor is unlikely to take any precipitate action without consultation with the client and it may be in some cases that the client will assume the risk rather than see his customer sued. In the last resort, however, the decision to take legal action will be that of the factor to whom ownership of the debt has passed. The assessment of credit risk is something at which the factoring company will normally be much more expert than the client. The staff of the factoring house is trained in the assessment of credit-worthiness and will have access to very extensive information on the financial standing and credit rating of individual customers and corporations. The assumption of the credit risk is, of course, of considerable value to the client. No figures are available for the total bad debt experience for trading concerns in the United Kingdom, but the volume of trade debt is believed to be of the order of £30,000 million so that even a modest bad debt experience can amount to a very substantial sum lost to British trading concerns in the course of a year. It would be wrong to think, however, that the factoring process merely transfers a bad debt experience from the client to the factor. When taking on a new client, the factor will examine the sales ledger closely and will not take on the responsibility for any debts which look 'doubtful'. A factoring house is not a debt collection agency and it cannot turn bad debts into good ones. What the factor does offer is credit control conducted in a very professional way from the outset of the client-factor relationship.

Factor financing

The third major aspect of the factoring role, although not an essential one, is the advancement of funds to the client against the debts which the factor has purchased. In this way the client turns a future debt into immediate cash. In earlier days the discounting of one's debts was looked upon as the last resort of a bankrupt trader – rather like taking one's watch to the pawnbroker. It was this attitude perhaps which gave a bad name to factoring or more correctly invoice discounting, because in many instances it was not a factoring operation. However, in more enlightened times it is recognised that book debts are as important an asset as any other and in some instances, such as companies with a very large turnover but few tangible assets, the book debts will form the principal asset. We have said that the essence of factoring is the purchase by the factor of the entire turnover of the trading operation. If payment is made by the factor to the client as and when the debts mature, there is no element of financing. The factor is providing a sales accounting and credit insurance facility, as explained above. In most cases, however, the factor will be willing to advance a proportion, say 80 per cent, of the outstanding debts ahead of the maturity dates. In such instances, the factoring operation becomes an additional source of finance for the client. The factor will charge interest on the funds advanced, probably at a rate of between 2 per cent and 4 per cent over bank base rate. The suitability of this form of finance will depend, as with any financing operation, on the nature of the business and the purpose for which the money is used. For obvious reasons it would be quite unsuitable to finance long-term capital needs from the factoring of trade debts. On the other hand, if an advance from a factor will permit substantial discounts to be obtained from trade creditors, this could be a profitable operation. In other cases, factor finance (because it increases the availability of working capital) might enable a company to make use of spare capacity or otherwise expand turnover. Traditionally the level of trade credit in the United Kingdom is considerably higher than the level of bank lending, but in recent years the gap has been greatly reduced. On average, trading companies in this country allow credit to their customers equivalent to approximately one-fifth of their annual turnover, or well over two months' credit. A survey conducted by the magazine *Business* some years ago showed that although approximately three-quarters of all customers were asked to settle their debts within thirty days, less than 10 per cent actually did so and 25 per cent took two months or more. Rather as one would expect the propensity to take extended credit increases in times of credit squeezes and other restrictions on bank lending. Certain industries traditionally allow, by force of circumstance, more trade credit than others. This is particularly true of the engineering industry, where in times of credit restriction, trade debts have been known to rise to levels of between 75 per cent and 100 per cent of the annual turnover. Three months' credit is not unusual among engineering concerns and it is not surprising therefore that such companies have turned increasingly to the factoring houses in recent years. It is obvious that a company which receives immediate payment (assuming for the moment 100 per cent finance) from a factor instead of waiting three months for customers to pay, is increasing its capital resources by a sum equal to 25 per cent of the annual turnover. Nor is this a once-for-all injection of capital because the product cycle is speeded up so long as the factoring operation continues. If in a typical case the cycle is six months from manufacture to date of payment, including three months' credit, the immediate factoring of the debt can reduce the product cycle by one-half or, in effect, double the circulation of capital in the business.

Not all companies are suitable candidates for factoring and, in general, the following would be excluded:

Small companies, e.g. those with an annual turnover of less than £250,000 and certainly those with less than £100,000 – in such cases the companies would normally find it more economical to run their own sales ledger.

Companies with large numbers of debtors for small amounts.

Companies with a speculative business.

Companies with unusual or highly specialist businesses where the factors would not have the experience to assess the credit risks.

Companies with an unusually high bad debt experience (although, if this arises from bad credit control, a factoring service may solve the problem).

Construction companies and others employing sub-contractors and requiring stage payments.

Companies selling a large range of small products to the general public.

Most factors would also exclude those companies where the management is patently inefficient and the supervision of the sales ledger could become a burden or even an embarrassment.

Some companies by nature lend themselves to the possibility of factoring. To quote one leading factor: 'Factoring is most suitable for goods which can be made, sold and forgotten.' In general terms, they are well-conducted, medium-sized companies selling not too diverse a range of products to a good spread of customers in a traditionally reliable sector. As we have seen, factoring began with the textile industry, but has long since been extended to a wide range of manufacturing and service operations. Although we have spoken here of client 'companies', incorporation as such is not a pre-requisite of factoring: some professional partnerships lend themselves to factoring, although such cases are more common on the continent of Europe than in this country.

As the business of factoring has grown in recent years, there has been a degree of specialisation among and within the factoring houses themselves. Factoring houses and officials within those houses continue to build up a wealth of experience of particular industries. They are also able to build up from their own experience a considerable fund of data which, in addition to the normal commercial sources of information, enables them to advise clients on specific credit risks.

Some legal aspects

Just as our modern mercantile law has evolved from the Law Merchant, itself a reflection of the practice of merchants in the Middle Ages, so the business of factoring is a good example of a modern commercial practice which exists in advance of any legal framework. It is true of course that there is an established body of law on the subject of assignment of debt. A debt is, as the lawyers would say, a 'chose in action', that is to say an intangible asset the right to which may be enforced by means of action in the Courts. There are various classes of choses in action and a debt is among those which arise from a contractual relationship. Like other choses in action, contractual debt was not assignable historically in English law until the Judicature Act of 1873, the relevant part of which was re-enacted in Section 136 of the Law of Property Act 1925. Under the Act the assignment of a debt from one person to another will be effective provided that the assignment is in writing and that notice of the assignment has been given to the debtor. An assignment which thus satisfies the Law of Property Act would be a statutory assignment. Where, however, an assignment has been made in a form which does not satisfy the Act, it may still take effect 'in equity' as between the assignor and the assignee and would be classed as an equitable assignment. If, for example, the creditor fails to give notice to the debtor, the assignment cannot be a statutory one and the debtor would not be bound by the assignment. If, therefore, he subsequently paid the amount of the debt to the original creditor, he could not be required to pay it again. Whether an assignment is statutory or equitable, the assignor can only transfer rights that he possesses himself – *nemo dat quod non habet.* If, for example, the debt in question is subject to some counter-claim by the debtor, the creditor can transfer or assign the debt only subject to that claim.

Applying these rules to factoring, it would be simple enough in the ordinary way to ensure that the trade debts of a company are assigned in writing and that notice is given to the debtors concerned. However, under the Stamp Act of 1891, as amended by subsequent Finance Acts, such an assignment would require to be stamped at the current rate of stamp duty on the value of the underlying debts. The cost of paying such a stamp duty would make factoring quite impossible in this country. In some cases the difficulty has been overcome by accepting an unstamped assignment (which would not be acceptable in evidence in civil proceedings), coupled with a power of attorney to the factor confirming the authority to execute a legal assignment in the factor's own favour (a document which would then be stamped if legal proceedings against the debtor became necessary). An alternative approach is that exemption from stamp duty may be claimed if the transaction is for a sum of money under £30,000 and does not form part of a series of transactions amounting in total to £30,000 or more. This exemption is secured by regarding each batch of invoices as a separate assignment.

In English law, factoring contracts and invoice discounting arrangements are essentially assignments of debt. The only other sphere of law – apart from bankruptcy and liquidation regulations – that relates to trade debts held for the benefit of a third party is a floating charge created under a debenture. Whereas a debenture is registrable, there is no provision in

English law for the registration of debt assignments and it is, therefore, impossible to tell from any public source whether or not a company has entered into a factoring agreement. A factoring house which acquired the trade debts of a company after the company had given a duly registered debenture to its banker may be postponed to the bank in a receivership situation. The point is not entirely free from doubt because, in the ordinary way, a company which has given a floating charge may continue to dispose of its assets in the ordinary course of business and there is some legal authority for the view that the factoring of book debts is in the course of business. If, on the other hand, a floating charge (given, for example, in a debenture to a bank) prohibits the sale or factoring of debts subject to the charge, it is essential that the book debts be released from the floating charge by agreement with the debenture-holder if the factor is to have priority of title to the book debts. From the bank's point of view, the obligation of the factor to the client company under the factoring agreement will be caught under the debenture representing a single and implicitly safer debt than would have been the case if the debts had not been factored.

In 1971, the Crowther Committee on Consumer Credit[3] recommended that all security interests should be the subject of public registration. This would enable the factoring houses to ascertain whether trade debts were in any way encumbered in priority to their own position as factors, and also to register their interest as assignees of the debts under the factoring agreement. However, the recommendation has not passed into law and in the meantime factors must continue to rely on their own investigations before entering into credit insurance arrangements.

Involvement of the banks

In the United States, there had been a link between factoring and banking since the First World War, but there was some doubt about the legitimacy of this occupation for commercial banks in America until, in 1963, the US Comptroller of the Currency ruled that the national banks had authority to engage in factoring business.[4] There was also apparently some doubt as to whether there was a demand for factoring services to be provided by the banks. In his book, *Law and Practice of Credit Factoring*,[5] Peter Biscoe refers to the survey conducted by *Fortune Magazine* in 1965 on the question whether or not factoring, as a bank activity, was saleable. The result, in the terms of the four possible answers, was:

Answer	%
Very saleable	17·8
Saleable	62·8
Not saleable	10·4
No answer	9·0

Encouraged by this survey and the Comptroller of the Currency's ruling on the legal aspect, twelve American banks entered into factoring activities in the five years from 1965 to 1970. Since then many more banks have entered the field, to such an extent that most factors throughout America and Europe are now owned by or associated with banks.

Notwithstanding the developments in America, it came as something of a surprise to the financial world when, in 1968, the then National Provincial Bank acquired through its subsidiary, North Central Finance, 75 per cent of the capital of Portland Group Factors, a company which had been founded five years earlier and which had helped to pioneer factoring services in the United Kingdom. The venture was not entirely successful, partly because of the troubles afflicting a number of the earlier factoring operations in this country, and on the merger of National Provincial Bank with Westminster Bank there was a major reorganisation. In 1970, an entirely new company was formed, Credit Factoring, and by 1971 this was fully operational having taken over the residual business of Portland Group Factors. The new company concentrated on sales accounting and credit protection rather than the advancing of funds, and it was perhaps this aspect that enabled good progress to be made in attracting larger companies which were not particularly seeking additional sources of finance. Through an associated company, Credit Factoring International, the National Westminster Bank group was the first of the British banks to move into international factoring and at the end of

1974 the bank's chairman was able to report that Credit Factoring International 'has established itself as a leading company in its field'. Today it has factoring operations covering many countries and services export sales on a worldwide basis. It is the largest factoring operation in the United Kingdom in terms of volume of business undertaken.

The first step by National Provincial Bank was a momentous one. In many ways it was seen as a complete departure from traditional banking, but in other respects it displayed a rationale which has not always been apparent in relation to other services. Three essential aspects of factoring, viz. detailed administration on a large scale, credit assessment and provision of funds, were all familiar to traditional bankers, and in the event factoring has proved to be a natural and complementary development of the older services.

International Factors, originally Towergate Securities, is a factoring company formed in 1960 by Tozer Kemsley & Millbourn, M. Samuel & Co. (now part of Hill Samuel) and the First National Bank of Boston. It was to become the largest of the factoring operations before the clearing banks entered the scene, and in 1968 Lloyds Bank and the Royal Bank of Scotland (through their joint subsidiary, Lloyds and Scottish Finance) acquired a 70 per cent interest (later to become a 75 per cent interest) in International Factors. The company is now wholly owned by Lloyds Bank. As the name implies, the company has developed internationally and is now part of a worldwide network.

The Midland Bank group moved into factoring in 1970 jointly with the First National City Bank of New York, but the new offspring, Midland-Citibank Factors, grew but slowly and in 1973 Midland Bank bought out their American partners and transferred the factoring business to Shield Factors, in which Midland Bank acquired a 50 per cent interest jointly with one of the original shareholders of Shield, the Anglo-African Shipping Company. The following year, Midland Bank acquired the Anglo-African shareholding and thus Shield became 100 per cent owned by the Midland Bank, the name having been changed to Griffin Factors, and at the present day it is third in the field among the clearing bank factoring companies in terms of total annual volume.

Alone among the clearing banks, Barclays Bank chose to develop their factoring business from within their own organisation rather than by purchase of an existing operation or by way of joint venture with a partner. A factoring division was set up in the bank's subsidiary company, Barclays Export & Finance Company, and it embarked on a steady programme of expansion under the trade name, Barclays Factoring. Barclays Bank already had an interest, however, in Mercantile Credit as a result of their acquisition of Martins Bank, and Mercantile Credit had been engaged in a factoring operation since the late 1960s. After the acquisition by Barclays Bank in 1976 of the balance of the equity of Mercantile Credit, it was appropriate to rationalise the factoring operations and they were brought together in a new subsidiary, Barclays Factoring, on 1 October 1978. It is believed that the volume of business at Barclays Factoring never exceeded 10 per cent of the total annual factoring volume in this country. For example, for the year to December 1982 Barclays share of the factoring business was approximately 6 per cent, i.e. significantly lower than the share of the other clearing banks. It was said around that time that 'Barclays showed a lack of commitment to factoring'. In February 1983, Barclays announced the transfer of Barclays Factoring Limited to Anglo Factoring Services Limited, a subsidiary of J. Rothschild & Company Limited.

Most of the major banks now have an interest, direct or indirect, in a substantial factoring activity as shown in table A, page 360. Of the eight major factoring companies, seven are subsidiaries of clearing banks or merchant banks.

The Association of British Factors

This Association consists of the eight leading factoring houses in the United Kingdom, who together account for 90 per cent of the total volume of factoring business, including invoice discounting. Table B on page 360 shows the growth in their business in the years from 1976 to 1985 and the level of factoring business of the clearing banks is shown in the Table of Statistics at the end of this work.

Table A

Company	Shareholders	Size of holding (%)	Method of international operations
Alex Lawrie Factors	Lloyds Bank	100	Part of International Factors network of associated companies
Anglo-Factoring Services Ltd.	J. Rothschild & Co. Ltd. Management	75 25	Factors Chain International
Arbuthnot Factors	Arbuthnot Latham Bank Ltd. Yorkshire Bank	75 25	Factors Chain International
Century Factors Ltd	Close Bros. PLC Management	95 5	—
Credit Factoring International	National Westminster	100	Own network of overseas offices
Griffin Factors	Midland Bank Finance Corporation	100	Factors Chain International
H & H Factors	Walter E. Heller Overseas Corp. Hambros Bank	95 5	Member of Walter E. Heller International factoring network
International Factors	Lloyds Bank	100	Part of International Factors network of associated companies

[Source: Association of British Factors.]

Table B—Growth of Turnover for Association Members 1976 to 1985

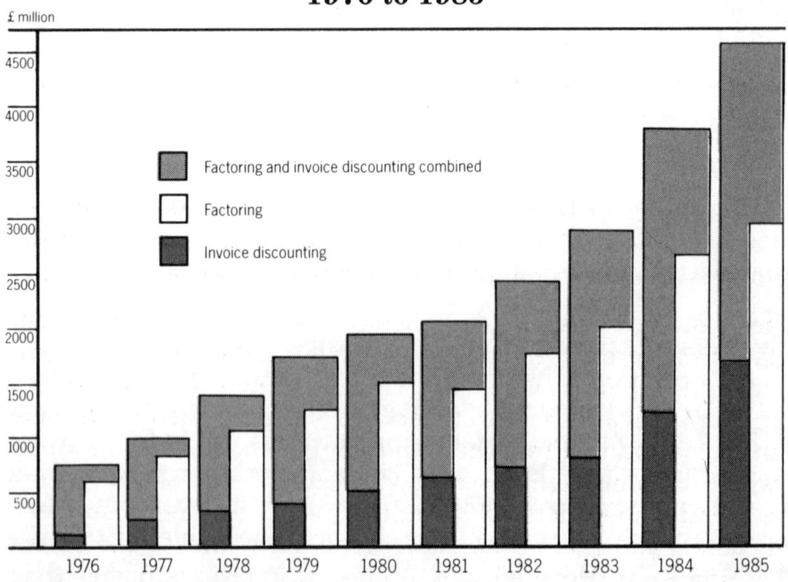

[Source: Association of British Factors.]

The banker-factor relationship

In former days, a banker would not always view with equanimity the news that his customer was factoring his debts. There would be a vague assumption that the customer was *in extremis* and that in some undefined way the customer's last remaining assets were disappearing through the window. In fact, a customer in such dire circumstances would be extremely unlikely to find a factor to take him on. Factoring is not in any sense a rescue operation – it is not finance of last resort.

In similar vein, the banker of bygone years did not like to think that his customer was obtaining finance from any other source but himself. Here again, times have changed. Many well-run companies obtain finance for a variety of purposes from a variety of sources. The banker whose customer has negotiated a factoring contract will at least know that:

1. the factoring house has a good opinion of his customer – it used to be said that only one out of every thirty or so companies who applied to factors were accepted, but the proportion tends to be higher now that factoring is better understood;

2. his customer's sales ledger will be well managed and the customer will have the additional help of the factor in matters of credit information;

3. bad debts, if any, will be eliminated and debts paid on time;

4. the covenant of the factor is being substituted for the multiple covenants of the trade debtors;

5. if required, an extra source of finance is available to aid the growth of the business, to take advantage of discounts from suppliers or, conceivably, to reduce the dependence on the bank.

The customer-banker relationship and the customer-factor relationship are not mutually exclusive – indeed they are complementary. This is particularly recognised now that the clearing banks are providing factoring services alongside their traditional banking function. From the standpoint of the banking group as a whole, the debt administration and credit control services are fee-earning operations which add strength to their customers' businesses and extend the influence of the bank. To the extent that finance is provided, the interest rate level is higher than that obtainable normally on bank overdrafts and the security is better than that which would otherwise be available to the bank on book debts.

If the roles of banker and factor are complementary, they are nevertheless different in concept. The banker lends money on the covenant and security of his customer. The factor, in so far as money may be advanced, is relying on the covenant and credit-worthiness of the client's debtors. Given that difference, the functions are compatible and the skills are similar. Factoring is a sensible and logical extension of the banker's role. It is here to stay and will no doubt be the subject of considerable growth in the coming years.

The risks

The early history of factoring in this country was a chequered one. Not only was the factoring of one's debts regarded, as we have said, as the last port of call before bankruptcy but the factoring companies themselves were not sufficiently selective. In some cases, the factored clients were quite unsuitable for a factoring service. On the clients' side there were instances of mismanagement or over-trading or failure to use the factor finance wisely or, in some cases, downright dishonesty. On the factors' side, there was a lack of experience of factoring in this country, inadequate administration on the sales ledger side, insufficient credit information and a general inexperience in matters of credit appraisal. In those early years, not all that long ago, considerable losses were written off by some of the factoring companies. In his book,[6] Melvyn Westlake has catalogued a number of case studies, not all failures by any means, which serve to illustrate some of the early mistakes.

Today the factoring houses, partly because of the influence of the banks, operate from better financial bases, have better back-up for their administrative services and have developed highly efficient systems of credit assessment and control. Nevertheless, factoring remains and always will be a risk business. Despite the systems of control, there is still the risk that through carelessness or fraud, invoices will be issued in respect of non-existent goods or to non-existent customers. Even the possibility of conspiracy to defraud on the part of the client company and the customer cannot be ruled out and has in fact been the cause of previous failures. However, the increased selectivity of the factoring houses has considerably reduced this area of risk. There remains the risk in 'with recourse' factoring of the failure of the client company or, in the more usual instances of 'without recourse' factoring, the failure of a major customer. As we have said, the factor is lending against the credit-worthiness of the customer, not of the client company (in a 'without recourse' situation) and even well-introduced, well-reported-on customers, have been known to fail. Here again, however, the processes of selectivity, aimed in part at seeking clients with a wide spread of customers, reduce the risk of an undue dependence on any one customer.

Lastly, there is the overall risk of business recession. The domino effect of business failures multiplies the factoring risk, particularly where (as was the case) factoring is concentrated on only a limited number of industries.

The risks are comparable to, but no greater than, those of traditional bank lending and the return in relation to resources employed can be as good or potentially better.

Profitability

Factoring finance taken in isolation as a money-lending operation enjoys the benefit of marginally higher rates than traditional overdrafts and thus provides the banks with an opportunity of improving their margins. On the other hand, there can be no factoring without the sales accounting side and this is work with high routine content. It is labour-intensive or computer-intensive and in either case the costs are considerable. There is a similarity here to company registration work and pension fund administration, and indeed to the money transmission services of the banks. It is exceedingly difficult for banks to provide an administrative or routine service for customers on a profit-making basis. This is largely because of the high standard set by banks in the running of their operations, whether for themselves or for their customers, and this in turn means high costs in terms of salaries, pensions, premises, systems of control and high quality generally in all the accoutrements of business. Factoring, therefore, suffers to a degree from carrying the burden of a large routine operation. So it must be doubtful whether the sales administration side would stand as a profitable operation by itself despite the very real advantages to the client company. It depends very much on the level of turnover.

In all its aspects, factoring may, however, be viewed as a profitable enterprise and, so far as figures are available, it would seem that the return on resources employed is as satisfactory in this side of the business as in the more traditional forms of banking. In any case, factoring must be seen as part of the wider banking function – particularly, as we shall consider now, in relation to the factoring of overseas business.

International factoring

'International factoring' is a loose expression denoting two or three developments of factoring business in overseas markets. It refers primarily to the factoring of exports from, say, the United Kingdom, the better term for which is probably 'export factoring'. It is also used to refer to the opening of offices or affiliates in other countries to undertake the factoring of both domestic and export business from those countries. Lastly, the term is used to describe the international groupings of the factors to undertake import-export factoring among trading nations generally, and this is more correctly referred to as 'multinational factoring'.

The factoring of export sales is fundamentally the same as for domestic business. The exporter may, however, have more need for factoring than in relation to his home trade. The problem is not necessarily one of finance, but rather of knowledge and expertise. The exporter may have no adequate means of assessing the credit-worthiness of his customer, and the language and documentation may be completely unfamiliar to him. There may be import duties and other local requirements, and the terms of trade may be much longer than those to which he is accustomed in this country. The factor who can take care of those problems as well as provide, as the larger houses do, information on local markets and introductions to agents and distributors, is giving the client a service which he would be hard put to match from his own resources. Thus it is that even the largest companies, who would not have recourse to factoring for their domestic business, have arranged to factor their exports.

For the factoring house, the work of export factoring opens up a whole new dimension, calling as it does for knowledge of overseas customs and the credit appraisal of the overseas buyers. The bank-controlled houses have perhaps a special advantage in this respect, drawing as they do on the international connections of the major banks. It was a natural extension of export factoring that the principal UK factors should set up offices in countries abroad.

Not surprisingly, the United States led the way in truly multi-national factoring. They were accustomed to the long distances and differing state laws of their own country and, in any case, were ahead of the rest of the world in having developed a modern factoring structure. Traditionally, the banks in the United States had not been involved in factoring apart from one or two minor instances before the Second World War. The First National Bank of Boston led the way in 1946, but it was not until the authorities finally approved factoring as a legitimate banking function in 1963 that the commercial banks in general moved into the field. Their involvement gave a great impetus to factoring in the United States in the following years, and at the present time over one-half of all factoring in the United States is undertaken by the bank-owned factoring houses.

The comparatively recent development of factoring in the United Kingdom was followed rapidly in most European countries, notably Sweden and West Germany. Factoring developed under the umbrella of existing financial institutions and was soon extended to a wide range of industries and professions.

International factoring has become centred on a handful of major groupings and it seems that this will continue to be the pattern. Three of the main groupings are the International Factors Group, dominated by the First National Bank of Boston but controlled as we have seen at the UK end by Lloyds Bank; the Walter E. Heller Overseas Corporation which is the largest factoring organisation in America; and Credit Factoring International, controlled by National Westminister group and having its world centre of operations in the United Kingdom. There is, additionally, a network of other leading factoring houses operating in association with each other under the title Factors Chain International. This 'association' of factors has approximately forty members throughout the world and has a permanent secretariat in Amsterdam. The aim is to achieve uniformity of standards and to assist members with legal and other technical information about the countries of operation. Factors Chain International enjoy a 'correspondent relationship' among their members, so that they are able to assist each other from their knowledge of the law, practice and language in each place, and the collection and guaranteeing of debts on behalf of members.

The potential

We have seen that not every company is suitable for factoring. Any sort of guess is probably meaningless, but it has been suggested that no more than 10 per cent of trading operations in this country would satisfy the stringent requirements of the factoring houses for the 'without recourse' factoring of their debts. Nevertheless, the market is very considerable and the arrival of the banks on the scene with their branch networks opened up possibilities that are reflected in the growth of factoring in this country in the last few years.

The number of companies using factoring services at the present time in Britain is of the order of 4,000. The size of the market can be no more than a guess, but it is thought to be between 80,000 and 100,000 firms. There is still a great ignorance in the business world about the true purpose of factoring and the considerable advantages which can accrue from it. Furthermore, the factoring companies have not yet entirely shaken off the image that they are the 'lenders of last resort'. It is perhaps a pity that the financial aspects of factoring have been emphasised over and above the 'service' aspects. Mr. F. R. Salinger of Anglo Factoring Services Limited, one of the leading authorities on factoring in this country has said:

> '... the service aspect of factoring seems to be relegated to a poor second place and only those who have difficulty in financing

their business by traditional means are considered as suitable prospects."[7]

Mr. Salinger continues:

> 'The fact that there may be many bank business customers, having credit funds on a permanent basis, which may benefit from or even be seeking, credit insurance or protection and a sales accounting service is rarely recognised.'

In an era such as the present, when so much emphasis is on the needs of small-to-medium sized businesses and there is a philosophical emphasis on the development of smaller industrial and commercial concerns, the factoring companies must have a special role to play. The administration of the sales ledger, the degree of credit protection and the improved cashflow can do so much to release the energies and capital of the proprietor to concentrate on the mainstream of his business.

If the potential for domestic factoring is considerable, that for multi-national factoring is absolutely vast. Only a small proportion of the total of world trade is so far factored. The large British and American banks with their worldwide networks have immense opportunities for facilitating world trade through their factoring operations. The biggest deterrents to world trade are ignorance of the markets, unfamiliarity with the procedures and the financial risk. The international factor is particularly well placed to remove those impediments and oil the wheels for increased trade.

References

1 Hamilton Finance Co. Ltd v Coverley, Westray, Walbaum & Tosetti Ltd, and Portland Finance Co. Ltd (1969) 1 Lloyds Rep. 53, at p. 58.
2 M. Westlake: *Factoring*. Pitman, 1975.
3 Report of the Committee on Consumer Credit (Chairman: Lord Crowther), Cmnd. 4596. HMSO, 1971.
4 US Comptrollers' Manual for National Banks, 1 June 1963. para. 1105.
5 P. M. Biscoe: *Law and Practice of Credit Factoring*. Butterworths, 1975.
6 M. Westlake: op. cit.
7 Finance Houses Association, Credit Quarterly Review, Vol. 22, September 1981.

CHAPTER 18

Corporate Trusteeships

Leaving the subject of asset financing, we turn to corporate trusteeships. The expression 'corporate trusts' is not in this country a very precise term. We use it here to differentiate between private trusts set up by an individual, as already discussed in Chapter 5 and trusts set up by corporate bodies for the purpose of their own business. In the United States the title has a more precise meaning to which we will refer later.

Trusts for corporate bodies may be classified under five particular headings, although the list is not exclusive. They are:

pension fund trusteeships,
custodian trusteeships,
debenture trusteeships,
consortium trusteeships, and
trusteeships for unit trusts.

Pension funds

The pensions services of the clearing banks will be considered in Chapter 19 and here we are concerned only with the trustee aspect. Occupational pension schemes fall into two categories, i.e. those which are self-administered invested funds and those which are underwritten or managed by a life assurance office. In the former category, it is necessary for a trustee to be appointed to hold the assets of the pension fund. In the case of an insured scheme the trustee will be responsible for the due administration of the scheme and the purchase of the pensions in due course, but will not hold the funds as such, these being part of the life fund of the insurance company. We are concerned here primarily with the self-administered fund. Pensions business is big business. The flow of new money into the pension funds of this country is enormous (see Chapter 19). The scope for trust business is also very considerable.

With the passing of the Social Security Pensions Act 1975 (effective from April 1978) every employed person, subject to minor exceptions, became automatically covered by the new State Scheme unless he or she had been contracted out of the State Scheme to the permitted extent and was covered by a private scheme approved by the Occupational Pensions Board. Thus, the pensions scene, which had been confused for some years, became much clearer. Some schemes continued as before, some were improved to satisfy the regulations and in all other cases employees were automatically covered by the State Scheme. Consequent upon the passing of the Social Security Act 1986, the relevant provisions of which came into force early in 1988, employees may elect to have a personal pension plan as an alternative to an occupational scheme or the State Scheme (see p. 396).

Every private pension scheme requires a trustee and the appointment of a corporate trustee is appropriate because of the advantages of continuity. In some companies the pension fund trustees are private individuals, perhaps directors of the company, but this is not an ideal situation. Indeed, many employees would probably prefer the fortunes of the pension fund to be handled outside the company.

We discuss in Chapter 19 the provision of pensions for 'controlling directors'. With the passing of the Finance Act, 1973 it became possible for controlling directors to become members of their companies' pension schemes or to benefit from separate pension arrangements. For a controlling director's scheme to be approved, certain undertakings are required by the Inland Revenue (see page 395) and, in the case of smaller schemes where the trustees will often be directors of a company, the Superannuation Funds Office requires one of the trustees to be what is now known as a 'pensioneer trustee'. This is a person or institution with professional experience of pension trusts, who must be approved by the Superannuation Funds Office as a suitable trustee. The role of pensioneer trustee is well suited to the banks and some of the larger banks now provide a service to smaller companies for setting up controlling director schemes.

The role of a pension fund trustee is to receive the contributions, whether from employer alone or from employer and employee, and to invest these in the pension fund according to the terms of the deed. In due time, the trustee is responsible for the payment of pensions to retired employees. To an extent the work is largely administrative. A 'full' trustee of a pension fund will also be responsible, however, for investment policy. There are usually very wide investment powers and thus the trustees have the very real responsibility of investing the trust fund, with virtually unlimited powers, in an attempt to combat inflation and keep the pension fund solvent.

In other cases the trustees will act on the advice of an investment committee or investment managers appointed by the company, but usually depending on the wording of the deed, the ultimate responsibility will still rest with the trustee. We shall discuss these investment matters at a later point.

The pensions legislation of recent times has thrown an additional burden on pension fund trustees, the full extent of which may not yet be apparent. For example, under the Social Security Act 1985, it became necessary with effect from 1 November 1986 for the trustees or administrators of occupational pension schemes to provide members automatically with the following information:

- basic information about the benefits under the scheme and how the contributions are calculated. (This must be supplied to all members on joining a scheme and to other members on request);
- the amount of benefit payable to members (to be notified just before benefit is payable or as soon as possible thereafter);
- the details of options open to the beneficiaries of members who have died;
- if the scheme is to be wound up, notification to members about their benefits under the scheme and details as to where information may be obtained after the winding-up.

In addition, the trustees or administrators must provide on request:

- the contents of the trust deed or rules governing the scheme (to be available for inspection at a reasonable place free of charge, and copies to be provided at a reasonable cost);
- the amount of a member's benefit and any survivors' benefit earned up to a particular date;
- an estimate of the amount of any transfer value available to the member calculated at a date close to the date of the request;
- information on whether, and if so in what circumstances, a member is entitled to a refund of contributions paid into the scheme and how it is calculated;
- the latest actuarial valuation of the scheme (to be available for inspection at a reasonable place free of charge, and a copy provided at a reasonable cost); and
- a copy of the latest annual report of the scheme (to be made available free of charge). This will consist of audited accounts, an actuarial statement and a full report of the trustees on the financial affairs of the scheme.

Yet again, with the introduction of the Social Security Act 1986, the main pension provisions of which came into effect early in 1988, the ability of employees to take out their own personal pension plans may well involve the trustees of occupational schemes to a greater extent than hitherto in ensuring that their schemes are attractive to the employees and to ensure that the interests of those who remain in the occupational schemes are fully protected.

Lastly, in these comparatively new areas of legislation, trustees of pension schemes will become increasingly involved in dealing with the subject of fund surpluses within the provisions of the Finance Act 1986.

Custodian trustees

The second area of corporate trusteeship is that of custodian trustee. In fact, this role is not limited to corporate situations, and in practice custodian trusteeships tend to be on behalf of companies and other corporations and unincorporated groups of people such as clubs and local societies. The office of custodian trustee is a statutory creation of the Public Trustee Act 1906 and, as we have seen, is the only instance where a corporate trustee has a statutory authority to charge fees. In practice, the statutory provisions are burdensome and it is normal for custodian trustees to be appointed under express powers in the trust deed rather than under the statutory power. It is a useful arrangement where the organisation concerned wishes to retain the managing function whilst having the benefit of a bank or other corporate body holding the trust assets. The custodian trustee retains custody of the trust property and documents, leaving the managing trustees to deal with the day-to-day administration of the trust.

Debenture trusts

The third main area of corporate trust work is that of debenture trusteeships. When a company seeks to issue debentures or debenture stock, or even unsecured loan stock, it is customary to appoint a trustee to protect the interests of the debenture-holders or stockholders. The issue is normally constituted under a trust deed entered into between the company and the trustee. The powers and duties of the trustee will be set out in the deed. In general, it is the concern of the trustee to see that the obligations of the company are duly performed. The debentures or stock may carry a fixed charge over certain fixed assets, or a floating charge over the undertaking generally, or both. The trustee would normally hold the documents of title to any specifically charged assets and in some cases may be required to ensure that the floating assets of the undertaking are maintained at a stipulated level. If there is a sinking fund for the redemption of the debentures or stock, the trustee will be responsible for seeing that the fund is operated in accordance with the deed. The trustee may have a particularly active role where there are a number of dealings in the charged assets by way of sales, purchases, leases, etc. The security property can be released only with the consent of the trustee and such consent would also be necessary where, for any reason, it is proposed to reduce the value of the security property by the withdrawal of

'. . . to protect the security property.'

assets from behind the debentures or stock without replacement. The trustee will also be responsible for seeing that freehold and leasehold properties are properly insured and that all outgoings are duly met.

The trustee's role will be comparatively passive unless and until the security becomes enforceable, when some action will be necessary by the trustee, usually the appointment of a Receiver, to protect the security property for the benefit of the debenture-holders or stockholders. The trust deed will specify the circumstances in which the security shall become enforceable and these will normally include default in payment of principal or interest on the debentures or stock, the winding-up of the company, the cessation of business or breaches of covenant by the company. It is fortunately rare that a trustee has occasion to appoint a Receiver, but it does of course happen from time to time and the responsibility of the trustee can then become an onerous one. The author had the unusual experience of appointing a Receiver for a well-known undertaking in Israel where the debentures were held worldwide – an interesting experience but not generally to be recommended.

Debenture trusts are usually of long duration and call for trustees of standing and business experience. The banks and insurance companies are therefore well equipped for the task and, in the ordinary way, the business is remunerative.

Whilst the duties are normally of an undemanding nature, they cease to be so if the security becomes enforceable and it is usual to provide that in such circumstances the level of remuneration shall be doubled, or even trebled.

As far as the banks are concerned, the business of debenture trusteeships has had a chequered career. It was not uncommon for a bank to accept debenture trusts in the pre-war and immediate post-war years, but it became a matter for comment in the Report of the Cohen Committee on Company Law Amendment in 1945, which suggested that a conflict of interest might arise in cases where a bank was both the creditor of a company and trustee for the debenture-holders. Following the Report, the Rules of the Stock Exchange were amended to provide that the trustee for the debenture-holders of a listed company must not have an interest in relation to the company which might conflict with the trustee's role as such.

Whilst recognising that a conflict of interest can arise where a banker is in the dual role of lender to a company and trustee for the debenture-holders, it should be noted that banks are not unaccustomed to apparent conflicts of interest between their role as banker and as trustee. In practice such issues are resolved with commendable independence by both sides and nothing is likely to deter the bank as trustee from acting in the best interests of its beneficiaries or, in this instance, debenture-holders.

After the Stock Exchange ruling it was therefore left to the banks to 'take in each other's washing', but in practice this did not happen. Some banks were reluctant to become trustee for debenture-holders in a large public company if it might inhibit the possibility of their becoming bankers to the company at some future date. Others felt that the conflict was more apparent than real and continued to take debenture trusteeships. In more recent times the Stock Exchange rule has been relaxed and the problem no longer remains, but in the years of uncertainty a considerable amount of debenture trusteeship business was lost to insurance companies.

Consortium trusts

Perhaps a more esoteric aspect of company trusteeship is the development in recent years of consortium trusts. They usually arise where a major development or exploration is financed internationally by a consortium of leading names. Provided the consortium are prepared to adopt the Anglo-Saxon concept of a trust, the appointment of a London clearing bank or trust company as trustee can solve a lot of problems. The day-to-day financial administration of the project becomes the responsibility of the trustee who will deal with stage payments under the contract, insurance, performance bonds, bank guarantees, currency conversion, investment of surplus funds and generally act as stakeholder for the parties. In such cases, the trust becomes the focal point for the legal, accountancy and administrative aspects of the project and a vehicle by which enforcement is ensured of the diverse legal rights of the contracting parties.

This is perhaps a good place to mention the development of corporate trusteeships in the United States. One important role there is the trusteeship of local authority bonds. This is similar to a trusteeship for debenture-holders in the United Kingdom, but there is no counterpart in this country in relation to local authorities. The local authorities in America enjoy a considerable degree of independence and autonomy and are responsible for their own local commitments such as schools, hospitals, roads and bridges. For these purposes money is raised in the market and there are over 80,000 municipalities issuing bonds in the United States. Corporate trustees are required to act in connection with such issues and this work falls to the banks and trust companies. They have an obligation to ensure that an issue is sound, but there is no legal liability on the trustee in the event of a failure of a local authority.

Unit trusts

We come then to the last major area of corporate trusts – the trusteeship of unit trusts. It is surprising that until recent times a large number of people, some of them in the business world, did not know what unit trusts were. In fact, market surveys show that the man in the street is remarkably ignorant on the subject despite having been bombarded by newspaper advertisements for a good many years. Perhaps many people would say 'I know what it is, but I can't describe it'. That is understandable because a definition is not easy and unit trusts are almost *sui generis* in that they do not fall naturally within the scope of company law or the vast body of trust law in this country. And while it is true that unit trusts have their origin in the basic trust concept – particularly in the use made of trusts to hold property for unincorporated associations – unit trusts on the whole owe little to the general body of trust law. Considering the growth of unit trust business, there is remarkably little statutory or case law on the subject. This is no doubt attributable both to the good sense of those engaged in the business, whether as managers or trustees, and to the very shrewd control exercised by the Department of Trade and Industry.

We have dealt more particularly with the nature and development of unit trusts in Chapter 7, but perhaps a brief historical note would be appropriate here. Dr Pennington, of Birmingham University, in his admirable book, *The Investor and the Law,*[1] refers to the trust funds set up in Victorian England for the purpose of spreading investors' risks, the equalisation of income, the gradual re-investment of capital and ultimate disbursement of capital profit. These foundered on the company law rule that associations 'formed for the purpose of carrying on a business that has as its object the acquisition of gain' may not have a membership exceeding twenty.[2] Although the decision was overruled in the later case of Smith v Anderson[3] and the way cleared for the development of investment trust funds, it was the investment company rather than the trust concept which was to be developed in England during the 1930s.

The subsequent development owes something to the experience of investment trusts in America, a large number of which were created in the 1920s, not all with satisfactory results. Some of them were very hazardous and became worthless when Wall Street collapsed in 1929. These early trusts (which were in fact companies) were 'fixed', in that the subscriptions from investors were committed to a stated portfolio which remained fixed throughout the life of the trust. When all the units of a trust had been issued, a second trust would be set up on identical terms with an identical portfolio, and so on with successive trusts. There was some confusion of terminology when these trusts were introduced into the United Kingdom because over here each separate trust was called a unit and the 'shares' held by the public were known as sub-units. The first British trust of this type was launched in 1931 by Municipal & General Securities Company Limited (now the M. & G. Group) under the name of First British Fixed Trust. In the ensuing years a number of other similar trusts were launched, but it soon became apparent that fixed trusts were too inflexible and that the managers could not vary the investments. Thus the flexible unit trust was introduced and the first of these was The Foreign Government Bond Trust, which was launched in 1934. By the beginning of 1938, seventy-three unit trusts were in existence in this country with a total market value of approximately £80 million.[4] All existing fixed trusts were either converted to flexible trusts or wound up, and all the newly-formed trusts were 'open-ended' in that the number of units in issue could vary according to the level of purchases and sales. The term 'sub-unit' was dropped in this country and the individual shareholdings became known as units or shares.

The principal difference between the British and the American pattern of development lay in the fact that, under company law in this country, it was not possible for a company to buy its own shares (although it has since become possible in certain circumstances under the Companies Act, 1981).[5] This limitation did not apply in the United States with the result that their mutual funds, as they are known today, grew out of the concept of the investment company.

In December 1935, the London Stock Exchange published a report on 'Fixed Trusts' and recommended that legislation be introduced for the protection of the investing public.[6] This was followed in August 1936 by a Board of Trade report which in turn recommended that there should be legislation on the subject of fixed trusts.[7] There was no statutory regulation of unit trusts however until some clauses were inserted at the Committee stage in the Prevention of Fraud (Investments) Bill 1939, which became law on 8 August 1944. Those provisions were updated and re-enacted fourteen years later in the Prevention of Fraud (Investments) Act 1958. Under the Act, the regulation of the unit trusts movement was brought under the then Board of Trade and is now the responsibility of the Department of Trade and Industry. Among other matters, the Act serves to emphasise the importance of the role of the trustee and it is that aspect with which we are principally concerned in this section.

In the following paragraphs we deal first with the law and practice as it is at the moment in relation to the trusteeship of unit trusts. As mentioned below, however, the regulatory regime for unit trusts will change in due course under the provisions of the Financial Services Act 1986.

Although the powers and duties of a unit trust trustee will be laid down in each case in the unit trust deed, the trust will not be 'authorised' (see Chapter 7) by the Department of Trade unless the deed complies with the requirements of the first Schedule to the Act.[8] Certain duties of a routine or procedural nature are also imposed on trustees by the Unit Trust Records Regulations.[9]

In general terms, we may summarise the functions of the unit trust trustee as follows.

1. To secure the vesting in the trustee or his nominee of the trust property prior to the issue of units.[10]

2. To be given reasonable time to consider or propose advertisements and related documents and to prohibit their issue if he, the trustee, disapproves.[11]

3. To require the managers to retire from the trust if he, the trustee, is satisfied that it is in the interests of the unitholders that they should do so.[12]

4. To hold the investments of the trust and any cash deposited by the managers, to collect and distribute the income from the trust assets, to sign and issue certificates to unitholders and to supervise the maintenance of the Register of Unitholders.[13]

5. To ensure general compliance with the terms of the trust deed.

The trustee of a unit trust does not have any specific responsibility for the content or performance of the portfolio, but if, for example, an investment were purchased outside the investment powers of the trust, it would be proper for the trustee to draw attention to the matter and require its rectification.

A trust deed will normally absolve the trustee from liability in respect of breaches of trust and he will not normally be liable for loss or damage to the trust property unless he has acted fraudulently or negligently. Nevertheless, the burden is an onerous one. The trustee must carry out his duties in a diligent and prudent fashion. It is not a passive role, it is not a perfunctory patrolling of a quiet street, it is not a mere custodianship. It is an active, day-to-day supervision of the manager's role to ensure that the terms of the trust deed and the Department of Trade regulations are observed, and that the interests of the unitholders are protected.

Chapter VIII of the Financial Services Act 1986 (Sections 75 to 95 of the Act) contains new provisions relating to collective investment schemes, i.e. unit trusts. The Act repeals the Prevention of Fraud (Investments) Act 1958, and it is understood that in most respects the control of the Department of Trade and Industry over unit trusts will pass to the Securities and Investments Board. The Act also brings regulations relating to unit trusts in this country in line with the Directive of the European Community on the subject of collective investment schemes. In 1986, in anticipation of the Financial Services legislation, the Department of Trade and Industry issued a consultative document on the proposed regulations for unit trust schemes. The document states:

> 'The trustee has an important dual role as the custodian of the scheme's assets and as the guardian of the participants interests. In the new regime the trustee will have an enhanced regulatory role, with more clearly defined responsibilities, to see that the manager acts in accordance with the regulations and the provisions of the trust deed'.

The following further extracts from the document illustrate the proposed tightening of the trustees' regulatory obligations:

— the trustee will have the power to replace the manager if the trustee considers this to be in the best interest of participants (this is so under the present law but the trustee will be *obliged* to dismiss the manager if either the unit trust participants so decide by extraordinary resolution at a meeting called for that purpose, or the manager becomes insolvent or ceases to meet the requirements of the Act).

— the trustee will be responsible for the safe custody of the scheme's assets (no significant change).

— the trustee will be obliged to check that the investments of the scheme are of the permitted kind and within the set limits (as mentioned above this would be done in practice by a trustee but the intention is that it would become a regulatory requirement).

— the trustee will have a duty to see that the transactions in units are properly carried out by the manager (this will require the trustee to ensure that there is an adequate system of internal control and to make spot checks to verify this).

It is also contemplated that the delegated agency, presumably the Securities and Investments Board, will be required to monitor the trustee's performance and the extent of a trustee's total exposure through all his trusteeships. Thus it would appear that, at least in theory, trustees may be restricted in the amount of new business which they undertake.

One positive change already enshrined in the Financial Services Act, Section 84, is that 'any provision of the trust deed of an authorised unit trust scheme shall be void in so far as it would have the effect of exempting the manager or trustee from liability for any failure to exercise due care and diligence in the discharge of his functions in respect of the scheme.'

The statutory requirements and the nature of the duties effectively limit the choice of unit trust trustees to the clearing banks, merchant banks and insurance companies. It is a role which has fallen naturally to the clearing banks because of their trustee experience over the years and at the present time, out of 1,021 unit trusts in this country, some 922 have English and Scottish clearing banks as trustees. The Midland Bank Trust Company actively sought unit trust trusteeships over the years and for a long time stood aside from active participation in the management of unit trusts. Perhaps for that reason the Midland Bank Trust Company had a larger number of unit trust trusteeships than its competitors.

Those banks which moved into the management of unit trusts in the early days did not however, necessarily, suffer in the development of their trusteeship business. For instance, Barclays Bank, although managers of the Unicorn Group of trusts, one of the largest in the country, was also for many years the trustee of the giant Save & Prosper Group. The two roles were exercised in separate pockets of the organisation and there was no apparent conflict and certainly no breach of confidence.

It is a statutory requirement that the effective control of the management company is 'exercised' independently of the corporation acting as trustee.[14] Thus a bank or other corporate body may not be trustee of a unit trust of which it is manager, even though the functions may be exercised separately in the same group. There are cases where the two roles are exercised side by side – indeed in some instances there are 'managing trustees' – but such trusts cannot be 'authorised', a subject which is dealt with in Chapter 7.

The business of unit trust trusteeships can be profitable if conducted on a reasonably large scale with streamlined methods of administration. The fees are a matter for negotiation between managers and trustees and are usually expressed as a percentage of the value of the funds under management. Where the trustee is a bank, the uninvested cash balances can be an added source of remuneration to the banking group, provision having been made for this in the trust deed, and such balances used to be very substantial although probably less so in recent years.

If there be any special problems of unit trust trusteeship, they almost certainly lie in the area of supervision and control. Troubles can soon arise if the management company does not have an adequate administrative system. There may also be problems over the monitoring of advertisements, but nowadays the Unit Trust Association (see p. 157) exercises a very firm influence on its members in such matters. Fortunately, it seems to have been exceedingly rare that a trustee has had to intervene to the point of requiring the managers to resign. (The author was closely involved in such an incident years ago, but knows of no other case.)

It has been said that unitholders are given less control in the management of their medium of investment than the shareholders of an investment trust company.[15] One might go further and say that unitholders have less 'say' in the affairs of their trust than a shareholder in any company. It is usual for the deeds of authorised trusts to provide that holders of, say, one-tenth in value of the units in issue may convene a meeting of unitholders. Such a meeting cannot, however, vary the terms of the trust without the approval of the managers, the trustees and the Department of Trade and Industry. The unitholders cannot remove either manager or trustee and they have no say in investment policy or any other matters concerning the day-to-day running of the trust. The unitholder has the right to request the Department of Trade to appoint inspectors to investigate a unit trust,[16] but the Department may do this only where it is satisfied that it is in the interests of unitholders and the matter is one of public concern. The remedies of two million or so unitholders in this country are minimal: thus the role of the trustee is an important one. (As mentioned above there are provisions in the pipeline for the tightening of unit holders' control.)

Although, as we have said, a bank or insurance company is a natural choice for the role of unit trust trustee, the business no longer enjoys the profits of former years. This is partly because the trustee must be near the management company, which usually means in London and partly because the business is still labour-intensive despite the use of computers. It is necessary also to maintain staffing levels appropriate to peak business periods. The business has also become very competitive and there is the fact, already mentioned, that large liquidity balances no longer accrue for the benefit of bank trustees, or if they do they are taken into account in the overall level of fees.

Other corporate trusteeships

The concept of the trust is one of the most versatile in English law and thus, in a changing environment, new forms of trust arise depending sometimes on fashion or ingenuity, but occasionally from statutory requirements. Two such examples are:

(a) trusteeships for insurance companies. Under a statutory provision,[17] the Department of Trade (or more correctly the Secretary of State) may require insurance companies to set aside in the United Kingdom a fund equal to the whole, or some specified proportion, of their domestic liabilities and may require the whole or part of the assets set aside to be held by a person, approved by the Secretary of State, to act as trustee for the company.

This enactment led for a time to a substantial flow of business to the banks who are, of course, natural custodians for this purpose. New business from this source, however, is now of little consequence.

(b) trusteeship of profit-sharing schemes. Although there is nothing new in the concept of profit-sharing schemes for employees, they were not widespread in the United Kingdom, partly because of taxation considerations until comparatively recent times. Under the 1978 Finance Act (as amended by subsequent Finance Acts), provision was, however, made for a degree of tax relief for profit-sharing schemes with effect from April 1979. Under the Act, an employer may make up to £1,250 per employee (or 10 per cent of the participants salary whichever is the greater, up to a maximum benefit of £5,000) available in shares, free of tax, provided a special trust has been set up for the profit-sharing scheme. The shares must remain with the trustee for a minimum period of two years. Thereafter, if the shares are sold, income tax will be payable on the original value or the sale price of the shares (whichever is the less) if they are sold within the third or fourth years and on 75 per cent of the value if sold within the fifth year.

In recent times such schemes have become increasingly popular and a large number of employers have now introduced profit sharing arrangements within the statutory framework described above.

All in all, the banks have few major competitors in the field of corporate trusteeships. It is a role they fill with great experience and efficiency and one which they will no doubt continue to carry out profitably, whether in relation to the particular areas described in this chapter or some future categories of trusteeship as yet not contemplated.

References

1 R. R. Pennington: *The Investor and the Law.* MacGibbon and Kee, 1968.
2 Sykes v Beadon (1879) 11 Ch.D.170.
3 Smith v Anderson (1880) 15 Ch.D.247.
4 M. J. Day and P. I. Harris: 'Unit Trusts'. *Oyez,* 1974.
5 Companies Act 1948, s. 54.
6 Report of The Stock Exchange Sub-Committee on Fixed Trusts, 1935.
7 Board of Trade: 'Fixed Trusts' – Report of a Departmental Committee, Cmd 5259. HMSO, 1936.
8 Prevention of Fraud (Investments) Act 1958.
9 Statutory Rules and Orders 1946. No. 1586.
10 Prevention of Fraud (Investments) Act 1958, Schedule 1, para. 2.
11 Ibid, para. 4.
12 Ibid, para. 7.
13 Unit Trust Records Regulations 1946, para. 5.
14 Prevention of Fraud (Investments) Act 1958, s. 17(d).
15 M. J. Day and P. I. Harris: op. cit., p. 174.
16 Prevention of Fraud (Investments) Act 1958, s. 12(1).
17 Insurance Companies Act 1974, s. 32.

CHAPTER 19

Pensions Services

Pensions business is a phenomenon of our times. Probably no other single branch of financial activity in modern times has seen such mushroom development. Today, pension schemes in their various forms are almost certainly the largest source of new investment in the various financial assets of this country, and have certainly become the largest single category of investor on the Stock Exchange. Sir Harold Wilson, Chairman of the Committee to Review the Functioning of Financial Institutions, remarked that pension fund investment might reach a point where the funds controlled both the affairs of British industry and the British economy. It is believed that the capital assets of pension funds stand at a figure of approximately £200 billion and new money flowing into pension schemes is of the order of £10/12 billion per annum. (In August 1986 the Economist Intelligence Unit estimated that pension funds in the UK and the USA had increased by 500 per cent in ten years.)

Until comparatively recent years, occupational pensions, i.e. those paid by employers, were regarded as a matter of 'grace and favour'. Charles Lamb's 'Superannuated Man' who expressed 'surprise and gratitude' at receiving a 'pension for life to the amount of two-thirds of my accustomed salary – a magnificent offer!' may well have expressed the same surprise in quite recent years. Many retired persons alive today have no benefit from any occupational pension scheme. Indeed it is estimated that out of the total work force of some 21 million employees, approximately 11 million are in occupational pension schemes, viz. 8 million men and 3 million women.

'A pension for life.'

Only in very recent years and then only with a bit of a push from the circumstances of various government wage freezes have pensions been looked upon as part of the total remuneration package. The concept of pensions being 'deferred pay' used to be forcefully denied by employers. In very few cases were pension schemes the subject of negotiation between the employer and employees, and seldom did trade unions show any interest in pensions, being much more concerned, understandably perhaps, with 'jam today'. One wonders whether there has ever been any major industrial dispute in the United Kingdom on the subject of pensions. Rather sadly, employee representation has been exclusively concerned with the working years, notwithstanding that it has been the retired employees, with or without pensions, who have borne much of the brunt of inflation. The lack of interest in occupational pensions is perhaps even more surprising in relation to the lengthening years of retirement occasioned partly by the lowering of retirement age and partly by greater longevity. It is not untypical for a man to work for forty years and to be retired for twenty. In the case of a woman, particularly if she happens to be a bank pensioner, it is perfectly possible that she will be as long a pensioner as she was on the active list. In fact, it is estimated that for both men and women the effect of earlier retirement and greater longevity will mean that by the turn of the century there will be one person in retirement for every two persons working.

It has also been a feature of our society that the clerical forms of employment have tended to be accompanied by pension rights, whereas manual labour has not. It was something special to have a job with a pension and the credit for leading the way with occupational pension schemes must go to the banks and insurance companies whose schemes have always been among the best that the legal and fiscal framework permitted. Despite the inadequacy and in some cases total absence of pension schemes, the emphasis on pensions in recent years has produced the upsurge in pensions business to which we have referred. A whole new dimension has been brought to the financial scene. New schemes have been formed and old ones re-designed. The pension funds of the large companies and public corporations have grown to enormous proportions because of the effect of inflation on salaries and therefore on pension contributions. The development of the nationalised industries led to the formation of some of the biggest pension funds in the country – in fact the eight largest pension funds are those associated with the nationalised (in some cases now privatised) industries.

The National Association of Pension Funds estimated that, whereas in the late 1960s only 2½ per cent of total wages and salaries in this country was paid into pension schemes, this proportion had increased by 1977 to 4½ per cent and was expected to become 5 per cent. Nevertheless, there was a considerable gap between the 'haves' and 'have-nots' and far too many people were retiring with no provision for their old age other than the retirement pension under the National Insurance Acts. It was left to government to bridge the gap and both the major political parties sought to introduce schemes in the early 1970s. After a few years of political differences and therefore great uncertainty in the pensions field, a measure of agreement was reached with the passing of the Social Security Pensions Act introduced by the Labour Government in 1975. We have already said that with the coming into force of the Act in April 1978 all employed persons automatically come within the new government pension scheme unless, by agreement with their employers, they have been contracted out of the state scheme and included in a satisfactory private scheme.

We may classify all pension arrangements under the two general headings of the state scheme and private schemes.

The State Scheme

This is by its nature outside the scope of this book and a brief note is included here merely as part of the general picture of pensions business. In broad terms the scheme provides that, in addition to the state pension which everyone will receive, those employees who are not contracted out of the scheme will receive an additional pension calculated by reference to their earnings. Thus there are two state pensions and it is customary to refer to the State Schemes. Here we are concerned, however, only with the scheme which provides an earnings-related pension, i.e. the State Earnings-Related Pension Scheme (SERPS). To the extent that an employee's earnings fall between a lower earnings limit (approximately the amount of the basic state pension) and an upper limit (approximately seven times the basic state pension) each year of earnings will qualify for an additional pension equivalent to 1¼ per cent of those earnings (now 1 per cent under the Social Security Act 1986) up to a maximum of twenty years. Thus, an employee who has contributed for twenty years would receive a pension equal to 25 per cent (now 20 per cent) of his earnings within the prescribed limits, in addition to the basic state pension. Furthermore, the calculation of earnings for this purpose was based on the employee's best twenty years earnings (now based, under the 1986 Act, on his lifetime's average earnings), which are revalued at the date of retirement in order to bring the actual earnings figure in line with the growth in earnings generally. The state scheme provides for retirement at age sixty-five years for men and age sixty for women. The scheme also provides for a widow to receive a pension based on her husband's earnings and also on her own earnings if she has been a contributing employee.

The state scheme is subject to certain limitations, in particular that (a) there is no provision for a lump sum on retirement, (b) there is no provision for dependants other than widows and (c) there is no provision for early retirement.

On the other hand, the scheme provides for pensions to be adjusted in line with the cost of living so that there is protection against inflation.

If an employer contracted out of the state scheme, his own and his employees' contributions were reduced by 4½ per cent and 2½ per cent respectively. It was not possible to contract out of the state provisions for the basic pension, but an employer could contract out of that part of the scheme which provides the additional earnings-related pension, provided his private occupational pension scheme was approved by the Occupational Pensions Board. To be approved the occupational scheme would have to provide benefits at least equivalent to the minimum benefits under the state scheme.

It is estimated that as many as 11 million employees were contracted out of the state scheme, a much higher figure than originally expected.

The Social Security Act 1986 introduced a new dimension to the pension scene. The Act provided, among other matters, that an employee could elect not to be a member either of the State Earnings Related Pension Scheme (SERPS) or of his employer's occupational scheme. Thus it became possible with effect from 1988 for employees to have their own personal pension plans as discussed in greater detail below.

Private schemes

Private pension schemes may be considered under the following broad headings:

Insured schemes
Managed pension funds
Self-administered schemes
Individual pension arrangements
Personal pension plans.

The first four of these are occupational schemes for employed persons including directors. The fifth category, personal pension plans, relates to self-employed persons and employed persons who elect to arrange their own personal pensions under the Social Security Act 1986 (see also Chapter 8).

We have already made reference to the difference between insurance schemes and those which are separately funded and self-administered. The more traditional insurance schemes are those where an insurance company agrees to underwrite certain pension benefits, which are fixed at the outset in relation to the premiums paid.

The second category, the 'managed' pension fund, is of later origin. It is normally a unit-linked insurance contract offered by a life assurance company, whereby the pension scheme participates in the investment performance of one of the life company's 'managed' funds. Such contracts are not insured schemes in the conventional sense in that they do not offer any guaranteed benefits other than provision for the purchase of an annuity when the pension becomes payable and, in some cases, a related life assurance benefit to cover death in active service. Such schemes are in the nature of a half-way house between a fully insured scheme and a self-administered scheme. They were introduced by life companies to meet the demand for participation in visible investment performance and are an extension of linked life assurance, which we have already discussed.

The third category is that of self-administered schemes. A company which wishes to retain the maximum control over its own pension matters will normally decide to have its own self-administered scheme, assuming that the amounts involved justify such a course. This will normally entail some degree of administrative costs, but this may be so even in the case of an insured scheme unless it is part of the arrangement that the insurance company will pay the individual pensions. Opinions vary on the relative merits of the various types of scheme, but in general the larger the amount of money involved the more economical it would be to manage the scheme internally as a separate fund. The relevant factors will be the number of employees, the size of the fund and the annual cash flow into the fund, the willingness of the company to undertake the administrative responsibility and the ability of the company to provide or pay for the necessary investment expertise.

The main variations among occupational schemes, whether they be self-administered or insurance schemes, usually lie in the following areas:

some schemes are contributory on the part of members: other schemes are non-contributory, the employer making the entire provision for pensions;

some schemes provide for pension units to be one-sixtieth of salary multiplied by the number of years service: others use a less generous factor, say one-eightieth;

pensions are based in some cases on final salary, but in other cases on the average of the last three years' salary or some similar formula;

some schemes provide for retirement for men at sixty-five and women at sixty: others provide for retirement at lower ages;

some schemes make provision for dependants: others do not;

in some cases there is provision for the commutation of a part of the pension in return for a capital sum: some schemes have no such provision (under the Finance Act 1987 a limit of £150,000 is imposed on the tax free element of such lump sums in the case of schemes approved on or after 17 March 1987);

in some cases there is provision for a discretionary payment in the event of death in active service: in other cases this is not so;

some schemes provide for early retirement on full pension: the majority do not.

Nowadays pension contributions, whether by the employer or the employee, are allowed in full for tax purposes and with some minor exceptions (e.g. development land tax, until this was abolished in 1985, and with-holding tax on some foreign investments) pension funds have enjoyed complete freedom from tax on income and on capital gains. The taxation aspect of pension funds has been the subject of varying legislation over the years, going back to the Finance Act of 1918. The provisions of more recent Finance Acts are embodied in the New Code governing Inland Revenue approval of pension schemes. Since the passing of the Finance Act 1970, as amended the following year, all new schemes have had to satisfy the New Code and with effect from 1980 all schemes, old and new, were brought within its provisions. These are principally:

retirement ages are normally to be between sixty and seventy for men and between fifty-five and seventy for women;

the maximum pension is normally to be forty-sixtieths of final salary, subject to a minimum of ten years' service (now 20 years' service under the Finance Act 1987);

maximum lump sum benefits are equivalent to one-and-a-half times final salary, provided twenty years' service has been completed – in cases of less service, the permitted maximum will be proportionately lower;

the maximum pension payable to a widow is two-thirds of the employee's maximum pension;

the maximum lump sum payable in the event of death in active service is four times the employee's salary plus a refund of any contributions he has paid.

Schemes for executives and directors

Individual pension arrangements can now be made on quite a

wide scale for directors and other senior executives where it is desired to provide supplementary benefits in addition to those available under the main scheme. The maximum benefits allowed for tax purposes listed above will still apply, but individual schemes permit of greater flexibility. There is for example no limit to the amount of contributions made by the employing company that would allow full tax benefits, with the result that the maximum pension benefits may be achieved over a shorter period of years. Prior to 1973, it was not possible for a director who held more than 5 per cent of the voting power of a company, which was director-controlled (i.e. where the directors held more than 50 per cent of the shares), to be a member of the company's pension scheme, nor was it possible for the company to take out a separate scheme on his behalf. With the passing of the Finance Act 1973, this rule was changed and it is now possible for such a 'controlling' director to join the company's scheme or to benefit from a separate individual pension arrangement.

In the case of controlling directors, such individual pension schemes enable substantial sums to be built up outside the company with complete freedom from Inheritance Tax, formerly Capital Transfer Tax, which would otherwise be payable on the director's death or other transfer of his interests in the company. The flexibility of the scheme also permits the company to make larger transfers in the more profitable years, thus reducing the company's Corporation Tax liability. Schemes of this kind are particularly attractive to family-controlled companies, but the Inland Revenue require an undertaking from the trustee of the fund that he will not agree to its winding up, other than in accordance with the terms of the trust deed.

Personal pension plans

The remaining category of pension provision is the personal pension plan. This terminology is usually applied in relation to people who are self-employed or partly self-employed. To the extent that a person is self-employed, up to 17½ per cent of his or her income (after deducting allowable expenses) may be set aside in an approved pension scheme, whether an insurance scheme or an individual pension fund, with the benefit of full tax relief.[1] Higher relief is available for older contributors. The contributor may elect to withdraw his pension at any time between the ages of sixty and seventy-five and to take part of his pension as a lump sum within the Inland Revenue rules. Employees who are in an existing pension scheme, but who undertake other private work in a self-employed capacity (e.g. consultants, lecturers and writers) may contribute to such personal pension plans from those earnings which would otherwise be non-pensionable. Employees who were not contracted out of the State Scheme and do not have the benefit of any occupational scheme may also take out a personal pension plan within the permitted limits in order to augment their state pension.

To this category of personal pension plans may now be added those who are employed (as distinct from being self-employed) but who choose under the Social Security Act 1986 not to be a member of their employer's occupational scheme nor of the State Earnings Related Pension Scheme. As mentioned below, this change in the pensions legislation has brought a whole new category of potential business to the financial services market.

Thus it is that pension schemes in their various forms have become something more than deferred remuneration or provision for old age. They have become one of the major means of saving in this country. To many people, the right to commute part of their pension gives them the one opportunity, with the exception of endowment assurance, to have a lump sum of their own to spend or not as they please. At the higher income levels, individual pension plans for the employed and self-employed have become major features of tax planning, perhaps the only remaining way of setting aside a tax-free fund out of profits or earnings which enjoys relief from tax at the highest rate.

The clearing banks in the United Kingdom have participated to a degree in the growth of pension fund business. The areas of their involvement are these:

Trusteeship for pension schemes

The nature of this function has already been dealt with in Chapter 18 on 'Corporate Trusteeships'. Although some companies appoint themselves or their senior officials as trustees of their pension schemes, this is not an ideal arrangement. The interests of a particular company are not necessarily identical with the interests of those employees past and present who are the members of the pension scheme. A company may go into liquidation, but the pension fund continues. A company may merge or be taken over, but the pension fund cannot, as such, be taken over, although there is provision in most modern pension fund deeds for the merging of pension funds where the need arises. In other cases, funds may be merged, either by agreement of the members, or if necessary by order of the Court. No act or default of the employer company can be allowed to vitiate the terms of the pension scheme without the approval of the members. It is desirable, therefore, that the trustees should be independent institutions of substance. The banks are well suited for this role, but do not in fact have a large share of this type of business. Many companies have no doubt hesitated to appoint banks or other outside trustees because they have preferred to retain the destinies of their pension funds within their own control. This, however, can give rise to conflict particularly if –

(a) a company invests pension fund monies in ways which benefit the company, e.g. in premises leased to the company; or

(b) pension fund monies are invested in the company's own shares in order to retain a degree of control over the shareholdings; and particularly if –

(c) a company seeks to use the pension fund voting power in a contested takeover situation; or

(d) a company seeks to make use of pension fund surpluses for the benefit of the company to the possible detriment of the fund beneficiaries.

It is desirable, therefore, that independent trustees of standing be appointed in order that these and other possible conflicts can be avoided.

It must be recognised, however, that the employer company has a very real interest in the well-being of the pension fund. If the assets of the fund become insufficient to meet the rising cost of pensions, the deficiency can become a burden to the employer. In the past, this burden has been assumed voluntarily by many companies in order to maintain the level of pensions.

Good performance of a pension fund can therefore save a company a lot of money so that employers will seldom wish to relinquish altogether the control of the pension scheme. The need remains however for strong trustees.

With the strong investment markets of the early 1980s a number of pension funds built up very substantial surpluses. In November 1985 the London Business School estimated that even adopting cautious assumptions the surpluses built up in pension funds amounted to approximately £50 billion in excess of the funds required to meet pension commitments. Apart from the occasional exception, the Inland Revenue have not allowed companies to withdraw surpluses from their pension funds for use in the company (although there would appear to be little doubt that such surpluses belong to the shareholders of the company following a decision on this subject in the Chancery Court in February 1986). In some cases the Inland Revenue allowed companies to suspend contributions to their pension schemes where the actuarial valuations have thrown up substantial surpluses. This trend merely strengthens the view expressed above that the investment performance of a pension scheme can be an important factor in the long-term performance of the company itself. The matter is now governed by the provisions of the Finance Act 1986 which in broad terms require trustees of occupational schemes to reduce to a reasonable level any undue surpluses which may arise in their funds. This may be achieved in some cases by an increase in benefits or by a reduction in contributions. In cases where a pension scheme's assets exceed its liabilities by more than 5 per cent the trustees will be required to reduce the surplus to a figure not exceeding 5 per cent. If a refund is made to the employer this will be taxable at 40 per cent in order to retrieve to some extent the tax benefits enjoyed on past contributions to the fund.

Investment management

This is the largest single category of pension fund business. All the larger pension funds and about 50 per cent of the medium sized ones are privately invested. All these require investment management. The options open to a company in the matter of the investment management of its pension fund are:

(a) to appoint a salaried manager to manage the fund,

(b) to appoint an independent advisor to assist the salaried officials, or

(c) to appoint an external investment manager such as stockbroker, merchant bank, actuary or clearing bank.

The choice very often depends on size. In smaller companies, the function of company secretary or a similar office will often be combined with that of pension fund manager. In the very large companies and nationalised industries, the company or nationalised board will appoint a salaried manager with the necessary staff to manage what in some cases will be a very large portfolio.

In the great majority of cases some outside help is sought on investment matters and traditionally the merchant banks have had the lion's share of this business, although stockbrokers too have had an increasing share of the investment management market for pension funds. For some time the banks did not put much muscle into the marketing of their pensions services. In recent times, however, they have been much more in evidence in this vast arena of pensions business and one estimate is that they have an investment responsibility for approximately £13,000 million of pension funds money. Even so, it is not a large proportion of the whole.

One advantage of appointing an external investment advisor or investment manager is that it is easier to make a change if performance is not satisfactory. With the increase in emphasis on pension fund performance in modern times, it has become increasingly the practice to place investment management business on a competitive basis – competitive, that is to say, in terms of performance and not merely in terms of fees charged. The practice, hitherto more common in America, of dividing large funds among two or three investment managers has also become a little more widespread in this country. The theory is that investment managers will be judged by the performance they achieve with that part of the fund for which they have responsibility. It is not always a satisfactory arrangement. Keenness of competition and the fear of losing the account can lead to over-anxious management, seeking in some cases short-term performance at the expense of the long-term strength of the fund. It can also encourage over-activity in the portfolio, whereas a more cautious approach often produces better long-term results.

The measurement of pension fund investment performance is a matter which has exercised the minds of experts over many years. Comparison of one fund with another is difficult. Between any two funds there may well be differing guidelines, quite different portfolio structure, differing proportions of new money in relation to existing funds and differences in the flow of money into and out of the fund. However, employers and trustees have become increasingly aware of the importance of performance and one or two institutions now provide performance tables based on data supplied by individual fund managers. Nowadays, most pension funds have very wide powers of investment. Historically, the investment clauses of pension trust deeds were very restricted. In many cases investment in equities was not permitted, but during the post-war years many deeds were widened to allow equity investment. Many funds, like the superannuation funds of local authorities, were restricted to the limited provisions of the Trustee Investments Act 1961. Some of the local authorities promoted their own Acts of Parliament to permit wider investment. From time to time most funds have taken the opportunity of widening their investment powers and many have powers which are now all-embracing.

The provision of investment vehicles

Despite the wide powers now available to pension fund trustees, many funds cannot call on either the resources or the expertise to invest in a wide range of assets. We have seen in Chapter 7 that the Department of Trade permitted property unit trusts to be formed for the convenience of pension funds. One or two of the banks were involved in the promotion of such unit trusts. They offered the advantages, compared with direct property investment, that (a) investment could be in smaller amounts, (b) the units could be sold back to the unit trust managers, (c) the portfolio contained a spread of properties and (d) the management was in the hands of property experts.

Another vehicle introduced by unit trust companies for the

benefit of pension funds was the exempt type of unit trust, which we have already mentioned in Chapter 7. Such funds enable pension funds, themselves exempt from taxation, to invest in tax-exempt unit trusts, thereby getting a wider spread of investments than might otherwise be possible.

Pension fund structure and administration

Pension funds are a changing scene. Many older funds have had to be brought up to date. Smaller funds have become large. Funds have become merged on takeover situations. Insured schemes have become managed funds or self-administered funds. Benefits have been improved and, as we have said, investment powers widened. This evolutionary process has enabled the banks to draw on their experience of pensions matters and to advise on the structure of new or changing schemes in co-operation with consultant actuaries. All the banks are able to provide administrative services for pension funds and are able to relieve employers of the day-to-day chore of pensions management. Perhaps most of all there is a need for a computerised service which will provide employer companies with records of their employees' contributions and pension entitlements. The banks had a particular advantage in this way, but this has been diminished by the wider use of computers even among smaller companies.

Insurance schemes

The insurance broking subsidiaries of all the banks advise their clients on group schemes for life assurance and pensions purposes and also market the personal pension plans for self-employed people.

So it is that the banks in total offer a very wide range of pensions services, but thus far the results have been disappointing. The clearing banks have not overtaken the merchant banks in obtaining investment business from pension funds; the specialist vehicles set up by the banks for pension fund investment have not on the whole grown so large or performed so well as those of other business houses; the advisory and management services have not been seized on by employer companies, many of whom have preferred to manage their own pension affairs; and the insurance broking arms of the banks have not as yet achieved a reputation as pensions consultants such as that enjoyed by some of the specialist broking firms.

Nevertheless, the market is enormous. The employed work force in the United Kingdom in normal times is of the order of 23 million. The total number of employers is not known, but there are believed to be over 90,000 occupational pension schemes (allowing for the fact that some employers might operate more than one scheme). Of these, 66,000 schemes are believed to have less than ten members.

So we can say that the total market for the banks' pensions services in all their forms consists of many thousands of occupational pension schemes (with approximately 11 million members), many companies which do not have pension schemes and 2½ million self-employed persons. Despite the range of pensions services offered by the banks including trusteeships, administrative services, investment management in all its forms and various insurance services, the banks act in a trustee or investment role for only 500 or so pension funds with a total value of less than £20 billion. It is surprising that the penetration of the market has been so modest, bearing in mind that over 90 per cent of all the employer companies in England have accounts with the clearing banks. Thus, it would seem that the banks miss out on the largest business phenomenon of our time. Why is this? We can only say that the banks did not make a sufficiently determined onslaught on the market. Traditionally the banks had not been noted for their pension fund business and some image-building was necessary for them to be accepted as pensions experts. There were those who saw the scope for pensions business and its long-term advantages in the development of banking connections. In at least one bank a major national pension scheme was prepared in outline, with full knowledge of the authorities, to provide employees with a private enterprise national scheme as an alternative choice to the statutory proposals to be introduced by the then Conservative Government. However, the marketing and administrative arrangements for such a scheme would have strained the resources of even a major bank and it was difficult to see that the end result would have been profitable. In any event, the subsequent legislation introduced by the Labour Government left no room for a private national occupational scheme of the kind contemplated. The three areas where the banks might have made better progress were investment management for funded schemes, administration services for pension schemes and consultative work as brokers for insurance schemes. As we have seen, some progress was made with the growth of investment management business. On the insurance side, however, the explosion in pensions business came at a time when the banks were organising themselves in the area of insurance broking. They were not equipped to compete in this highly specialist market with those firms who had led the field for many years in the designing and placing of insurance-based pension schemes.

After the upheaval of the new pensions legislation, the dust has now settled. All employed people above the minimum earnings level are now covered by the state schemes or their own occupational scheme. As time goes by there will be further refinement and upgrading of existing schemes, but the market for new occupational schemes will be limited to those cases where companies decide to contract out of the state scheme and introduce their own occupational scheme, and those cases where employers decide to 'top up' the benefits under the state scheme by introducing their own supplementary scheme. There is also a very considerable market for private pension plans for self-employed people and, following the Social Security Act 1986, for those employees who choose to have a personal pension plan rather than stay in an employer's scheme or fully in the State Earnings Related Pension Scheme. We have referred above to the benefit of such plans – and the banks' insurance broking subsidiaries, as well as their in-house life offices, are well placed to offer personal pension plans to their self-employed customers. The majority of self-employed people still have no private pension arrangement and yet the tax savings are such that these schemes provide one of the best savings packages of our time.

At the time of writing a new dimension is opening up for banks and other financial institutions in the field of pensions business. The Social Security Act 1986, provides for a range of financial institutions, e.g. banks, building societies and unit trusts, to provide personal pension plans whereas in the past this has been the exclusive province of insurance companies. It will be interesting to see the extent to which the banks are able to take advantage of this new source of pensions business.

Fund management

The main area for the banks must remain, however, that of investment management. It is increasingly difficult for companies to manage their own invested funds. The breadth of knowledge now required of a fund manager is such that there is a shortage of such men and they are very expensive. Furthermore, an investment manager who hopes to compete in modern markets with worldwide investment powers needs back-up resources for research and distillation of investment data. There is also a degree of isolation about in-house investment managers which can make it difficult for them to anticipate market trends. To employ a man to manage a modest-sized pension fund of, say, £500,000 would cost approximately £50,000 annually, including his own salary, his pension, his secretary's salary and pension, and a modicum of assistance in the office. For managing the investments of a fund that size, a leading bank would charge approximately £5,000 and in some cases less. Even for a much larger fund of, say £5 million, when a bank's charge might be £25,000 per annum (but in fact is usually much less), the 'do-it-yourself' resources required by the employer company for that level of fund would be increased correspondingly. Some pension fund experts estimate that a fund would have to be of at least £50 million and probably as high as £100 million for it to be economical to employ its own investment staff.

We have referred to the scope of present-day pension fund investment. It includes equities and fixed interest stocks or bonds in all the major stock markets of the world; in addition many funds undertake property investment and property development in this country and overseas, and some funds undertake investments of a more entrepreneurial nature in North Sea oil, new and developing companies, commodities and works of art. Only the largest companies and nationalised industries can afford the resources to manage such diverse portfolios. A large number of pension funds are run by company officials who would not claim to be other than amateurs in investment matters. With the narrower investment powers of former years this was perhaps acceptable, but nowadays it is very much a matter for the professional. The large banks, with their day to day contact with the market, their considerable research facilities and their worldwide contacts, are better equipped than most to deal with the realities of present-day pension fund investment.

In a survey conducted in 1972[2] approximately one-quarter of all respondents among companies with pension schemes could think of no disadvantages of employing outside investment management. Strange as it may seem, 28 per cent (the largest single category) thought that there was 'too much risk' in employing outside management, but only 6 per cent thought it would be too expensive. Presumably the 28 per cent who thought there was too much risk considered that there was less risk if they did the job themselves. It would be strange if the clearing banks with their fuddy-duddy image of the past in matters of investment management, were now categorised along with other institutions as too risky. However, that was 10 years ago and the banks have made progress since then. The sad thing is that many of the respondents to the survey, when thinking of 'outside investment management', would not have been thinking of the clearing banks at all. Indeed, of all those companies who thought it likely that they would change their investment management arrangements in future years, none envisaged changing to a clearing bank! That is not so now.

References

1 Finance Act 1980.
2 Opinion Research Centre: 'The Pension Fund Market'. 1972.

CHAPTER 20

Business Advisory Services

Some time before midnight on 31 December 1984 the number of incorporated companies in the United Kingdom passed the one million mark. Of these, approximately 10,000 are public companies, 2,500 of which are quoted on the Stock Exchange. Even these substantial figures do not of course constitute the entire business life of the country. Although we are no longer a nation of shopkeepers, a considerable amount of business is conducted by private individuals and partnerships. The total number of private people and partnerships assessed for income tax on trading profits in the year 1982–83 was over 2·3 million.[1] It has been estimated that between one-sixth and one-fifth of business assets (excluding the public sector) are owned by private companies and private individuals.[2]

All businesses, large and small, require advice at one time or another and the availability of advice has tended to vary according to the size of the concern. Large companies have traditionally had access to the merchant banks and leading firms of accountants, and from their own resources they have been able to marshal and distil all the available advice. Smaller firms and those in the middle range have not in general known where to turn for guidance on the more sophisticated aspects of modern business, nor indeed could the comparatively small number of experts in the corporate advice field have coped with such a large demand.

The problem of smaller businesses was considered in great depth by the Bolton Committee on Small Firms. Among a large

'... according to the size of the concern.'

number of far-ranging recommendations, the Committee made the following comment:

> 'We hope, however, that the Clearing Banks will consider whether they could further improve their services to the small businessman in two particular respects. First, if it were possible for the banks to impose as a normal condition for the grant of an overdraft to a firm the production of regular cash-flow statements, or the employment of adequate estimating and budgetary systems, and if such disciplines, valuable in their own right, came to be recognised as being helpful for obtaining bank finance, the efficiency of small firms might be much increased. We do not suggest that a control system should be insisted on as a kind of bureaucratic formality, but rather that the bank manager might be able to improve the efficiency of his customers, in their interests and his own. He could also help them by pointing out the benefits of regular attention to certain simple indices of the health of a business – the profit/sales ratio, the debtor/sales ratio, the stocks/turnover ratio, return on capital employed and so on. In this way he would give powerful support to the efforts of the accountant in improving the performance and hence the overall viability of the small firm sector. Second, the bank manager should be ideally placed to advise small businessmen on the availability, the cost and the advantages of different forms of finance, in cases where an overdraft facility is not the appropriate kind of finance for the purpose in mind. The Clearing Banks have represented to us that their branch managers are already providing advice of this kind, especially as regards the facilities offered by the Banks' own subsidiary and associated companies, and we do not doubt that many branch managers now go to considerable trouble to keep themselves informed about the terms on which other financial institutions are prepared to do business with small firms. Nevertheless we have repeatedly been told by the specialist finance institutions that the quality of the advice on available sources of finance given to most small firms by their bank managers is poor. The same was said, often with greater force, of accountants. Certainly the strong prejudice of many small businessmen against any form of borrowing other than by overdraft, and their ignorance of the terms on which it is likely to be possible, suggest that there is great scope for improvement in the advice they receive on financial matters.'[3]

At a later point, on the subject of sources of finance, the Committee reported:

> 'We have found that small firms have suffered and still suffer a number of genuine disabilities, by comparison with larger firms, in seeking finance from external sources.'[4]

A number of the banks saw in the Bolton Report a new challenge and an opportunity to do some good for themselves and their customers. In his Chairman's Address to the stockholders of Barclays Bank in 1972, Sir John Thomson said:

> 'The ordinary customer will require sympathetic and skilful understanding of his needs and frequent quick decisions. The Bolton Report on Small Firms has a special message for us because we see it as placing firmly on the shoulders of the branch manager this task of servicing a most important sector of the economy. Local staff, having adopted a project, are also in the best position to keep an eye on future progress. There has been criticism that banks have been too slow in diagnosing problems before it is too late to save their customers from complete failure, resulting in dire trouble for owners, employees and creditors. It has not always proved advisable for bank managers to have been the first to intervene because such intrusion has been resented and the business taken to a competitor. On recovery, a valuable account will have been lost. Many remedies have been prescribed, but it is important that we should train our staff not to be slaves of historical statistics of past performance but truly to understand cash flow and the assessment of future prospects. Any such assessment must involve close contact and exchange of information with customers.'

In 1971 Barclays Bank had announced its new Business Advisory Service. In a preparatory six months' period a team of managers had been set up 'able to investigate and find solutions to financial planning and control problems which face their customers and to advise on and help instal management accounting systems'. In due time the service was extended to every district of the bank. By 1984 the bank had 45 Business Advisory Managers around the country and had completed over 20,000 reports.

It was stated at the time that this was the first occasion a major bank had drawn together its various services for the purpose of advising smaller companies. Barclays Bank provide the service free to customers of the bank, but make an appropriate charge for non-customers.

In 1971, Midland Bank had in fact organised its Finance Management Service designed not specifically for small customers, but for corporate customers generally. Sir Archibald Forbes, Chairman of Midland Bank, said in his Statement to Shareholders in 1972:

> 'Early last year we set up a Finance Management Service with which customers can discuss the whole range of their financial requirements and determine the most appropriate methods of meeting them. The officials of this Service are thoroughly versed in the more specialised activities of the Group, including for example not only the various lending facilities and outlets for surplus funds, but also insurance, the provision of equity finance and the introductions to such activities as mergers and flotations. The part played by this Service will surely become increasingly important as the financial problems of our customers become more and more complex. The Service will, we think, be found of particular value to medium sized and small business undertakings which are often handicapped by lack of knowledge of the range of financial facilities available to them. This was emphasised in the Report of the Committee of Inquiry on Small Firms presented last year.'

Although only Midland Bank and Barclays Bank formalised their advisory services in the wake of the Bolton Report in this way, all the banks would now claim to give financial advice to their business customers in one way or another. Lloyds Bank set up a business advisory service and also advertise the services of their Trust Division to assist family businesses with taxation, insurance and pension problems. In other cases, the advisory services are an extension of the existing merchant banking function. National Westminster Bank chose not to formalise its business advisory services, preferring to regard the branch manager as the main link with business customers. Most of the banks have issued brochures or 'kits' to assist the owners of smaller businesses and National Westminster Bank have issued a quarterly publication, the *Small Business Digest*.

What then is the sum and substance of the advice offered by the clearing banks to their business customers? We have already commented on the reluctance of banks to give advice and until comparatively recent times it would have been unthinkable that any bank should presume to tell its customers how to run their businesses. Bank managers at local level would assist in a variety of comparatively minor ways. Certainly some small businesses would lean quite heavily on their bank managers, but it is no disparagement to say that few if any managers were equipped to give advice at other than a very unsophisticated level.

Even now it would seem that a large number of proprietors of businesses do not consult their bank managers on business matters. One survey of twenty-three London branches, which provided banking facilities to over 8,000 small firms, showed that 45 per cent of the owner-managers had not conferred with their branch managers during the previous year.[5] The survey also showed that in the case of firms without borrowing facilities, over 60 per cent of the owner-managers had not conferred with their bank managers during the year. Of those who had any discussion with their banks, understandably as high a proportion as 94 per cent were seeking advice on borrowing and 72 per cent on the economy generally. On the more detailed aspects of the customer firm's business, only 56 per cent had discussion with their banks on the subject of debtors, 45 per cent on taxation matters, 45 per cent on inventories, 24 per cent on budgeting and as few as 4 per cent on such subjects as leasing and factoring. Out of the total of only 45 per cent who conferred at all with their banks, only 8 per cent discussed the investment of surplus cash. Perhaps an even more telling comment from the survey was that 'there was a wide range of opinion among the bank managers concerned as to the subjects on which they should be advising'.

It would never be possible, nor necessarily desirable, to train bank managers throughout the country in modern business techniques to a point where they could advise all sorts and conditions of customers. Bank managers have their own branch business to run and they cannot all become business consultants. So it is that the banks chose the obvious course of training small teams of chosen officials to run their advisory services.

Nevertheless, as Mr Timothy Bevan, then Deputy Chairman of Barclays Bank, said in his address to The Institute of Bankers' 1978 Cambridge Seminar:

> 'It is difficult to see the branch manager ever being totally supplanted by the small business adviser or any other non-line specialist.'

Mr Bevan went on to stress the need for selected bank staff to be given appropriate training in business advisory matters before progressing in the normal way into branch management.

To go into the 'business' of business advice was a major, unprecedented step – a complete departure from banking as such but nevertheless an activity which fits well enough with the basic business of the lending of money. It was yet another example of the ways in which the banks can respond to pressures or suggestions from outside their ranks – in this case from the Bolton Committee. We can now say that the clearing banks are prepared to help in an advisory way anyone large or small engaged in a legitimate business activity. The type of problem, the nature of the advice and the infrastructure within each banking group will vary according to the size of the firm in question. (We were taught in our youth that a firm was a partnership and a company was a limited company. The distinction has much to commend it, but has long since gone by the board.)

Any dividing line between large companies and small ones must necessarily be an arbitrary one. The Research Unit set up by the Bolton Committee of Inquiry into Small Businesses defined 'small' at different levels according to different types of business. In the case of manufacturing industries, for example, any company with assets of less than £250,000 and a turnover of less than £1 million would be classified as 'small'. It would be meaningless to say that large companies are those which have a public quotation and 'small' companies are those which do not. On the other hand, quoted companies and those companies which hope for a quotation in the foreseeable future are, as our American friends say, in a different ball game. The scene changes very considerably with the transition from 'private' to 'public' and even more so when 'public' is accompanied by an official listing on the Stock Exchange, or a quotation on the Unlisted Securities Market. There is another reason for this differentiation between the public and the private company. The business of corporate advice began with merchant banks and in general a merchant bank would not seek an advisory role for an unquoted corporate client unless there was some prospect of leading that client along the road to a public quotation. Merchant banks were entrepreneurs and their interest in giving corporate advice was not altruistic. They would give their support to an up and coming, well-managed company, taking or placing a share of the equity and possibly taking a seat on the board, in order to enjoy one day the substantial fees for bringing the company to the market and more particularly a handsome return on their investment which would then be in a marketable form.

There is another difference in the nature of the advisory function depending on the size of the business. A large company engaging a merchant bank as corporate advisor would be entering into a continuing relationship until such time as it might change to another advisor. In the case of a clearing bank advising a small business, this would normally be a once-for-all operation (with a follow-up arrangement if required) and although naturally the banker-customer relationship would continue, the bank would not assume a continuing consultative role. However, these are peripheral matters. The point is that for one reason or another a company customer seeking advice will be dealt with either by the bank's merchant banking operation, or by a special business advisory team, depending on the size of the company and the nature of the problem.

For a publicly quoted company, the merchant bank will often be required to advise on such matters as:

> the capital structure of the company including the sources of available capital, and the pros and cons of equity capital and long-term debt;
>
> dividend policy;
>
> investment appraisal and cost-benefit analyses;
>
> merger or take-over possibilities;
>
> management of liquid resources;
>
> development of overseas business and import and export financing.

For a company approaching public status the bank will advise on:

> overall strategy;

profit planning;

constitution of the board;

the general structure and organisation of the company;

the raising of capital and the placing or offering for sale of shares to the public.

Turning to smaller companies, we may quote from the evidence of the clearing banks to the Wilson Committee:

> 'The clearing banks are the main, and in many cases the only, point of contact with the financial system for the 1¼ million businesses in the country believed to meet the Bolton Committee's definition of a small firm ... small firms still contribute about 20 per cent of Gross National Product and provide employment for about 6 million people or 30 per cent of the working population.'[6]

And in a later paragraph:

> 'One of the most important features of the development of the clearing banks over the past 20 years has been the increasing range of facilities available through their branch outlets to meet the needs of smaller businesses at each successive stage of their development.'[7]

Because of the great diversity and range of activity of smaller companies, there is almost an infinite variety of subjects on which the banks might be called upon to advise. Only when the bank's representative has made an initial survey will the problem areas be identified. The student of these matters will wish to know something of the areas covered by the advisory services and they include in particular the following:

Philosophy and objectives: overall business strategy, long-term and short-term planning, the setting of targets, the communication of objectives and performance measurement;

Budgeting: the importance of budgeting in relation to corporate objectives, budgeting assumptions and the quantifying of variable factors, the monitoring of progress and analysis of variations;

Costing: the choice of a costing system, the setting up of records, the application of standard costing, marginal costing or absorption costing techniques, contract costing and estimating and allocation of overheads;

Pricing policy: methods of fixing product prices, market data, elasticity of demand and price sensitivity generally;

Credit control: the terms of trade, the credit-worthiness of customers, the efficiency of debt collection, the bad debt experience and the suitability for factoring or invoice discounting;

Cash flow: the importance of cash flow forecasting, relationship to the budget, performance monitoring and reporting of variances;

Stock control: determination of stock levels, liaison with production units and sales force, stock recording methods, methods of perpetual stock valuation, stock insurance and valuation of work in progress;

Management control: management information and management accounting systems to facilitate day-to-day control of the business;

Bookkeeping and financial accounting: the choice of system, electronic aids, audit procedures and preparation of accounts;

Use of resources: the management of assets and liabilities, better utilisation of assets, return on resources employed and methods of productivity measurement;

Financing: possible sources of finance, increase in capital, gearing or medium-term loan finance, sale and leaseback of property, factoring, leasing or bill discounting;

Import/export business: methods of financing, market information, choice of agents and distributors, export credit guarantees and international factoring.

No list is exhaustive, but these examples will serve to show the breadth of the business advice now available from the clearing banks. In many ways, these matters are a natural extension of the more modest role played by the traditional bank manager on the review of a customer's overdraft. But the bank manager was never expected to be an expert in business methods and indeed such expertise can only be concentrated at any one time in a comparative handful of specialists, as has now been done in the banks.

Why should the banks have taken on this extra responsibility? The answer does not lie in terms of an immediate profit because such services are costly to provide and in some cases are given without charge. The benefits to the banks may be summarised thus:

1. A successful customer is a more valuable customer and so the banks hope to reap the long-term benefit from the advice they give. At its lowest, the bank's lending risk will be reduced – at its highest, the banks will share in the growth prospects of an increasing number of successful customers.

2. The banker-customer relationship is strengthened because the customer receives from his bank, possibly without charge, a service which is not readily available elsewhere.

3. The investigation in depth of a customer's business provides the bank with opportunities of offering a wide range of services, e.g. medium-term loans, leasing and factoring, insurance, pensions and family trusts.

4. The advisory services can be a means of securing new accounts.

5. The bank is seen to be offering a highly professional service in the whole field of business administration, which in itself encourages confidence in that banking group – it is seen as a bank which understands business problems.

The giving of advice is often associated, directly or indirectly, with the provision of finance. At one time, the clearing banks would have pointed the way to one or other of the specialist institutions for the provision of long-term loan or equity finance. This might be through the banks' jointly owned subsidiaries, Industrial and Commercial Finance Corporation (ICFC) or Finance Corporation for Industry (FCI), both of which became subsidiaries of Finance for Industry (FFI) in 1973 and which in turn became the Investors in Industry Group (3i) on 1 July 1983. Alternatively, the bank customer may have been introduced to one of the merchant banks or investment trusts specialising in equity finance. Nowadays, these specialist services are augmented by the banks' own willingness to provide loan finance under a variety of schemes, as described in Chapter 3 or equity funding through their merchant banks, as outlined in Chapter 14.

In total, the banks will now assist their customers or potential customers in virtually every aspect of financial and business life. In some cases, they run a 'marriage bureau' for companies seeking to merge. In other instances, they will advise on marketing techniques, factory layout or deployment of the labour force – all matters beyond the cognisance of the clearing banks until recent years. In many cases, they are using the language of techniques which were foreign to the banks themselves only a few years ago. Not all that many years ago, no major bank had an adequate costing system; none of them was marketing-minded nor knew much about their markets. Corporate strategy, management by objectives and performance measurement were as foreign to British banks two decades ago as they are to many of the businesses to whom they are introducing these matters today. That is not a matter for cynicism and certainly not a subject for reproach. If anything, it is yet another indication of the quite remarkable resilience and adaptability of our massive banking institutions.

There is one area of 'advice' which should more correctly be called 'information'. That is the provision of economic and business data on almost every developed country and every sector of business throughout the world. The economic information services of the banks are impressive and perhaps far too few customers have recourse to them. The importance of such data has taken on a special significance in relation to the European Community. The clearing banks now have up-to-date information on file relating to all relevant aspects, legal and fiscal of business in the Common Market countries. Anyone with an interest in overseas countries – whether as importers or exporters, members of trade missions, executives taking jobs abroad, lecturers, writers and schoolboy essayists – now has the opportunity of tapping, through their banks, the reservoirs of information on overseas countries. And it is all free.

References

1 Board of Inland Revenue Survey of Personal Incomes 1982/83.
2 Research Report No. 4 of the (Bolton) Committee of Inquiry on Small Firms. HMSO, 1971.
3 Report of the Committee of Inquiry on Small Firms [Chairman: J. E. Bolton], Cmnd. 4811. HMSO, 1971. para. 10.14.
4 Ibid, para. 12.98.
5 R. D. Back: 'The Branch Manager as an Adviser to Small Firms'. *Journal of The Institute of Bankers,* December 1977.
6 Committee of London Clearing Bankers: 'The London Clearing Banks' – Evidence to the (Wilson) Committee to Review the Functioning of Financial Institutions. Longman, 1978. para. 9.1.
7 Ibid, para. 9.20.

CHAPTER 21

Off-shore Services

It is a widely held view that the offshore islands of the British isles are populated by wealthy Britons who, having made their fortunes in this country, put themselves beyond the tax-collecting arm of successive governments. This popular image is not wholly without justification. But there are of course far more people who have left the United Kingdom to live in other tax-favourable countries around the world than have moved to the Channel Islands and the Isle of Man. The point is, however, that a large number of people have for tax reasons chosen to leave the United Kingdom and taken up residence and domicile in the off-shore islands, thus enjoying the freedom of exchange within the sterling area during the days of Exchange Control, the continuation of a predominantly British way of life, the convenience of frequent visits to the home country and, in some cases, the facility for running their UK businesses from a safe distance. Whether or not the tax loss to the Inland Revenue is of significant proportions will no doubt continue to be a matter of debate. Such is the constitutional independence of the Islands, however, that the introduction of any system by which they could become tax-gatherers for the UK Inland Revenue is extremely unlikely.

In fact, the 'independence' of the Isle of Man was demonstrated in 1981 in an important law case where the Inland Revenue in the UK (of which the Isle of Man is not part) had sought to have access to bank records in Barclays in the Isle of Man to assist in criminal proceedings in connection with a building company in the UK. Although the High Court in this country gave the Inland Revenue an Order requiring Barclays to divulge details of the account, the Manx Court obtained an injunction restraining Barclays from so doing. In the Court of Appeal, the ruling of the Manx Court was upheld, i.e. that a UK Court could not require a bank in this country to divulge information on the books of a branch in the jurisdiction of a foreign country. It is particularly interesting that the information in question was available, at least in part, on the central computer records in the UK (and therefore within the UK Court's jurisdiction), but the jurisdiction of the Manx Court on the subject was held to be paramount.

To the extent that the Islands are seen as sanctuaries for fugitives from the British tax system, it must seem strange that the English and Scottish banks have established off-shore bases in the Islands, as indeed they have in other so-called tax havens around the world. The truth is, however, that the British banks have refused to allow their off-shore services to be used for tax-avoidance purposes for persons of continuing UK residence and have certainly not taken a positive role in encouraging people to forsake the UK and remove to the off-shore islands. Intending residents of the Islands will be given every assistance by the local subsidiaries of the UK banks in matters of local information and, as in this country, will be helped in arranging their affairs to the best advantage.

A 'Gentleman's Agreement'

There has been for many years, however, a 'gentleman's agreement' between the English clearing banks and the States of Jersey that the off-shore subsidiaries would not be used to assist UK residents in the avoidance of taxation. Additionally, there was a firm understanding between the Channel Island States and the UK Inland Revenue that companies would not be registered in the Channel Islands for the purpose of avoiding UK tax liabilities. Indeed, the off-shore services of the UK banks are more for the convenience of business customers than for the relief of private taxpayers and thus we include them here under the heading of business services rather than the personal category.

Any contemplation of these matters requires some definition of the terms used. In everyday parlance, the Channel Islands

'. . . prefer to be called Financial Centres.'

and the Isle of Man and other similar locations around the world are referred to as 'tax havens'. This is a slightly emotive term suggesting an element of escape, or at least refuge, and understandably enough the Islands prefer to be called financial centres. This latter description is no doubt reasonable in relation to the principal off-shore centres around the world, but is a little euphemistic when referring to some of the wind-swept isles which claim to be 'low tax areas'.

The meaning of off-shore

The expression 'off-shore' has also acquired its own special meaning in the financial world. Naturally enough it was of geographical origin. People who moved their residence or their business affairs from some political land mass to a nearby tax-efficient base were usually moving to the nearest convenient haven within reach. It was literally off-shore – the British to the Channel Islands, the Americans to the Bahamas, the Chinese to Hong Kong and the Australians to the New Hebrides. In time, however, the term acquired a wider significance and was used to apply to any centre where international business may be done in a favourable tax climate. This may be an on-shore independent state, e.g. Panama, Liberia, Liechtenstein, but it may also be a state within a state – usually a situation where a country allows international business to be conducted free from the burden of its own tax laws. For example, non-resident companies may operate in Jersey free from Jersey's own income tax (modest though it is) and in a number of countries it is possible for overseas nationals, whether personal or corporate, to conduct business in a way which is reasonably free from the local fiscal legislation. Indeed, it is argued by some that the United Kingdom is one of the best 'off-shore' centres in the world because there is more international business conducted there, untrammelled by British taxation or other restrictions, than in any other place.

In general terms, we may say that there are three categories of business in which British banks and other international financial institutions engage in the various financial off-shore centres of the world. They are:

1. Personal financial services, whether for the local residents of

the off-shore centre or, more likely, for the residents of other countries around the world.

2. Corporate financial services for those institutions in various parts of the world who can with advantage conduct some part of their business from an off-shore centre.

3. Those activities which, for the convenience of banks or other financial institutions themselves, may better be conducted off-shore.

Personal services

Taking first the broad area of personal financial business, we should note the particular requirements of the typical international customer. They are:

(a) He wishes his affairs to be managed in a low tax area in order to minimise the effect of income taxes, inheritance taxes and capital gains tax.

(b) He expects a standard of expertise which may only be available in the more sophisticated off-shore centres.

(c) The local currency should be reasonably stable, or it should be possible to conduct transactions in the currency of the customer's choice.

(d) There must be politically stable conditions.

(e) The off-shore centre should be sufficiently agreeable scenically and climaticallly, and enjoy sufficiently good communications to encourage the customer either to live where his money is, or at least make occasional visits.

(f) Complete confidentiality is essential.

Some typical examples of personal off-shore business are:

The management of personal trusts. These may be set up by a customer for the benefit of himself, his family or other persons. It may be to the advantage of the settlor not only that the settled funds enjoy a favourable tax climate, but also that the trust funds may be beyond the reach of the political system of his own country. To some extent, a trust may do the work of a will in so far as it facilitates the transfer of assets on death without incurring the time and expense of proving title and changing the title to assets in a number of different countries.

The management of investment companies. In those centres where there is a degree of personal taxation, but little or no tax on companies, it may be an advantage to the customer concerned to have his or her investments or other assets held in a company in the off-shore centre.

The management of investments. Most of the off-shore centres conduct portfolio management for private clients on an international basis, offering secrecy, international expertise, freedom from local taxation and to varying degrees, freedom from exchange control restrictions.

The management of mutual funds and unit trusts. These have been set up in most of the principal off-shore centres, partly because of the freedom from local taxation and partly, in the case of UK promoters, to facilitate transactions in non-sterling securities without the need for payment of the dollar premium in times of Exchange Control. There are, for example, approximately 450 international unit trusts or investment companies in the Channel Islands, which are now believed to have more of this type of business that any other off-shore centres in the world.

These various activities are very much the same as each other in substance. They provide a worldwide service to enable customers of means to locate some part of their personal resources in a politically stable environment with a favourable taxation system.

Corporate services

The second category of activity, corporate services, or perhaps more correctly called business services, is more sophisticated and in some cases more tortuous. An increasing number of business houses are finding it an advantage to centre some part of their activities in off-shore locations, perhaps to avoid recording taxable profits in the parent company or perhaps to circumvent some other legal requirement of the company's country of origin. The following are examples of services offered by the off-shore centres to international or multinational businesses:

1. *Company registration services*
These include the setting up of subsidiary companies for international companies and the provision of secretarial arrangements and sometimes the provision of local directors, to enable companies to establish some part of their business in a tax-favourable area. Although it may not always be possible to transfer a manufacturing process to a tax haven, there are instances where consultancy services and intellectual property such as copyrights and patents, have been transferred off-shore in order to allow royalties to build up in a tax-free situation.

In the Channel Islands and the Isle of Man, companies set up in this way (or investment companies, as described on page 426) are referred to as 'corporation tax companies'. This is because they are not subject to income tax on profits, except locally earned profits, but pay a flat rate of corporation tax, now £500 per annum in the Channel Islands and in the Isle of Man. At the time of writing, there are approximately 25,000 companies registered in Jersey and new registrations are running at a level of over 2,000 a year. In Guernsey, there are nearly 7,000 registered companies and the number is increasing at over 1,000 a year.

2. *Invoicing*
In its simplest form this involves the routing of invoices through an off-shore centre where a further margin is added to the price in order to accumulate profits in the neutral tax area. In other instances, the invoicing or re-invoicing procedure is used to circumvent exchange control regulations in the principal country of operation. The banks will not of course lend their name or assistance to any scheme which transgresses the local laws of any of the countries concerned.

3. *Captive insurance companies*
This type of company has been known in the United States of America for fifty years or more, and in more recent times has been introduced to other parts of the world. A so-called 'captive' insurance company is usually a subsidiary company set up by a large corporation to handle the group's insurance risks. In other words, the group undertakes its own insurance, thereby retaining for itself the profit element of the insurance contracts, although larger risks would be laid off in the re-insurance

market. It has become the fashion to establish a captive company in such places as Bermuda, Guernsey or the Bahamas in order that the company may operate in a tax-free environment and build up untaxed reserves for the benefit of the group generally. There are many advantages of setting up captive insurance companies, although this is not perhaps the place to pursue the subject in detail. It is noteworthy, however, that there has been a considerable growth in this type of business in recent years with consequent benefit to the off-shore centres.

4. *Cash management*

One of the problems of multinational companies is the management of cash flow in the various countries of operation and the 'netting' of cash balances in order to achieve maximum benefit from the group's liquid resources.

Some international banks operate a worldwide clearing system to enable inter-company payments to be made in local currencies on a settlement day each month (or more frequently, if desired). The inter-company and group liquidity position is available at a glance from a computer print-out and so maximum use can be made of cash resources. Similarly, it is possible to operate a collection system for trade debts by the use of a single account in each customer country, the worldwide balances being netted by the bank operating the service. Thus it is possible to obtain a daily cash position for the group as a whole, notwithstanding the variety of currencies in which transactions have been conducted. If services of this kind are operated through a company set up for the purpose in one of the off-shore centres, it is possible for net balances to be built up for investment purposes in a neutral tax situation.

These are but examples of services which are being developed on an increasing scale for international companies. As world trade develops, more and more companies are attracted to the possibilities of channelling some part of their business through those centres which have a favourable tax climate. In some cases, this merely postpones the payment of tax until such time as the profits are remitted to the home country, but in other instances it permits the accumulation of tax-free reserves for the further development of a group's international business without any occasion to repatriate funds to a high-tax country.

The banks' involvement

What then is the role of the British banks in all this? Most of the UK banks have subsidiary companies operating in the principal off-shore centres throughout the world, partly as a service to local residents but more particularly, in modern times, for the development of such international services as we have described. It must be emphasised again that the banks will not lend their name or support to any transactions which are illegal in any of the countries involved. More than that, however, the banks will not participate in any activities which, although strictly legal, are contrary to the known views of the governments or central banks of the countries involved. The British banks are themselves concerned, to varying degrees, in international banking activities and thus will not prejudice their own presence or potential presence in particular contries by operating nefarious schemes to the detriment of those countries. For example, an international bank represented in, say, Italy will not do its image any good by encouraging Italian companies to operate elaborate re-invoicing schemes off-shore in order to defeat the Italian taxation laws or exchange control regulations. Similarly, in the area of personal wealth the banks will not facilitate the flight of capital across national boundaries in contravention of local regulations.

There is no objection however, to the opening of banking accounts in the off-shore islands in the name of United Kingdom residents. Such accounts usually have the advantage that the interest is paid gross, whereas bank interest in the mainland on personal accounts is now paid after deduction of Composite Rate Tax (CRT). Such interest paid on off-shore bank balances is of course taxable in the hands of the UK resident but these accounts can be convenient for children and others who may not be liable to British income tax and who would not be able to recover the CRT deducted in this country.

Nevertheless, as the world contracts, more and more people will seek to develop their personal fortunes in the most favourable fiscal climates; and corporations, in the pursuit of international business, will seek to administer it from, or channel it through, those parts of the world which offer the most attractive return. One may indeed argue that world trade is encouraged by the particular facilities which the off-shore centres offer.

So it is that the British banks have sought to provide a complete range of legitimate services, not only in the immediate off-shore bases of the Channel Islands and the Isle of Man, but in the Bahamas, Bermuda, the New Hebrides, Hong Kong, the Cayman Islands and even the small island and former German colony of Nauru in the Central Pacific.

Banking business

The third aspect of off-shore business is that which relates to the business of the banks themselves as distinct from services to customers. One of the earliest examples of this was the setting up by the British banks of finance companies in the Channel Islands at the time of the interest rate cartel on the mainland. The finance companies were not governed by the agreement on interest rates, nor indeed were they subject to the liquidity ratios then applying to the clearing banks. It was possible for these finance company subsidiaries to offer a service not only to the local population and other overseas depositors, but also to residents of the United Kingdom who were thus able to obtain a higher rate of interest than was available in this country. That was a minor example of a use which the banks made of the off-shore centres for their own bookkeeping purposes.

Of far greater importance in quite recent times was the practice of international banks of 'booking' substantial loans in the off-shore centres, whether for reasons of tax efficiency or in order to take advantage of the freedom from regulatory provisions in a bank's home country. The result was a considerable upsurge of business on the books of the principal off-shore centres, notwithstanding that the effective control of the lending had remained with New York or London or elsewhere. A particular example of this occurred in the Bahamas in 1976 following an increase in New York State bank taxes in the previous year. It was reported that in the first half of 1976 more loans by American banks were 'booked' in the Bahamas than in London. In the same year, UK bank loans 'booked' in the Bahamas increased by over 28 per cent and deposits taken through the Bahamas increased by 77 per cent.

From the standpoint of international banking, the choice of

an off-shore centre will depend on such factors as (a) local exchange control regulations, (b) the freedom of foreign banks to operate, (c) the freedom to operate in non-local currencies, (d) the freedom from onerous local taxes, whether direct taxes or withholding taxes, and (e) the freedom from reserve ratios or other regulatory provisions in relation to international business. At the time of writing, more that 300 banks have branches in the Bahamas and as many again in the Cayman Islands. Bermuda has specialised more in shipping and insurance services, but has introduced a financial futures exchange. In the Channel Islands, Jersey has approximately 50 banks and in Guernsey there are 45. In the Isle of Man, legislation has been introduced to permit insurance companies to operate with freedom from Manx tax. This will facilitate the development of 'captive' insurance companies, which hitherto have been a feature of Guernsey where there are believed to be about 150 such companies. There are now approximately 50 licensed banking companies in the Isle of Man.

There will always be off-shore financial centres. Like water finding its own level, entrepreneurial business, when constrained in one place, will emerge in another. When the restrictions in one place become too burdensome, too discouraging and perhaps too punitive, the businessman will look elsewhere. Ship owners soon appreciated the taxation advantages of registering their vessels in Liberia or Panama. Mutual fund operators found they could set up their funds in centres where there was no capital gains tax and no withholding tax. The equalisation tax and domestic interest rate regulations in New York led to the development of London as the centre for the Eurodollar and Eurobond markets. If bearer securities cannot be issued in one place, they will be issued in another. And so on. As one door closes, another is opened. Even within the off-shore centres themselves the rules change from time to time. What is possible today in the Bahamas, Bermuda, Jersey or Grand Cayman, may not be possible tomorrow. The term 'off-shore' shorn of its original meaning will no doubt continue until someone finds a better one. As with flags of convenience, perhaps we ought to call them countries of convenience – countries where we can run businesses or manage our private finances in a way which seems advantageous to us at the moment and which is denied to us somewhere else. One thing is certain, that the banks will wish to be where the action is. They will seek to meet a demand and cultivate a demand wherever there is the opportunity of doing legitimate business for themselves and their customers – whether it be in Bermuda or Bootle.

CHAPTER 22

Finance of Foreign Trade

'In the infancy of commerce' wrote J. W. Gilbart[1]

> 'all trade was carried on with ready money. Before good roads are formed, and posts are established, the trade between distant places is carried on by merchants, who associate together in considerable numbers, and meet at fixed times at particular places, whence they commence their journey to the country with which they intend to traffic. When arrived at the place where the market is held, they dispose of their goods for ready money; they then lay out their money in the purchase of other goods, with which they return.'

And again:

> 'The labour of carrying money from one country to another was considerably diminished by the invention of bills of exchange.'

Bills of exchange are believed to have had their origin among the Jews and Lombards in the fourteenth century as a means by which they transferred funds from countries from which they were expelled. They are said to have existed, however, in the thirteenth century as a common method of payment among Venetian merchants and used even earlier by the Florentines in the twelfth century. The earliest reference to bills of exchange in use in this country is in the reign of Richard II in 1379.

Every student of banking learns (or ought to learn) by heart the definition of a bill of exchange in Section 3 of the Bills of Exchange Act, 1882 and carries the memory throughout his career and well into retirement and old age. It has stood the

'. . . merchants meet at fixed times at particular places . . .'

test of time and is as relevant today as 100 years ago, coming as it did from the pen of the draftsmen of that 'perfect' Act of Parliament, the Bills of Exchange Act.

The nine ingredients of the definition flow almost like poetry:

an unconditional order in writing
addressed by one person
to another
signed by the person giving it
requiring the person to whom it is addressed
to pay
on demand or at a fixed or determinable future time
a sum certain in money
to, or to the order of, a specified person or to bearer

A 'bill drawn on London' was the hallmark of reliability in the development of international trade not only throughout the old sterling area as such, but also in relation to 'third-country' trade. It must now presumably have a limited life, for international payments in these days of advanced electronic gadgetary and in its more popular domestic form, the cheque (which will no doubt give place to plastic card banking as discussed in the next chapter) are replacing it, and young bankers of today will have learned the definition in vain.

Overseas trade

We are concerned in these pages with the services of the British banks from their UK base and not with the wider spectrum of international trade as such. Thus, from the standpoint of the UK customer, foreign trade means either exporting from this country or importing to this country. The need for finance, as it says in the London Clearing Banks' Evidence to the Wilson Committee with commendable simplicity:

> 'is either to bridge the gap between the exporter making shipment and the importer taking delivery, or to provide short-term finance to the buyer pending resale of the goods.'

It is understood that about 90 per cent of exports from this country are settled in cash or near cash, but the bill of exchange still plays a major part in meeting the need for short-term credit. The great majority of bills vary between 'sight' and 90 days, but some are drawn as long as 180 days.

We are essentially a trading and a net exporting nation, but it is not known how much of the total banking activity is directed towards the finance of foreign trade. This is because a considerable amount of trade is financed from customers' own resources or overdraft facilities and only if finance is specially arranged through a bank, or insured through the Export Credits Guarantee Department (see below), is there necessarily any separate record of the transaction. Various methods of financing exports from, and imports to, the United Kingdom are discussed below.

Export finance

Payment from overseas buyers may be effected in the following ways:

Cash or deposits;
Open account;
Bills of exchange;
Documentary letters of credit;
Acceptance credits;
Forward contracts;
Export guarantees.

Cash or deposits

This may take the form of an outright payment of 'cash with order' which would be unusual, or, more likely, a payment in advance of an agreed proportion of the contract price, e.g. 10 per cent. This might be followed by further payments on account of the purchase price during the period of manufacture, particularly in the case of capital goods. The overseas importer paying cash in this way will usually require some form of guarantee from the exporter's bank in the event of non-performance of the contract.

Open account

This method accounts for the great majority of export sales from the United Kingdom. It usually means that the buyer will pay for the goods on receipt. Payment may be in sterling or in a foreign currency and may be by telegraphic transfer, which is quick or by cheque, banker's draft or mail payment order, which can cause delay. The 'open account' method is appropriate only for known buyers of undoubted integrity and creditworthiness. Pending payment, the exporter is financing the transaction either from his own working capital or from a bank overdraft for that purpose.

Bills of exchange

The bill of exchange still remains one of the most effective ways of ensuring payment for exports. It has the advantages of simplicity and a time-honoured procedure. The bill, drawn on the buyer of the goods, is sent with the shipping documents through the exporter's bank to the overseas bank, who will release them to the buyer when the bill is paid if it is a 'sight' bill or when it is 'accepted' by the buyer if it is a 'time' bill. If, pending payment of the bill, finance is required by the exporter, his bank may either buy the bill from him or lend to him against the security of the bill.

In the last resort, the payment of the bill depends on the financial standing of the overseas buyer, but in most trading countries it is possible to sue on a bill of exchange in the event of its dishonour.

Documentary letters of credit

To be effective, a documentary letter of credit must be 'irrevocable'. It is an arrangement whereby the overseas importer of goods instructs his bank in this country to set up a credit in favour of the exporter. Under the terms of the letter of credit, the buyer's bank will undertake to pay or accept bills of exchange drawn in accordance with the letter of credit provided they are accompanied by the required documents, usually bills of lading, insurance certificates and invoices. A 'time' bill accepted in this way may be discounted by the London bank, i.e. the bank will buy it from the exporter and usually sell it on to a discount house. Thus, the exporter is put in funds without waiting for the bill to mature.

In most countries, documentary credits are now subject to a standard code of practice set up by the International Chamber of Commerce. Such documentary credits will be stated to be 'subject to uniform customs and practice for documentary credits (1984 Revision), International Chamber of Commerce'.

Acceptance credits
This method of payment is more correctly known as the London acceptance credit. They are a form of irrevocable documentary letter of credit and are established by exporters in this country with the accepting houses, i.e. members of the Accepting Houses Committee whose acceptances have the accolade of being discountable at the finest rate by the Bank of England.

Forward contracts
This is not strictly a method of payment for exported goods, but a means by which the exporter can protect himself against an adverse change in the exchange rate. If payment under the contract is to be made in foreign currency at some future date, the exporter can enter into a forward exchange contract with his bank which determines the amount of sterling which will be received for the foreign currency at that future date. Whatever the movement in the exchange rate in the meantime, the exporter will neither lose nor gain.

In a similar way, the exporter may borrow foreign currency up to the amount of the export contract and sell this for sterling. When payment is received under the contract, the currency loan is repaid and thus the exchange risk is covered.

Export guarantees
In the years since the War, there has been a quite unprecedented increase in world trade. This has been occasioned no doubt partly by the emergence of new nations, partly by the increase in economic growth in some areas of the world resulting in greater prosperity, partly by the emergence of the European Economic Community, partly by the development of new and, in some cases, very large markets and partly by the rise of multinational corporations. This has all been accompanied (whether it be cause or effect) by the dismantling of trade barriers and an increased willingness of nations to overcome national obstacles in the way of trade (although nationalism in other ways is as strong as ever). From the UK point of view, this was accompanied by the gradual contraction and eventual

disappearance of the sterling area and a notable shift in our trading pattern from the old Commonwealth countries to continental Europe. Furthermore, in the 1960s and 1970s there was a very substantial increase in the export from the United Kingdom of those capital goods which, by their nature, require medium to long-term financing. To quote from the Radcliffe Report in 1959 (well before the major boom in the export of capital goods):

> 'The exporter of capital goods has not merely to find credit, often for a period extending well beyond the completion of the contract; he has also to bear unaccustomed risks throughout the entire period from the commencement of manufacture until final payment.'[2]

And again:

> 'Since governments in all countries are now expected to accept some measure of responsibility for the balance of payments and exchange situations of their countries, the credit terms demanded and offered on purchases of capital goods concern not merely the buying and selling concerns but their respective governments.'

So it is that nowadays the governments of most trading countries provide a degree of credit protection, the terms of which are a matter of broad consensus among the member countries of the Organisation for European Co-operation and Development (OECD).

In the United Kingdom, the Export Credits Guarantee Department had been in existence since 1919 and was designed originally to provide cover for a variety of trade risks, which were not otherwise insurable. The scope of the Department's powers was widened considerably by Statute over the years, enabling the Department to cover up to 90 per cent of most commercial risks, e.g. the insolvency or default of the buyer, and up to 95 per cent of risks of a political nature, e.g. government action which prevents payment. Following the Radcliffe Report, a number of schemes were introduced under the aegis of the Export Credits Guarantee Department to support the banks in the provision of finance for export and provide credit protection for the exporter. These provisions are set out below:

ECGD insurance cover

When the ECGD provides protection to an exporter against the risk of non-payment, the Department will usually require all that company's export business to be so insured in order to spread the risks. There are two main categories of policy, viz.

(i) *Comprehensive short-term policy.* This covers contracts with credit terms up to six months. As mentioned above, the cover is for 90 per cent of loss due to insolvency or other default by the buyer and up to 95 per cent for political frustration of the contract. The cover will normally apply from the time the goods are shipped.

(ii) *Supplemental extended terms policy.* This covers contracts in excess of six months and up to five years duration. Each contract must be separately approved by the ECGD (whereas the short-term policies operate under a blanket discretionary arrangement so that the exporter does not need to inform the ECGD of each contract unless some problem arises).

(iii) *Capital goods and capital projects policy.* Major contracts for capital goods or construction work on credit terms extending over two years may be insured individually with the ECGD. It is necessary for the Department to be brought into the negotiations from the begining and they will confirm the creditworthiness of the buyer and whether or not cover is available for the country concerned. Cover is not normally given against the failure to take up the capital goods on the part of a non-government purchaser.

(iv) *Other policies.* ECGD cover is also available in certain cases against escalation of UK manufacturing costs for contracts of £2 million or over, extending over at least two years. Cover is also available for the insolvency of sub-contractors or consortium members. The Department is, in fact, willing to look at virtually any legitimate trading risk involving the export of goods or services from the United Kingdom, including losses on overseas investments through political intervention and failure to pay royalties on patented inventions.

ECGD guarantees

Contracts which are insured under an ECGD policy may also be financed with the benefit of an ECGD guarantee. In that case, the British bank will provide the finance either directly to the exporter or, if it is a major capital contract overseas, direct to the overseas buyer (or other approved borrower) with the benefit of an ECGD guarantee. This may take the form of either:

(i) short-term supplier credit for:
  (a) contracts covered by bills of exchange or promissory notes for periods up to two years, or
  (b) contracts on open account (see above) where the credit period does not exceed six months;

(ii) medium-term supplier credit:
This is available to exporters of capital goods and services where the contract provides for credit of two years or more.

In the case of short-term supplier credits, the rate charged to the exporter by the bank for the export finance is at a very fine rate (currently ⅝ per cent over base rate). In the case of medium-term supplier credits, the interest rate is fixed at the outset by the ECGD depending on the circumstances of each contract. When the interest received by a bank under medium and long-term loans falls below current market rates, an interest adjustment in favour of the bank is received from the ECGD. An adjustment is made in favour of the Department if interest rates fall below the fixed rate under the guarantee.

The exporter must agree to indemnify the ECGD in respect of any sums which the Department has to pay to the financing bank under the guarantee. The exporter will then be able to claim correspondingly under his ECGD insurance policy up to 95 per cent of the amount involved depending on the circumstances.

ECGD support services

Where banks have entered into performance bonds for overseas contracts these may be covered by the ECGD if they are for amounts of £1 million or over.

Similarly, the Department will indemnify banks in respect of 'tender guarantees', i.e. where the bank has guaranteed to the overseas buyer that the U.K. exporter will comply with the conditions of his tender and enter into a contract if it be accepted, and 'advance payment guarantees' where the bank guarantees that if the exporter fails to complete his contract, any advance payments which the buyer has made may be recovered.

In all these cases, the indemnity support of the ECGD is available only if:

the contract value is £250,000 or more;
payment under the contract is in cash or near cash, and
ECGD credit insurance has been effected.

Buyer credit guarantees

In some cases, the ECGD will guarantee a bank loan to the overseas buyer of British goods in order that the UK exporter may be put in funds straight away. This is known as a 'buyer credit' and it is available only for high value goods and services, i.e. those where the contract value is in excess of £1 million. The amount of the loan and of the guarantee will be up to 85 per cent of the contract value. The ECGD will investigate the credit-worthiness of the buyer and may require a guarantee from an overseas bank or the parent company of the buyer.

Buyer credit may be (a) for single contracts, (b) for multiple contracts – general purpose line of credit where there are a number of UK exporters as well as a number of overseas buyers (even though the individual contracts may be for quite small amounts) and (c) for a multiple contract – project line of credit which is to cover purchases from a number of UK exporters to one overseas buyer provided it is in connection with a particular project.

In the case of a buyer credit, there is no liability on the UK supplier for the amount of the loan unless he fails to fulfil his part of the contract. It is not necessary, therefore, for the supplier to take out ECGD insurance because his only responsibilities are the fulfilment of the contract and payment of the premium for the guarantee.

Export finance houses

A number of banks in the UK have their own export finance subsidiaries. These have their own omnibus ECGD policy covering both the possibility of buyers' default and political risks. It is not necessary, therefore, for an exporter dealing through one of the export finance houses to have his own ECGD policy. The export finance house will make finance available for either short-term contracts, e.g. up to six months or will provide medium-term credit up to five years. The finance house will extend credit to the overseas buyer usually repayable, in the case of medium-term credit, in six monthly instalments against bills of exchange. There are a number of export finance houses in the country in addition to those owned by the banks. The attraction from the exporter's point of view is that the finance house deals with most of the paper work, he does not require his own ECGD cover and he is virtually receiving payment in cash.

A forfait finance

This is a form of export finance which has traditionally been more common among banks in continental Europe but which some British and US banks have actively developed in recent years. The term (meaning literally to relinquish, e.g. a right, to something) applies to a type of export facility where a bank on behalf of an exporter, agrees to buy the debt due from the foreign customer. Generally, *a forfait* finance, or forfaiting is appropriate to fixed-price contracts for, say, two to five years, e.g. for manufactured goods. It is also used, however, for shorter-term commodity finance. It is not appropriate to contracts under which payment depends upon performance clauses. The advantage to the exporter is that he receives payment more or less immediately and he is no longer concerned with obtaining payment under the contract. The return to the forfaiting bank lies in the discount at which the trade debt is purchased. To that extent there is a similarity to factoring (q.v.).

Over the years there was comparatively little interest in forfaiting in Britain because of the overall coverage for exports provided by the Export Credits Guarantee Department but the practice has developed in more recent times with the active encouragement of a number of leading banks.

Export factoring

The subject of factoring is dealt with in Chapter 17. The factoring subsidiaries of the British banks provide export factoring services to suppliers in this country, which can take much of the time and trouble and risk out of the business of exporting. In addition to operating the sales ledger, the factoring company will be able to draw on its knowledge of overseas markets, local conditions, credit-worthiness of customers and the terms of trade.

Import finance

All the commercial banks offer facilities to finance imports, whether by the acceptance of bills of exchange drawn by foreign exporters or by the setting-up of documentary credit facilities for the UK buyer. The making of produce loans to finance the purchase of goods on the sea has long been a feature of British banking and usually involves the 'pledging' of the produce to the bank against payment for the goods in due course.

Other supporting services

International trade has always been greatly facilitated by the ease with which London banks can make international payments, whether by mail transfer, banker's draft or telegraphic transfer as already described. The system of correspondent banking is worldwide and virtually permits the payment of funds to the account of a payee anywhere in the world. Since 1977, most of the British banks have been able to operate through SWIFT (Society for Worldwide Interbank Financial Telecommunication), which allows payments to be made between banks instantaneously by computer.

We have referred in Chapter 20 to the advice available from the British banks to their business customers and this extends to the provision of advice on economic conditions in almost all trading countries. Almost any business, however modest, seeking to develop overseas trade may benefit from the rich resources of their banks in such matters as local economic conditions, local markets, currency and Exchange Control regulations and, perhaps most important of all, introductions to the right people.

We may conclude as we began with J. W. Gilbart:

> 'It is not the banks that give rise to the trade, it is the trade that gives rise to the banks: though, after the trade is established, the introduction of the bank extends the trade.'

References

1 'The History and Principles of Banking', J. W. Gilbart (1871).
2 Report of the Committee on the Working of the Monetary System (Chairman: Lord Radcliffe), Cmnd. 827, HMSO, 1959.

CHAPTER 23

Money Transfer

Government Committees and Royal Commissions are not much given to the coining of new words, but the Radcliffe Report of 1959[1] gave us an expressive word which unfortunately has not been adopted into our language, at least not into the Oxford English Dictionary. The Report said:

> 'above all, the bankers' service consists of the cheque service. It is the *moneyness* of the bank balance that is the basic attraction to the depositor, and the more perfect his service in this direction the more readily will the banker find his resources growing.'

Moneyness is a good word. It describes not the dormant deposit account but the busy current account. It describes the unending and every-growing flood of payments in modern society. It describes the special, and historically unique, role of the clearing banks in Britain in the operation of current accounts and the facility for making payments by cheque and cash anywhere in these Islands. The number of payments made in Britain each year exceed 50,000 million (on average four per day for every adult) and virtually all these payments, whether by cash, cheque or other voucher depend on the services of the English and Scottish clearing banks. In their Evidence to the Wilson Committee, the banks estimated that the resources of the banks engaged in money transfer, whether by cash or cheques, amounted to approximately 60 per cent of the total clearing bank staffs, about 120,000 people, and a total annual cost, at that time, of approximately £800 million.

Methods of payment

Anyone in the United Kingdom wishing to make a money

transfer to another person will normally do so by one of the following methods:

Cash
Cheques
Banker's Draft
Standing Orders or Direct Debits
Credit Card
Travellers' Cheque
National Giro Credit
Postal Order or Money Order

Anyone wishing to make a payment to someone overseas will normally do so by international money orders, telegraphic transfers, Eurocard, travellers' cheques and, in the case of urgent business transfers, he may use SWIFT. (See page 444.)

Payments in cash

All that is necessary for a commodity to be used as money is that it should be accepted as such by a community. Money becomes necessary in a primitive society when there are surpluses of goods of one kind or another, or in one area or another, beyond the level where exchange can be by barter. In the transition from barter to coinage, the artifacts of particular societies may be used as a medium of exchange as metallic tools were used by the early Chinese. In other societies, cattle have often been the means of exchange as have shells, and in more recent times cigarettes and postage stamps.

Although metal coins were in use in the seventh century B.C. in Asia Minor, China and India, it was in the reign of rich Croesus, last King of Lydia, in the sixth century B.C. that a bi-metallic system of coinage was first introduced, i.e. gold and silver, and in time this led to a system of exchange throughout the Persian Empire and later the Greek and Roman worlds.

The use of metallic tokens or coins as a means of exchange has the advantage of durability, portability, homogeneity and the facility for the supply to be controlled.

Metallic coins were not supplemented by the use of bank notes to any significant degree until this century – indeed, not until the Currency and Bank Notes Act of 1928. A bank note is a promissory note 'made' by a banker, payable to bearer and payable on demand. Bank 'notes' issued by the private banks were in limited circulation from the late sixteenth century onwards, but the rights of private banks to issue notes was gradually reduced by successive Bank of England Acts from 1800 to 1844. Messrs. Fox, Fowler and Co. of Wellington, Somerset (which amalgamated with Lloyds Bank in 1921) was the last bank in England and Wales possessing the right to issue its own notes. By the Currency and Bank Notes Act, 1928 the Bank of England was empowered to issue £1 notes and 10/- notes. Prior to that Act, bank notes under £5 were prohibited in England.

Out of the 50,000 million or so payments made each year, over 90 per cent are made in coin or notes. One of the most fundamental services rendered by the banks in this country is the collection of cash from the Bank of England and its distribution through the hundred or so cash centres of the banking system to the bank branches. The banks are responsible for the entire cash distribution system, not only for the benefit of their own customers but for other financial institutions, including the building societies and the Post Office.

Despite the introduction of electronic methods of payment discussed below, there is little likelihood, as we have already said, of there being a cashless society for as far ahead as anyone can see. Payment by cash is for most people convenient, quick and efficient for the smaller payments of everyday life. It is interesting that even in the United States, which is looked upon as a society living on credit, 87 per cent of all payments are made in cash (over 200,000 million payments per annum) even though in *value* these payments represent only 3 per cent or so of the total.

Apart from the distribution of cash around the country, the banks provide an over-the-counter service at all their branches. This means the receipt of cash deposits and the payment of cash withdrawals, whether for private customers or business customers.

Traditionally, this is something which had to be done 'over the counter'. There is still no very practical way of depositing cash with a bank other than over a counter or by use of a night safe. Withdrawals of cash from a bank would normally have to be made from the branch where the customer's account was kept unless he or she had an open credit at some other branch or bank. With the introduction of cheque cards, however, (see Chapter 10), the banks have entered into reciprocal arrangements for the encashment of cheques drawn on other banks or other branches of their own bank. In May 1981, however, after discussions with the Office of Fair Trading the banks were advised that this reciprocal agreement may be regarded as restrictive practice. The arrangement was thus terminated and Barclays introduced a charge of 50p for cashing cheques on behalf of the customers of other banks, and in time most of the other banks introduced a similar charge. At the same time, charges were introduced for the payment of household bills such as electricity accounts over the counters of the banks.

Perhaps one of the most significant developments of recent years has been the introduction of automatic cash dispensers. The first of these to be introduced anywhere in the world was in this country in 1967. The early dispensers were designed to receive vouchers of £10 each purchased by the customer from his bank and used in the dispensers when the need arose. These machines were soon replaced, however, by more advanced designs 'on line' to the main computer centres of the banks. By inserting a plastic card and keying in a personal identification number, the customer is enabled to draw cash, usually up to £100, provided the computer accepts the debit. If the computer says 'No', this can be embarassing if there is a queue of people. There is something rather severe about a computer's refusal – human cashiers are usually more tactful.

At the time of writing, there are over 8,000 cash dispensers in use in this country and the banks and building societies have plans for increasing the number substantially. As with many services which we have discussed, the banks have gone by different routes to arrive at the same objective. Each bank has its own cash card, whilst the principal credit card groups, Access and Barclaycard also have their own cash dispensers which debit the cardholder's credit card account rather than his current account with the bank. A significant feature of automated teller machines (ATMs) in the UK is that there was a reluctance on the part of the banks to share their machines. This was contrary to the general experience in the United States where there is widespread sharing. If this tendency were extended to the use of cash dispensers in stores (see below), there would be some strange consequences, e.g. only Midland customers would be able to obtain cash in, say, one store and a Lloyds customer may have to be directed across the road to a machine at a competitor's store. This in itself would not encourage the banking habit, particularly among those who are at present 'unbanked'. However, the likely development of 'point-of-sale' banking will almost certainly be on a sharing basis as discussed below. An important development is that a Barclaycard has come to fill three roles, viz. a credit card, a cheque card and a cash card. We shall discuss the significance of this a little later.

More recently a degree of reciprocity has developed in the use of automated teller machines. For example, Barclays, Lloyds, Royal Bank of Scotland and Bank of Scotland have moved towards a shared network of machines as have National Westminster, Midland, Northern, Ulster Bank and Clydesdale Bank. Similarly in the building society sector there have been two main groupings in order to share ATM facilities. After the failure of an initial attempt by the building societies collectively to establish a national network of ATMs two separate groupings emerged in the building society movement. In January 1985, it was announced that the LINK Organisation had been set up to provide a shared network and that the original members would be Girobank PLC, the Abbey National Building Society, the Co-operative Bank PLC, Nationwide Building Society and a consortium of 19 other building societies, card issuers and other financial institutions. It was estimated that by the end of 1987 there would be approximately 1,100 LINK cash dispensers available in the United Kingdom to more than five million cardholders. Similarly, a consortium of seven other building societies launched a national network of cash dispensers known as Matrix. The founder members were Alliance, Anglia, Bradford & Bingley, Leeds Permanent, Leicester, National & Provincial and Woolwich Equitable building societies. In the meantime, the largest building society, the Halifax, has stood aside from any shared arrangements and has developed its own extensive network of over 300 ATMs throughout the country.

Another development in the dispensing of cash is the introduction of cash machines in stores. The Co-operative Bank, through its link with the Co-operative stores, was the first of the banks to introduce 'in-store banking' with their Handybanks. More recently, Barclays have experimented with in-store banking under the name of 'Supercash'. These machines are similar to other cash dispensers in that the bank customer uses a Barclaybank card or Barclaycard and enters a personal identification number, but the machine is manned by a cashier who deals with the cash withdrawal. The machine is on line to the bank's computers and will only dispense the cash if funds are available. If the customer wishes to check this first, he or she may do so at a private booth nearby. The advantage of this particular system is that machines are very much cheaper than the fully automatic cash dispensers and the intention is that the costs will be shared by the stores because it is to their advantage that customers should be able to draw cash without going to the bank and without relying on bank opening hours.

We have already referred to the fact that approximately 40 per cent of employees in this country are paid weekly in cash. Those who are so paid have no need for in-store banking or automated teller machines, nor for the most part any need to withdraw cash from a bank or building society except for special expenditure such as holidays and Christmas. If, however, the move towards payment of wages by credit transfer gathers momentum, there will be an increasing need for cash dispensers in convenient locations around the country.

So it is that at the present time any customer of a bank requiring cash may obtain it in one of the following ways:

- by cashing a cheque over the counter of his branch;
- by cashing a cheque over the counter of another branch or bank, supported by a cheque card;
- by using a cash card in a cashier-operated telling machine in a branch;
- by using a cash card in a cash dispenser outside a branch;
- by using a cash card at a cashpoint in a store;
- by drawing cash on a credit card at one of the Visa or Mastercard outlets;

by drawing cash at a Post Office (Girobank and National Savings Bank customers).

Payments by cheque

Cheques are bills of exchange (see page 435) drawn on a banker and payable on demand. They, therefore, have their origin in the early days of banking in this country and came into use as cheques rather than as other forms of bills of exchange in or about 1780. Thomson's Dictionary of Banking suggested that the name is derived from the French 'echecs' meaning chess, similar chequer-boards being used for the counting of money: hence, the expression 'to check an account'.

Although an uncrossed cheque may be used, and frequently is used, to draw cash over a bank counter, we are concerned with it here as a means of making third party payments. Approximately 3,000 million cheques and other vouchers are handled by the British banks each year and the number continues to grow. When a cheque is paid into a customer's account at a particular branch, that bank is said to 'collect' the cheque for the customer which means that it is sent off through the 'clearing' system to the branch of the bank on which it is drawn, i.e. the 'paying' bank. If, for any reason, the paying bank is not prepared to pay the cheque, either because there are no funds to meet it or the signature is irregular or there is some other defect, payment will be refused and the cheque will be returned to the collecting bank who will debit the customer's account. If the cheque is in order, it will be 'paid' the day it is received at the paying bank and the payee's account will be debited. Some would argue that this procedure belongs to a former age, that cheques are dealt with nowadays by account number rather than by signatures, that signatures are not checked as they used to be years ago and that in any case very many cheques nowadays are supported by a cheque card and thus cannot be returned. These and many other points are relevant to the introduction of 'plastic card' banking. In any case, some streamlining of the system is necessary or it will break down under the sheer weight of paper.

The very terminology 'clearing bank' has its origin, of course, in the system of 'clearing' cheques. In olden days, clerks from the private banks would meet together in the coffee houses of Lombard Street to exchange cheques drawn on each other's banks This led in time to the system of local clearings which existed in the principal cities until 1969. The clearing system on a national basis as we know it today originated in or about 1770. In recent times it has operated under the auspices of the Bankers' Clearing House which is a limited company owned by the members of the Committee of London and Scottish Bankers.

The criteria established by the clearing banks for membership of the Clearing House are: (1) the existence of a branch network, (2) a sufficient volume of items passing through the clearing system (this proportion was fixed at one per cent of the total volume), (3) an ability to accept and conform to the functional requirements and timetable of the clearing system, including the setting-up of a town clearing branch and a clearing department within a reasonable distance of the Clearing House and (4) an acceptance of the costs of participation.

Membership of the Clearing House is not synonymous with membership of the Committee of London and Scottish Bankers.

In 1984, a committee set up under the auspices of the Committee of London Clearing Bankers, published its report which proposed that a new bank clearing system be set up which would permit institutions, in addition to the existing clearing banks, to become members, subject to certain criteria, the main one being that the institution concerned was dealing with at least ½ per cent by volume of total clearings passing through the new company. Such institutions would have full membership of the new umbrella body, alongside the existing members. Additionally, it was proposed that other institutions accounting for a smaller amount of total clearings be enabled to join with other institutions in applying for associate membership of the new body.

Today there are two clearing systems, viz. the Town Clearing which deals with cheques for £10,000 or more drawn on 100 or so branches in the City of London, and the General Clearing which deals with the rest of the country. The purpose of the Town Clearing is to enable major transfers of funds to be dealt with in London on the same day. Although the number of items is small in relation to the whole country, the value of cleared items on the Town Clearing is enormous and represents approximately 90 per cent of the total value of cleared cheques in the country. The clearing system throughout the country is now automated to the extent that cheques are automatically sorted and listed on computers but, as we have said, the volume and weight of paper moving round the country is very considerable. (See also Clearing House Automated Payments System (CHAPS) below.)

The credit clearing

So it was that the clearing system evolved around the payment of cheques. It is thus a *debiting* process because a cheque ends up as a debit to an account, even though in the mind of the drawer of the cheque it is issued with the intention of crediting the payee. There was thus no system other than the issuing of a number of cheques for a person to initiate credit transfers to other people. In the 1930s, however, the banks developed, somewhat tentatively, a system of 'traders' credits', a means by which a business customer could instruct his bank to make a number of payments, in accordance with a list supplied by the customer, to the banking accounts of the creditors concerned. Out of this grew the 'credit transfer' system, which in time enabled the customer of any branch of any bank in the country to pay in money for the account of a third party at any branch of any other bank. Each 'credit' was sent to the branch concerned accompanied by a branch payment voucher, i.e. a *debit* voucher for the amount involved which was then passed through the clearing system. The facility for making payments to branches of other banks in this way led to a very considerable increase in the number of standing orders (see page 00) and other recurring items such as monthly salary payments. The volume of these transactions led to the formation in 1960 of the credit clearing. This operates in the same way as the debit clearing system, the only difference being that the net balances which the banks settle among themselves in the course of the clearing process represent the difference in the value of credit vouchers instead of debit vouchers.

The name of the credit clearing was changed in 1967 to Bank Giro in anticipation of the foreseen competition from the National Giro introduced the following year. The Bank Giro embraced the newly devised system of 'direct debiting' (described on page 52). This enabled business customers, e.g. insurance companies to initiate regular monthly payments which hitherto had been initiated by the customer as part of the standing order system.

The credit clearing or Bank Giro thus became the normal means of making credit transfers over bank counters for customers of other banks and other branches (as was the origin of the credit transfer system) both for (a) the immense volume of standing order payments and direct debits used for all regular periodic payments in both the private and public sector and (b) the vast majority of all regular payments initiated in the business sector for salaries, pensions, trade debts and the like. The credit clearing now handles well in excess of one million items each day.

The Bankers' Automated Clearing Services Limited (BACS)

In April 1968, the clearing banks set up the Inter-Bank Computer Bureau later to become a separate company, Bankers' Automated Clearing Services Limited (BACS) to handle payments between banks on an electronic basis. This has become the largest automated clearing house in the world. It deals with those transfers between banks which are entirely automated to the extent that they are on magnetic tape rather than vouchers. With the computerisation of current accounts throughout the banks, it became possible for inter-bank and inter-branch transfers to be effected by the exchange of magnetic tapes. Nearly all standing order payments are now processed in this way, as are a large volume of direct debits and an increasing volume of individual automated credit transfers. Within each bank magnetic tapes are prepared daily in respect of transfers to be made between banks, or between branches of the bank. In the case of inter-bank transfers, the tapes are sent to BACS where they are integrated and a tape produced for each bank for credits to be made to its own customers.

BACS is, however, much more than a process of settlement and distribution of credit payments between banks. It provides a similar service to other financial institutions and to the customers of the banks. Thus, a company which has a large volume of credit transfer payments to be made regularly may deliver an electronic tape direct to BACS. From the banks' point of view, there are considerable savings in the use of BACS instead of the older methods of transfer. It has been estimated that the cost of processing a paper voucher such as a cheque is three times that of making the payment through BACS.

In 1986 BACS dealt with over 900 million automated money transfers and accounted for approximately 25 per cent of all interbank clearings in the United Kingdom. It is anticipated that by the year 1990 BACS will deal with over 1,900 million transactions.

Clearing House Automated Payments System (CHAPS)

In 1977, the clearing banks took the decision to proceed with the development of an electronic system for the Town Clearing (see above). This would enable banks using the Town Clearing to initiate payments by electronic means, thus dispensing with paper vouchers and achieving almost instant money transfers. Under the CHAPS system ultimately agreed, each of the British clearing banks and the Bank of England subscribe to an electronic payment system using the British Telecom network for payment-switching. Each member bank can make immediate payments to other member banks and the daily differences between banks are adjusted in the books of the Bank of England at the close of business. A non-member bank, e.g. an overseas bank may make arrangements with a member bank for the transfer of funds to another member bank for the credit, e.g. of a non-member bank's account. Each member bank is free to make its own arrangement with its own customers on a commercial basis for the instantaneous transfer of funds through CHAPS. This has considerable possibilities for the settlement of security transactions and may be used in those cases where a banker's draft would otherwise be necessary. For example, the use of banker's drafts on the settlement of property transfers is particularly cumbersome where there is a chain of property transactions to be completed. The Trustee Savings Bank has in fact offered solicitors the facility of settling property transactions through CHAPS and there could well be similar developments in other fields.

At the time of writing only 50 or so banks (out of approximately 700 banking institutions of all kinds in the City) have joined CHAPS. Because of the risk of breaking the rules of the Office of Fair Trading in matters of competition each of the settlement banks has had to devise its own computerised system for its 'gateway' into banks. This has had the result that participant banks and company treasurers, etc., have been faced with a choice of conducting all their sterling settlements through one only of the member banks or investing in a diversity of computer equipment in order to deal through other member banks. Discussions have continued in the hope of achieving a common interface with a standardised system of communication, but so far this has not been achieved.

Other money transfers
Other methods of money transfer have been dealt with in other chapters, e.g. Credit Cards (see Chapter 10), Travellers' Cheques (see Chapter 13) and International Money Transfers including SWIFT (see Chapter 22).

Bank charges

The charges made by the banks for their money transmission services depend, in general terms, on the degree of activity on the account and the balances held. There is no published tariff for business accounts and the level of charges is usually a matter of negotiation. The charges may be expressed as a rate per item passing through the account, or as a percentage charge on turnover.

In the case of personal accounts, the banks publish their respective tariffs. Nowadays banks usually make no charges on personal customer accounts provided the accounts are maintained in credit. If bank charges are made (e.g. because the balance has become overdrawn) credit will normally be given for the average balance maintained, i.e. most banks will deduct from their charges a notional figure for interest on the average balance. It is usual for credits to a bank account to be free of charges, but service charges are made for withdrawals and electronic payments. The charges per item vary from bank to bank and range approximately between 15p and 35p. Bank charges are usually applied quarterly.

In their Evidence to the Wilson Committee the banks estimated that only about 20 per cent of the total costs of money transmission was recouped in the form of bank charges. In 1978, the Price Commission enquired into the subject of bank charges for money transmission and recommended that the charges should more closely relate to the cost of the service provided and that fuller credit should be given to the customer for the benefits accruing to the bank from investment of the balances. In more recent times, the banks have sought to bring their charges more into line with the true costs of the service, but costs have escalated considerably and there is little doubt that those who use the very extensive money transmission services of the banks are subsidised by the rest of the banks' current account customers.

Plastic money

Money transfer is a subject which lends itself to a Wellsian contemplation of the future. It is amusing and quite exciting to dwell on the scope for electronic money transfer to a point which could even nullify the branch banking system as we have known it. We touch on some of these more surrealist possibilties in a moment. There is one development, however, which seems destined to play a major role in the immediate future, that is the use of a plastic card instead of a paper cheque for the purpose of making both debit and credit transactions. On the face of it, the advent of the credit card brought a new dimension to retail banking. This may be too simplistic a view bearing in mind that in the United States a plastic card method of money transfer was almost bound to arise sooner or later in a country with no inter-State banking and, therefore, no counterpart of our cheque clearing system. Nevertheless, we must credit the Visa and Mastercard Groups with demonstrating that a plastic card works very efficiently as a means of money transfer and indeed as a source of personal credit without the need for the retail banking system as we have known it. Secondly, the major credit card companies led the world in the settlement of transactions by electronic data transmission on a truly international basis.

Taking Barclaycard as an example, it is already a means of money transfer (although, at the present time, a paper voucher is usually necessary to pay the card company's account each month); it is used as a cheque card (although this is irrelevant to the argument for plastic money); it is a source of obtaining personal credit and it is a means of obtaining cash. In 1980, the card was introduced in a pilot scheme in Norwich as a *debit* card for the payment of petrol. This scheme, known as Counterspeed ran for an experimental period of twelve months. The customer had the choice of paying by Barclaycard or Barclaybank card. By means of advanced electronic equipment and a personal identification number, it was possible for petrol to be paid for by a debit to the customer's banking account (using a Barclaybank card) or Barclaycard account (using a Barclaycard). Thus, for the first time in this country a plastic card was used as a point-of-sale debit card, i.e. with not only immediate payment to the merchant but almost immediate debit to the customer. (The details were recorded on discs and transmitted by telephone line each day with a debit to the shoppers' accounts the following day. With an 'on-line' system, the debit would be made to the customer's account immediately.) There would appear to be no technical obstacles in the way of point-of-sale on-line banking transactions and, indeed, successful operations have been conducted in both France and Belgium. The principal problems seem to be those of cost and security, as discussed below. (See also the discussion of credit cards in Chapter 10.)

EFTPOS

In 1980, the banks set up a working party to consider the possibility for introducing a national Electronic Funds Transfer, Point of Sale (EFTPOS) system and contemplated that this would be at least a 10 year investment programme. A pilot scheme planned for Southampton was not pursued in it original form, but a second point-of-sale scheme (POS 2) was devised and accepted in principle by the clearing banks (see below). We have seen that it has been possible to install cash dispensers in stores, partly because these machines are not quite so expensive and partly because the costs are shared with the store concerned. It is obviously in the interests of stores that their customers should be able to have ready access to cash. The introduction of on-line point-of-sale equipment for the purchase of goods is not necessarily so advantageous to the shopkeeper or merchant who is already perfectly satisfied with payment in cash, by cheque with a cheque card or by credit card. The machines are very expensive and the capital cost of introducing them on a large scale would be gigantic. An off-line system is less expensive, but involves sending the tapes to the computer centres of the banks with risk of delay or loss. Also, with an off-line system there is no immediate check that the card is valid or, indeed, that the holder of a valid card has funds available in his account. The use of personal identification numbers (PIN) reduces of course the risk of fraud, but a person who wrongfully obtained another person's number could play havoc, using an off-line system, before he was detected.

The mark 2 point-of-sale scheme depended not, as was originally contemplated, on any centralised electronic system of settlement, but rather (like CHAPS) it was designed to make use of the British Telecom network for the transfer of payments. Membership of the scheme would be limited to the clearing banks and to those card-issuing companies associated with the clearers. The point-of-sale machines, whether they be installed in stores, airports or on garage forecourts, etc., would be universal to the extent that they would accept the cards of any of the banks or the card-issuing companies (unlike the automated teller machines to which we have referred above).

Under an EFTPOS scheme a typical customer, Mr. Smith holding any of the plastic cards acceptable under the scheme may make a purchase from the ABC stores where point-of-sale machines have been installed. By inserting his plastic card in the machine and using his personal identification number, he will initiate a message to the store's banker, e.g. Barclays through the British Telecom network, effectively crediting the store's account. Barclays will imediately seek confirmation from the card issuer, whether it be another bank, e.g. Midland or a card-issuing house, e.g. Access that the payment is in order. On receiving that confirmation, the entry will be logged immediately by the card-issuing bank or company and by the store's bankers,

Barclays. Confirmation of the payment will be sent immediately to the store where the customer is waiting. The whole process will take a matter of seconds. Whether the customer is buying a shirt or obtaining cash, the process is the same. If, however, he wishes to check the balance of his account before making the purchase, he may have to use a separate cubicle as already described on page 000.

Early in 1985 the English and Scottish clearing banks announced that they had reached agreement in principle with the Retail Consortium for the introduction of a nationwide system of electronic funds transfer at the point of sale (EFT-POS). This system, planned in co-operation with British Telecom and IBM, was designed to have 250,000 terminals in stores, shops and other retail outlets, transmitting in time up to 1,000 transactions per second. This agreement with the Retail Consortium did not mean that any particular retailers were committed to the scheme. Indeed it was emphasised that EFTPOS is to be regarded as an additional and optional method of payment for those who wish to take advantage of it.

There were two main factors on which the future of EFTPOS would depend. The first is a matter of consumer attitudes and the second is the allocation of costs for running the system.

A survey conducted by Gallup among 1,000 adults in 1985 indicated (not surprisingly) that 8 out of 10 people were ignorant on the subject of EFTPOS. Of those who professed to know about it 60 per cent were less than enthusiastic. The then Committee of London Clearing Bankers claimed to have conducted a survey with much more favourable findings and in some respects the Gallup responses were not all that surprising in relation to the questions which were asked. It does seem, however, that so far as the consumer is concerned there will have to be a cultivated demand which will only arise when the system is live and working.

The division of costs is perhaps more difficult. It is anticipated that member banks will have to negotiate terms with individual retailers and obviously the latter will not wish to contribute to the costs of expensive equipment unless they can see a reasonable long-term advantage.

In December 1986 the Association for Payment and Clearing Systems representing the twelve clearing banks announced an agreed strategy for an EFTPOS system in which all members would participate. It was proposed that 2,000 counter-top terminals would be installed by the end of 1988 in three cities, viz Southampton, Leeds and Edinburgh, with the intention that, after the prototype services had been established, the members would choose whether to continue the system co-operatively or independently. Thus a basic national framework would be established and thereafter the member banks would be free to go their own way and there would be provision for other institutions to join the system. A company, EFTPOS Administration Limited, was established under the ownership of the member banks to control the proposed new system.

In July 1987 the banks announced that a common debit card would be used by all the institutions which joined the system and those cards would bear a common logo signifying that they could be used in all EFTPOS terminals. The EFTPOS card would be the only one which participating retailers would be required to accept – beyond that they could continue to accept other cards if they so wished as at present. The member banks would be able to choose which of their cards was to be adapted for the EFTPOS system and it is feasible that in time the EFTPOS debit cards would phase out the existing credit cards. Of particular significance, therefore, was the introduction by Barclays of its own debit card, known as Connect.

The 'Connect' card

The introduction by Barclays of their Connect card deserves special mention because it was a major development in the field of money transfer. News of the new card leaked in October 1986 but was not announced officially until the following June. Connect is a debit card. For all practical purposes it replaces a cheque in that (a) it can be used to purchase goods and services (with no £50 limit) and the transaction is immediately debited to the card holder's account, (b) it can be used to pay bills over a bank counter, (c) it may be used to obtain cash (as with existing cash cards) and (d) it may be used to order goods and services by telephone (as with existing credit cards). The card is linked to the customer's current account and thus provides a plastic (and electronic) alternative to the cheque. At first there was disagreement with The Retail Consortium over the proposed system of charging for Connect but eventually the differences were resolved. At the time of writing Barclays have a target to issue one million Connect cards by the end of 1987.

Home banking?

In 1978, the Post Office announced the introduction of its Viewdata Service by which the linking of a telephone line to a home television set would permit a considerable array of goods and services to be offered on the screen. In 1980, this was followed by the introduction by the Post Office of Prestel, the world's first public viewdata service. This required a special television set which is connected to a Prestel computer. By means of a keyboard, the viewer can select any 'page' of information he requires from the wide range of data covered by the service. This includes travel information from airlines and British Rail as well as up-to-date information on the services of various financial institutions. It also covers a wide range of consumer goods which the customer may order and pay for by keying in his credit card number. On the whole, consumer response to the scheme was disappointing. By December 1981, only 13,000 terminals had been introduced, almost entirely for business users. There were 20 Prestel computers at various places around the country in anticipation of a wider market, but quite a number of these had to be put into 'cold storage' for the time being. In the meantime, an extension of Prestel has been introduced under the name Gateway. Using this service, it is technically possible to transfer money between bank accounts, confirm travel bookings, order financial services of various kinds and make retail purchases. This, at least in theory, will enable a bank customer, who subscribes to Prestel to obtain on the screen his up-to-date bank statement, or a note of the current balance, or details of a particular item and by means of the keyboard to make money transfers. A small number of West German banks have introduced a degree of home banking on these lines, as have two major American banks, Citibank and Chemical Bank. Other American banks are expected to follow suit. It is interesting that in America the provision of banking

'Home banking.'

services on television screens across State boundaries is thought to transgress the restrictions against inter-State banking.

In the United Kingdom credit for the introduction of the first home banking service must go to the Bank of Scotland who, jointly with the Nottingham Building Society, launched in 1983 the Homelink service. This was followed in 1985 by the introduction by the Bank of Scotland of its own Home and Office banking service. Both of these services are available through the Prestel network. In the case of the Bank of Scotland home banking service there are four particular features. First, it is possible to obtain on the screen not only the balance of an account but detailed statements showing all transactions, including standing orders, direct debits, etc. Secondly, transfers may be made between accounts and if effected before 5 p.m. interest may be earned overnight. Thirdly, the bills may be paid on prescribed dates up to 30 days ahead, and fourthly a higher interest investment account enables transfers to be made from a current account in order to maximise interest.

Another significant experiment conducted in home banking is that introduced late in 1983 by Midland Bank. This uses a view data system separate from the national Prestel service. This service was introduced experimentally with approximately 1,200 customers in order to gain experience of customer reaction and the market generally for this type of service. It is understood that early impressions were very favourable.

In January 1987 the Clydesdale Bank introduced its home banking service known as Telebank and in April that year the TSB announced the introduction of Speedline enabling customers to enjoy a home banking service by telephone. Lloyds bank also announced the introduction of a telephone-based service with effect from the end of 1987.

One of the most important aspects of home banking must be the ability to conduct banking transactions without a branch presence. It is not so much that the customer is spared a journey to the bank: it is rather that the bank itself becomes less dependent on a costly branch network, a subject to which we return in the next chapter.

The main hurdles in the way of this do-it-yourself banking

are once again cost and security. At this stage, not many people will be prepared to pay the fairly heavy costs of a Prestel unit in their homes (as evidenced by the slow response to the original Prestel service). The banks themselves recognise the enormous scope for home banking, but do not regard it as a matter of priority. Indeed, any extensive use of a viewdata service must almost certainly depend on the development of cable television in this country. The development of in-store plastic card banking is certainly much higher on the list. No doubt some temporary advantage will accrue to the first bank to introduce home banking (the Verbraucher Bank in Germany secured a very substantial increase in customers when it started its home banking scheme), but (a) the costs would be very considerable, (b) the public response would be uncertain and (c) it would not in itself be a substitute for the enhancement and innovation which is already taking place in the money transfer system at very considerable cost.

Here again, the security risks are very real. There will be a mind-blowing amount of information stored in the viewdata system, some of it highly sensitive and confidential. It will not merely be the time of the next train to Basingstoke, but will for example include the personal financial details of the customers of those financial institutions, whether banks or not, who subscribe to the service. By the use of a special but expensive adapter designed for the purpose, the Prestel user will be able to enter into any of the 'gateways' to the various user categories in the System. There will no doubt be a 'fail safe' system of personal identification numbers, code names and passwords. As we said at the beginning, someone will have to re-write the Bills of Exchange Act.

The future

The future trend of the British money transfer system is to some extent unresolved. It must be doubtful whether any one person sees the end result in the form which will in fact be realised. No one doubts the availability of the technology. The costs of change, however, are enormous as are the risks of being wrong. Even the requisite degree of conformity is difficult to obtain in these days of restrictive practices regulations. Also, the behavioural patterns of the community are, as always, unpredictable. At the centre of it all is the costly branch network. The human and financial resources committed to 13,500 or so banking branches in the United Kingdom is very considerable. Almost any advance on the lines currently debated in the matter of money transmission, whether it be truncation of clearings, plastic card banking, in-store banking, home banking or whatever, must inevitably have an impact on the branch system as we have known it.

In the meantime, let it be acknowledged that the British clearing banks operate a money transfer system of a size and reliability quite unparalleled elsewhere in the world – a system on which money payments large and small, by cash, cheque or credit card, whether by bank customers or not, entirely depends.

Reference

[1] Report of the Committee on the Working of the Monetary System (Chairman: Lord Radcliffe), Cmnd. 827, HMSO, 1959).

CHAPTER 24

Selling the Services

This final chapter is in the nature of a tailpiece to what has gone before, for it seems appropriate that some reference should be made to the methods of selling bank services and to some of the problems involved. The point must, however, be made that we are concerned here only with selling, not with the total marketing concept. Selling is merely part of marketing. Marketing, as the distinguished business philosopher, Peter Drucker, has said: 'encompasses the entire business. It is the whole business seen from the point of view of its final result, that is, from the customer's point of view.'[1] It is too vast a subject to deal with here and in any case would be outside the scope and purpose of this book.

It is a pity that there has been such a shortage of works on the subject of bank marketing in the United Kingdom, although we now have the excellent book by Mr McIver and Mr Naylor.[2] Even in the United States, there was such a comparative shortage of literature on the subject that in 1974 Professor Leonard Berry and Mr L. A. Capaldini recognised the need for a marketing book which 'puts it all together' for the bank executive.[3]

The marketing mix

As we have already said, the term 'marketing' was unknown in British banking until the late 1960s. In fact it was not in much earlier use in North America. It was only in the early 1960s that marketing attitudes and the language of marketing were introduced into American banks. The so-called marketing mix (not to be confused with the product mix) refers to the major ingredients of the marketing concept. They have been defined for bankers in the same phraseology now used in the marketing world in general: they are the four Ps of marketing – product, place, promotion and price.[4]

Marketing as applied to banking has been defined by Lord Seebohm[5] as:

(i) identifying present and future markets for services;
(ii) selecting which markets to serve and identifying customer needs within them;
(iii) setting long and short term goals for the progress of existing and new services;
(iv) managing the services so as to persuade customers to use them at a profit, and controlling our success in so doing.

These matters and indeed the whole approach to marketing in the clearing banks will repay detailed study. What would no doubt emerge is the extent of the pragmatism (and also conservatism) and the sensitivity (and also inconsistency) which has characterised the rapid development of bank services. Here, however, we are concerned only with the P of promotion – the selling of the products.

The first edition of this book was concerned only with the non-traditional banking services, so the comments on selling were logically confined to those services and not to banking as a whole. Such a distinction was not easy to preserve because, to use the National Westminster Bank's terminology, these 'related' bank services have been very much related to the traditional banking function when it comes to the processes of selling.

Bankers as salesmen

Some bankers are good salesmen by nature, others would never be good salesmen in a thousand years. Some regard selling as fun, some regard it as vaguely unclean. There are those who, long before 'marketing' was introduced to banking, regarded themselves as salesmen – and some were better salesmen that bankers. There are others who to this day, with Ralph Emerson, believe that if a man offers a better service than his neighbour 'though he build his house in the woods, the world will make a beaten path to his door'.

The traditional view was summed up long ago by George Rae:[6]

> '. . . it is for its customers to come to a bank, and not for the bank to go to them . . . the Manager has to be as much a fixture in the office, during the business hours of every business day, as the office desks or the bank counter.'

And again:

> 'You ask, if you are thus to pass the remainder of your days inside your office, how are you to push the business? But banking is a business to which the business of pushing must be applied if at all with the utmost circumspection.'

Bank officials on both sides of the Atlantic were not on the whole regarded as salesmen. The typical view was given light-hearted expression in an article published in 1965 by the Financial Public Relations Association from which the following is a short extract:

> 'Our bank offices are nice and my chair is soft. I like my chair and its softness. People come to my desk to see me and I make lots of loans and open their accounts – all in my chair. I don't like to leave my chair.
>
> 'We have lots of customers all over town. I know they like my bank as much as I do because we are so nice. Almost everyone likes us. Some customers send people to the bank for them and have no more contact with us than their monthly statement. Some nervy people from those other banks go to call on *our* customers and ask for their business. But they won't get it because we are such nice folks. I understand some of those other banks even go out to see prospective customers instead of letting them come in themselves. We have branches all over town. It is convenient for them so they will come to see us at our nice offices.
>
> 'Some of those other banks even have *officers* who go out to "sell" bank services. Anyone knows a BANK OFFICER IS NOT A SALESMAN. Salesmen are pests. We're executives. I've even heard that some banks have special meetings to promote selling of bank services. They show films and talk about "prospects". None of those gimmicks for me. I'm a bank officer and people come to me and my bank because we're nice.
>
> 'But, where have they been lately?'

There were good reasons why bank managers should not be

seen in the role of salesmen. We shall consider in a moment the ways in which their role has changed, but it must be recognised that historically the bank manager saw himself as a professional man offering a professional service. He was similar to the solicitor or accountant or doctor or surveyor. He was not running a shop and he did not see himself in charge of an emporium with row upon row of shelves full of various products.

Perhaps understandably something of the traditional attitude still lingers. We have referred earlier (see p. 412) to a survey of twenty-three bank branches in London whose customers included over 8,000 small firms. The survey tells us that 'one subject on which there was almost unanimous agreement was their (the bank managers') dislike of the marketing approach that they consider was being forced on them'.

The need to sell

Amongst banks in the United Kingdom, the need for aggressive selling may be attributed to three main causes:

1. The historical inability to compete on interest rates, coupled with long periods of credit restriction in the 1950s and 1960s when it was equally impossible to compete as lenders. It seemed, without justification in the event, that traditional banking was to be proscribed for ever.

2. The disclosure of bank profits which brought a sharper edge to competitiveness with an increased profit awareness on all sides.

3. The changes brought about in 1971 under the heading of 'competition and credit control', which as we have already mentioned brought about freedom from the interest rate cartel, uniformity of liquidity ratios among banking houses generally and a greater encouragement to compete for business.

It was the first of these factors which gave rise to the proliferation of banking services, but the two subsequent developments gave new emphasis to the need for developing those services in an energetic and profitable way.

In more recent times, however, the pressure on domestic banking has come from the competition, principally from the building societies but also from the Trustee Savings Bank, the National Savings Department and other financial institutions.

In the mid-1980s the competition to offer financial services increased very considerably. The Building Societies Act gave the societies increased powers and both the Government and the Bank of England encouraged the City to be more competitive. Thus emerged the financial conglomerate. We have discussed in earlier chapters the acquisition by the banks of securities houses and estate agencies and we have referred to the dramatic increase in the banks' home mortgage business. Almost every category of financial institution moved simultaneously into related (and sometimes unrelated) areas of financial services, and with the passing of the Banking Act 1987 even the right to be called a bank became much easier than hitherto. The effect of all this was that the commercial banks had even more services to sell, but the competition became even more intense.

The Markets

The markets for bank services are considerable and in some cases almost infinite. The first and obvious point is that there is not one market but many. The market for personal taxation advice is not the market for leasing or factoring. The market for world travel may overlap only sightly with the market for executorship work. The market for linked life assurance has no relevance to the market for large funded pension schemes. And so on. In short, the size and location of each market will vary from service to service and readers may wish to make their own calculations and draw their own conclusions on the size and nature of the different markets. To some extent the subject is discussed under the various chapter headings.

Some services – for example, trusts and estates, taxation advice, company registrarships and insurance broking – tend to follow the existing banker-customer relationship. They are services designed primarily but not exclusively for existing customers. Many other services however – for example, credit cards, instalment credit, factoring, leasing, travel services and life assurance – cut across the banker-customer relationship in that they are offered equally to customers of other banks and are available to the world at large. Thus, a city corporation may bank with A but lease equipment through Bank B; a private customer of Bank C may buy his car through the hire purchase company of Bank D; the traveller may carry the travellers cheques of Bank E but book his holiday through the travel agency associated with banking group F.

Customer response

Defining the individual markets is one thing: identifying the market responses and attitudes is something different. Quite a lot of market research has been done in the field of traditional banking and other organisations have financed a considerable amount of research into savings habits generally. Only a modest amount of research has been undertaken so far in relation to the newer banking services. Some of the banks have undertaken 'in depth' surveys with random groups in order to define consumer attitudes to banks and banking. Transcripts of the tapes make remarkable reading, but the samples are inevitably small and are of limited value. It is comparatively easy to find out why Smith banks with a clearing bank: it is difficult to establish accurately why Jones does not.

If it is difficult to establish consumer attitudes to traditional bank services, it is seemingly impossible at the present time to establish a meaningful cross-section of responses to all the other services. The potential consumers for the majority of bank services are so unaware of the nature and scope of those services that the problem is primarily one of education. In many instances, the need has not yet become a demand.

'Salesmanship,' says Dr Paul Nystrom in his *Handbook on Marketing,* 'is the skill or art of presentation of goods so as to convert neutral or even negative attitudes into positive wants or demands.' The salesmanship of the clearing banks is conducted through four main channels and these we will consider in turn. They are (a) the branch network, (b) advertising, (c) direct mail and (d) extra-branch salesmen.

The banking branches

The network of 13,500 or so branches operated by the English and Scottish clearing banks is, or ought to be, the envy of every retail business. They are in prime locations in virtually every town and a good many villages. The systems of regional or district control are highly developed and the staff are of a high standard of intellect and integrity, but the style of the premises and the hours of business are not necessarily conducive to the development of the business and, as we have questioned elsewhere, 'is there any other trading organisation which would retain 11,000 or 12,000 properties in town centres all over the country and open the doors for a mere thirty hours a week?'[7]

Mr D. V. Weyer, former Chairman of Barclays Bank in the UK summed the matter up when he said:

> 'If 20 years ago the industry had thought of itself as running a huge network of retail outlets, it might have developed on a shop hours basis.'[8]

More recently, the Price Commission in a report on bank charges suggested that 'there should be greater flexibility with regard to opening hours so that retail bank services can be available to the public whenever there is a commercially justifiable demand'.[9] Since the publication of the report, one or two banks have experimented with extended opening hours on weekdays and most of them now have limited opening on Saturdays.

The location of a branch may be important in developing the basic banking business in the town, but it is the customer list which is important when it comes to developing the related services. The bank branches around the country have a captive market of about 25 million customers. For the most part those customers, a little anachronistically perhaps, consider that they bank personally with their branch in the High Street and not with Barclays Bank or Midland Bank or whatever bank. Some think, however absurdly, that their money is deposited in that place and that their overdraft (if they have one) is granted out of the local kitty. Thus, there is a local banker-customer relationship, on which the banks would have been foolish not to build as they developed their new services.

The key figure is essentially the manager and his role is so important that we shall look at it separately in a moment. As Mr L. C. Mather has said:

> 'More than ever before, the bank manager, supported by his branch team, will have to be the marketeer ever on his toes to produce new business for the entire family group.'[10]

It is part of his everyday task to offer to his captive market the ever-growing services of his bank. He will do this in conversation and in correspondence. He will take opportunities and he will make opportunities. He will seek tirelessly to recognise his customers' needs and to match them with the services on his shelf. When reviewing an overdraft, he may mention opportunities for insurance, savings plans or taxation advice; when talking about holidays, he will mention the related travel agency and the need for insurance; when talking about the burden of taxation, he will mention Inheritance Tax and the need to make a will; when talking about future retirement, he will suggest a pension plan. In talking to business customers, the manager will try to have regard to the considerable range of business services which the bank has to offer, whether it be merchant banking, leasing, factoring or to offer the services of BACS. And because the manager, even in the best ordered branch cannot hope to meet all his customers, he will teach his staff to take or make the same opportunities over the counter.

In recent times, Barclays Bank has introduced a new 'Personal Banker' service in selected branches. These are the large, predominantly urban branches where it is difficult for the manager to maintain personal contact with his customers. Under the Personal Banker scheme, customers receive a plastic card bearing the name of the member of the banking branch staff who will look after that particular customer's requirements. These 'personal bankers' are normally seated at desks in the banking hall and not behind the counter, and will assist customers with all their banking enquiries. In 1981, Barclays were able to report that as many as 1,000 of their staff had been trained in customer liaison and that 'personal bankers' were installed on the customer side of the counter in 250 branches.

In all banks there are those customers, an increasing number, who do not visit their branches, but receive the occasional leaflet – irreverently known as 'a stuffer' – with their bank statement. It will pinpoint some appropriate service, and invite further enquiry and discussion. Those customers who do visit their branches will see from time to time the visual displays mounted nowadays by the banks in relation to their varied services. On other occasions, a little more formally, they will be invited to receptions or 'bank-in's' either in the bank's premises or at a local hotel, where they can partake of a sherry and chat or be chatted to about unit trusts, life assurance, financial planning, household insurance, investment management and everything else that the bank has to offer.

All in all, it amounts to a careful cultivating of the existing connections, to the advantage of bank and customers alike, seeking to make the best use of the bank's presence in that place.

Like Goldsmith's village schoolmaster ('And still they gaz'd and still the wonder grew, that one small head could carry all he knew'), the bank manager has the impossible task of seeking to be up-to-date and well-informed on all his bank's services. In this he is aided not only by a steady flow of circulars and handbooks, but by the specialist help of others in the group. In Barclays Bank, for example, the local manager may call on the help of the local consultant representing the bank's insurance broking subsidiary, the area manager of the unit trust company, the representative of the in-house life office, the local manager of the business advisory service, the local representative of Mercantile Credit Company, a regional director of Barclays Merchant Bank and the local Trust Company manager (for matters of investment, taxation, testamentary arrangements and pensions).

Obviously, the manager must have sufficient 'product knowledge' to recognise the customer's need before he can call in the specialist. He has a daunting task.

Advertising

If the spearhead of the marketing attack is the branch network, it is advertising which provides the main support role. In advertising everyone is his own expert. There are few subjects on which there are so many diverse opinions and so many inconclusive answers. Despite the use of modern scientific aids, advertising remains very unscientific. The results of advertising are unpredictable and often unquantifiable.

The view is sometimes advanced that if the banks agreed among themselves to cease advertising, only the agencies and the media would lose. There may have been an element of truth in this at one time, but less so nowadays. The banks are in competition, not only among themselves and not only collectively for the business of non-banked customers; they are also in competition with a considerable number of institutions, including foreign banks, for a wide range of services.

Bank advertising falls into a number of different categories. In the first place, considerable expenditure is incurred merely to keep the name before the public. This is sometimes known as prestige advertising and, in other spheres of activity, is usually undertaken to establish a brand name or maintain a brand image. It is difficult to see that this is so necessary among the handful of well-established clearing banks in the United Kingdom. It is unlikely that anyone will ever say: 'Whatever happened to the Natwest Bank?' Nevertheless, the experts can show that when a name disappears from the advertisement pages, there is sooner or later a falling off in business. In this category of advertisement one may include sponsorships. For a umber of years banks did not look with much favour on the sponsoring of sporting or other events and indeed, some banks withdrew altogether from this form of advertising. There has perhaps been a change of attitude in recent years as evidenced, for example, by the Natwest cricket trophy and, at the time of writing, the sponsorship by Barclays Bank of the English Football League at a cost thought to be in the region of 10 per cent of the Bank's total advertising budget.

Secondly, there is the advertising of specific products, usually to establish a new service in the market, but thereafter to maintain and improve its competitive position. Thus the banks advertise their various advisory services, their credit cards, their instalment credit facilities and so on. Thirdly, there is an element of 'instant response' advertising, although financial services in general are not the subject of impulse buying and an advertisement on television is unlikely to produce a queue at the High Street branch to open new accounts the following morning. Some services lend themselves, however, to 'off the page selling', i.e. advertisements requesting the completion of a coupon asking for further information, and in some cases it is possible to include an application form inviting an immediate response. The latter would apply particularly to advertisements for unit trusts and single premium life policies. Fourthly, a considerable amount of bank advertising in recent years has been aimed at 'product awareness'. One of the biggest obstacles to the development of bank services is the lack of market awareness of the products being offered. Many companies do not appreciate that banks can help them with their pensions problems, or the issuing of capital, or the provision of alternative forms of finance such as leasing or factoring. Many private customers have but a hazy knowledge of the investment services or the insurance broking facilities offered by their banks. In many cases, they are not aware of a basic need such as the importance of making a will. In other cases, they are aware of a problem but are confused by the number of products on the market.

The fifth and last area of bank advertising is that undertaken from time to time by the banks collectively such as the 'bank manager in the cupboard' advertising undertaken as a counter to the possible threat from the then National Giro, and in the advertising campaign against bank nationalisation. Using the established methods for measuring consumer response, the 'feedback' on such advertising has been good but it is of course outside the field of advertising of bank services as such. This category of advertising is more in the area of public relations and has been used, for example, by the insurance industry in an effective way to show the socially desirable ways in which insurance company funds are invested.

One American critic of bank advertising, Mr N. W. Pope, has written:[11]

> 'Bank advertising has been traditionally noted for its obvious, almost intentional lack of creativity. Most bankers felt, perhaps wisely and perhaps not, that a bank's image through its advertising must be conservative, straight-arrow, soft-sell or no real sell at all. Any so-called "off-beat", creative approach would degrade the bank, its offices, personnel and maybe even its customers.'

And more stringently:

> 'Too few bankers who spend money to advertise genuinely understand advertising's purposes. Too often, the bank's money goes towards advertising creation and placement as a reaction to the competition, or in panic. Many banks advertise to advertise. It is accepted as the thing to do. It is expected. Therefore we run ads. And in so doing we often waste a good deal more than we produce. Then the obvious occurs. Someone in authority becomes upset and arbitrarily blames advertising *per se* for the failure.'

This last, aimed at American banks some years ago, would certainly not be true of UK banks today. They are very much aware of what advertising is all about and employ some highly skilled people in their advertising and marketing departments. At the same time, because many of the services we are concerned with are new, the advertising of those services is new. It is in a formative period and to some extent its success or otherwise cannot yet be judged.

In some areas, as we have said, the response can be measured. If, for example, a unit trust advertisement contains an application form, the response can be measured in terms of the number of applications returned. Better still, the profitability of the advertisement can immediately be gauged. During the comparatively euphoric unit trust period of the late 1960s and early 1970s, it would be rare for a unit trust advertisement not to produce sufficient applications and sufficient immediate income to show a profit even after allowing for an elementary costing of unallocated overheads. On the other hand, television advertising for linked life assurance has been known on occasions to produce no identifiable response. The cost may have been justified in terms of building up a brand image, but that kind of advertising requires some very shrewd and carefully controlled budgeting.

Some bank services show such a narrow margin of profit that extensive advertising would be prohibitive, except as part of an overall picture of the all-purpose bank. We have already seen that the main selling thrust is in any case through the branch network, and a lot of bank advertising is in support of the selling effort put in by the bank branches. If a full allocation of branch costs were taken into account in the marketing of the individual services, there would certainly be little to spare for advertising, particularly with the increase of advertising costs in recent years.

The purpose of advertising is to inform. The aim is to tell the potential consumer about the product in such a way that he becomes aware of his own need and of the suitability of the product to meet that need. That process must go on and to some extent it has hardly begun. Relatively few people are aware of the range and variety of modern bank services and their suitability to meet the varying needs of individuals and corporations alike. Even the bank staffs up to quite senior levels find it difficult to keep informed in terms of product knowledge.

Many of the markets for the individual services are but lightly tapped and none is near saturation. With many of the services, to borrow a phrase from an old advertisement, the world is indeed 'our market'. If advertising is too expensive for some individual products, they may have to be included in packages and advertised, as it were, in bulk. Some traditional forms of advertisement may have to be discarded and new ones adopted. Research will continue on consumer attitudes and consumer responses in order to find out which advertisements 'get through' to the market. But the need for advertising will continue as part of the total marketing process. The basic need will remain – to inform, inform, inform.

Direct mail

After the two main selling weapons – the branch network and advertising – we come to two methods of direct selling which are comparatively new in the banking world: they are direct mail and the employment of sales representatives. Some form of advertising is of course direct selling, but generally advertising is mass communication through the mass media: it is not selective except in a broad sense. A so-called 'mail shot' is much more selective. It is aimed at individuals because of certain known facts about them. A section of the market will be isolated because it displays certain common characteristics. It may be merely that they are all customers of a particular bank or of a particular branch, and they may perhaps receive what we have already referred to as 'stuffers' with their bank statements. On the other hand, the target group may be existing unitholders of a bank unit trust, in which case they may receive a communication inviting them to buy more units. Yet another example would be a 'mail shot' to the bank's credit card holders with information about some new insurance package put together by the bank's broking subsidiary.

The particular advantage of direct mail is that it is comparatively selective. It is good marketing in that the opportunity is taken of building on an existing relationship. Although postage and printing costs are high, direct mail is proving itself to be much more cost effective than many other forms of selling. It does not depend on expensive branch outlets and it is not so wasteful as blanket advertising through the mass media.

On the other hand, unsolicited mail can cause offence and damage existing connections, and also there are occasions when customers become caught in the cross-fire of a number of bank departments or subsidiaries seeking to sell their own wares. These are perhaps no more than the normal hazards of zealous salesmanship.

An extension of the 'mail shot' is the circulation of newsletters or magazines designed to promote the bank's business. There have been a number of these promoted by the clearing banks and on the whole they have not been a great success. This may be no more than a failure to strike the right note. Other organisations have successfully developed the concept of a regular magazine as a means of promoting their goods or services. The contents should be down-to-earth and appropriate to the needs of the consumer. Esoteric articles on the state of distant economies are too remote for the High Street customer and 'fluffy' articles written by humorous celebrities probably do little to convince the customer of the seriousness of the bank's products. The television studios teach one not to smile when expounding on the subjects of religion, death or money – particularly money, which for most people is a serious matter.

Sales representatives

Lastly, we come to direct selling by representatives. We have discussed this at some length in connection with life assurance, but the banks also employ salesmen in the development of their credit card and hire purchase activities. Similarly the insurance broking consultants or representatives are also engaged in direct selling, but in their case it is to a professional sector of the market rather than to the general public. A highly trained and well-controlled sales force can be very effective; a good salesman will often achieve better results than, say, a bank manager who may not have the right temperament, probably has not had the right training and in any case has other things to think about. The professional salesman does not enjoy the respect in our society which he deserves. According to a survey among 3,000 college students in America, the words which most came to mind in connection with the word 'salesman' were 'travel', 'money', 'personality', 'sales', 'fast talker', 'commission'.[12] The public concept of direct selling is very often that of persuading people to buy something they do not want. To quote, however, from the July 1976 issue of the Royal Bank of Canada monthly letter:

> 'The top-ranking salesman is a gold-mine of information and help. He has studied the merchandise he sells until he is an expert judge of quality, fit, good taste and appropriateness. He has absorbed ideas from the experience of customers. His function, as he sees it, is to help the buyer get the best for his money. He has respect for what he is selling and that respect is contagious.'

The presence of a professional sales force lies a little uncomfortably among professional bankers. Furthermore, direct sales organisations have become rather expensive. By their nature they are labour-intensive and the costs of salaries and commissions, social security and pensions, training and supervision have escalated in recent years. There is a tendency among insurance companies to move away from this method of selling, but it may well become more common in one or two particular areas of bank services. Whilst a sales force is cheaper to maintain than a branch network, the banks are not faced with that choice. The branch network already exists and an independent sales force is not only an extra expense but it does not fit easily into the established structure of banking in this country.

The role of the bank manager

This is perhaps a good point to turn from the professional

salesman to the role of the bank manager in promoting the proliferation of bank services.

The traditional role of the bank manager is that of lending banker. He has of course to manage the bank branch as such, but his technical training over the years has been in the lending of money. It would no doubt be generally agreed that he now has to have a wider knowledge of financial matters. This is partly because the financial scene has become more diverse and partly because the manager has more services to offer. As we have seen, he has always acted in an advisory way to his customers and now when a customer has a financial problem, a manager is very often offering a solution from his own stock-in-trade. As a result, there are those who say that the manager of a bank branch should be primarily a salesman. We would respectfully disagree with this view, although it is of course a matter for the individual banks to determine the function of their managers. We prefer the view that the bank manager is running a business – a business which consists of matching a wide range of financial products to the needs of a variety of customers.

We have said that the bank manager's place in the local town has been that of a professional man, not unlike that of the solicitor, doctor and accountant. His professional skill has been, in a broad sense, the care of his depositors' money, the conduct of their banking arrangements and, more specifically, the lending of money. In a comparatively short space of time, he has been required to be much more than that. Whilst discarding none of his traditional skills, he now has to run a shop: he has to mix the *professional* skills of lending money and giving advice with the *trade* of selling products from his shelf. He need not of course do all this himself. His task as the manager of the business in that place is to see that it is done, and to organise his staff and other resources to that end.

The all-purpose bank calls for the all-purpose banker. It is not an easy task and there are those who would regard it as near-impossible. The running of a branch usually involves the strictest attention to internal disciplines and compliance with a massive book of instructions, and one may add to this the responsibility for lending money in a variety of situations in

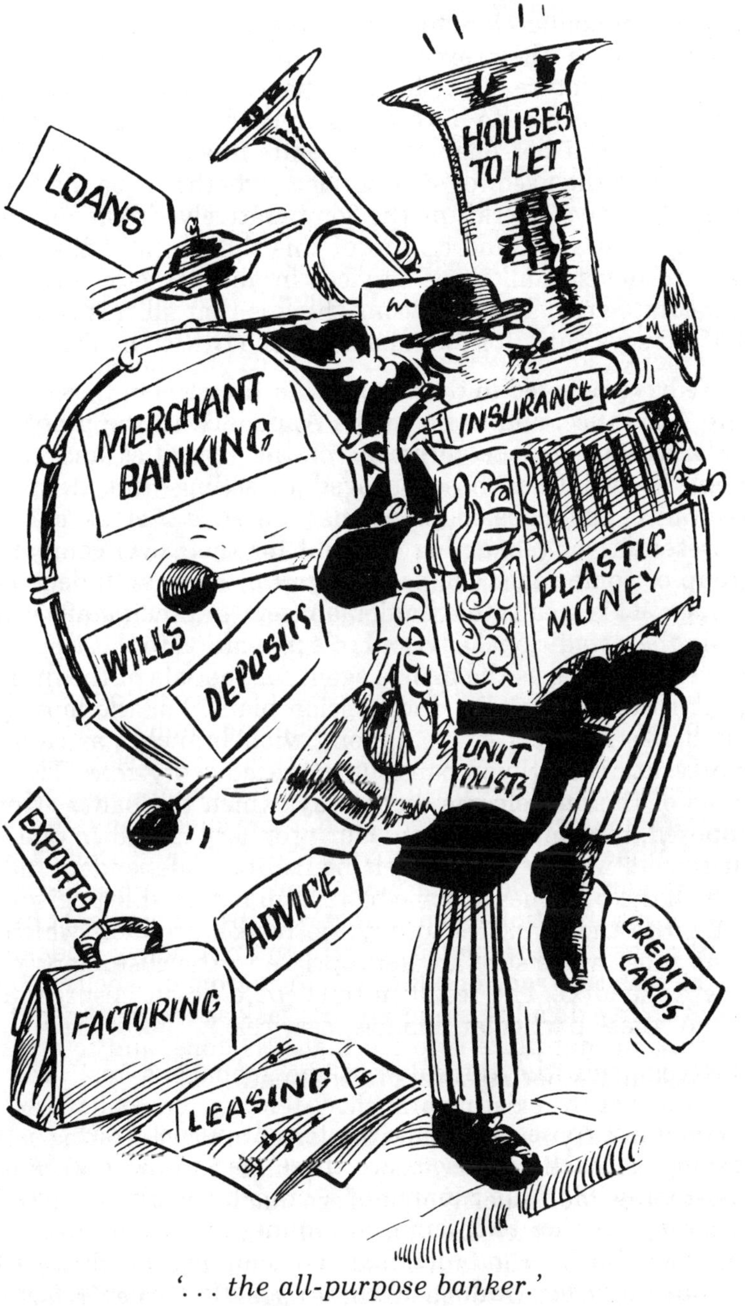

'. . . the all-purpose banker.'

varying economic climates and the need to assist customers generally with their everyday financial affairs. That is the established picture of the bank manager. One must now add to it the need for him to have an up-to-date knowledge of almost every aspect of personal and corporate finance; the facility for recognising the need for such services, whether it be the leasing of an executive aircraft or the comparatively simple matter of holiday insurance; and on top of this there is now the overall need to develop all those services in an energetic way in his immediate area. The surprising thing is that all this is done so well – it says much for the capacity of the British bank manager.

We have referred in the chapters on Investment Services and Life Assurance, and again in the Appendix, to the problem of 'polarisation' – the requirement of the securities and Investments Board that those engaged in selling unit trusts, life assurance and pension plans may do so *either* as company representatives (i.e. acting as agent for their own company or group or some other company or group) *or* as an independent advisor. This means that bank managers and their staffs cannot act in their traditional advisory role in relation to those products as well as acting as the bank's agent for the sale of the in-house unit trusts, life policies and pension plans. For the most part, the banks have chosen to appoint their branches as company representatives, thus abandoning the advisory role. The outcome of this unwelcome dichotomy, which the banks strongly opposed, remains to be seen. Our prophecy is that in due time customers will go less to their banks for 'independent' advice (which the branches of some banks will not be able to give), but will go to the branches to buy the bank's products which the bank must make sure are appropriate to the customer's needs (see Appendix). The result in time could be an upsurge in the sale of these particular financial services.

Recognising the difficulty of the manager's task and the costliness of the existing branch system, the banks have experimented in varying degrees with plans for concentrating certain services in particular branches. If there be a natural division among the multiplicity of modern bank services, it must lie between those which are of a corporate nature and those which are designed for the individual. To some extent, that pattern has been followed throughout these pages. It can never, however, be a clear-cut distinction. For example, in considering the affairs of a director of a private company, it is impossible to divorce his own personal situation from the fortunes of the company as such. Nevertheless, one can draw a line between business needs and personal financial needs. Midland Bank, in particular, conducted an experiment in Newcastle, Sunderland and Southampton, and subsequently extended this to other areas of the country. This involved setting up centralised Area Offices to deal with the more specialised needs of business customers, leaving the other branches to operate as so-called 'service branches'. Somewhat similar schemes are being tried in other banks. The concept is not by any means new, having been introduced in some North American banks many years ago. Early in 1986 National Westminster Bank announced a major reorganisation of its branch network. This was to involve the creation of over 100 corporate banking centres in the busier commercial areas of the country. These would provide corporate banking services and specialist advice to the larger business customers. Approximately 2,000 of the smaller branches would be developed to cater specifically for personal and small business customers and these would be grouped around 450 or so locations throughout the country. Barclays too have announced an extensive five-tier reconstruction of the branch network, in which the branches are categorised according to the type of customer banking services which they provide. The concentration of particular services in one office must lead to an accumulation of the relevant skills in that place. The knowledge and experience of the bank staff is not spread so thinly and, therefore, there will be a better use of resources. In time, such schemes will no doubt lead to some 'streaming' or categorising of bank officials according to whether they are equipped to manage 'business' or 'service' branches. It remains to be seen whether this is practicable and, in the meantime, no doubt all career staff will be required, as hitherto, to acquaint themselves, through professional education and internal training, with the total banking scene.

Although the bank manager remains the focal point, he is in some cases no more than a source of introduction to certain of his group's services. A continuing problem of bank marketing is the offering of the relevant services at the right level to the right customer in the right area. This also has led to the division of the market into the two main areas for personal and corporate services. A private customer may well look to his local bank manager for a variety of personal financial services, but the large corporate body will probably deal with the bank at a higher level and it is at that level that the channel must be found for the cross-selling of corporate services. So it is that some of the banks have created a number of 'account executives' – senior officials with the responsibility for the financial needs of a number of companies and institutions. In the ordinary way, the official would expect to be kept informed of the various contacts throughout the group with the customers on his list and he, rather than the local bank manager, will become the focal point for co-ordinating the various services as between the bank and those particular customers.

Packaged services

In similar vein and for similar reasons the banks have moved increasingly towards the packaging of customer services. Private customers will be offered for example, insurance packages to cover a variety of their insurance needs. One bank offers a combination of investment advice and financial planning. Another bank has offered a package of investment management and taxation advice. On the corporate side, attempts have been made to win accounts or to cultivate existing connections by offering all-in packages embracing such services as corporate advice, company registrarship and pension fund management. However, many of the services do not lend themselves to packaging. In each bank there are many different profit centres and cost centres, and it becomes a mammoth task of so-called transfer pricing to mix a number of services at an all-in rate. Furthermore, many customers resist packages. They sometimes feel that they are being offered, and therefore would have to pay for, more services than they require, and in any case most people and institutions prefer to look at each item in isolation, and in some cases to 'shop around' for particular services.

Whether or not packaging is the answer, the banking groups all have a similar aim – to be the all-purpose bank for their private and corporate customers. Ideally, for the private customer, the bank would be the modern counterpart of the Victorian 'man of affairs' – the bank would be on hand to help the customer with every imaginable financial problem. Much modern advertising is directed in this way. Similarly, with corporate customers, the aim is that the all-purpose bank will look after the institution's every need, drawing as necessary on the considerable resources of the banking group at home and abroad. It may be in that situation that the provision of traditional facilities will have a less than paramount place. We said at the beginning that many of the services described in these pages were often termed 'ancillary'. But in fact, in the total concept of bank services, the basic banker-customer relationship may become subsidiary. There are two aspects of modern banking which the student or observer of these matters may wish to consider.

New relationships

The first is that new relationships have been created quite outside the legal relationship of banker and customer. The bank manager looks upon each customer as 'his' customer and quite reasonably has tended to consider all other banking services as subsidiary to that basic relationship. He may feel aggrieved if his customer is sold a life policy or is offered computer services or receives financial planning advice from elsewhere in the group without his knowledge. This may be a commendable possessiveness on the manager's part, but it must be realised that many of the new relationships cannot be appended to the traditional one of banker and customer. In the new order of things, the banks enter into a great variety of relationships, including the following:

Lessor and lessee
Trustee and beneficiary
Factor and client
Credit card promoter and merchant
Investment manager and client
Insurer and insured
Broker and client
Travel agent and client
Computer bureau and client
Pension fund manager and client
Registrar and company
Unit trust manager and unitholder.

None of these necessarily depends on an underlying banker-customer relationship. Many such services are offered by institutions who are not in any sense bankers. In the case of credit card holders, the relationship may still be that of banker and customer but it is *sui generis* – it is not dependent on any other underlying relationship. A large number of the 10 million or so card holders in the United Kingdom will not necessarily have a banking account with the group whose card they carry. A very large number of them will never have been seen face to face by anyone from that group.

In other words, the banks are all the time entering into a number of diverse relationships with people and institutions and, in some instances, those relationships will be very long term. For example, a life policy may be for twenty-five or thirty years. In many cases, the local bank manager will have no particular part to play in that continuing relationship, although he may at the outset have been responsible for the introduction of the business to the group. In many cases, the particular service in question may be taken up by someone who is not a customer of the banking group. This will apply frequently, for example, in the case of unit trusts, insurance policies, hire purchase finance, credit cards and leasing contracts. This may apply even more so in the case of international services where, for example, factoring contracts, the sale of off-shore funds and credit card operations may be entered into where the banking group has no retail outlet and there is no question of an existing banker-customer relationship. Thus, we may note one of the major changes in modern banking – that many of the newer services have no particular relevance to and certainly are not dependent on the traditional banker–customer connection.

The bank account

The second point for consideration is that in the total concept of financial management, the operation of a banking account is no longer the most important item in the eyes of the customer, whether the customer is a private person or institution. Taking the case of a private individual who has all his financial needs provided by his clearing bank – including such matters as life assurance, house mortgage, car and household insurance, investment and taxation advice, pensions advice and executorship arrangements, overseas travel and, if desired, advice on his business – the day-to-day operation of his banking account becomes of comparatively minor importance. This is particularly so if he makes frequent use of credit cards. Even in the case of an institution, although the operation of a current account and the provision of overdraft facilities will always be important, they will not necessarily have any special priority in the mind of the company customer which may also be receiving from its bank certain computer services, company registration services, and pensions services, and may well have entered into major leasing contracts and factored its debts (which reduces the activity on the current banking account), and may even be engaged on a major capital issue or merger situation with the assistance of the merchant banking arm of the group.

If that be so, what does it matter? There is no reason why it should matter: indeed, in these various ways the UK banks have extended their business influence. It does mean, however, that some major re-thinking has been necessary in relation to bank marketing in general. At present, people go into the High Street branches of the clearing banks only if they are customers. It may become important that banks should open their doors in a more welcoming way to allcomers – to anyone who may have occasion to use the services we have sought to describe, regardless of whether or not they have a banking account. Traditionally bank branches have been designed primarily for the purpose of receiving and paying out cash and it could be that the counter may have to be pushed to one side. Obviously the counter as such becomes less important with the increased introduction of cash dispensers, automated teller machines, in-store banking and plastic card banking generally. Perhaps a time will come when the public will 'drop in' on the banks in the High Street as they might visit the supermarket, not necessarily because they are already a 'customer' there but because they have a financial problem and from somewhere on its shelves the bank can provide the answer. That will indeed be all-purpose banking.

Postscript

The one matter which must surely exercise the mind of bankers possibly more than any other is the 'shape' of the bank branches of the future. The traditional purposes of the branches were:

to receive deposits, whether in cash or cheques;
to pay cash out;
to lend money;
to advise customers and
to be a channel for the bank's services.

We may pose the question (a little 'tongue-in-cheek') whether a branch network is necessary at all for these purposes. With the ability to pay in or draw out by machine, to transfer money by cheque, plastic card or some form of viewdata keyboard, to borrow on personal account by credit card or some other form of 'formal' credit appraisal and to negotiate business loans at the special branches set up for that purpose, there would appear to be a need only for (a) cash centres and (b) an advisory and selling organisation.

Ex hypothesi some branches, as we have known them, will be closed and perhaps fewer staff will be required. But the essentials will still remain – the ability to sell and to administer the services of the all-purpose bank.

References

1 P. F. Drucker: *The Practice of Management*. Pan, 1968.
2 C. McIver and G. Naylor: *The Marketing of Financial Services*. The Institute of Bankers, 1979.
3 L. L. Berry and L. A. Capaldini: *Marketing for the Bank Executive*. Leviathan House, 1974.
4 J. S. Hensel: The Essential Nature of the Marketing Management Process: An Overview, L. L. Berry.
5 Sir Frederick Seebohm (now Lord Seebohm): The Marketing Programme *in* 'The Marketing of Bank Services', Cambridge Seminar 1971, The Institute of Bankers.
6 G. Rae: *The Country Banker*. Murray, 1885.
7 D. G. Hanson: Money Shops – or Not? *Journal of the Institute of Bankers*, April 1973.
8 D. Vander Weyer: Clearing Bank Marketing: 'The Practical Issues Today'. *The Banker*, October 1970.
9 Price Commission: 'Banks; charges for money transmission services'. HMSO, 1978.
10 L. C. Mather: Commercial Banks: Evolution of Services *in* International Banking Summer School, *Banking in the 1970's*. The Institute of Bankers, 1970.
11 N. W. Pope: A Philosophy of Bank Advertising *in* L. L. Berry and L. A. Capaldini, *Marketing for the Bank Executive*. Leviathan House, 1974.
12 *Harvard Business Review*, January 1972.

Table of Statistics

(as at end 1986)

	Number	£ million
Deposit Banking		
Number of accounts:		
London and Scottish Clearing Banks:		
Current Accounts	32,631,000	
Deposit & Savings Accounts	21,756,000	
Total deposits (sterling and other currencies):		
London and Scottish Clearing Banks' Groups:		
UK personal sector		63,217
Other non-bank UK residents		53,310
Bank Lending		
Total advances (sterling and other currencies):		
London and Scottish Clearing Banks' Groups:		
UK personal sector		40,320
Other non-bank UK residents		68,626
Credit Cards		
Number of cards in issue:		
Access	9,846,000	
Visa	12,121,000	
Diner's Club	282,000	
American Express	951,000	
Building Societies		
Number of societies	149	
Number of branches	6,950	
Deposit and Share Accounts		117,610
Life Assurance		
Number of policies in force 1985 (millions):		
(a) Ordinary branch	23·4	
(b) Industrial branch	42·3	
(c) Linked	7·8	

		Number	£ million
Insurance Broking			
Total premium income (all insurance companies)			27,800
Total premium income of London and Scottish Clearing Banks (estimated)			400
Unit Trusts			
Unit Trust Groups		150	
Authorised Unit Trusts	(approx.)	1,050	
Bank-owned Unit Trust Groups		5	
Bank-owned Unit Trusts		74	
Total value of units in issue			32,131
Total value of units in issue (Clearing Banks)			3,600
Total number of unit trust holders		3.4m.	
Executorships and Trusts			
(London and Scottish Clearing Banks)			
All trusts		61,835	4,353
New estates in 1985/86		9,718	£65,000*
Will appointments of living customers		1,084,000	
Investment Management			
Private portfolios		62,000	5,140
Institutional portfolios		1,269	37,000
Pension Funds			
Trusteeships		199	5,424
Investment responsibility		320	14,000
Taxation Cases		137,328	
Capital Issues			
(a) Company issues (new money)			
Total value			9,148
(b) Rights issues			
Total value			5,790
Company Registrarships		1,700	
representing (no. of accounts) (approx.)		17,000,000	

* Average value.

	Number	£ million
Factoring		
London and Scottish Clearing Banks:		
Companies	3,400	
Volume		4,362
Association of British Factors (est.)		5,000
Leasing Services (total leased assets at cost)		
London and Scottish Clearing Banks		13,800
Equipment Leasing Association		23,800
New Leasing Contracts (1986)		
London and Scottish Clearing Banks		3,600
Equipment Leasing Association		5,180
Money Transfer (London and Scottish Clearing Banks)		
B.A.C.S. (see p. 456)		
Value of clearings		£251,000 million
Number of articles		943 million
CHAPS (see p. 457) and Town Clearing		
Value of clearings		£12,317,000 million
Number of articles		7,489,000 million
Cheques and credit clearing		
Value		£847,000 million
Number		2,136 million

Appendix

The Financial Services Act 1986

The Financial Services Act received the Royal Assent on 7 November 1986. Certain of its provisions, principally those relating to insider-dealing, have now passed into law. Other provisions notably those relating to the carrying on of investment businesses are expected to come into effect in April 1988. Those aspects of bank services which are most affected by the Act are investment services (Chapter 6), unit trusts (Chapter 7), life assurance (Chapter 8), insurance broking (Chapter 9), merchant banking (Chapter 14), pensions services (Chapter 19) and the selling of those services (Chapter 24).

The provisions of the Act and the attendant Rules of the Securities and Investments Board are exceedingly complex and far-reaching and are in course of changing the face of the financial services industry in this country arguably more than in any other piece of legislation. The full impact of the Act and the Rules of the SIB is yet to be seen but as far as practicable references have been made to the new legislation in the relevant chapters of this work.

The following pages contain a brief commentary on the Act and the Rules based on articles by the author in *Banking World* in the summer of 1987.

The Act

For the most part the Financial Services Act had its origins in Professor Gower's 'Review of Investor Protection' undertaken at the request of the Secretary of State for Trade in July 1981, the first part of which was published in January 1982. That excellent document covered some of the ground which had already been touched on by the Wilson Committee which reviewed the 'functioning of Financial Institutions' in the report of 1980. For the most part therefore, the Act is concerned with consumer protection but it is more than that. There was also a desire to provide a better regulatory framework within which the financial sector could operate and to achieve this in addition to the provision of investor protection it was decided that the Act should cover the entire securities scene governing the relationships of 'professionals' in the financial sector as much as protecting the life savings of Aunt Agatha. Other provisions relate to the listing of securities, insider-dealing and collective investment schemes.

The previous legislation

To a considerable extent the legislation was, and still is, fragmented. For example, the business of banking was governed by the Banking Act, 1979 (now mostly replaced by the Banking Act 1987), the business of building societies was governed by the Building Societies Act 1962 (now replaced by the Building Societies Act 1986), insurance companies are governed by the Insurance Acts, and companies in general were regulated by successive Companies Acts (now principally the Companies Act, 1985). Investment in listed securities was governed by the Rules of the Stock Exchange and the only significant 'investment' legislation was the Prevention of Fraud (Investments) Act, 1958 – a remarkable piece of legislation which remained virtually unaltered by the legislature for nearly 30 years but which was itself a consolidation of previous Acts and which served as an umbrella for the Department of Trade not only to regulate licensed and exempted dealers but also to govern the unit trust industry, consisting now of approximately 1,000 trusts. That Act, which is to be repealed by the Financial Services Act, was never intended to provide a regulatory framework for the entire securities industry. The new Act is so intended. Thus it is described in the preamble as:

> 'An act to regulate the carrying on of investment business; to make related provisions with respect to insurance business and business carried on by friendly societies; to make new provision with respect to the official listing of securities, offers of unlisted securities, takeover offers and insider-dealing; to make provision as to the disclosure of information obtained under enactments relating to fair trading, banking companies and insurance; to make provision for securing reciprocity with other countries in respect of facilities for the provision of financial services; and for connected purposes.'

The Scope of the Act

As we have said, the Act is a very complex piece of legislation which was in itself the subject of much controversy and amendment in the course of its ten month passage through Parliament. (At one point there were as many as 581 amendments to the Bill under consideration in the House of Lords.) Whilst it is probably true to say that the central theme and purpose of the Act has remained intact it would seem that in a desire to cover all eventualities the legislature has imposed a very considerable burden on some institutions and companies engaged in perfectly legitimate commercial and financial transactions. In order to catch those who might transgress, some impeccably managed businesses in the financial sector will be subjected to some exceedingly burdensome regulations.

The main burden of the Act is the regulation of investment business and the prohibition of the carrying on of investment business other than by authorised or exempted persons. The Act also introduces new rules for the regulation of collective investment schemes, e.g. unit trusts, replacing the Prevention of Fraud (Investments) Act, 1958. The Act further contains new regulations relating to insurance companies and friendly societies, new provisions relating to the listing of securities and the offering of unlisted securities, new regulations relating to insider-dealing and various other related matters. For the moment we may confine our attention to investment business.

Investment business

Under Section 1(1) of the Act 'investment' means 'any asset, right or interest falling within any paragraph in Part I of Schedule 1 to this Act'. The definition includes stocks and shares, debentures, gilt-edged stocks, local authority securities, unit trusts, options, futures and certain life assurance policies. Bank accounts are not investments for the purpose of this Act, nor are land and buildings and such tangible assets as works of art, coins, stamps, etc.

Section 1(2) of the Act defines investment business as the business of engaging in one or more of the activities listed in Part II of Schedule 1. These include dealing in investments, arranging deals in investments, managing investments, giving or offering or agreeing to give investment advice, establishing and operating etc., collective investment schemes and acting as a trustee of such schemes.

Exemptions

Part III of Schedule 1 lists a number of activities which are excluded from the general definition of investment business. They include:

(i) Dealings by a person as a principal provided he does not hold himself out as willing to deal in investments at prices determined by himself nor holds himself out as engaging in the business of buying investments with a view to selling them nor regularly solicits members of the public for the purpose of inducing them to enter into transactions of an investment nature and the transaction is entered into as a result;
(ii) employees' shares schemes;
(iii) transactions between companies in the same group;
(iv) participators in certain joint enterprises;
(v) investment transactions by trustees and personal representatives (except to the extent that such a person holds himself out as providing a service of buying and selling investments or is remunerated for his services in addition to any remuneration he receives for discharging his duties as trustee or personal representative, and
(vi) investment advice contained in newspapers, magazines etc., if the purpose of the publication as a whole is not to lead persons to invest in any particular investment.

The Concept of Authorisation

The main provisions of the Financial Services Act are based on the concept of self-regulation (by authorised bodies and persons) within a statutory framework. The supervisory powers under the Act are delegated by the Department of Trade and Industry to the Securities and Investments Board (SIB). The SIB will authorise a number of Self Regulating Organisations (SROs) who, in turn, will authorise and regulate their members. The Act also contains power for the SIB to 'recognise' professional bodies. Members of such recognised professional bodies (RPBs) e.g. solicitors and accountants, will thus be authorised for the purpose of the Act but only in relation to the conduct of investment business incidental to the practice of that particular profession.

A person may be authorised direct by the SIB to carry on investment business and it would seem that this may be the only route for those persons who are not members of an SRO or of one of the recognised professional bodies, e.g. an overseas resident carrying on investment business in the United Kingdom without having a permanent place of business here.

The Act contains separate provisions for authorisation of insurance companies and friendly societies and for certain investment operations conducted by persons resident in the Member States of the European Community.

In general terms there are thus seven ways of becoming authorised under the Act to carry on investment business, viz:

1. Direct authorisation by the SIB.
2. Membership of a recognised SRO.
3. Membership of a recognised professional body.
4. Authorisation as an insurance company under the Insurance Companies Act, 1982.
5. Authorisation as a friendly society registered under the Friendly Societies Act, 1974.
6. Operating as a recognised collective investment scheme constituted in another Member State of the European Community.
7. Authorisation in another Member State of a body which has its Head Office in that State and no permanent place of business in the United Kingdom.

The consequences of carrying on investment business without authorisation

Any person who carries on investment business without authorisation under the provisions of the Act or without being exempted under the Act commits a criminal offence and is liable to imprisonment for up to two years or a fine or both. It is a defence to such a charge however, to show that the person concerned took all reasonable precautions and exercised due care to avoid committing the offence.

Any agreement entered into by a person in the course of unauthorised or unexempted investment business is unenforceable and any money paid or property transferred to him may be recovered by the other party unless it can be shown to the court that the person committing the offence believed that the agreement was not a contravention of the Act and the court is satisfied that it would be just and equitable for the agreement to be enforced or for the money or property paid or transferred to be retained. It is not clear whether 'reasonable belief' that there was not contravention includes 'reasonable ignorance' that the Act applied to the transaction.

There are a number of persons and institutions exempted from the need to be authorised under the Act. These include in particular the Bank of England, Lloyd's and Lloyd's underwriting agents, listed money market institutions, holders of public offices, e.g. the Public Trustee, and appointed representatives acting as agents for authorised firms, e.g. agents for life assurance companies, in those cases where the agent's principal has accepted responsibility in writing for the agent's activities. Recognised investment exchanges and clearing houses are also exempted from authorisation.

The Securities and Investments Board

Chapter XIII of the Act contains provision for the most of the authorisation and regulatory powers contained in the Act to be transferred to a 'designated agency' to be known as the Securities and Investments Board Limited (SIB) provided that the Secretary of State is satisfied that the SIB is 'able and willing' to discharge the delegated functions. The constitution of the SIB provides that its members are to be appointed by and are removable by the Secretary of State and the Governor of the Bank of England acting jointly. The membership must include persons experienced in investment business, persons who are regular users of financial services and others who are totally independent. There must be a proper balance between the interest of those engaged in investment business and the general public.

The SIB is a private limited company. In February 1987 it submitted its formal application to the Secretary of State for Trade and Industry for delegation of the statutory powers under the Act. The application was supported by the draft Rules consisting of some 430 pages – Rules which have now been approved and which will have the force of law and will govern the authorisation and conduct of virtually all investment business in the United Kingdom, other than the specific exemptions mentioned above.

The self-regulating organisation

At the time of writing it is understood that the following organisations will be recognised as SROs subject to approval of their applications to the SIB.

The Association of Futures Brokers and Deals (AFBD) covering firms and individuals broking and dealing in financial and commodity futures and options and providing investment services incidental to that business.

The Financial Intermediaries, Managers and Brokers Regulatory Association (FIMBRA) covering independent intermediaries dealing direct with the public in such matters as unit trusts and life assurance.

The Investment Management Regulatory Organisation (IMRO) covering investment managers and advisors including managers and trustees of collective investment schemes and pension funds.

The Life Assurance and Unit Trust Regulatory Organisations (LAUTRO) covering those involved in the marketing of life assurance and unit trusts (but such membership will not of itself authorise the undertaking of investment business). Thus, for example, unit trust management companies will need to obtain authorisation through FIMBRA (see above) or IMRO (see above) and LAUTRO.

The Securities Association. This was formed as a result of a merger of the Stock Exchange and The International Securities Regulatory Organisation.

It is possible that in due time other SROs will emerge seeking recognition by the SIB for the purpose of regulating the investment activities of their particular members. In particular, the Building Societies Commission will have a supervising role in relation to building societies but their subsidiary companies will be regulated by the appropriate SRO.

Applications for authorisation

Under Section 26 of the Act an application for authorisation may be made by:

(a) an individual;
(b) a body corporate;
(c) a partnership, or
(d) an unincorporated association.

Whether the application for authorisation is made direct to the SIB or to one of the SROs the same standards will apply in determining whether or not the authorisation should be granted. Under the Act the applicant must show that he is a 'fit and proper' person to carry on investment business and the rules of the SIB interpret that to mean that the person or firm will deal honestly and fairly and aspire to best market practice in all its dealings. The application form will have to cover such matters as the structure of the organisation including names of directors, audited accounts and a statement of capital adequacy; the applicants business record, including such matters as solvency, litigation and disciplinary proceedings; the compliance arrangements including the names of senior personnel and the procedure for dealing with complaints; and details of the experience and record of controlling shareholders, directors and key personnel.

Authorisation will be granted and thereafter continued only if the business is conducted within the general guidelines laid down in Schedule 8 of the Act and the more detailed Conduct of Business Rules issued by the SIB.

The Conduct of Business Rules

These Rules are set out in Chapter III of the Board's Rule Book. Strictly speaking these Rules apply only to persons authorised by the Board itself. SROs may draft their own rules but they must give 'equivalent' protection to those provided by the Rules of the SIB. The Rules are too extensive to detail here. They include such matters as business plans, 'know your customer' requirements, customer agreements, 'appointed representative' and 'company representative', advertisements, custody of investments, dealing by officers and employees, compliance procedures and maintenance of records. The list is not exhaustive.

In addition to the Conduct of Business Rules, there are rules regarding unsolicited calls, cancellation of contracts, clients' money, compensation for investors and investigation of complaints.

The Business Plan

An applicant for authorisation will be required to submit to the SIB or the appropriate SRO a plan describing the investment business to be undertaken. Generally the business plan will be required to show that the applicant is a 'fit and proper' person to undertake investment business. The details of the activities to be undertaken will include a profile of the category of customer with whom it is proposed to do business. In the business plan the applicant will be required to demonstrate the ability to comply with the regulations governing the conduct of investment business and to identify a senior person with overall responsibility for such regulatory matters. It also will be necessary to show the arrangements which have been made for dealing with and recording details of customer complaints.

An authorised person may carry on only the type of investment business authorised in the business plan and the nature of that business must be set out in the authorised person's business letters and publications. For example, a person whose business plan provides for the giving of advice on life assurance and unit trusts should not describe himself as an 'investment adviser' in a wider field.

'Know your customer'

The Conduct of Business Rules impose a 'know your customer' obligation on the authorised person. Generally this means that he must not advise on, or act in, investment matters without first considering whether the investment or the particular transaction is appropriate to the customer's needs. This imposes on the authorised person an obligation to enquire into the customer's financial circumstances including, it is thought, his or her tax position. It will also be important to ensure that the customer understands the risks involved in a particular investment transaction. If a particular client or prospective client refuses to answer questions relating to his or her financial circumstances, the authorised person offering the investment service need not pursue the inquiries.

The Customer Agreement

The Conduct of Business Rules also require the authorised person to enter into a 'customer agreement' with each customer, to maintain a record of investment recommendations to demonstrate the suitability of those recommendations in relation to each customer's circumstances and to maintain a record of such steps as may be necessary to ensure that transactions effected on behalf of customers are on 'best terms'.

In all cases the authorised person, when acting as an agent must subordinate his own interests to those of the customer notwithstanding that in some cases the authorised person may be acting also as a principal in dealing off his own book for the customer.

A self-regulatory system

The new Act and the underlying regulations are based on the concept of a self-regulatory system. This has been described as a kind of privatisation because the Securities and Investments Board is, as we have said, a private limited company and for the most part the process of regulation will operate through the Self-Regulating Organisations (SROs). The self-regulatory approach was chosen because it was thought right that the City should have maximum control of its own affairs and it was also argued that practitioners involved on the day to day business of the financial markets would perhaps make better regulators than civil servants. There is also the point that the costs of a self-regulatory system are borne directly or indirectly by the promoters and users of the financial services, whereas a full statutory system similar to the Securities and Exchange Commission in the United States would be paid for presumably by the taxpayer. The result is a self-regulatory structure within a statutory framework.

The enforcement of the statutory powers

There are in effect different levels of supervision and enforcement. In the front line the self-regulating organisations have the primary responsibility for controlling their members. Breach of the rules may result in disciplinary sanctions up to and including the withdrawal of the authorisation of the member firm. Supervision will take the form of spot checks and detailed returns from the members to their SRO. The Regulations contain provisions for the investigation of complaints and it may be that an Ombudsman will be appointed. A breach of the rules of the Board or an SRO will *prima facie* give the investor a right of action in the courts. The Board will also have the right to take up cases on behalf of investors.

Where fraud is suspected the Board has extensive powers of investigation and may compel witnesses including bankers and auditors to appear before it and to produce documents. Special investigatory powers are also available for suspected offences of insider-dealing (see below). The Board also has power to bring prosecutions under the Act and in fact the Act creates a number of new criminal offences as well as re-defining some existing offences.

The right of appeal

Where authorisation has been refused, withdrawn or suspended an investor has the right to appeal to the Financial Services Tribunal set up under Section 96 of the Act. This right however relates only to authorisations to carry on investment business. Any civil or criminal proceedings arising from the SIB's enquiries are subject to appeal in the normal way through the courts.

The Compensation Fund

Section 54 of the Act and the rules of the SIB provide for the setting up of a Compensation Fund to cover those cases where firms carrying on investment business are unable or are likely to be unable to meet their civil liabilities to investors. The amount payable to an investor from the Compensation Fund is limited. Where the total amount of the liability to the investor exceeds £50,000 the maximum compensation will be £30,000 plus 90 per cent of the excess and where the total amount of the liability does not exceed £30,000 compensation is payable in full. The Fund will be a private limited company funded by the various regulatory bodies which in turn will be financed by members' contributions.

The effect on banks and other financial institutions

The Act and the delegated regulations apply in greater or lesser degree to all financial conglomerates. Within any banking group the services now offered would conceivably include investment management, unit trust management, life assurance, insurance broking, pension fund management, trusteeships, the offer of securities and applications for listing. All these and, not least important, the day to day giving of advice by a bank manager to his customer come within the stringent requirements of the legislation. In that area one of the more controversial rules of the SIB came to be known as 'polarisation'.

Polarisation

In simple terms it means that a person selling or advising on life assurance contracts and unit trusts (including pension plans based on such investments) must do so in one of two basic categories, i.e. either as an *independent intermediary* or as a *company representative*. In these fields of activity no-one may act in both roles. In the past, bank managers have responded to their customers' requests for investment advice (a role akin to that of 'independent intermediary') but in doing so would quite often sell their customers products from the bank's own ranges of unit trusts and life policies (as *de facto* 'company representative'). Bank customers were accustomed to this apparent ambivalence – they believed the advice to be as 'independent' as it would be from any source and they were happy that the solution to the problem should come, at least in part, from the bank's own shelves. This duality of role, whether for banks, building societies or anyone else, is no longer possible under the polarisation rules. It is of the very essence of the financial services regulations that if a person or firm acts as both an independent intermediary and a company representative the investor will be confused as to the nature of the service available to him and as to the position of the person advising him and accordingly liable to make decisions based on erroneous assumptions. Thus the two roles must be kept apart and this policy of 'polarisation' has been written into the SIB's rules notwithstanding the view of the Director of Fair Trading that the 'proposal bites particularly on the banks and building societies' and will reduce considerably the independent advice available.

The effect of polarisation

First of all, there would appear to be no objection to the giving of so-called generic advice by banks or by any other advisers. In other words they may give general advice on the broad outline of investment for a capital sum. When however it comes to the point of giving more detailed or particular advice the branches of banks and building societies will have to operate as 'company representatives' or 'independent intermediaries' but not as both. An institution like a bank will obviously wish its branches to serve as outlets for its wide range of investment products and thus most banks are pursuing the route of 'company representative' (although National Westminster Bank and Bank of Scotland have decided that their branches will operate on the 'independent intermediary' basis). Under the 'best advice' rules a company representative must recommend only a product which is at least as good as any other product available from his company or group.

The duality of role

A person or firm may not be a company representative for in-house products and as independent intermediary for the products of another business house. For example, most banks operate unit trust groups but do not necessarily own life companies. A branch of the bank, if designated as a company representative, may sell the in-house unit trusts but may not adopt the posture as an independent intermediary in recommending another group's life assurance contracts or pension plans. Whilst a bank branch may act as a company representative *another part of the group* may act as independent intermediary. Thus a bank branch may sell investment products as company representative and may introduce the customer to, for example, the bank's insurance broking subsidiary for 'advice' in the role of independent intermediary.

This is subject to the stringent rule that an independent intermediary who is part of a conglomerate group may recommend a product of another part of that group only if the customer would be *disadvantaged* if such in-house product were not recommended. In other words, an *independent intermediary* must normally recommend only a product which is at least as good as any other product available on the market but an *independent intermediary within a conglomerate* may only recommend an in-house product if there is nothing else as good on the market (e.g. if an insurance company's annuity rates are currently the best in the market). As a company representative the manager of a branch will be able to sell the in-house products but, beyond that, any 'advice' must come from an independent intermediary within the group. The branch may act as a 'post office' for that advice but may not qualify it in any way nor advise on the merits of the intermediary's recommendations. The reference to the independent intermediary in the group must not be used as a device to give the whole transaction the mere appearance of independence – what has been called the 'halo' effect. The important point is that the customer must always know the capacity in which the branch or professional adviser is acting, i.e. whether as a company representative or as an independent intermediary.

The sale of pension plans

Banks and building societies are among those who will be able to manage pension schemes for their customers when the new Social Services legislation comes into operation in 1988, but this can only be done within the 'polarisation' rules. This is because pension plans based on life policies and unit trust contracts are deemed to be 'investments' under the Act. Thus a person (or for example a bank branch) may act as an appointed representative of a life office or unit trust group for the purpose of selling pension plans, but may not act in a dual role as independent intermediary offering the plans of other groups.

Branches which are 'company representatives' may offer the group's own pension plans, but not the products of another group even though these may have been 'broked' by the bank's insurance broking subsidiary. On the other hand, a subsidiary may pass on a recommendation to a customer via a bank branch acting purely as a post office. The situation is the same as explained above in relation to unit trusts and life asssurance policies.

Pension plans linked to deposits in building societies or banks are not investments for the purpose of the Act and thus do not come within the 'polarisation' rules. Thus, whether a branch of a bank or building society is an independent intermediary or an appointed company representative, it will be able to promote its own *deposit-linked* pension plans. This is something of an anomaly because logically a deposit-linked pension plan is as much an 'investment' as a unit-linked scheme.

Direct marketing

Bank subsidiaries offering unit trusts, life assurance or pension plans may sell them by advertising, direct mail and other direct marketing regardless of whether the branches in the group are designated company representatives or independent intermediaries.

Personal Equity Plans (PEPs)

These do not come within the 'Polarisation' rules. They are regarded as matters of investment management rather than investments as such. Thus, a bank or building society may promote its own or other group's PEPs regardless of whether its branches are appointed representatives or independent intermediaries.

Banks as investment managers

This will be done invariably through a separate department or subsidiary company. The service will be provided within the framework of a customer agreement as already described and the regulations regarding 'best terms' and 'know your customer' will apply. The investment manager will be able to invest in unit trusts managed by the same group if this is provided for in the customer's agreement. In such a case, the portfolio manager looking after the investments may invest the client's funds in unit trust products within the group or indeed, in the unit trusts of outside groups. Banks and other institutions or persons acting in an investment management role will have to be authorised by the appropriate self-regulating organisation (SRO) which in this case is the Investment Management Regulatory Organisation (IMRO).

The management of pension fund investments

Banks and others engaged in the business of managing pension fund investments must be authorised under the regulations. It would appear, however, that under Section 191 of the Act anyone managing the assets of a pension scheme will require authorisation (even if they are not engaged in the *business* of managing pension schemes), unless day-to-day investment management decisions are taken by some authorised person on their behalf. Thus, the in-house manager of a pension fund must be authorised. Furthermore, the trustees of a pension fund will have to be authorised if they are regularly involved in the decisions regarding the sale or purchase of particular investments. This would not apply, however, if the trustees are involved only in strategic decisions such as the balance between income and growth, or the proportion of investments in particular sectors.

Banks acting as trustees of other funds

Anyone acting as a trustee or personal representative need not be authorised under the regulations in respect of investments which he manages as a trustee or personal representative, unless he holds himself out as offering investment management services or is receiving remuneration for providing such services additional to any remuneration he receives for the more customary duties. There can be little doubt that banks offer their services as trustees on the basis that they can provide investment advice and also that some part of their fee relates to the provision of that advice. On either of these grounds, they would be deemed, under Paragraph 22 of Schedule 1 of the Act, to be conducting investment business and thus must be authorised.

Advertisements

Under Section 57 of the Act, no person other than an authorised person may issue or cause to be issued an investment advertisement in the United Kingdom unless its contents have been approved by an authorised person. In this context, 'advertisement' means any form of advertising including that which may be done by television or radio. Any investment advertising in contravention of Section 57 would constitute a criminal offence and also any money made as a result of the advertisement may be recovered together with, if appropriate, compensation. However, the Court may decline to disturb whatever obligation has been entered into and not require the return of any money or property transferred if the investor was not influenced to a material extent by the advertisement *or* the advertisement was not misleading as to the nature of the investment and fairly stated the risks involved.

Investments sold 'off the page'

If investments are made by signing and returning a 'coupon' at the foot of an advertisement, there is obviously not the same scope for enforcing the conduct of business rules such as 'know your customer', 'best advice', etc. The regulations provide that the only investment products which may be sold in this way are life assurance policies, units in authorised unit trusts and Personal Equity Plans, and in all these cases the regulations specify the particulars which must be included in the advertisement and in the application form. All investment advertisements, whether for selling 'off the page' or not, must conform to the stringent rules of the Securities and Investments Board and, in particular, must be 'clear and not misleading'.

Unsolicited calls

The Act provides that the only investment agreements which may be entered into as the result of so-called 'cold calls' are those which are permitted by the SIB regulations and in essence this means life assurance policies, personal pension plans and authorised unit trusts. In addition, unsolicited calls in relation to investments of any description may be made on investment businesses and business investors by each other and by would-be customers of investment business.

Cancellation rights

Under the regulations the sale of life assurance policies, personal pension contracts and authorised unit trusts will be subject to the requirement that the investor must be notified of his or her right to cancel the agreement and notice of this right must be given within seven days of the original agreement to issue the policy or the units. The investor will be entitled to cancel the agreement within fourteen days of receiving the notice, or within fourteen days of the day on which he first became aware that the agreement had been entered into and that the first payment under the agreement had been made. If the investor cancels the agreement within the permitted time, the contract is rescinded and moneys paid under the agreement must be returned. In the case of industrial life policies, the notice of the right to cancel may be handed to the other party instead of being sent by post.

Clients' accounts

Another particular requirement of the legislation is that which relates to the keeping of clients' money. Section 55 of the Act provides for regulations to be made on this subject and these are now set out in the Rules of the Securities and Investments Board. It is required that any person engaged on investment business within the meaning of the legislation must provide for the segregation of clients' money from that of other clients and from that of the business itself. Such segregated balances will have the status of trust moneys and there will be no question of their being available to creditors in the event of the liquidation of the investment business. Such clients' balances must be subject to regular audit and be held with an approved bank. Interest on the balances must be held for the clients concerned unless the individual amounts of interest are less than £10. The provisions relating to clients' money do not apply in relation to customers who are professional, business or experienced investors who choose to waive their rights to segregation of the balances.

Assets other than money are not susceptible to such segregation. Where, therefore, securities or other property are held by an investment business on behalf of clients, there is no absolute rule requiring segregation although, as already mentioned, there are strict rules as to maintenance of records.

Compliance

The Financial Services Act and the attendant Rules are extremely complicated and far-ranging. Many investment firms, particularly smaller ones, will no doubt have difficulty in becoming acquainted with and thereafter observing the statutory requirements. It will be the responsibility of the regulatory bodies, as authorised by the Securities and Investments Board, to ensure compliance by their members and to some extent these regulatory bodies will provide a valuable digestive process in assimilating the complex requirements of the legislation and translating them into everyday business terms. To ensure that each officer, employee and appointed representative complies with the statutory regulations these procedures are to be set out in a compliance manual (except in the case of small firms where the total number of persons employed does not exceed 10) and the compliance procedures are to be reviewed no less frequently than once in every twelve months. The review of those procedures must extend to the records kept by the investment firm, its compliance procedures, its procedures for supervising its officers and employees and appointed representatives and a review of customer accounts. It follows that a compliance officer should be a senior person and, in the larger organisations, it will be someone of very senior rank.

Insider-dealing

The main provisions relating to insider-dealing are contained in the Company Securities (Insider-Dealing) Act, 1965. In broad terms it means dealing in the securities of a company by a person connected with that company whilst in possession of unpublished price-sensitive information. Connected persons not only include directors and senior officials but also auditors, solicitors, merchant bankers and other professional persons acting on the company's behalf. More particularly, the new Act empowers the Secretary of State to appoint inspectors to investigate suspected insider-dealing offences and confers on the inspectors wide powers to compel attendance before them and the production of documents etc. Under the Act a person carrying on the business of banking is not required to disclose any information or produce any document relating to the affairs of a customer unless the customer is a person who the inspectors have reason to believe may be able to give information concerning a suspected contravention *and* the Secretary of State is satisfied that the disclosure or production is necessary for the purpose of the investigation. The provisions of the Act relating to the investigation of suspected cases of insider-dealing came into force in November 1986 and there have already been prosecutions under the Act.

Unit trusts

Unit trusts, hitherto governed by the Prevention of Fraud (Investments) Act, 1958 (which is to be repealed) will be brought within the provisions of the Financial Services Act, Chapter VIII of which deals with 'Collective Investment Schemes'. This Chapter of the Act (Sections 75 to 95) deals with the authorisation, management and promotion of unit trusts and brings the law in line with the relevant EEC Directive. The powers of the Secretary of State under the new provisions will be delegated to the Securities and Investments

Board who will in due course issue their Rules on the subject. It is envisaged that most of the supervisory powers at present exercised by the Department of Trade and Industry will in due time be taken over by the SIB.

The official listing of securities

Part IV and Part V of the Act deal with the official listing of securities and the offer for sale of unlisted securities. These provisions replace the Stock Exchange (Listing) Regulations, 1984. The Stock Exchange (or, more correctly, the International Stock Exchange) will continue to be the competent authority for the issuing and administration of the rules but for the first time the regulations governing the listing of securities are set out in statutory form and embrace the relevant EEC Directives. Those provisions of the Companies Act 1985 and the Prevention of Fraud (Investments) Act 1958, relating to prospectuses and the offer of securities for sale are to be repealed and are now brought within the new legislation.

Further Reading

A list of books and articles that readers of this book may find helpful and interesting.

Chapter 1. Service Banking

Institute of Bankers: *Bank strategies for the 1990s*. The Institute of Bankers, 1986.
Klein, Gerald, and Lamber, Janice: *The business of banking*, Methuen, 1987.
Widlake, Brian: *In the City*. Faber, 1986.

Article
'UK banking: a survey'. *Financial Times*, published annually.

Chapter 2. Deposit Banking

Chartered Institute of Bankers: *Banking through the looking glass*. The Chartered Institute of Bankers, 1987.
Institute of Bankers: *The banks and personal customers*. The Institute of Bankers, 1983.
Howcroft, J. B. and Lavis, J.: *Retail banking: the new revolution in structure and strategy*. Blackwell, 1986.
National Consumer Council: Banking services and the consumer: a report. Methuen, 1983.

Chapter 3. The Lending Banker

Banking Information Service: *The banks and small firms*. 4th ed. B.I.S., 1985.
Dyer, L. S.: *A practical approach to bank lending*. 3rd ed. The Chartered Institute of Bankers, 1987.
Holden, J. Milnes: *Law and practice of banking*. Vol. 2: securities for bankers' advances. 7th ed. Pitman, 1986.
Perry, F. E.: *Law and practice relating to banking*. 5th ed. Methuen, 1987.

Article
'Small businesses: a survey'. *Financial Times*, published annually.

Chapters 4 and 5. The Administration of Estates and Private Trusts

Sladen, Michael: *Practical trust administration*. 2nd ed. Europa, 1983.
Soares, Patrick C.: *Trusts and tax planning*. 3rd ed. Longman, 1987.
Vickery, B. G.: *Law and accounts of executors, administrators and trustees*. 21st ed. Cassell, 1987.

Chapter 6. Investment Services

Allied Dunbar: *Allied Dunbar investment guide 1986–87.* Longman, 1986 (annual).
Hamilton, J. Dundas: *The new securities industry and the banks.* The Institute of Bankers, 1985.
Lomax, David F. *London markets after the Financial Services Act.* Butterworths, 1987.
Trade and Industry, Department of: Review of investor protection: report. (Chairman: L. C. B. Gower.) H.M.S.O., Part I, 1984, Part II, 1985.
Whittaker, Andrew and Morse, Geoffrey. *The Financial Services Act 1986: a guide to the new law.* Butterworths, 1987.
Winfield, R. G. and Curry, S. J.: *Success in investment.* 3rd ed. Murray, 1987.

Articles

'Investment trusts: a survey'. *Investors Chronicle,* published annually.
M. S. Mendelsohn: 'Investment trusts seek out a role'. *The Banker,* December 1986.

Chapter 7. Unit Trusts

Trade and Industry, Department of: The regulation of authorised unit trust schemes: a consultative document on the proposed regulations for unit trust schemes under the Financial Services Bill. H.M.S.O., 1986.
Financial Times: *The unit trust year book 1986.* Financial Times Business Information, 1986 (annual).
Wedgwood, A. J. and Pell, G. A.: *A guide to the Financial Services Act 1986.* Financial Training, 1986.

Chapters 8 and 9. Life Assurance and Insurance Broking

Clews, Roderick ed.: *Textbook of insurance broking.* Woodhead-Faulkner, 1980.
Dickson, G. C. A. and Steele, J. T.: *Introduction to insurance.* 2nd ed. Macdonald & Evans, 1984.
Hansell, D. S: *Elements of insurance.* 4th ed. Macdonald & Evans, 1985.
Hodgson, Godfrey. *Lloyds of London: a reputation at risk.* Rev. ed., Penguin, 1986.

Articles

'Broking services from the big four'. *Planned Savings,* May 1986.
R. Harvey: 'Financial services: life assurance companies drive ahead'. *Banking World,* December 1986.
'Insurance and insurance broking: a survey'. *Financial Times,* published annually.

Chapter 10. Credit Cards

Drury, A. C. and Ferrier, C. W. *Credit Cards,* Butterworths, 1984.
Frazer, Patrick: *Plastic and electronic money: new payment systems and their implications.* Woodhead-Faulkner, 1985.
Goode, R. M.: *Electronic banking: the legal implications.* The Chartered Institute of Bankers/Centre for Commercial Law Studies, 1985.
Joint Credit Card Company: *A guide to credit cards.* Rev. ed. The Company, 1986.

Articles
M. Brandenburg: 'Credit cards are here to stay'. *Accountancy,* January 1987.
J. P. Friedman: 'The changing world of plastic cards: a revolution in perspective'. *Journal of Retail Banking,* Spring 1987.

Chapter 11. Hire Purchase and Consumer Credit

Bennion, F. A. R.: *Consumer credit control.* Longman, 1976 – (loose-leaf).
Ivamy, E. R. Hardy: *Casebook on sale of goods.* 5th ed. Lloyds of London Press, 1987.
Karpinski, Jan and Fielding, Stephen: *Consumer credit agreements: a working handbook to truth in lending.* Waterlow, 1985.
Leder, M. J.: *Consumer law.* 2nd ed. Pitman, 1986.

Articles
M. Blanden: 'Point-of-Sale or direct selling?'. *The Banker,* April 1987.
G. Borrie: 'The credit society; its benefits and burdens'. *Journal of Business Law,* May 1986.

Chapter 12. Personal Advisory and Agency Services

Hanson, D. G.: *Moneyguide: the handbook of personal finance.* Kluwer, 1981 – (loose-leaf).
Homer, Arnold and Burrows, Rita. *Tolley's tax guide 1987–88.* Tolley, 1987 (annual).
Rayer, John: *Robson Rhodes personal financial planning manual.* 3rd ed. Butterworths, 1986.
Sinclair, W. I.: *Allied Dunbar tax guide 1987–88.* Longman, 1987 (annual).

Article
M. Wright and T. Watkins: 'Banks and developments in the personal financial services market: evidence from a questionnaire survey'. *International Journal of Bank Marketing,* Vol. 4 no. 2, 1986.

Chapter 13. Money and Travel

Chawla, Roger: *The travellers cheque game: what every banker should know.* The Author, 1983.
Frazer, Patrick: *Plastic and electronic money: new payment systems and their implications.* Woodhead-Faulkner, 1985.
Swinglehurst, Edmund: *Cook's tours: the story of popular travel.* Blandford Press, 1982.

Chapter 14. Merchant Banking

Bannock, Graham and Doran, Alan: *Going public: the markets in unlisted securities.* Harper & Row, 1987.
Clay, C. J. J. and Wheble, B. S. eds.: *Modern merchant banking.* 2nd ed. Woodhead-Faulkner, 1983.
Panel on Take-overs and Mergers: City code on take-overs and mergers and rules governing substantial acquisition of shares. The Panel, 1985 – (loose-leaf).
Wright, Mike and others: *Spicer and Pegler's management buy-outs.* Woodhead-Faulkner, 1987.

Articles
'Corporate finance: a survey'. *Financial Times,* published annually.
'UK banking: a survey'. *Financial Times,* published annually.
'Unlisted securities market: a survey'. *Financial Times,* published annually.

Chapter 15. Share Registration and Computer Services

Charlesworth, J.: *Company law.* 13th ed. Stevens, 1987.

Chapter 16. Leasing and Industrial Hire Purchase

Clarke, Tom ed.: *Leasing finance.* Euromoney, 1985.
Gmur, Charles J. ed.: *Trade financing.* 2nd ed. Euromoney, 1986.
Sowler, Richard: *Taxation of leasing transactions.* Butterworths, 1984.

Article
C. Ferrier: 'UK leasing finance: down but not out'. *The Banker,* July 1986.

Chapter 17. Factoring

Cox, Anthony N. and Mackenzie, John A. *International factoring.* Euromoney, 1986.
Chrichton, Susan and Ferrier, Charles: *Understanding factoring and trade credit.* Waterlow, 1986.
Salinger, F. R. *Tolley's factoring and the lending banker.* Tolley, 1986.

Chapter 18. Corporate Trusteeships

Barnes, Michael and Spill, Ronald: *The pension scheme trustee.* Guild Press, 1978.

Article
R. Abramson: 'What the trustees do'. *The Accountant,* 30 October 1985.

Chapter 19. Pension Services

Bean, Barry and others: *Allied Dunbar retirement planning guide.* Longman, 1987 (annual).
Hosking, Gordon Albert: *Pension schemes and retirement benefits.* 5th ed. Sweet & Maxwell, 1985.
Oldfield, Maurice: *Understanding pension schemes.* 3rd ed. Format Publishing, 1987.
Pension funds and their advisors. A.P. Financial Registers (annual).
Seres, J. S. D. *Pensions: a practical guide,* 2nd ed. Longman, 1987.

Articles
'Life assurance company and private pension fund investment, 1962–84'. *Bank of England Quarterly Bulletin,* December 1986.
'Pensions: a survey'. *Investors Chronicle,* published annually.

Chapter 20. Business Advisory Services

Bank of England: *Money for business.* 5th ed. The Bank of England, 1985.
Banking Information Service: *The banks and small firms.* 4th ed. B.I.S., 1985.
Chartered Institute of Bankers: *Financing new technology.* The Institute of Bankers, 1984.
Davis, A. J.: *The banking revolution: the banks and industry.* The Institute of Bankers, 1986.
Doran, Alan and Hoyle, Michael: Lending to small firms: a study of appraisal and monitoring methods. National Economic Development Council, 1986.

Article
'Small businesses: a survey': *Financial Times,* published annually.

Chapter 21. Off-shore Services

Diamond, Walter H. and Diamond, D. B.: *Tax havens of the world.* New York: Matthew Bender, 1974 – (loose-leaf).
Doggart, Caroline: *Tax havens and their uses.* Rev. ed. Economist, 1985.
Eastaway, Nigel and Miller, Jonathan: *Allied Dunbar expatriate tax and investment guide.* 2nd ed. Longman, 1986.

Chapter 22. Finance of International Trade

Export Credits Guarantee Department: *ECGD services.* E.C.G.D., 1986.
Gmur, Charles J.: *Trade financing.* 2nd ed. Euromoney, 1986.
Watson, Alasdair. *Finance of international trade.* 3rd ed. The Institute of Bankers, 1985.
Whiting, D. P.: *Finance of international trade.* 5th ed. Pitman, 1987.

Chapter 23. Money Transfer

Frazer, Patrick: *Plastic and electronic money: new payment systems and their implications.* Woodhead-Faulkner, 1985.
Goode, R. M.: *Electronic banking: the legal implications.* The Institute of Bankers/Centre for Commercial Law Studies, 1985.
Kirkman, Patrick: *Electronic funds transfer systems: the revolution in cashless banking and payment methods.* Blackwell/Institute of Chartered Accountants in England and Wales, 1987.
Robinson, David: *Payment systems: a means or an end?* The Chartered Institute of Bankers, 1987.

Articles
J. Harris: 'All change in the clearings'. *Banking World,* March 1987.
'Recent developments in the UK payment clearing systems'. *Bank of England Quarterly Bulletin,* August 1987.

Chapter 24. Selling the Services

Andrew, Kenneth: *The bank marketing handbook.* Woodhead-Faulkner, 1986.
Channon, Derek F.: *Bank strategic management and marketing.* Wiley, 1986.
McIver, Colin and Naylor, Geoffrey: *Marketing financial services.* 2nd ed. The Institute of Bankers, 1986.
Richardson, Linda: *Bankers in the selling role.* 2nd ed. Wiley, 1984.
Watkins, Trevor and Wright, Mike: *Marketing financial services.* Butterworths, 1986.

Articles
N. A. L. Brooks: 'Strategic issues for financial services marketing'. *International Journal of Bank Marketing,* vol. 5 no. 2, 1987.
M. K. Lewis: 'The provision of retail services'. *International Journal of Bank Marketing,* vol. 5 no. 2, 1987.

Index

ABERDEEN TRUST *144*
ACCEPTANCE CREDITS *291, 292, 296, 438*
ACCEPTING HOUSES *291, 292, 296, 438*
ACCEPTING HOUSES COMMITTEE *438*
  evidence to Radcliffe Committee *292*
  regulatory and disciplinary body *291*
ACCESS CARD *218, 219, 224, 225, 230, 277, 450*
  see also CREDIT CARDS
ACCIDENT AND SICKNESS INSURANCE *172*
ACCOUNT EXECUTIVES *310, 488*
ACCOUNTING STANDARDS COMMITTEE 1984 *332*
ACCOUNTING SYSTEMS
  computer services for *321*
ADMINISTRATION, LETTERS OF *94*
ADMINISTRATION OF ESTATES *83–102*
  market *86, 89, 92, 98, 100*
  profits *95–7*
ADMINISTRATORS *87*
ADVERTISING *477–81, 508*
  bank deposits *45, 48–9*
  coupon advertising *185, 508–9*
  credit cards *223*
  life assurance *184–5*
  linked life assurance *185*
  taxation services *262*
  trust services *99*
  unit trusts *159, 383, 480*
ADVISORY SERVICES *see* BUSINESS ADVISORY SERVICES, PERSONAL ADVISORY SERVICES
AGENCY SERVICES *270–2*
AGRICULTURE MORTGAGE CORPORATION *63*
AIRLEASE INTERNATIONAL *336*
ALDENHAM, LORD, Chairman of Westminster Bank on purchase of interest in Mercantile Credit *335*
ALEX LAWRIE FACTORS *360*
AMERICAN EXPRESS *281*
  credit cards *215–16, 277*
  Gold Card *234–5*
  travel and entertainment cards *215, 216*
  travellers cheques *278, 279*
AMMIDON, HOYT
  on investment management *128*
ANCHOR RELOCATION SERVICES *271*
'ANCILLARY SERVICES'
  description no longer acceptable *3*
ANGLIA BUILDING SOCIETY *34*
ANGLO-AFRICAN SHIPPING CO. *358*
ANGLO FACTORING SERVICES *359, 360*
ANNUITY
  certain *172*
  deferred *172*
  reversionary *172*
ARBUTHNOT FACTORS *360*
ASDA GROUP *34*
ASSET FINANCE
  provision of *63*
ASSOCIATION OF BRITISH FACTORS *359–60*
ASSOCIATION OF CORPORATE TRUSTEES *94*
ASSOCIATION OF INSURANCE BROKERS *194*
ASSOCIATION OF UNIT TRUST MANAGERS *see* UNIT TRUST ASSOCIATION
ASTLEY INDUSTRIAL TRUST *9*
AUTHORISED DEPOSITARY *118*
AUTOMATED TELLER MACHINES (ATMs), AUTOMATIC CASH DISPENSERS *450–2*
  shared networks *451*

BAGEHOT IN *LOMBARD STREET*, collection of customers' income from bearer securities *118*
BAILEE, GRATUITOUS *52*

BAILEE FOR REWARD *52*
BANK AMERICARD *215*
BANK GIRO *455–6*
BANK OF AMERICA *215, 279*
BANK OF ENGLAND
Banking Act 1979 *1, 32, 45–6, 49*
Competition and Credit Control 1972 *21, 35, 38, 72, 77, 299, 336*
guidance to banks *64, 72*
rescue of Barings in 1890, the first 'lifeboat' operation *294*
BANK OF IRELAND *217, 235*
BANK OF SCOTLAND
cheque cards *217*
hire purchase *9, 256*
Home and Office banking service *466*
Homelink service *466*
insurance broking *199*
leasing *336*
Managed Portfolio service *134*
merchant banking *298*
money market account *36*
share registration *314*
unit trusts *144*
BANK OF SCOTLAND FINANCE CO *298*
BANKERS AUTOMATED CLEARING SERVICES (BACS) (formerly INTER-BANK COMPUTER BUREAU) *51–2, 321, 456–7*
BANKERS CARD *see* CHEQUE CARDS
BANKERS' CLEARING HOUSE
Clearing House Automated Payments System (CHAPS) *457–8*
clearings *454–6*
membership *4, 454*
BANKERS' OPINIONS, STATUS ENQUIRIES *53–5*
BANKERS' ORDERS, STANDING ORDERS *51, 456–7*
BANKING ACT 1979 *1, 32, 45–6*
Deposit Protection Scheme *49*
BANKING ACT 1987 *1, 33, 46–9, 473*
BANKING SUPERVISION, BOARD OF *47*
BANKS AND BANKERS
all purpose bank, the *3, 12, 484, 489, 492*
as Trustee *3, 108, 116*
balances generated by
—personal trust work *97*
—receiving bankers for capital issue *305*
bank charges and commission *40–1, 458–9*
banker/customer relationship
—new *489*
—traditional *49–51, 417, 475, 489–90*
—under Financial Services Act 1986 *503*
banker/factor relationship *361–2*
banking habit *41–4*
branches in UK, number of *8*
business, off-shore *422, 430–1*
Committee of London & Scottish Clearing Bankers
—agreement on taxation services *262, 263*
—membership *4, 454*
company registrarships *314*
computer services *320–2*
'cradle-to-grave' service *83*
customer, no definition *49*
'customer, not client' *2*
deposits, banks' share of *21–3*
EFTPOS *451, 460–3*
guidance from Bank of England *64, 72*
hours of business *475*
in-store *33–4*
investment manager, banks as *507*
life assurance *165–6*
liquidity ratios *71–2*
managers
—as financial advisor, *121–3, 259, 264, 270, 409, 410, 415*
—as salesmen *99–100, 179–80, 470–2*
—role in selling services *11, 475–6, 483–8*
mergers with insurance companies, possibility of *190*
origins *19*
participation in equity *306–7*
personal accounts *12, 20, 41–2, 69–71*
'free banking' *40*
regulations for banking business *46–9*
Reserve Asset Ratio *72*
services, extension of *1–17*
share of personal savings *6*
sites *475*
stockbroking firms, acquisition of *135*
see also MERCHANT BANKING
BARCLAYCARD *217, 224, 230, 238, 240, 450*
control of card issue *229*
DARTS *240*

first credit card on American pattern *9, 218*
Petrol Cards *236, 460*
Pinpoint machines *235*
see also CREDIT CARDS
BARCLAYS BANK, BARCLAYS BANK TRUST CO
Barclaycare *226*
branch re-organisation *487*
bureaux de change *284*
business advisory service *410*
business start loan scheme *68–9*
cash card, cheque card (triple role of Barclaycard) *451*
Connect card *237, 463–4*
Counterspeed *460*
credit cards (Martins Bank) *9*
estate agency *272*
exempt unit trusts *154*
export finance for smaller companies *69*
factoring *359*
Gateway *464*
Higher Rate Deposit Account *36*
hire purchase *8, 256*
home savings plans *36*
In-house cards *226*
insurance broking *199, 202*
investment report service *123*
leasing *335, 336*
linked life assurance *181*
loans to small businesses *68, 69*
'Personal Banker' service *476*
personal financial planning
—estate planning service *266*
—football pools winners *268*
—money doctor service *266*
Premier Card *235*
Prime account *36*
share registration *314, 319*
Shareline *120*
stockbrokers *15–16, 300*
stock jobbers *15–16, 300*
Supercash *452*
tax aid service *263*
travellers cheques *279*
'unauthorised' property unit trust *163*
unit trusts *142, 144, 382*
BARCLAYS DE ZOETE WEDD *120, 125, 135–6, 300, 303*
BARCLAYS EXPORT & FINANCE CO *335, 359*
BARCLAYS FACTORING *359*
BARCLAYS INSURANCE BROKERS INTERNATIONAL *199, 202*
BARCLAYS INSURANCE SERVICES CO *199, 202*
BARCLAYS MERCANTILE INDUSTRIAL FINANCE *335*
BARCLAYS MERCHANT BANK *297, 300*
BARCLAYS UNICORN GROUP *143, 144, 161, 166, 168*
BARING BROTHERS *294*
BASE RATE *294*
banks *77*
finance houses *341*
BEARER SECURITIES *118*
BEEHIVE LIFE ASSURANCE CO (now BLACK HORSE LIFE ASSURANCE CO) *166*
BEVAN, TIMOTHY, Deputy Chairman of Barclays Bank on business advisory matters *412*
on investment services *117*
BIDDING SUBSIDIARY *299*
BIDS AND DEALS *294–5*
'BIG BANG' *1, 14–15, 117, 118, 300*
events leading up to *13*
BIGGINS, JOHN
credited with introducing the bank credit card *215*
BILLS OF EXCHANGE *291, 433, 435–6, 437*
BILLS OF EXCHANGE ACT 1882 *433, 435*
BISCOE, PETER
Law and Practice of Credit Factoring *357*
BISGOOD, BISHOP *16, 300*
BLACK HORSE AGENCIES *271*
BLACK HORSE LIFE ASSURANCE CO *166*
BLOCK DISCOUNTING *342–3*
BOLTON COMMITTEE ON SMALL FIRMS *67, 407, 409–10, 413*
BOSTON TRUST AND SAVINGS *34*
BOWMAKER *8, 256*
BRITISH HOME STORES *34*
BRITISH INSURANCE ASSOCIATION
Code of Conduct *183*
BRITISH INSURANCE BROKERS' ASSOCIATION (formerly BRITISH INSURANCE BROKERS' COUNCIL) *194, 195, 209–210, 211*
BRITISH LINEN BANK *144*
hire purchase *8*
merchant banking *298*

BRITISH WAGON CO *8*
BUDGET ACCOUNTS *37*
BUILDING SOCIETIES
ATM facilities *451*
competition for deposits and personal savings *12, 22, 23, 40*
conveyancing services *26*
estate agencies *26, 272*
financial services *26*
growth *23*
—reasons for *24–7*
house purchase *70*
income tax treatment of interest *24–7*
insurance services *26, 211*
total assets figure *23*
BUILDING SOCIETIES ACT 1986 *1, 13, 26–7, 473*
BUILDING SOCIETIES COMMISSION *27*
BUILDING SOCIETY ACT 1962 *26*
BUREAUX DE CHANGE *283-4*
BURTONS *33*
BUSINESS ADVISORY SERVICES *407–19*
corporate advice departments *294–5, 307*
'off-shore' *426–8*
BUSINESS SECTOR
lending to *62, 66–9, 73, 74, 77*
BUSINESS, SMALL *see* SMALL BUSINESSES
BUYER CREDIT GUARANTEES *442*

CANADA LIFE ASSURANCE CO *166*
CAPITAL GAINS TAX *see* TAXATION SERVICES
CAPITAL ISSUES *291–2, 294, 303*
CAPITAL TRANSFER TAX *see* INHERITANCE TAX, TAXATION SERVICES
CAPTIVE INSURANCE COMPANIES *427–8, 431*
CARDLINK *236*
CARTE BLANCHE *215*
CASH DISPENSER *see* AUTOMATED TELLER MACHINES
CASH DISPENSER CARDS, CASH CARDS *215, 450–2*
CASH MANAGEMENT
off-shore services *322–3 428*
UK services *322–3*
CENTRAL TRUSTEE SAVINGS BANK *30*
CENTURY FACTORS LTD *360*
CERTIFICATES OF DEPOSIT *35, 119*
CHANNEL ISLANDS
off-shore services *422–32*
CHARGE CARD SERVICES LTD *233*
CHARITABLE TRUSTS *111*
CHARITIES
exempt unit trusts *154*
investment business *128*
property unit trusts *163*
CHARLES CASE (R v CHARLES) 1981 *232*
CHARTER HOUSE DEVELOPMENT *298, 300*
CHARTERED TRUST *32*
CHEMICAL BANK *464*
CHEQUE CARDS *9, 215, 216–18, 228, 232, 237–8, 450*
see also CREDIT CARDS
CHEQUES *453–5*
CHILDREN'S ASSURANCE *172*
CITIBANK *32, 225, 279, 464*
CITICORPORATION *216, 279*
CITY CODE ON TAKEOVERS & MERGERS *308*
'CITY REVOLUTION' *13*
CLEARING HOUSE *see* BANKERS CLEARING HOUSE
CLEARING HOUSE AUTOMATED PAYMENTS SYSTEM (CHAPS) *457–8*
CLEARINGS *453–6*
CLOSE BROS. PLC *360*
CLYDESDALE BANK
Access card *218*
insurance broking *199*
share registration *314*
Telebank *466*
COHEN COMMITTEE ON COMPANY LAW AMENDMENT 1945
conflict of interest, debentures *375*
COMMERCIAL BANK OF SCOTLAND *8*
COMMERCIAL UNION ASSURANCE CO *166*
COMMITTEE OF LONDON CLEARING BANKERS
agreement with Institute of Chartered Accountants *262, 263*
proposal for new clearing system *454*

COMMITTEE OF LONDON & SCOTTISH CLEARING BANKS *4, 454*
COMPANIES ACT 1948 *45*
COMPANIES ACT 1980 *308*
COMPANIES ACT 1981 *379*
COMPANIES ACT 1985 *316, 317, 332*
COMPANY REGISTRARS *315–17*
profitability *317–19*
COMPANY REGISTRATION SERVICES
off-shore *427*
COMPANY SECURITIES (INSIDER DEALING) ACT 1985 *308*
'COMPETITION AND CREDIT CONTROL' 1971 *21, 35, 38, 72, 77, 299, 336*
COMPOSITE RATE OF INTEREST *24, 429*
COMPUTER SERVICES *320–2*
COMPUTERISATION, TRUST DEPARTMENT *93*
CONDUCT OF BUSINESS RULES *502–3*
CONNECT *237, 463–4*
CONSORTIUM TRUST, TRUSTEESHIPS *376–7*
CONSTRAINTS ON LENDING *71–2*
CONSUMER CREDIT *63, 229, 234, 248, 253–4, 255*
CONSUMER CREDIT ACT 1974 *220, 227, 245, 249, 255*
CONSUMER HIRE PURCHASE *63, 250, 253*
CONTRACTING-OUT
of Government Pensions Scheme *208, 370, 391*
CONTROLLING DIRECTORS
pension schemes for *370*
COOK, THOMAS & SON *279, 280, 281*
CO-OPERATIVE BANK
business loans *69*
competition for savings *31–2*
credit card *224*
Handybanks *31, 38, 452*
Handycard *31, 226*
hire purchase *256*
history of *31*
interest on current account *38*
leasing *336*
short-term deposits *31, 36*
travellers cheques *279*
CO-OPERATIVE TRAVEL *282*
CORPORATE ADVICE *294, 414*
CORPORATE ADVICE DEPARTMENTS *see* BUSINESS ADVISORY SERVICES
CORPORATE FINANCIAL PLANNING
off-shore services *425, 426–8*
CORPORATE INVESTMENT BUSINESS *128, 130*
CORPORATE SECTOR
deposits *20, 21–2*
CORPORATE TRUSTEES *see* TRUSTEES, CORPORATE
CORPORATE TRUSTEESHIPS *369–385*
CORPORATION OF INSURANCE BROKERS *194*
'CORPORATION TAX COMPANIES' *427*
'CORSET' *21, 25*
COUNTERSPEED *460*
COUNTY BANK *297, 299, 300, 303*
COUPONS, COLLECTION OF *118*
CREDIT AND MONETARY CONTROL
Competition and Credit Control, 1971 *21, 35, 38, 72, 77, 229, 336*
'Corset' *21, 25*
CREDIT BROKERS *255*
CREDIT CARDS *213–241*
advantages
—to cardholder *220*
—to merchant *221–2*
card companies *222–3*
card holders *218, 219–21*
company schemes *225*
consumer credit *63, 70, 229, 234*
early developments *9, 213, 214*
floor limit *222*
fraud, losses due to *227–8*
'free' credit *219–20*
in-house cards *225*
legal aspects *220, 227, 231–3*
market *223–5*
merchants *221–2, 230–1*
monopoly aspect *227, 229–31*
overseas *218, 277–8, 279*
profitability *222–3, 233–4*
recent developments *234–7*
risk aspects *221, 226 0*
sales representatives *483*
settlement by electronic transmission *238*
statistics, table of *239*
the future *237–8*

three parties to the operation *219–23*
travel and entertainment cards *215, 216*
Trustee Savings Banks *224*
CREDIT CLEARING, BANK GIRO *455–6*
CREDIT FACTORING, CREDIT FACTORING INTERNATIONAL *357, 365–6, 360*
CREDIT SCORING *75–6*
CREDIT TRANSFERS *see* MONEY TRANSFER
CROCKER NATIONAL CORPORATION *281*
CROSS-SELLING OF BANK SERVICES *264*
CROWTHER COMMITTEE ON CONSUMER CREDIT, 1971
bank overdraft *69*
factoring *356*
finance house *248*
hire purchase *243, 245, 253–4*
CURRENCY AND BANK NOTES ACT 1928 *449*
CURRENT ACCOUNTS *35, 37–8, 59–62*
CUSTODIAN TRUSTEES *86, 372–3*

DARTS (DATA CAPTURE AUTHORISATION TRANSMISSION SERVICE) *240*
DEBENHAMS
in-house card *33, 225*
DEBENTURE TRUSTS *373–6*
DEBIT CARDS *237, 460–4*
DECLARATION OF TRUSTS
over investments *124*
DENNING, LORD, in United Dominions Trust Ltd v Kirkwood—difficulty of defining a banker *1, 289*
DEPARTMENT FOR NATIONAL SAVINGS (formerly POST OFFICE SAVINGS DEPARTMENT) *12, 27–9*
DEPARTMENT OF TRADE
insurance companies *384*
property unit trusts *163*
report on role of unit trust trustee *381*
responsibility for unit trusts *145–6, 147–9, 158, 160, 163, 379*
DEPOSIT BANKING/DEPOSITS *19–55*
advertising *45, 48–9*
bank charges *40–1*
banker/customer relationship *49–51*
banking habit *41–4*
basic bank function *19–20*
competition for *21–3, 40*
constraints *20–1*
currency *20*
current accounts *35, 37–8, 40–1*
deposit accounts *34, 35*
financial outlets *34*
foundation of clearing banks' business *12*
Higher Rate Deposit Accounts *36*
historical developments *19*
home savings plans *36*
income tax treatment of interest *24*
institutions' share of *22*
interest on current accounts *37–8, 40–1*
interest, rates of *38–41*
investment accounts *36*
larger deposits—bidding subsidiaries *299*
legal aspects *44–9*
market rate *119*
money market *36*
off-shore *430–1*
savings accounts *36*
sources *20*
sterling *20*
term *35–6, 40*
types of account *34–8*
DEPOSIT PROTECTION BOARD *49*
DEPOSIT PROTECTION SCHEME *49*
DEPOSIT RECEIPTS *119*
DEPOSIT-TAKING INSTITUTION *see* LICENSED DEPOSIT-TAKING INSTITUTION
DE ZOETE & BEVAN *15, 300*
DINER'S CLUB, THE
credit cards *9, 277*
travel and entertainment cards *215, 216*
DIRECT DEBITS *52, 456*
DIRECT MAIL *481–2*
DIRECTOR OF FAIR TRADING *see* OFFICE OF FAIR TRADING
DISCRETIONARY ACCOUNTS *see* INVESTMENT SERVICES
DISCRETIONARY TRUSTS *107–8*
DISTRICT BANK *9, 297*
DOCUMENTARY LETTERS OF CREDIT *437*

DOMICILE
off-shore services *421–2*
DRAYTON GROUP *11*
DRAYTON MONTAGUE PORTFOLIO MANAGEMENT *300*
DRUCKER, PETER
on marketing *469*
DU CANN, RT HON EDWARD
post 1939–45 war development of unit trusts *143*

ECONOMIC INFORMATION SERVICES *418*
ELECTRONIC FUNDS TRANSFER POINT OF SALE SYSTEM (EFTPOS) *460–3*
EMERSON, RALPH
on salesmanship *470*
ENDOWMENT ASSURANCE *170, 174*
EQUIPMENT LEASING ASSOCIATION *340*
EQUITY BOND, EQUITY-LINKED POLICY *174*
EQUITY PARTICIPATION *306–7*
ESTATE AGENCY *271–2*
ESTATE DUTY *106, 107*
ESTATE PLANNING *see* PERSONAL FINANCIAL PLANNING
ESTATES *see* ADMINISTRATION OF ESTATES
EURO TRAVELLERS CHEQUES INTERNATIONAL (ETCI) *279, 280*
EUROCARD *218, 279, 280*
EUROCHEQUES *277*
EUROCURRENCY, EURODOLLAR *293, 299*
EUROPEAN COAL AND STEEL COMMUNITY
finance of loan schemes *69*
EXCHANGE CONTROL REGULATIONS *276*
authorised depository *118*
EXECUTOR
choice of *88–91*
definition *87*
duties *87*
banks as *87–8*
EXECUTOR AND TRUSTEE SERVICES
cost of *91–3*
earliest of new services *83*
early advertisement of services *99*
ideal qualities of executor, trustee *88*
market *98*
marketing methods *98–101*
EXECUTORSHIPS *87–8*
EXEMPT UNIT TRUSTS *154*
EXPORT CREDITS GUARANTEE DEPARTMENT *439, 440–3*
guarantees *440–1*
insurance cover *436, 440*
support services *441–2*
EXPORT FINANCE *436–9*
EXPORT FINANCE HOUSES *442–3*
EXPORT GUARANTEES *436, 438–9*

FACTORING *345–67*
banker/factor relationship *361–2*
credit protection *350–1*
debt administration *349–50*
export *364–5, 443–4*
financing *351–4*
history *345–8*
international *364–6*
involvement of banks *63, 356–9*
legal aspects *354–6*
market *366–7*
nature of *348–9*
potential *366–7*
profitability *363–4*
risks *362–3*
FACTORS ACT 1889 *345*
FACTORS CHAIN INTERNATIONAL *366*
FAIR TRADING ACT 1973 *13, 227*
FEDERATION OF INSURANCE BROKERS *194*
FIELDING, NEWSON-SMITH *16, 300*
FINANCE ACT 1918 *394*
FINANCE ACT 1956 *175*
FINANCE ACT 1969 *249*
FINANCE ACT 1970 *394*
FINANCE ACT 1971 *327, 329*
FINANCE ACT 1972 *110*
FINANCE ACT 1973 *370, 395*
FINANCE ACT 1978 *384*
FINANCE ACT 1980 *148*
FINANCE ACT 1982 *108, 110, 113*
FINANCE ACT 1986 *372, 398*
FINANCE ACT 1987 *394*
FINANCE CORPORATION FOR INDUSTRY (FCI) *417*
FINANCE FOR INDUSTRY (FFI) *63, 417*
FINANCE HOUSE BASE RATE (FHBR) *341*

FINANCE HOUSES *248–9, 251, 355*
FINANCE HOUSES ASSOCIATION 248, 254, 256
FINANCE LEASE *333–4*
FINANCE MANAGEMENT SERVICE
Midland Bank *411*
FINANCE OF FOREIGN TRADE *433–45*
buyer credit guarantees *442*
ECGD guarantees *440–1*
ECGD insurance cover *440*
ECGD support services *441–2*
export factoring *443–4*
export finance *436–9, 443*
export finance houses *442–3*
import finance *444*
overseas trade *435–6*
FINANCIAL OUTLETS
number of *34*
FINANCIAL SERVICES ACT 1988 *1, 13, 49, 136, 158, 163, 169, 173, 183, 210–11, 269, 308, 379, 380–1, 382*
see also APPENDIX
FINANCIAL INTERMEDIARIES, MANAGERS AND BROKERS REGULATORY ASSOCIATION (FIMBRA) *211, 501*
FINANCIAL SERVICES
banks' diversification into *5*
FIRST BRITISH FIXED TRUST *378*
FIRST CO-OPERATIVE FINANCE *39, 256, 336*
FIRST NATIONAL BANK OF BOSTON *358, 365*
FIRST NATIONAL CITY BANK OF NEW YORK *358*
FORBES, SIR ARCHIBALD, Chairman of Midland Bank on Bank's 'Finance Management Service' *411*
FOREIGN CURRENCY *275–6*
FOREIGN CURRENCY ACCOUNTS *276*
FOREIGN TRADE *see* FINANCE OF FOREIGN TRADE
FORFAIT FINANCE *443*
FORWARD CONTRACTS *438*
FORWARD LEASING *335*
FORWARD TRUST GROUP
hire purchase *8, 256*
leasing *335*
FOWLER A W (BILL)
post 1939–45 war development of unit trusts *143*
FRANKLIN NATIONAL BANK *215*
FRAUDULENT USE
of cheque cards *228*
of credit cards *227–8*
FUND FOR THE BANKS FOR SAVINGS *29*

GATEWAY *464*
GENERAL CLEARING *454*
GILBART J W
in *The Principles and Practice of Banking* on
—branches of business of modern banking *19*
—relationship between trade, money and banks *433–4*
—replacement of money by cheques *37*
—the Lombards *58–9*
GILT BONDS *174*
GIRARD LIFE INSURANCE, ANNUITY & TRUST CO (now GIRARD BANK) *85*
GIROBANK (formerly NATIONAL GIROBANK) *8*
credit card *226*
competition for personal savings *22, 31*
post cheques *277*
GLYN MILLS & CO *217, 297*
GODDARD, LORD former Lord Chief Justice
banking as a 'trade' *2*
GOWER REPORT
Review of Investor Protection *136, 169, 183*
GREAT WESTERN RAILWAY v THE LONDON & COUNTY BANKING CO *49*
GRESHAM, SIR THOMAS
the goldsmiths' banker *19*
GREVILLE INSURANCE *166*
GRIFFIN FACTORS *358–9, 360*
GRIFFIN LIFE ASSURANCE CO *166*
GRINDLAYS
American Express *235*
GUARANTEED INCOME BONDS *188*
GUARANTEES, THIRD PARTY *76–7*

H & H FACTORS *360*
HAILEY, ARTHUR
in *The Monechangers*
credit card forgeries *227*

HAMBROS BANK
estate agency *272*
factoring *360*
foreign loans *292*
unit trusts *9, 142*
Westminster Hambro unit trust group *9, 142*
HANDYBANK *31, 38*
HARRODS *33–4*
HEDLEY BYRNE & CO v HELLER & PARTNERS *53*
HELBY v MATTHEWS (1895) *246*
HENDERSON ADMINISTRATION *144*
HIBERNIAN BANK *217*
HIRE PURCHASE *243–57*
clearing banks and *8–9, 255–6*
consumer *250, 251*
finance houses *248–9*
hiring of railway wagons *246–8*
history *245–8*
industrial *250-1*
instalment credit, categories of *249*
market *252–5*
nature of *243–5*
profitability *251–2*
sales representatives *252*
see also CONSUMER HIRE PURCHASE, INDUSTRIAL HIRE PURCHASE
HIRE PURCHASE ACT 1965 *249*
HOARE & CO *91*
HOBHOUSE, LORD
early Bill, 1889, to establish trust corporations *85*
HOLDER FW
on entry of Lloyds Bank into unit trusts *162*
HOME AND OFFICE banking service *466*
HOME BANKING *464-7*
HOME LINK *466*
HOME SAVINGS PLANS *36*
HOUSE MORTGAGES
banks *26, 70–1*
building societies *25–6*
home savings plans *36*

ICL *336*
IMPORT FINANCE *444*
INCOME TAX
treatment of interest on
—building society accounts *24*
—National Savings Bank ordinary account *28*
—Trustee Savings Bank accounts *30*
see also TAXATION SERVICES
INDUSTRIAL AND COMMERCIAL FINANCE CORPORATION (ICFC) *417*
INDUSTRIAL AND PROFESSIONAL SERVICES
computer services for *321–2*
INDUSTRIAL HIRE PURCHASE *63, 250–1, 340–3*
block discounting *343*
market *342–3*
motor industry *342*
INHERITANCE TAX (formerly CAPITAL TRANSFER TAX *106, 261, 395*
INSIDER DEALING *308–9*
INSTALMENT CREDIT
categories of *249*
INSTITUTE OF CHARTERED ACCOUNTANTS
agreement on taxation services *262*
INSTITUTIONAL INVESTMENT BUSINESS *128, 130*
IN-STORE BANKING
cash dispensers *452*
competition for savings *33–4*
INSURANCE/INSURANCE BROKING *193–212*
banks' share of market *200*
banks, involvement *165, 179, 184, 198–202, 211*
banks, criticism of involvement *202–4*
broker
—definition of *193, 194–5*
—number of *183*
—registration of *209, 210*
—regulatory bodies *209–211*
categories of *195*
companies
—captive, off-shore *427–8, 431*
—possibility of mergers with banks *165*
—trusteeships for *384*
customer attitudes *204–6*
insurance consultant *193*
Lloyds of London *105–7*
managers' agencies, purchase of *201*
market *206–7*
marketing *207*
'pad' schemes for bank branches *205*
pensions business *208, 392*

'polarisation' *211*
professional bodies *194–5*
profitability *207–8*
reasons for banks' involvement *200–202*
widespread business *197–8*
see also LIFE ASSURANCE
INSURANCE BROKERS' (REGISTRATION) ACT 1977 *209, 210, 211*
INSURANCE BROKERS' REGISTRATION COUNCIL *209*
INSURANCE COMPANIES ACTS 1974 & 1982 *182, 210*
INSURANCE COMPANIES (AMENDMENT) ACT 1973 *182*
INSURANCE COMPANIES REGULATIONS *182*
INSURANCE CONTRACTS *121*
INTER VIVOS SETTLEMENTS *106–7*
INTERBANK CARD ASSOCIATION (now MASTERCARD) *218*
INTER-BANK COMPUTER BUREAU *see* BANKERS AUTOMATED CLEARING SERVICES
INTER-BANK RESEARCH ORGANISATION
building society accounts *27*
INTEREST RATE CARTEL *21, 299 430*
INTEREST RATES *38–41, 77–8*
composite *24*
constraints 1973–75 *21*
hire purchase
—consumer *252*
—industrial *341*
London Bankers' deposit rate *38*
London Inter-Bank Offered Rate (LIBOR) *78*
INTERNATIONAL CHAMBER OF COMMERCE *437*
INTERNATIONAL FACTORING *364–6*
INTERNATIONAL FACTORS formerly TOWERGATE SECURITIES *347–8, 358, 365, 360*
INTERNATIONAL MONEY ORDERS (IMOs) *276*
INTERNATIONAL PAYMENT ORDERS (IPOs) *276*
INTERNATIONAL STORES
first supermarket in-house card *226*
INTESTACIES *100, 105*
INVESTMENT ACCOUNTS *36*
INVESTMENT BUSINESS, definition of *499*
INVESTMENT COMPANIES
management of, off-shore *426*
unitisation of *152*
INVESTMENT MANAGERS REGULATORY ORGANISATION (IMRO) *158, 501–2, 507*
INVESTMENT SERVICES *117–139*
advice *121–3*
banks' competitors *137*
banks—conflict of functions *134–5, 307–9*
bearer securities, custody of and collection of income *118*
deposit receipts *119*
discretionary accounts *125*
insurance contracts *121*
institutional business *128, 130*
investment
—compared with saving *118*
—management *123–38*
—off-shore *425–6*
—problems *131*
—policy *126–8*
—vehicles for, provision of *400–1*
Investment Report Service *123*
investments
—certificates of deposit *119*
—local authorities *121*
—market rate deposits *119*
—stock exchange securities *119–20*
—Treasury Bills *121*
—valuation of *119*
market *137*
nominee companies *118*
Personal Equity Plans (PEPs) *125–6*
INVESTMENT TRUSTS *378*
INVESTOR PROTECTION
gower Report *136, 169*
INVESTORS IN INDUSTRY GROUP *417*
INVOICE DISCOUNTING *348–9, 351, 355*
INVOICING
off-shore services *427*
UK computer services for *321*
ISLE OF MAN
branch of UK bank outside UK courts' jurisdiction *421–2*
off-shore services *422–32*
ISSUING HOUSES *291–2, 294, 301–2*

ISSUING HOUSES ASSOCIATION, THE *292*

JERSEY, STATES OF
Gentleman's agreement with clearing banks *422*
JOHN MENZIES *33*
JOINT CREDIT CARD CO *218, 230*
JUDICATURE ACT 1873 *354*
JUDICIAL TRUSTEE ACT 18946 *85*

KEETON, PROFESSOR G W
definition of 'trust' *105*
KELLETT RICHARD
The Merchant Banking Arena *289, 292*

LADBROKE & CO v TODD *50*
LAMB, CHARLES
Superannuated Man *387*
LAMBIE CASE (R v LAMBIE) 1981 *232–3*
LAW OF PROPERTY ACT 1925 *354–5*
LAW SOCIETY
liaison with the Trustees Departments' Committee of the Committee of London Clearing Bankers *100*
LEASEUROPE *340*
LEASING *325–40*
clearing banks and *63, 334–337*
growth of business *338–40*
history *325–6*
lease buy decision *337–8*
nature of *326–7*
source of finance *331–2*
taxation aspects *327, 329–30*
types of contract *333–4*
LENDING BANKER *57–79*
analysis of UK bank lending *63–6*
basic bank function *2*
bridging *70*
constraints *71–2*
credit card *63*
credit scoring *75–6*
development of lending business *58–9*
export finance for smaller businesses *69*
house purchase *26, 70–1*
interest rates *77–8*
Lombards *58–9*
nature of bank lending *59–63*
principles *72–5*
schemes financed by European Coal Steel Community *69*
technical training *57–8*
to business sector *62, 66–9*
to personal sector *63, 69–71*
to smaller businesses *67–9, 409*
total to UK residents by all London & Scottish clearing banks *66*
LEWIS'S BANK *34*
bureau de change *284*
cheque card *217*
LIBOR (LONDON INTER-BANK OFFERED RATE) *78*
LICENSED DEPOSIT-TAKING INSTITUTIONS *32–3, 46–9*
LIFE ASSURANCE *165-91*
advertising *184–5*
categories of *170–2*
competition for savings *22*
consumer protection *180, 183*
growth *208*
historical aspects *169–70*
market *185–6*
profitability *186–7*
purpose of *172–4*
risks, minimal *188–9*
selling methods *179–85*
LIFE ASSURANCE ACT 1774 *169*
LIFE ASSURANCE & UNIT TRUSTS REGULATORY ORGANISATION (LAUTRO) *158, 211, 502*
LIFE POLICY
as security for loans *76*
number in existence *206*
trusteeship of *115*
LIFETIME TRUSTS *106–7*
LINK, cash dispensers *225, 451*
LINKED LIFE ASSURANCE *393*
advantages to unit managers *153*
advertising *185*
categories of *174–5*
compared with conventional life policy *167–8*
definition *167*
origins *153, 167*
personal pension plans *175–8*
profitability *186–7*
selling methods *181*
switching facility *174*
LIQUIDITY RATIO *71–2*
LITTLEWOODS *33*
LIVING TRUSTS *111, 115*

LLOYD'S *see* LLOYDS OF LONDON
LLOYDS ASSOCIATED AIR LEASING *336*
LLOYDS ASSOCIATED BANKING CO *299*
LLOYDS BANK
- Access card *218*
- American Express Gold Card *234–5*
- bureaux de change *284*
- business advisory service *411*
- business loan scheme *69*
- cashflow accounts *38*
- cheque cards (bankers card) *9, 216*
- credit cards *218*
- endowment mortgage scheme *166*
- estate agency *271*
- exempt unit trusts *154*
- factoring *358, 360, 365*
- High Interest Cheque account *36*
- hire purchase *8, 256*
- home banking *466*
- home loan market *271*
- In-House cards *226*
- insurance broking *199*
- investment management *124*
- leasing *335, 336*
- linked life assurance *166*
- merchant banking *16, 298, 299*
- Option Deposits *36*
- securities business *16*
- share registration *314, 319*
- Sharedeal *120*
- travel and entertainment cards (American Express) *216*
- travellers cheques *279*
- unit trusts *9, 141, 142, 144, 162*

LLOYDS BANK INSURANCE SERVICES *199*
LLOYD'S BROKERS *195–7, 200, 202, 205, 207*
LLOYD'S INSURANCE BROKERS ASSOCIATION *194, 197*
LLOYDS LEASING *335*
LLOYDS OF LONDON *195–7*
LLOYDS MERCHANT BANK *298, 303*
LLOYDS & SCOTTISH FINANCE *256*
- factoring *358*
- hire purchase *256*
- In-house cards *226*
- leasing *335*

LLOYDS & SCOTTISH FINANCE v CYRIL LORD CARPET SALES *343*
LOANS
- Barclays Bank Business Start Loans *68–9*
- bridging *70, 73*
- fixed rate *78*
- fixed term *7, 62, 63*
- for consumer durables *7*
- house purchase *66, 70*
- interest rates *77–8*
- medium term *62*
- off-shore *430*
- personal *63, 78*
- secured *76–7*
- unsecured *75*

LOCAL AUTHORITY INVESTMENTS *121*
LOMBARD BANKING *247, 335*
LOMBARD NORTH CENTRAL *256*
- hire purchase *247*
- leasing *335*

LOMBARDS *58–9*
LONDON & EDINBURGH INSURANCE CO *153, 166, 168*
LONDON JOINT STOCK BANK v MCMILLAN & ARTHUR *50*

MCIVER C & NAYLOR G
- on marketing financial services *469*

MACMILLAN REPORT 1931
- increase of financing Bills of Exchange *291*

MAIL ORDER
- consumer credit *70*

MAIL ORDER TRANSFER *437, 444*
MANAGED BONDS *173–4*
MANAGED FUND *149*
MANAGEMENT BUY-OUTS *303–4*
MANAGING TRUSTEES *382–3*
M & G GROUP *378*
MARINE INSURANCE COMPANY *198–9*
MAINWARING, RANDLE, former Vice-Chairman, Midland Bank Insurance Services
- on insurance *201*

MARKET
- bank services *473–4*
- credit cards *223–5*
- executor and trustee services *86, 89, 92, 98, 100*
- factoring *366–7*

hire purchase
—consumer *252–5*
—industrial *342–3*
insurance *206–7*
investment services *137*
life assurance *185–6*
pension business *402, 403*
personal pension plans *178*
unit trusts *158–60*
MARKETING *507, 509*
insurance broking *201, 207*
life assurance *179–86*
pension services *402*
trust services *98–101*
unit trusts *158–60*
MARKS & SPENCER
In-house credit card *33, 225–6*
'MARRIAGE BUREAU'
for companies seeking to merge *418*
MARRIAGE SETTLEMENTS *107*
MARRIED WOMEN'S PROPERTY ACT 1882 *115*
MARSH D R *Corporate Trustees* *84*
MARTINS BANK
Cheque cards (Bankers cards) *9, 217*
factoring *359*
hire purchase *8*
insurance broking *201–2*
investment management *125*
investment research *124–5*
leasing *335*
linked life assurance *166*
personal financial planning
—estate planning service *265*
—football pools' winners *268*
travel and entertainment cards (American Express) *216*
unit trusts *9, 142*
MASSACHUSETTS HOSPITAL INSURACNE CO OF BOSTON *85*
MASTERCARD *218, 240, 277, 278, 279*
MASTERCHARGE CARD *215*
MASTER'S TRAVELLERS CHEQUES *278*
MATHER L C in *The Journal Of The Institute Of Bankers*
on branch manager's role in estate planning *264*
on marketing *476*
MATRIX cash dispensers *451*
MEINHARD & CO *348*
MERCANTILE CREDIT CO *256*
factoring *359*
hire purchase *8, 256*
leasing *335*
MERCHANT BANKING *289–311*
accepting houses *290–1*
banks—conflict of functions *307–11*
clearing banks' involvement *295–300*
corporate advice *294–5, 413–4*
diversity of business *292–3*
issuing houses *291–2, 294, 301–2*
management buy-outs *303–4*
MIDLAND BANK
Access card *218*
area offices and service branches *487*
bureaux de change *284*
Capital Investment accounts *36*
cash management service *323*
cheque cards *9, 216*
Cook, Thomas & Son *279, 281, 284*
Croker National Corporation *281*
estate agency *272*
exempt unit trusts *154*
factoring *358*
Finance Management Service *411*
Gold Mastercard *235*
High Interest Cheque account *36*
hire purchase *8, 256*
home banking *466*
home savings plans *36*
In-house cards *226*
in-store banking *33*
insurance broking *199–200, 202*
leasing *335, 336*
linked life assurance *166*
managed fund *149*
merchant banking *297, 298, 300*
personal financial planning
—Financial Planning Service *268*
—football pools' winners *268*
Readicash *38*
share registration *319*
stockbrokers *16, 300*
trust film 'Why not Uncle Willie?' *99*
trustee for unit trusts *9*
unit trusts *9, 11, 144, 166, 300*
MIDLAND BANK FINANCE CORP *335, 360*
MIDLAND BANK INSURANCE BROKERS *200*
MIDLAND BANK INSURANCE SERVICES *199*
MIDLAND BANK TRUST CO *3, 268, 382*
MIDLAND-CITIBANK FACTORS *358*
MINISTERIAL TRUSTS *107*

MINTEL RESEARCH
on financial advisers *121*
MOCATTA, MR JUSTICE
on factoring *345*
MONETARY CONTROLS *see* CREDIT AND MONETARY CONTROLS
MONEY AND TRAVEL *275–85*
MONEY BONDS *174*
MONEY MARKET DEPOSITS *36*
MONEY SUPPLY *37*
MONEY TRANSFER *447–68*
BACS *456*
bank charges *450, 458–9*
Bank Giro *455–6*
cash *448–53*
CHAPS *457–8*
cheques *453–5*
EFTPOS *460–3*
home banking *464–7*
payments
—methods of *447–8*
—number of *447*
plastic money *459–60*
MONEYLENDERS ACT 1900 *59*
MONEYLENDERS ACT 1927 *245*
MONEYSHOPS *12, 22*
competition for savings *32*
MONOPOLIES & MERGERS COMMISSION
Report on credit card companies *230*
MONTAGU TRUST *11*
MORGAN GRENFELL & CO *292*
MORRIS, LORD
duty of care when special skills possessed *54–5*
MORTGAGE PROTECTION ASSURANCE *172*
MORTGAGES *see* HOUSE MORTGAGES
MORTMAIN STATUTES *104*
MUNICIPAL & GENERAL SECURITIES CO *see* M & G GROUP
MUTUAL FUNDS *see* UNIT TRUSTS

NADLER, PROFESSOR PAUL
on American Banks *5*
NATIONAL ASSOCIATION OF PENSION FUNDS *390*
NATIONAL BANK *217*
NATIONAL COMMERCIAL BANK OF SCOTLAND *217*
NATIONAL CONSUMER COUNCIL
Banking Services and the Consumer 93, 98, 101
NATIONAL GIROBANK
(formerly NATIONAL GIRO)
see GIROBANK
NATIONAL PROVINCIAL BANK
cheque cards *9, 216*
factoring *348, 357*
hire purchase *8, 247, 335*
leasing *335*
NATIONAL SAVINGS *27–9*
NATIONAL SAVINGS BANK
(formerly POST OFFICE SAVINGS BANK)
competition for
—corporate deposits *22*
—personal savings *27–9*
income tax, treatment of interest *28*
NATIONAL SAVINGS—DEPARTMENT FOR—*see* DEPARTMENT FOR NATIONAL SAVINGS
NATIONAL WESTMINSTER BANK
Access card *218*
branch re-organisation *487*
bureaux de change *284*
Business Development Scheme *69*
estate agency *272*
factoring *357–8, 360, 366*
hire purchase *256*
In-house cards *226*
insurance broking *199*
interviews, charge for *260*
leasing *336*
linked life assurance (Westminster Bank) *166*
merchant banking *297, 299*
share dealing services *120*
share registration *314, 319*
Small Business Digest *411*
stockbrokers *16, 300*
stockjobbers *16, 300*
travel and entertainment card (Diner's Club) *216*
travellers cheques *279*
unit trusts *144, 299*
NATIONAL WESTMINSTER BANK INSURANCE SERVICES *199*
NATWEST INVESTMENT BANK *125, 300*
NEGOTIABLE CERTIFICATES OF DEPOSIT *35, 119*

NEGOTIATED ORDER OF WITHDRAWAL (NOW) *37*
NOMINEE COMPANIES *118*
NON-CONTENTIOUS PROBATE RULES *94*
NORFOLK, DUKE OF NORFOLK'S TRUSTS
  Lord Justice Fox on increasing trustees' remuneration *110*
NORTH BRITISH SECURITIES *256*
NORTH CENTRAL WAGON CO *8, 247*
NORTH CENTRAL WAGON & FINANCE *335*
  factoring *357*
  hire purchase *247*
  leasing *335*
NORTH WEST SECURITIES *9, 256, 336*
NORTHERN BANK *218*
NOW (NEGOTIATED ORDER OF WITHDRAWAL) *37*
NYSTROM, DR PAUL in *Handbook on Marketing* *474*

OCCUPATIONAL PENSIONS *see* PENSION SCHEMES
OCCUPATIONAL PENSIONS BOARD *370, 391*
OFFICE OF FAIR TRADING *183*
  Director of Fair Trading *93, 204*
OFF-SHORE SERVICES *421–32*
  meaning of *424–5*
OFF-SHORE TRUSTS *115*
OLDS DISCOUNT *9*
OMNIUM LEASING *336*
ON LINE CARD SERVICES LIMITED *236*
OPEN CREDIT/STANDING CREDIT
  abroad *276*
  UK *53*
OPERATING LEASE *334*
ORGANISATION FOR EUROPEAN CO-OPERATION & DEVELOPMENT (OECD) *439*
OVERDRAFT *35, 59–62, 66, 69*
OVERSEAS PAYMENTS *276*
OVERSEAS TRADE FINANCE *435–6*

PACKAGED SERVICES *488–9*
PAGE COMMITTEE 1973
  Trustee Savings Banks *29*
PAGE, JOHN, MP
  Insurance Brokers (Registration) Act 1977 *209*
PAYMENT OF WAGES BY CHEQUE ACT 1960 *43–4*
PAYROLL SERVICES
  computer services for *320, 321*
PENNINGTON, DR *The Investor and the Law*
  investment trusts and unit trusts *378*
PENSION BUSINESS *387–405*
  clearing banks' participation in growth of *396–7*
  growth in *208, 387, 396*
  insurance brokers involved in *184, 208, 401*
  market for *402, 403*
PENSION FUNDS
  administration services *401*
  competition for savings *22*
  exempt unit trusts *154*
  flow of new money into *370*
  investment management *398–400, 404–5, 508*
  investment policy *370*
  largest single category of investors on Stock Exchange *387*
  National Association of *390*
  property unit trusts *163*
  provision of investment vehicles *400–1*
  scope for new business *370*
  trusteeships for *269–72*
PENSION SCHEMES *172, 512–3*
  commutation *393*
  'controlling directors' *370*
  death in service *394*
  desirability for corporate trustee *370*
  desirability for independent trustees *397*
  for executors and directors *394–5*
  Government scheme *390–2, 396*
  maximum allowable benefits *394*
  merits of self-administered schemes *393*
  new code *394*
  occupational and private schemes *370, 392–4*
  —individual pension arrangements *396*
  —insured schemes *369, 392*
  —managed pension funds *392*
  —personal pension plans *395–6*
  —self-administered schemes *369, 393*
  pensioner trustee *370*

provision for dependants *393*
State scheme *390–2, 396*
Superannuation Funds Office *370*
supplementary benefits *395*
tax relief on contributions *394, 395, 396*
unit linked *392*
PENSION SERVICES *387–405*
marketing *402*
PERPETUITY LAWS *105*
PERSONAL ACCOUNTS: 'FREE BANKING' *40*
PERSONAL ADVISORY SERVICES *259–70*
effects of legislation *269–70*
insurance advice *203*
investment advice *121–3, 260*
personal financial planning *264–9*
taxation *261–4*
PERSONAL BANKER SERVICE *476*
PERSONAL EQUITY PLANS (PEPs) *125–6, 507*
PERSONAL FINANCIAL PLANNING *264–9*
categories of people for whom appropriate *268–9*
Estate Duty Savings Schemes *265*
estate planning *265–6*
Estate Planning Service, banks' competitors *266*
—Martins Bank *265*
Financial Planning Service, Midland Bank Trust Co *268*
football pools' winners *268*
Money Doctor Service, Barclays Bank Trust Co *266–8*
off-shore *424, 425–6*
profitability *265, 268*
PERSONAL IDENTIFICATION NUMBERS *225, 450, 461*
PERSONAL LOANS *63, 78*
PERSONAL PENSION PLANS *172*
categories of person eligible *175, 178*
commutation *176*
features *176–7, 178*
types *177–8*
PERSONAL SECTOR
competition for savings *22–3*
deposits *20–1*
lending to *63, 69–71, 73, 75–6*
PETROL CARDS *236*
PINPOINT MACHINES *235–6*
'PLASTIC CARD' BANKING *240, 280*
'PLASTIC MONEY' *459–60*
POLARISATION *505–6*
POPE, N W
on bank advertising *479–80*
PORTLAND GROUP FACTORS *357*
POST CHEQUES *277*
POUND-COST AVERAGING *150*
PRESTEL *464, 466, 467*
PREVENTION OF FRAUD (INVESTMENTS) ACT 1958 *147, 162, 379, 381*
PRICE COMMISSION
bank charges *41, 459*
banking hours *475*
fees for administration of estates *95*
money transmission *459*
PRIVATE TRUSTS *103–16*
PROBATE, GRANT OF *93–4*
PROFITABILITY
administration of estates *95–7*
credit cards *222–3, 233–4*
factoring *363–4*
hire purchase *251–2*
insurance broking *207–8*
linked life assurance *186–7*
money and travel *282–3*
personal financial planning *265, 268*
share registration *317–20*
taxation services *264*
trustee fees *91–3, 97–8*
trusteeship of unit trusts *383*
unit trusts *383*
PROFIT-SHARING SCHEMES *384*
PROPERTY BOND, PROPERTY-LINKED POLICY *173–4*
PROTECTION OF DEPOSITORS ACT 1963 *45*
PROTECTIVE TRUSTS *107*
PROVIDENT MUTUAL LIFE ASSURANCE ASSOCIATION *166*
PRUDENTIAL ASSURANCE CO *170, 185*
PUBLIC TRUSTEE *86, 92*
PUBLIC TRUSTEE ACT 1906 *86, 373*

RACKHAMS *34*
RADCLIFFE COMMITTEE 1959
bank lending *61, 62*
building societies, total assets *23*
commercial banks *6*
merchant banks *292*
'moneyness' of bank balance *447*
need for export finance *439*

RAE, GEORGE
on benefit of security *76*
traditional view on salesmanship *471*
RECEIVER, APPOINTMENT OF, BY DEBENTURE TRUSTEE *375*
RECEIVING BANKER
capital issues *305*
REGISTRARS, COMPANY *see* SHARE REGISTRATION
RESERVE ASSET RATIO *72*
RIGHTS ISSUES *302–3*
RETAIL CONSORTIUM
agreement with banks on EFTPOS *462*
Connect card *464*
ROTHSCHILD, J & CO LTD *359*
ROTHSCHILD, NATHAN
foreign loans *291, 292*
ROTHSCHILD, N M & SONS *291, 294*
ROYAL BANK OF SCOTLAND
Access card *218*
American Express *235*
Cashline *38*
cheque cards *217*
factoring *358*
High Yield Deposit Scheme *36*
hire purchase *8*
insurance broking *199*
leasing *336*
merchant banking *298*
premium account *36*
stockbrokers *16, 300*
unit trusts *144*
ROYAL BANK LEASING *336*
ROYAL COMMISSION ON LEGAL SERVICES *94*
ROYAL INSURANCE CO *166*

SAFE CUSTODY *52–3*
SAINSBURYS *33*
ST LEONARDS, LORD
on paid trustees *85*
ST MARGARET'S TRUST *256*
SALESMEN *see* BANKERS, managers as salesmen SALES REPRESENTATIVES *482/3*
SALINGER, F R of ANGLO FACTORING SERVICES
on service aspect of factoring *366–7*
SALMON, MR JUSTICE
in Woods v Martins Bank Ltd *259*
SAMBACH v DALSTON 1634 *104*
SAMUEL, M & CO *358*
SAMUEL MONTAGU & CO *16, 202, 297, 298, 300, 303, 335*
SAVE & PROSPER GROUP *382*
SAVINGS ACCOUNTS *36*
SAVINGS, COMPETITION BETWEEN BANKING AND INSURANCE INDUSTRIES *189*
SAVINGS PLANS *149*
SCHRODER WAGG *294*
SCOTT COMMITTEE REPORT 1973 *167, 168, 182*
SCOTTISH MIDLAND GUARANTEE TRUST *8*
SCOTTISH UNIT MANAGERS LTD *144*
SEARS ROEBUCK *33, 215*
SECOND SCOTTISH MIDLAND GUARANTEE TRUST *8*
SECURITIES
bearer *118*
definition of, for unit trusts *147*
purchase of, Stock Exchange *119–20*
SECURITIES & INVESTMENTS BOARD *158, 163, 180, 183, 211, 269, 270, 381, 382, 500, 501*
SEDGWICK FORBES GROUP *202*
SEEBOHM, LORD
definition of marketing *470*
SELECTIVE INCOME PLANS *150–2*
SELF-EMPLOYED PENSION PLAN *see* PERSONAL PENSION PLANS
SELF REGULATING ORGANISATION *500, 501, 504*
SELLING THE SERVICES *469–92*
see also MARKETING
SETTLED ESTATES *105–6*
SETTLEMENTS
marriage *107*
trusteeships for *87*
SHARE EXCHANGE SCHEMES *152*
SHARE REGISTRATION *313–20*
off-shore *427*
SHAREHOLDERS
number of *138*
SHIELD FACTORS *358*
SHORT, ERIC, Insurance correspondent of the Financial Times
on insurance and insurance brokers *193*
SMALL BUSINESSES *407, 413, 415*
lending to *67–9, 409*
SMALL FIRMS LOAN GUARANTEE SCHEME *68*
SMART CARDS *235*

SMITH v ANDERSON *378*
SOCIAL SECURITY ACT 1985 *371*
SOCIAL SECURITY ACT 1986 *175, 178, 208, 370, 391, 392, 396, 403*
SOCIAL SECURITY PENSIONS ACT 1975 *205, 370, 372, 390*
SOLICITORS
attitude towards bank trustees *100*
liaison between Law Society and banks *100*
preparation of legal documents *93, 94*
SOLICITORS' ACT 1974 *94*
SOUTH SEA COMPANY *84*
SOUTHERN COUNTIES FINANCE CORPORATION *247*
SPEEDLINE *466*
STAFF, number of in clearing banks *8*
STAMP ACT 1981 *355*
STANDARD CHARTERED BANK *32*
STANDARD LIFE ASSURANCE CO *190*
STANDING CREDITS *see* OPEN CREDITS
STANDING ORDERS *see* BANKERS' ORDERS
STATE EARNINGS–RELATED PENSION SCHEME (SERPS) *390–2, 396*
STATISTICS, TABLE OF *see* APPENDIX
STATUS ENQUIRIES *see* BANKERS' OPINIONS
STATUTE OF USES, 1535
attempt to stop formation of 'trusts' *104*
STIRLING D A, Chairman of Westminster Bank on launch of their first unit trust *142*
STOCK CONTROL
computer services for *321*
STOCK EXCHANGE (COMPLETIONS OF BARGAINS) ACT 1976 *315*
STOCK EXCHANGE (LONDON)
Central Stock Office *319*
dealing by company directors *308*
involvement of financial institutions *15–16*
membership categories
—broker-dealers *15*
—inter-dealer brokers *15*
—market-makers *15*
—money brokers *15*
minimum commissions abolished *15*
number of private shareholders *315*
number of quoted companies *314, 407*
proposal for eliminating share certificates *319–320*
purchase of securities *119–20*
rule 163(2) *304–5*
restrictive practice proceedings by Office of Fair Trading 1979 *13*
re-structing 1986 *13–15*
STOCK EXCHANGE'S AUTOMATED QUOTATION SYSTEM (SEAQ) *15*
STOCKS AND SHARES
as security *76*
SUPERANNUATION FINDS OFFICE *370*
SUPERCASH *452*
SWIFT (SOCIETY FOR WORLDWIDE INTERBANK FINANCIAL TELE-COMMUNICATIONS) *444*
SWISS BANK CORPORATION v JOACHIMSON *50*
SWITCHING FACILITY *174*

TARGET FINANCIAL SERVICES GROUP *144*
'TAX HAVENS' *see* OFF-SHORE SERVICES, TAXATION SERVICES *261–4*
advertising *262*
Capital Gains Tax *154, 157, 261*
profitability *264*
tax aid service *263*
TELEBANK *466*
TELEGRAPHIC TRANSFERS (TTs) *277, 437, 444*
TERM ASSURANCE *170*
convertible *170*
TESCO STORES *33*
TETHER C GORDON, Lombard Columnist of the Financial Times 1963 on merchant banks *294*
THEFT ACT 1968 *232*
THOMSON, SIR JOHN, Chairman of Barclays Bank on Barclaycard *218*
on business advisory services *410*
on developing bank services *8*
TILNEY & CO *16, 300*
TOURNIER v NATIONAL PROVINCIAL & UNION BANK OF ENGLAND *50–1*
TOWN CLEARING *454–5, 457*
TOZER, KEMSLEY & MILLBOURN *346, 358*

TRADED OPTIONS MARKET *148–9*
TRADERS' CREDITS *455*
TRAVEL AND ENTERTAINMENT CARDS *215, 216*
TRAVEL BUSINESS *280–5*
TRAVEL ENTERPRISES *281*
TRAVELLERS CHEQUES *275, 278–80*
TREASURER'S DEPOSITS *36*
TREASURY BILLS *121*
TREVELYAN, G M
  on Jews as moneylenders *58*
TRUCK ACT 1831 *43*
TRUST POLICIES *115*
TRUST, TRUSTS
  charitable *111*
  conveyances to 'uses' *104*
  declarations of *124*
  definition, no satisfactory *105*
  discretionary *107*
  investment *109*
  lifetime *106–7*
  living *111, 115*
  ministerial *107*
  off-shore *115, 425*
  origins *103–5*
  private *103–116*
  protective *107*
  trust business today *86–7*
  will ('settled estate') *105–6 see also* UNIT TRUSTS
TRUSTCARD *224*
TRUSTEE ACT 1925 *107*
TRUSTEE INVESTMENTS ACT 1961 *133*
TRUSTEE SAVINGS BANKS
  competition for personal savings *12, 28*
  credit card—Trustcard *224*
  early developments *29–30*
  estate agency *272*
  hire purchase *256*
  home savings plans *36*
  leasing *335*
  linked life assurance *166, 181*
  Page Committee *29*
  public flotation *30*
  settlement of property transactions through CHAPS *458*
  Speedline *466*
  term deposits *36*
  travellers cheques *279*
  unit trusts *142, 144, 166*
TRUSTEE SAVINGS BANK ACT 1976 *30*
TRUSTEE SERVICES *see* EXECUTOR AND TRUSTEE SERVICES, TRUSTEES, CORPORATE
  as investment experts *109*
  banks have few competitors *385*
  charging system for *97–8*
  continuity, importance of *109*
  cost of appointing *91–2*
  development in Australia, New Zealand, South Africa and U.S.A. *85*
  expense of operation *91–3*
  Financial Services Act 1986 *508*
  historical background *84–6*
  older fee scales *109–11*
  remuneration—increase by Court *110*
  resistance to fee levels *100*
  South Sea Company *84*
  wrongly thought to be impersonal *89–91*
TRUSTEESHIP
  consortium *376–7*
  corporate *369–85*
  custodian *372–3*
  debentures, unsecured loan stocks *373–6*
  insurance companies *384*
  life policy *115*
  local authority bond in U.S.A. *377*
  pension funds *369–72, 396–8*
  profit-sharing schemes *384–5*
  unit trust *377–84*

ULSTER BANK *218*
UNICORN GROUP *see* BARCLAYS UNICORN GROUP, UNICORN SECURITIES *9, 142*
UNICORN TRUST *153, 159*
UNION OF LONDON & SMITHS BANK *86*
UNIT TRUST ASSOCIATION *157–8, 383*
  advertising *157*
  objects *157, 158*
  representations on charges *160–1*
UNIT TRUSTS *141–164, 510–11*
  advantages *156–7*
  as alternative to small individual portfolios *152*
  authorised trusts *147–9*

banks involvement *9, 141–3, 382*
charging structure *160*
competition for savings *22*
control by Department of Trade *145–6, 147–9, 158, 160, 379, 381, 383*
exempt unit trusts *154, 401*
for children *153–4*
for pension funds and charities *154*
future *163–4*
growth of *143–4, 161, 377*
investment aspects *154–6*
limited rights of unitholders *383*
linked life assurance *152–3*
managed fund *149*
management, off-shore *426*
market *158–60*
nature of *144–5*
powers and duties of trustees *379, 380–2*
profitability *161, 383*
property unit trusts *163, 400*
records & regulations *380*
regulatory organisations *158*
savings plan *149–50*
share exchange scheme *152*
traded options market *148–9*
trusteeships for *377–84*
unauthorised trusts *162–3, 383*
unitisation of investment companies *152*
unit price *145–7*
Unlisted Securities Market *148*
withdrawal plans (selective income plus) *150–2*
UNITED DOMINIONS TRUST *256, 335*
hire purchase *8*
leasing *335*
UNITED DOMINIONS TRUST LTD v KIRKWOOD 1966 *1, 289*
UNITED STATES OF AMERICA
anti-trust laws *190*
UNITED STATES TRUST CO *128*
UNITISATION OF INVESTMENT COMPANIES *152*
UNLISTED SECURITIES MARKET (USM) *148, 304–5*

VALUATION SERVICES *119*
VALUE ADDED TAX *110*
VARIATIONS OF TRUSTS ACT 1958 *109*
VERBRAUCHER BANK *467*
VIEWDATA SERVICE *464*
VINCENT, SIR HOWARD, MP
passing of the Public Trustee Act 1906 *86*
VISA GROUP *240, 277*
code of practice for issue of credit cards *229*
travellers cheques *278, 279*
VISA INTERNATIONAL SCHEME *218*

W GREENWELL & CO *300*
WAGES ACT 1986 *43*
WAGES—PAYMENT BY CHEQUE OR CREDIT TRANSFER
analysis of payments *42–4*
WALTER E HELLER OVERSEAS CORPORATION *360, 365*
WARBURG, S G & CO *289*
WEDD DURLACHER MORDAUNT & CO *16, 300*
WELLBECK FINANCE *33*
WESTERN SAVINGS & TRUST *32*
WESTERN STATES BANKCARD ASSOCIATION *215*
WESTLAKE, MELVYN in *Factoring*
growth of factoring *346*
risks *362*
WESTMINSTER BANK
hire purchase *8*
insurance broking *199, 201*
leasing *335*
merchant banking *296–7*
travel and entertainment card (Diner's Club) *9, 216*
unit trusts *9, 142*
WESTMINSTER HAMBRO UNIT TRUST GROUP *9, 166*
WEYER, D VANDER
on banking hours *475*
on credit cards *240*
WHOLE LIFE ASSURANCE *170, 174*
WILCOX, MALCOLM G Assistant General Manager, Midland Bank
on travel business, 1973 *283*
WILLIAMS & GLYN'S BANK
Access card *218*
hire purchase *256*
insurance broking *199*
linked life assurance *166*

WILLIAMS & GLYN'S INSURANCE CONSULTANTS *199*
WILLIAMS DEACONS BANK *217*
WILLS
drawing up by banks *95, 100*
number of bank appointments *86*
WILSON COMMITTEE
advisory services for small businesses *415*
bank charges for money transmission *459*
bank lending *61, 63–4*
building societies, total assets *23*
companies' reluctance to release equity *306*
competition for deposits *7, 23*
customers of banks and finance houses *343*
disinvestment in equities by individuals *137*
loan finance for small businesses *67–8*
medium-term lending *262*
National Giro Bank and National Savings Bank *31*
need for foreign trade finance *435*
resources engaged on money transfer *447*
securities' markets
—availability to small companies *304*
services other than banking *11–12*
Trustee Savings Bank *30*
WITHDRAWAL PLANS, UNIT TRUSTS *150–2*
WOODS v MARTINS BANK 1958 *122, 259*
WORLD INSURANCE CONFERENCE 1974 *202*

YORKSHIRE BANK *32*
cheque card *217*
factoring *360*
hire purchase *256*
share registration *314*

NOTES

NOTES

NOTES

NOTES

NOTES

NOTES

NOTES

NOTES

NOTES

NOTES

NOTES